The Newspapers Handbook

KU-052-025

'Rich   eeble's handbook is a superb guide for those who believe in free journalism.'
John   .

'This   *y* is a superb book and a "must have" for any aspiring journalist.' *Jane Taylor,*
Head   Journalism, the Surrey Institute of Art & Design, University College

'Eacl   lition of this key textbook gets better. It is a mine of information from
whicl   ing journalists can extract nuggets of gold, managing to be both comprehensive
and d   d while combining a sense of history with up-to-date events. Most important of
all, R   d Keeble consistently points to the need for improvements to journalistic ethics.
Quite   ly, it's a must-read.' *Professor Roy Greenslade, Department of Journalism, City*
Unive

The i   *papers Handbook* remains the essential guide to working as a newspaper
journa   t examines the ever-changing, everyday skills of newspaper reporting and
explo   e theoretical, ethical and political dimensions of a journalist's job.

The ,   *apers Handbook* encourages a critical approach to newspaper practice.
Thoro   *y* updated for the fourth edition and using a range of new examples from tabloid,
compa   nd broadsheet newspapers, non-mainstream and local publications, Richard
Keebl   ines key journalistic skills such as the ar of interviewing, news reporting,
reviev   feature writing, using the internet and fr   cing. New chapters from John
Turne   k Nuttall and Mark Hanna explore the   ms of local and national government   ting, investigative journalism and cr   courts.

The N   *aners Handbook* includes:

* Int   s with journalists about their   rac ces
* Ex   s of writing from a range of   ion
* A   to training and career opr
* Th   portance of new technolog   ustry
* An   dated glossary of key ter   phy.

Richa   ble is Professor of   y of Lincoln and former director
of unc   ate studies for tr   sm at City University. He is the
author   *hics for Journali   rnalism: critical introduction.*

Media Practice

edited by James Curran, Goldsmiths College, University of London

The *Media Practice* Handbooks are comprehensive resource books for students of media and journalism, and for anyone planning a career as a media professional. Each handbook combines a clear introduction to understanding how the media work with practical information about the structure, processes and skills involved in working in today's media industries, providing not only a guide on 'how to do it' but also a critical reflection on contemporary media practice.

The Newspapers Handbook 4th edition

Richard Keeble

The Radio Handbook 2nd edition

Carole Fleming

The Advertising Handbook 2nd edition

Sean Brierley

The Television Handbook 3rd edition

Jonathan Bignell and Jeremy Orlebar

The Photography Handbook 2nd edition

Terence Wright

The Magazines Handbook 2nd edition

Jenny McKay

The Public Relations Handbook 2nd edition

Alison Theaker

The Cyberspace Handbook

Jason Whittaker

The Newspapers Handbook

Fourth edition

Richard Keeble

Routledge
Taylor & Francis Group

LONDON AND NEW YORK

First published 1994 by Routledge
2 Park Square, Milton Park, Abingdon, Oxon OX14 4RN

Simultaneously published in the USA and Canada
by Taylor & Francis Inc
270 Madison Ave, New York, NY 10016

Reprinted 1995, 1997
Second edition published 1998
Reprinted 1999, 2000
Third edition published 2001
Reprinted 2004
Fourth edition published 2006

Routledge is an imprint of the Taylor & Francis Group

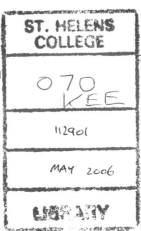

Typeset in Times and Helvetica by
Florence Production Ltd, Stoodleigh, Devon
Printed and bound in Great Britain by
The Cromwell Press, Trowbridge, Wiltshire

British Library Cataloguing in Publication Data
A catalogue record for this book is available from the British Library

Library of Congress Cataloging-in-Publication Data

Keeble, Richard, 1948–
  The newspapers handbook/Richard Keeble.—4th ed.
    p. cm.
  Includes bibliographical references and index.
  1. Newspaper publishing – Handbooks, manuals, etc.
  2. Journalism – Handbooks, manuals, etc. I. Title.
  PN4783.K44 2005
  070.1′72–dc22   2005010474

ISBN10: 0–415–33113–7 (hbk)
ISBN10: 0–415–33114–5 (pbk)

ISBN13: 9–78–0–415–33113–5 (hbk)
ISBN13: 9–78–0–415–33114–2 (pbk)

Contents

Notes on contributors

Mark Hanna is a lecturer in the Department of Journalism Studies, Sheffield University. He worked for eighteen years as a journalist for regional daily newspapers, specialising in crime and investigations, and for the *Observer* as northern reporter. His awards and commendations include Provincial Journalist of the Year in the British Press Awards. He is treasurer of the Association for Journalism Education.

Nick Nuttall is a senior lecturer at the University of Lincoln School of Journalism where he teaches mass media writing, investigative reporting and feature writing. Travel writer, record-shop owner, PR consultant, he worked for many years in East Africa, the Middle East and Cyprus, writing on communication issues for many local and regional papers. His research interests include press history, and the journalism of Allen Ginsberg and the 'Beat' writers. He was journalism course leader at Southampton Institute before moving to Lincoln in 1999.

John Turner is a Senior Political Consultant with ICM Research, a major polling organisation. He carries out opinion surveys and organises focus groups for a number of political and media organisations, including the *Guardian*, the *Observer* and Channel 4 News. He is also a Research Fellow in the School of Social Science and Law at Oxford Brookes University.

Preface

....

I had many ambitions when I sat down to write the first edition of this textbook in the early 1990s. I saw journalists and media theorists living in completely separate (and often antagonistic) 'worlds'. So by linking theory and practice I was hoping to encourage dialogue between the two. I wanted to root the study of practical skills in an awareness of the political economy of the media. And I wanted to build on the day-to-day experiences of journalists. Hence, near the start, I carry profiles of five journalists: male and female, black and white, mainstream and alternative.

I was concerned at the narrow, Anglocentric focus of journalism education in many places, and so my examples and cuttings focus on foreign as well as UK events. Ethics (which I ground in a political understanding) is not buried at the end but, because of its importance, symbolically high up there near the start. And I wanted to celebrate and critique the work of journalists in all sectors. So I don't just focus on Fleet Street but look at local mainstream newspapers as well as the ethnic, leftist, alternative press.

In some respects, the media have gone through revolutionary changes since 1994, and it is still too early to assess the overall impact of the internet. Yet the main focus of the text, the basic skills of writing lively, coherent, accurate, engaging copy in a range of genres, remains the same. All the historical sections have been updated for this new edition. And most of the newspaper examples I use to highlight various skills and issues have been changed. But not all: in some cases, the examples from the third edition appear to illustrate perfectly the issues under discussion and so they remain.

A number of important textbooks have been published in the UK since 1994 (such as Hicks 1998, Frost 2002 and Harcup 2004) while the field of journalism ethics has seen publications by Frost 2000, Hargreaves 2003, Sanders 2003, Alia 2004, Lloyd 2004 and Richards 2005. These, together with a wide range of recent articles from newspapers, magazines, websites and academic journals, are referred to. John Turner has updated his chapter on covering local and national politics while Nick Nuttall and Mark Hanna contribute excellent new chapters on investigative reporting and the courts. To them: sincere thanks.

In other respects, despite the internet revolution, news values since 1994 have hardly 'progressed', remaining stubbornly sexist, racist and elitist. To highlight the changes to the conventions of news writing, in each edition I have, sadly, been able to focus on a *Times* report of a recent US–UK military attack. This edition allows for no exception – and so the 2003 assault on Iraq falls under the spotlight. One of my hopes is that, if there is another edition, there will be then no new series of US–UK attacks on defenceless Third World countries for me to consider in my analysis of news discourse and values.

The other major change in my life since the last edition has been my move to the University of Lincoln in April 2003 after teaching for nineteen years at City University, London. I have felt privileged to be part of such a lively, friendly and creative faculty (under the inspirational leadership of Professor Brian Winston). It was during a sabbatical that I was able to complete this new edition. And so to all my colleagues and students at the university I dedicate this new edition. Special thanks should also go to Valeria Alia, Rebecca Barden and Katrina Chandler (Routledge), Robert Beckett, Claude-Jean Bertrand, Peter Cole, Martin Conboy, Vicky Cottam, Julie-ann Davies, Bob Franklin, Chris Frost, Richard Garner, Jon Grubb, David Houlton, Ippy (of *Peace News*), Angella Johnson, Philippa Kennedy, Phillip Knightley, Kristine Lowe, Mike Lyon, Tessa Mayes, Fuad Nahdi, Fotini Papatheodorou, John Pilger, Yvonne Ridley, Simon Rogerson, Karen Sanders, Jon Slattery, Jane Taylor, Milverton Wallace, Sharon Wheeler, Chris Willey. And, as always, to Maryline Gagnère and Gabi Keeble-Gagnère.

Withcall, Lincolnshire
January 2005

Acknowledgements

The author and publishers gratefully acknowledge permission to reproduce copyright material from the following:

The *Scunthorpe Telegraph* for permission to reprint Nick Cole, 'Corus restored to prestigious index', *Scunthorpe Telegraph*, 30 November 2004.

Peace News for permission to reprint the front covers of *Peace News,* No. 2457 (December 2004 – February 2005) and No. 2458 (February 2005).

The *Bury Free Press* for permission to reprint Mark Baxter, 'Please end this misery', 7 April 2000, front page.

Mirrorpix for permission to reprint Jenny Johnston, 'Virginie's secret', *The Mirror*, Wednesday, 23 February 2000, page 3.

The *Daily Star* for permission to reprint the review of Michael Moore's *Fahrenheit 9/11*: the *Daily Star* (9 July 2004) by Alan Frank.

World Entertainment News Network for permission to reprint the picture of Virginie Ledoyen and Louis used in 'Virginie's secret', *The Mirror*, Wednesday 23 February 2000, page 3.

The Voice for permission to reprint Vic Motune, 'Youngsters flock to praise Christ', *The Voice*, 20 and 27 December, 1999.

Times Newspapers Ltd for permission to reprint 'On this day', *The Times*, 1 January 1992. Orig. 1 January 1855.

Times Newspapers Ltd for permission to reprint 'On this day', *The Times*, 18 January 1940.

Times Newspapers Ltd for permission to reprint Catherine Philp, 'US paratroopers send Saddam a dramatic message', *The Times*, 28 March 2003.

The *Daily Express* for permission to reprint the text of Polly Dunbar, 'We knotted hotel sheets together to escape flames of death: Britons tell story of holiday inferno ordeal', *Daily Express*, 27 October 2004.

Albanpix for permission to reprint the pictures used in Polly Dunbar, 'We knotted hotel sheets together to escape flames of death: Britons tell story of holiday inferno ordeal', *Daily Express*, 27 October 2004.

Guardian Newspapers Limited for permission to reprint Patrick Wintour, 'Brown to offer a vision of Britain's Destiny', *The Guardian*, 1 December 2004.

Matthew Parris and Times Newspapers Ltd for permission to reprint Matthew Parris, 'Portillo hunting party targets early birds', *The Times*, 24 November 1999.

Tessa Mayes and Times Newspapers Ltd for permission to reprint Tessa Mayes, 'Women "rent" wombs to beat hassle of pregnancy', *Sunday Times*, 8 July 2001.

Cambridge Newspapers Ltd for permission to reprint 'Bingo: eyes down for that elusive jackpot', by Richard Keeble, *Cambridge Evening News*, 15 January 1977.

The Morning Star for permission to reprint Mike Parker, 'A few wisps of smoke', *The Morning Star*, 4 May 2000, page 9.

Every attempt has been made to obtain permission to reproduce copyright material. If any proper acknowledgement has not been made, we would invite copyright holders to inform us of the oversight.

1 Behind the Hollywood myths

....

The journalist's job

One of the most striking features of the British press is its diversity. There are many 'journalisms'. The poorly paid journalist on a local freesheet is living almost in a different world from a top columnist on a national. The reporter on an ethnic-minority weekly, similarly, has little in common with a freelance travel writer. Their salaries, sources and working routines will all be different. So might their ethical values and notions of what they expect to achieve through their jobs.

The London-based national mainstream press comprises twelve Sundays and eleven dailies (*Today* being the most recent casualty, closed by Rupert Murdoch in November 1995). Three out of every four national newspapers are bought unordered from newsagents each morning: hence the hyper-competition between the titles.

In 1990, there were 1,333 local newspapers. By 2004, the regional mainstream press incorporated 1,300 titles: including 25 morning dailies (19 paid and 6 free), 75 evening newspapers, 21 Sundays (11 paid and 10 free), 529 paid weeklies and 650 free weeklies (Franklin 2005: 140). Some 42 million local newspapers are sold every week while 30 million are distributed free. In all, 84 per cent of adults read a regional newspaper, 40 per cent of those never buying a national (Preston 2004a).

Behind the diversity: DOMINATION

....

Yet behind the façade of extraordinary diversity lies an industry dominated by monopolies and conformism. There is a lively 'alternative' press including leftist, religious, municipal, trade-union and ethnic-minority publications. But their circulations are relatively small and their impact on the national debate only marginal. Power, influence and financial resources lie with the mainstream local and national press. Here competition has not promoted variety. By 1974 only London, Edinburgh and Belfast had directly competing paid-for local morning or evening papers. Since then, the concentration of media ownership has intensified, reducing many newspapers to tiny outposts of vast, highly profitable multinationals (G. Williams 1994; Sarikakis 2004). As John Pilger stressed in an interview in *Socialist Worker* (20 November 2004): 'In 1983 there were 50 multinational companies effectively controlling the world's leading media. Today there are six. The "new global media" is less diverse than ever before.'

Yet even in the face of the internet-inspired technological revolution of the late 1990s the local press remained the country's second-largest advertising medium. In 2003 alone, advertising spend in the local-newspaper sector amounted to a massive £2.986 trillion (Preston 2004a). As Colin Sparks (1999: 46) comments:

> Newspapers in Britain are first and foremost businesses. They do not exist to report the news, to act as watchdogs for the public, to be a check on the doings of government, to defend the ordinary citizen against abuses of power, to unearth scandals or to do any of the other fine and noble things that are sometimes claimed for the press. They exist to make money just as any other business does. To the extent that they discharge any of their public functions, they do so in order to succeed as businesses.

Monopolies rule: AT THE LOCAL LEVEL

The mid-1990s witnessed a major shake-up in the ownership structure of the regional press. In November 1995, the Chester-based Trinity International Holdings, which grew out of the *Liverpool Post* group in the 1980s, purchased Thomson Regional Newspapers (for £327.5 million), making it the largest group in the UK with well over 130 titles, while Newsquest bought out Reed Regional Newspapers, the UK's largest free-newspaper publisher (for £205 million). Also in this month, Southnews bought Portsmouth and Sunderland Newspapers for £12.95 million.

Then, in July 1996, Johnston Press paid £211.1 million for Emap Regional Newspapers while in the following month Pearson sold its regional newspaper business, Westminster Press, to Newsquest for £305 million. In all, 77 per cent of the regional press changed ownership between 1996 and 1999. Yet the overall monopoly structure of the regional press remained intact. In June 1998 a survey by the Newspaper Society, representing UK regional and local newspapers, showed the top twenty publishers accounted for 92 per cent of the total weekly audited circulation.

In the late 1990s the financial successes of the local press began to attract the attention of US companies, and in June 1999 the US media giant Gannett (owner of 74 papers including *USA Today* and 22 television stations all with their interlocking websites) purchased Newsquest, the UK's largest local group with 63 paid-for titles and 120 frees, for £904 million. The following month Trinity became the UK's largest newspaper group with its £1.5 billion merger with the Mirror Group. The new company, named Trinity Mirror, included the *Mirror*, the *Sunday Mirror*, the *Sunday People*, along with the *Sunday Record* and the *Sunday Mail* in Scotland and 155 regional papers. Johnston consolidated its position in March 2002 with the purchase of Regional Independent Media for £560 million. Thus, by 2004, just four companies – Northcliffe (part of Associated Newspapers), Trinity Mirror, Johnston Press and Newsquest – controlled 73 per cent of the regional market while the top twenty publishers accounted for 85 per cent of all local and regional newspapers and 96 per cent of the total weekly audited circulation (Greenslade 2004a).

Monopolies rule: AT THE NATIONAL LEVEL

Monopoly ownership has similarly intensified at the national level. In 1947, the three leading corporations accounted for 62 per cent of the national daily circulation and

60 per cent of national Sunday circulation. By 1988 these figures had increased to 73 and 81 per cent. Kevin Williams (1998: 228) comments: 'In the post-war period the press has become integrated into British finance and industry. So much so that today there is no national newspaper or major regional newspaper group that does not have a tie through cross-ownership to interests outside publishing and the media.'

Overall, the trend in ownership of the British press since 1945 has been towards concentration, conglomeration and internationalisation. By 2000, Fleet Street was dominated by just four companies. This trend is best-typified in Rupert Murdoch, head of News Corporation, whose personal wealth amounted to $6.9 billion in 2004, according to *Forbes* magazine. In 1954, following the death of his father, Sir Keith Murdoch, his company comprised the *Adelaide News* in South Australia, with a circulation of just 75,000. By 2004, his four London-based newspapers (*The Times*, the *Sunday Times*, the *Sun* and the *News of the World*) amounted to 37 per cent of the national market. Yet they constituted a small subsidiary of a vast empire which included:

- A principal, 35.4 per cent share in British Sky Broadcasting (BSkyB) satellite TV company which distributes programmes throughout Europe to more than 6.6m subscribers with exclusive screening rights to many top sporting events such as Premiership football, golf's Ryder Cup and the cricket World Cup. The *Guardian* (27 March 2000) described him as having 'an iron grip on sports broadcasting'.

- 175 newspapers worldwide in New York, Australia (including the *Australian* and the *Herald-Sun*), Fiji, Papua New Guinea and Hong Kong. Significantly, all bar one backed the US–UK invasion of Iraq.

- 20th Century Fox Hollywood studios (producers of *Titanic*, *Independence Day* and *Star Wars*) and 35 US TV stations. Programmes include *The Simpsons* and the *X-Files*.

- Asia's dominant satellite company, Star TV (by satellite to more than 50 countries and 95.4 million subscribers), purchased in July 1993 for £525 million; and stakes in television companies in the United States, New Zealand and Latin America (Page 2003). In China, Murdoch holds a 38 per cent share of Phoenix Satellite Television. The satellite broadcaster DirecTV (with 12.9 million subscribers in North and Latin America) was purchased for £4.1 billion in April 2003 (Cassy 2003). And, in July 2004, Sky Italia pay TV was launched in Italy as a direct challenge to Silvio Berlusconi's Mediaset and the state broadcaster RAI.

- Book publishing (HarperCollins) in the US, the UK, Europe and Australasia.

- A growing interest in internet services in the UK, the US and Australasia. In June 1995 Murdoch's company, News Corporation, announced the launch of a joint deal with the *People's Daily*, the powerful newspaper of the Chinese Communist Party, to develop the information technology sector including electronic publishing, online information databases, data transmission networks and digital mapping.

- In March 1998 Murdoch's Fox Entertainment Group purchased the LA Dodgers baseball team for $350 million (£212 million) and then sold it for $430 million in January 2004 to real-estate developer Frank McCourt. In English football, Murdoch has stakes in Sunderland, Chelsea, Leeds United, Manchester City and Manchester United, though his plan to take over Manchester United was blocked by the Blair government.

- In April 2004, Murdoch shifted his headquarters from Adelaide, Australia, to Delaware in the US.

What it takes

Journalism remains a job carrying enormous personal rewards. It is difficult, challenging (politically, ethically, physically) and fun. It can be dominated by routine: it can also be very exciting. It requires a formidable range of knowledge and skills. Reporters must be both literate and numerate. They need to master the law as it affects newspapers and the social skills to develop contacts and interview different kinds of people. Many will want to speak at least one foreign language. All will need to possess computer and internet searching skills. Reporters should be inquisitive, persistent, imaginative and daring.

Or, in the words of Nicholas Tomalin, the *Sunday Times* foreign correspondent killed aged 41 on the Golan Heights in 1973, journalists should cultivate 'rat-like cunning, a plausible manner and a little literary ability'. In addition, he said, they should be able to display 'an ability to believe passionately in second-rate projects' and possess 'well-placed relatives' and 'an implacable hatred of spokesmen, administrators and public relations men'. There is a glamorous side to the job which Hollywood has helped to promote. No wonder the queues for entering the industry are so long.

The jobs revolution

Since the arrival of new technology, the job has been through many changes – not all of them positive. Staffing levels have been reduced at both national and local levels. In the regions, newspapers lost hundreds of jobs as owners 'downsized', reducing staffing levels in advance of selling off titles to the emerging conglomerates. At the same time, working hours have been extended, with early-Saturday-morning 'sunrise' editions adding further demands to provincial journalists.

Accompanying the attacks on trade unions has been growing casualisation. Many staffers have been turned into 'permanent part-timers'. Managements have found it cheaper, while job insecurity always promotes conformism.

Local branches (chapels) of the 34,000-strong National Union of Journalists (NUJ) have been left struggling for recognition, and personal contracts have been increasingly forced on staffers. But in recent years the NUJ has been fighting back: the recognition deal signed by the NUJ with T. R. Beckett, part of the Johnston Press, in March 2000, was significantly its first with a regional newspaper group for more than a decade. On Fleet Street, a strike by journalists at the *Express* and the *Star* in March 2002 was the first at national newspapers for 15 years. And following the Employment Rights Act 2000, giving bargaining rights to unions where they had 50 per cent or more of the workforce in membership, recognition had been gained in 46 provincial newspaper centres by 2004.

Multi-skilling or de-skilling?

One consequence has been 'de-professionalisation', with reporters forced to perform promotional, distribution and other non-professional tasks. 'Multi-skilling' schemes are being introduced on some papers with reporters, photographers and subeditors (those handling text and layout) learning from each other – and sparking fears of further job cuts and a decline in standards. Many local papers are training reporters in subediting skills, not primarily as a way of improving their overall journalistic skills, but so they can fill in during absences. 'Flexibility' is the buzzword.

As newspapers move increasingly into the internet and cable television, the demands on journalists are likely to mount. Anthony Thornton, editor of http://www.nme.com, one of Britain's most popular websites, commented: 'Now the journalist needs to be a writer, sub editor, designer, photographer, camera person, editor, technician and radio presenter to carry out online journalism effectively.' In the United States, reporters are increasingly having to write a story, appear on television, broadcast on radio and then file a quick update for the newspaper's internet site.

How long will it be before these multimedia demands are routinely faced by British journalists? Young reporters have had to fund their own training; some work without any contractual protection. Many entrants, desperate to get their foot in the door, are being cynically exploited by managements, having to work long periods on unpaid attachments. 'Commercial features' geared to promoting business and info-tainment specials (reflecting the growing power of market researchers on editorial content) have mushroomed; serious investigative journalism has been marginalised.

The tabloid values of junk journalism (and trash TV) have crept into the serious and the regional press. As Harold Evans, the legendary former editor of *The Times* and the *Sunday Times*, commented: 'Sexual allegations make the front pages and the decision to do that is defended on the grounds the story is about "character". This is no more than prurience on stilts.' He continued: 'If only one tenth of the energy spent on snooping on private lives can be spent on monitoring real power, on analysis, on improving the writing and the accuracy, we will be a helluva lot better off.'

Many press commentators have argued that, in a period of hyper-competition, profits are the prime concern of managements rather than editorial quality. Roy Greenslade, former editor of the *Mirror*, *Guardian* media analyst and Professor of Journalism at City University, London, argues: 'The pressure is constantly on managing directors and directors. They must cut costs, they must make savings. This means redundancies and greater productivity from those who stay.' And he adds: 'The most important person on a newspaper is no longer the editor. It is the managing directors. They rule the roost.' Foreign staffs have been cut to the bone, with the over-fifties the most likely to be chopped.

Money matters: THE SCANDAL OF LOW PAY

Salaries for many in the newspaper industry remain scandalously low: for trainees they can be appalling. A 2002 survey by the Journalism Training Forum found that while the average salary was £22,500, one in ten journalists earned less than £12,500 a year. The survey also identified significant gender differences, as women's pay lagged behind men's by £5,000 per annum. Moreover, the average working week was 41.6 hours per week, compared with 35 hours across the UK working population (Hargreaves 2002). In 2004, a survey by the National Union of Journalists found that almost half of Britain's journalists earned below the national average of £26,151 while almost three-quarters earned less than the average professional's salary of £35,766 (Greenslade 2004b). Not surprisingly, strikes over pay were spreading, with newspapers in Blackpool, Bradford, Bolton, Rotherham, Spalding, Birmingham and Coventry affected.

At the same time top executives and columnists on national newspapers can earn £200,000 plus. According to Andrew Marr (2004: 43), former editor of the *Independent* and the BBC's political editor, 'a very few top journalists are earning salaries that would be regarded as good even in the City. One tabloid columnist is said by colleagues to be on £500,000. There is a broadsheet writer on £300,000.' In contrast, for many freelances salaries have either stood still over recent years or dropped, while payments to them can take up to a year.

Colin Sparks (2003: 47) argues that the media hierarchy, based around marked differences in status and salary, is 'a powerful mechanism of control'. 'In particular, the possibility of very substantial financial rewards for those who are professionally successful acts as a strong incentive on journalists and other creative staff to toe the management line.'

The news machine

Reporters work in close liaison with their news desk. The number of titled executives on the desk will differ according to the size of the operation. A weekly free-sheet may have just one news editor doubling up as deputy editor and feature writer. An evening paper may have a city desk headed by a news editor alongside a district desk organising (through computer link-up) the operations of the district offices. In contrast a national may have as many as five journalists assigned to the home news desk. They will be drawing up the diary and the news lists, liaising by phone with reporters out on stories and feeding follow-up ideas into the operation. In addition, they will be monitoring the news agency wires, the other media and the flow of copy from staff reporters, and attending news conferences to review past issues and plan future ones.

The amount of initiative allowed to individual reporters differs from paper to paper. General reporters on local weeklies and dailies will be 'fed' a considerable number of their stories by their news editor. They will arrive in the office at 7.30 a.m., say, often with no idea of what they are to cover until they are briefed by the news editor. Specialists, who are generally more experienced reporters, will tend to originate far more of their own material. An evening might have them assigned to crime, education, industrial, local government, farming (where relevant) and environment beats. A national broadsheet's specialisms, on the other hand, might include education, the environment, crime, arts, the media, consumer affairs, the countryside, defence, Westminster, health, religion, politics, transport, the law, Ireland, social services, technology (but significantly neither peace nor race relations).

At the core: the conference

At the centre of the news operations of all but small weeklies will be the conference. A national broadsheet may have as many as six in one day; a regional evening two or three; a weekly just one at the start of an operation. Attendance differs from paper to paper. At a small newspaper all the staff will attend. At a national, one meeting may be open to all staffers while at other times only heads of departments such as features, sports, finance, news, foreign and arts together with top executives (often called the backbench team) will be present. Discussions tend to focus around the news list extracted from the diary with reporters and where relevant photographers, graphic artists and cartoonists being assigned tasks.

In and out of the office?

One of the consequences of new technology and the staffing cuts has been the increased amount of newsroom-based work by reporters. Many local reporters say that as much as 90 per cent of their work is done by phone; national reporters can spend 70 per cent of their time and more in the office. Reporting is an increasingly desk-bound job. As investigative reporter Nick Davies says of working journalists: 'They spend such a lot of time trapped in newsrooms where they are not allowed to be real reporters. They simply process PA copy and PR quotes and have no time or encouragement to go and dig-up old-fashioned stories.'

The role of the subs

Once the story has passed the news editor, it will go through the computer system to a copy taster (often in a group of copy tasters), the much-analysed media content 'gatekeepers' of sociological theory (Niblock 1996: 34–5). They will check for accuracy, see, for instance, if someone or some group criticised has had the opportunity to answer any allegations, establish whether the intro is the strongest one and decide, finally, whether the story is worth using. The story at this stage may be sent back to the reporter for revision. If the story is not rejected ('killed' or 'spiked' in the jargon) by the taster, it then moves on to the subeditors, who work entirely at the screen manipulating text and images with their mouse.

The subeditors will further check for accuracy, with the reporter contacted if there are queries, and for legal problems such as libel and contempt. (In addition, nationals have teams of lawyers to offer advice, provincials usually have lawyers just a phone call away.) They may re-jig the story if a clearer structure is required or reduce its length if necessary. They will ensure style is followed throughout and compose any accompanying headlines, captions, standfirsts and panels (see Hicks and Holmes 2002). They design the pages, normally using the QuarkXpress, InDesign or Tera desktop publishing programs and PhotoShop for image manipulation.

This basic structure has many variants. For instance, in some newspapers the news editor and deputy operate as 'tasters'. At the *Western Morning News* reporters type their stories straight into the page and add the headlines, with the subs checking for errors on a full-size tabloid page proof. Other former subs spend their time developing content. In some provincial operations, subbing has been taken away from individual offices with a centralised group handling copy from a number of journals.

The amount of subbing of copy differs from paper to paper and from section to section. But all reporters have to accept that their copy may be hacked about. News copy on a national tabloid might be almost entirely rewritten to fit the small space available, though features on the same paper may be only slightly touched by the subs. National broadsheets are 'reporters' papers' and their copy is generally only lightly subbed. Given the number of words, there is not the time to do regular re-jigs. Journalists new to local papers will tend to have their copy subbed a lot as they get used to house style. Once settled, their copy will tend to be heavily subbed only rarely. Indeed, reporters come to sub their own copy (checking style, clarity, conciseness, flow, punctuation, spelling and factual accuracy) before passing it on.

Writing with a visual sense

Designers and art editors are responsible, particularly in large publications, for the overall appearance of the newspaper: its use of pictures, fonts, column widths, even the use of white space in the layout, together with features such as graphs, maps and sophisticated computer-generated artwork. Their work is becoming increasingly important as newspapers reduce the text and extend their picture/graphics elements.

Accordingly reporters are having to consider the representation of their stories on the page more and more as they write. A reporter composing a long feature, for instance, will often accompany it with a smaller one. This will help add tonal variety to the text on the page and also provide the sub with the material for an interesting layout. Or a reporter will help research details for a complex graphic. At the *Eastern Daily Press* (*EDP*), reporters and photographers are encouraged to think together about the best ways of displaying their stories. As Pete Waters, *EDP* special projects editor and author of *The Guide to the Tabloid: Best Practices for a Better EDP*, commented: 'If the best form [of presenting a story] is a graphic and the reporter is asked to research details rather than write a story, then that is what we must do.'

To illustrate the day-to-day practicalities of the job, journalists from differing sectors talk about the challenges, routines, stresses, necessary skills and rewards of working in the media. A local evening, a local free weekly, a national tabloid, a national broadsheet and an 'alternative' newspaper/journal are represented.

Importance of the enriching role

Profile | *Scunthorpe Telegraph*

Local newspapers' three major tasks are to inform, entertain and enrich, according to Jon Grubb, editor of the *Scunthorpe Telegraph*:

The modern newspaper has to do more than simply inform and entertain. By enriching we are taking basic stories and adding fact boxes, background, colour and graphics. For instance, a local restaurant is celebrating its anniversary with a special truffle night. We report the story in a colourful way, add a box on 'Ten things you didn't know about the truffle'; explain how it's made and even add a graphic and pictures.

Or take a story about the council tax. We don't simply say it's rising by so much and show each band's payments. In addition, we show how the tax has moved over the last decade; we break it down to show what's going on social services, combating crime, schools and so on. We compare it with the tax in neighbouring council areas; we ask how the opposing party would set its rate and accompany all this with graphics.

This new emphasis on 'enrichment' is having an enormous impact at the *Telegraph*. For instance, instead of the daily news conferences, the staff now operate a system with conferences held at 4 p.m. two days before publication. Thus a meeting on Tuesday afternoon will be planning for the Thursday edition. As Jon explains:

> Scunthorpe is not what you might call a hotbed of breaking news stories. The vast majority of our stories come through contacts, following up agendas before meetings, phone conversations, letters. To carry out all those 'enriching' tasks, we need time – though our system is obviously flexible enough to accommodate major breaking stories when they do occur.
>
> It also means the traditional split between hard news and features is breaking down. All my reporters, in effect, now have to be writers: they have to be able to use both their eyes and ears, making stories both informative and entertaining.

Of the 22,000 daily sales (making a readership of around 60,000), 40 per cent are through casual outlets:

> This means the front page becomes highly important. We have to be out there scrapping every day for the attention of readers. And many of the younger ones are internet savvy; they are used to whizzy graphics and less committed to the local press. Somehow we have to appeal to them – as well as our older readers. It's not easy.

Jon, 37, became editor in August 2002 and acknowledges the changes he is introducing at Scunthorpe are radical with at least two years needed to 'get the culture right'. But he is confident he has the skills and processes in place to achieve his ambition. Of the 33 editorial staff, ten are reporters (with specialists in crime, health, local government, education and the courts). Seven of these are trainees with a range of backgrounds: NCTJ college, postgraduate diploma, local college or freelancing. In addition there are three photographers, one graphic artist, a production editor with six production staff; a sports editor and four specialist sports staff who write and sub around 50 pages every week.

Trainees start on a salary of around £13,500 rising to £16,000 when they pass their proficiency test. Seniors earn on average £19,000, with subs on £20,000.

The reporting bug hit Jon when he was just 13. He always enjoyed writing and was inspired to become a journalist by the example of his uncle, Frazer Ansell, of the *Watford Observer*. After taking a degree in English and History at Ripon College, he obtained a copy of *Willings Press Guide* and wrote off asking for a job to as many newspapers as possible. He finally secured a position at the *Buckinghamshire Advertiser*, a small weekly based at Chalfont St Peter, where he stayed three and a half years rising to become assistant editor. After another three years at the *Gloucester Citizen* (where he ended as head of content), he moved to the Nottingham *Evening Post* for seven years, ending as deputy editor.

Jon is outspoken on local newspaper campaigns. 'Let's be honest: they are mostly done for PR reasons. They help identify the newspaper as a brand but I don't believe any campaign ever helped sell a newspaper except in the short term.'

He continues: 'Trust does not sell newspapers. Death, shock, horror: that's the reality we live in.'

How email is 'depersonalising' the journalist's job

Profile

Vicky Cottam, chief reporter
the *Scunthorpe Telegraph*

Vicky Cottam, chief reporter of the *Scunthorpe Telegraph*, is concerned that the increasing use of emails for interviews is 'depersonalising' the journalist's job:

> About 25 per cent of my interviewing is now done via emails. In the past, I would build up a personal relationship with my sources and often ring them either daily or weekly. Now, whenever possible, I talk to my sources before emailing them to make that personal contact.

Vicky, 27, works closely with the news editor and deputy news editor on the news desk. They have established a rotating system of shifts starting at 7.30 a.m., 8 or 8.30, and work is hectic for all three until the single edition of the day goes at 9.40 a.m.

She admits to still 'getting a buzz' seeing her name in print alongside a story. 'I don't know if that's kind of sad – but I still get immense satisfaction from the job.'

After studying law at Derby University, Vicky worked for her father until landing a job at her local weekly paid-for, the *Worksop Guardian*, where she rose to be chief reporter and then news editor, passing her NCTJ exams first time. The 100 wpm shorthand she still finds 'absolutely invaluable'.

A WEEK IN THE LIFE OF VICKY COTTAM

Wednesday: the thirtieth anniversary of the explosion at the Flixborough chemical plant near Scunthorpe, in which 26 people died, approaches and Vicky has been given a free hand over two weeks to build up a portfolio of features. 'We sent out an appeal for survivors to recall their memories and we were inundated with calls.' Vicky manages to track down a surviving elderly woman through www.192.com and drives out to meet her at her home. 'It was heart-breaking to hear her talk. She had lost everything in the disaster and was still in the process of picking up the pieces.'

After spending two and a half hours with the woman (much more than her usual interview time), she drives back to the office and immediately writes up the story. 'I like to do that while the interview is fresh in my mind.' It takes her about an hour but she broods on the story overnight (allowing time for small changes and corrections) before handing it over to the news editor the following morning.

Thursday: drives out to interview steelworker at 11 a.m. 'He was just an ordinary bloke caught up in something horrific. He found he had bumps on his head and when operated on they were found to be small pieces of glass embedded in his skull. I spent just one hour with him. I like to get the job done and leave: some people can talk and talk to no great purpose.'

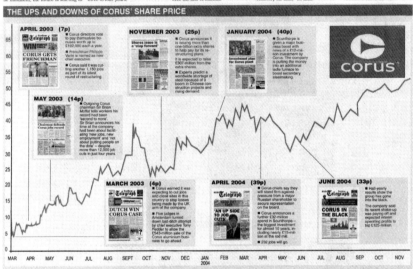

Figure 1.1 An 'enriched' page from the *Scunthorpe Telegraph*, with page lead, graphic and question box

2 p.m.: interviews fireman, one of the first on the scene of the disaster, for an hour and a half.

4 p.m.: back to the big, open-plan offices and writes up interviews until 5.45 p.m.

Friday: 7.30 a.m. start. Three pages have to be filled before the 9.40 deadline. The news desk receives up to 100 emails every day and while more than 95 per cent are 'binnable' they still have to be checked. Trainee reporters have to be briefed and advised to carry a mobile so they can be contacted while out on a story. Vicky operates as a sort of 'gatekeeper', checking stories for accuracy, asking for a 'balancing' quote if necessary, and making sure the stories are legally safe. The newspaper's lawyers, Foot Anstey Sargent, of Exeter, have to be contacted at least once a week. And she liaises with Caroline Wheeler, the Northcliffe group's parliamentary correspondent with a special brief for the *Telegraph*. The afternoon conference plans the editions for the following week.

Sunday: the reporter on the calls to the police, fire brigade and ambulance service rings Vicky at her Lincoln home with news of a suspected murder. She advises him to get as much information as possible from neighbours and the police.

Monday: in at 7.30 a.m. Checks BBC Lincolnshire website and monitors the radio and television coverage of the suspected murder. Lengthy negotiations with the police for a photograph of the victim begin. Just before the deadline one is secured.

Tuesday more pages to fill. Liaises with graphic artist Jane Cuthbert-Moss. And organises a vox pop on 'Should the king-sized Mars bar be reduced?' 'We obviously do serious vox pops but it's good to have some on a lighter theme.'

Professional and compassionate

Profile : *Lincoln Chronicle*

After just two weeks as a cub reporter on the *Gainsborough News*, Mike Lyon was thrown in at the deep end. 'It was terrifying,' says Mike, now editor of the free weekly *Lincoln Chronicle*.

> An asthmatic girl had died in the town centre simply because she could not get access to an inhaler. I was asked to doorstep the family. But I'd never done anything like that before. In the end, my experience captured the two reactions you can have doorstepping: the father could not stop talking about his daughter, the mother could not stop crying.'

It was also an early lesson in how professional journalism could be compassionate. He remembers a recent story in which he highlighted the plight of a severely disabled man who had lost the help from social services he so desperately needed to bathe himself, breakfast and get to work. 'So I ran a front page exclusive on his predicament complete with a picture of him sitting at his desk looking bewildered. Within two weeks, the authorities had responded and the situation was resolved. So I could run another exclusive story, this time showing the man smiling.'

For Mike, 42, journalism is about integrity ('always telling the truth') and public service. In recent years, the *Chronicle* has run a 'Light up a Life' Christmas appeal for Macmillan Cancer Relief. For £5 people can sponsor one of the three thousand lights on a giant Christmas tree in Lincoln city centre and have the name of someone they wish to be remembered listed in a book open to the public in a shopping centre.

But journalism is also about providing 'interesting, relevant, lively news'. 'We are tending to steer away from features of any length. The consensus is that people don't want big reads from their weeklies.' On the news pages the one story of length, the lead, may be up to 20 cm but it will always be accompanied by an image. And there will usually be a column of nibs to boost up the story count on the page.

The *Chronicle* has also launched a monthly 'Reporter' insert of stories provided by journalism students at the nearby University of Lincoln. 'It's very difficult providing students with work experience on the paper. They have tended to be left writing up press releases and that's not going to fire their enthusiasm for the job. I have enjoyed very good relations with the university's press department and given some lectures to the PR department on how to compose effective press releases. Running the "Reporter" is another way of extending that good relationship.'

After studying English at Newcastle University from 1979 to 1982, Mike dropped childhood dreams of becoming a poet and novelist and took the one-year NCTJ training course at Richmond College, Sheffield. He enjoyed the experience 'hugely' and was recruited by the Lincolnshire Standard Group, then based in Boston, even before the course had ended.

Mike has a shorthand speed of 130 wpm 'on a good day', and that proved invaluable during his time at the twice-weekly *Gainsborough News* when he did long stretches of court reporting ('along with writing up the weddings and obits'). In 1987, he moved to the *Lincoln Chronicle* as chief reporter, becoming editor in 1992. During his years in Lincoln the newspaper has had a chequered history, as ownership – and even its title – has changed.

Worst of all, this has been disorienting for the readership. One owner decided the paper should become a paid-for and adopt a style of 'sex, drugs and rock 'n' roll'. On the front page of the first edition we ran a story about wife swapping on the internet. Sales of the second edition were just a fraction of the first. The people of Lincoln just didn't want it. We battled on against the odds and worked all hours. But it never took off, and after a year the strategy was simply dropped.

For the last three years, the newspaper has stabilised under the ownership of Johnston Press with a weekly circulation of 46,500. The latest venture is to boost up the website (www.lincolntoday.co.uk) with daily updates and a 'Stop Press' column of stories which did not make it to the print edition. 'All this is good. It gives the website its own identity – and it means all the hard work we put into stories is not wasted.'

A pin-up strategy for contacts

Profile   ## Chris Willey, reporter
the *Lincoln Chronicle*

Chris Willey, reporter at the *Lincoln Chronicle*, has an unusual strategy for handling his contacts list. 'I found a notebook difficult to refer to so I pin A4 sheets up on a pinboard. It's now full,' he says.

Chris, 24, started on the *Chronicle* in November 2003 with no previous knowledge of the city, so has been busy building up his contacts in the area. 'Most of the people I meet on other regionals say they have to drive around all the time. Here I can walk virtually everywhere so I'm able to meet a lot of my contacts and not rely just on the phone or email.'

The city is relatively crime-free, he says. 'Journalistically that's a pity but I don't mind. There're a lot of other sources for news: the city and county councils, schools, the university, colleges, the police and amateur dramatics clubs – while a lot of regional bodies have their headquarters here.'

After studying history at Roehampton University, south-west London, from 1998 to 2001, Chris worked one day a week for a sports news agency. But within two months he had demonstrated his abilities and was working all hours five days a week. 'It was great. I was doing three 100-word stories on four football teams every day. The duty news editor would tear them apart, but I certainly learned that way how to write quickly and concisely.'

He then decided he needed to hone his reporting skills and joined the NCTJ postgraduate course at Cornwall College, Camborne, before returning to his home town of Letchworth and working in the local district council's press office for six months. Finally, following up job advertisements on holdthefrontpage.co.uk, and, much to his delight, he landed the Lincoln post.

On covering stories involving people's emotions, he says:

> I can deal with business and political stories without a problem. But when it comes to interviewing people about death or other tragedies I feel nervous and worry if I'm intruding or offending. Recently, I had to interview a local teacher whose daughter had died of cancer and who was campaigning to raise money for a health foundation. She was, actually, very happy to speak to me. But I still found it difficult. I am sure that as I grow in experience I will be able to handle those situations more confidently.

A WEEK IN THE LIFE OF CHRIS WILLEY

Wednesday: in at 9 a.m. (finishing at 5.30 p.m.). The weekly edition goes to bed at 10.15 a.m., so there may well be a last-minute race to get a late-breaking story on to page one or three. This week, the news comes just in time that Jim Speechley, former leader of Lincolnshire County Council, has failed in his appeal against an 18-month jail sentence for misconduct. Rest of the day is spent building up stories for the week ahead. As the newspaper's sole reporter (along with editor Mike Lyon) there's a lot to cover. 'I'm particularly keen on creating a culture in the local schools where they think automatically of contacting us about anything newsy: say a sporting event, an international day, a play.' Some 75 per cent of his week is spent in the office (in Lincoln's busy High Street) 'but that 25 per cent of my time spent out on stories is really productive. And I can use my camera to take pictures.'

Thursday and Friday: more time spent planning and writing stories for the inside pages. Many press releases now arrive on his computer via emails – from the local councils, hospitals, Territorial Army and the Blood Service, for instance. The best he follows up.

Monday: a lot of time spent working on the back, sports pages. Rugby, boxing, hockey, snooker, football teams (Lincoln City and United) and badminton are among those covered regularly by a team of freelances. 'We don't expect perfectly clean copy. I will tend to have to work on them to make them usable.'

Tuesday: another very busy day. Meets editor Mike Lyon to discuss content of pages one and three. Proofs of pages arriving via fax from the subbing centre in Louth will be checked for accuracy and spelling.

'A little racier and pacier': ON THE JOYS OF SWITCHING FROM BROADSHEET TO TABLOID

Profile   ## Angella Johnson, features writer
the *Mail on Sunday*

'I like it very much. It's a little racier, a little pacier and more opinionated.' This is how Angella Johnson compares her writing today on the tabloid *Mail on Sunday* with the copy she produced earlier in her career for the broadsheet *Guardian*.

> For instance, I interviewed a woman whose estranged husband took their four young boys to a beauty spot in Wales and killed them before killing himself. He was upset she was involved in another relationship and had become pregnant. I was able to stress the guy's wickedness and how his actions impacted on her in a much more critical way than if I had been writing a news story for a broadsheet.

The features section of the *Mail on Sunday* is directed particularly at women readers and celebrity-led. Does she worry about a trivialisation of news values? 'No, after all, the whole world's celebrity obsessed.' So a lot of her time is spent interviewing soap stars, society people, models, a ballerina (once) 'and, of course, there are ordinary people with tragic or moving stories to tell'. Each week she will tend to produce one major feature of up to two thousand words and sometimes two.

Angella is clearly pressed for time, so we meet briefly over lunch in Northcliffe House, the swish headquarters of Associated Newspapers, just round the corner from High Street Kensington Tube station in central London.

She travels a lot: recently she has been to Australia (twice), to New Zealand to interview Michael Barrymore, to India for a story on Elizabeth Hurley and her lover Arun Nayar, Ethiopia (twice) following Bob Geldof's campaign on famine, and to Germany for an interview with soccer star Dwight Yorke about his relationship with model Jordan and their child (in the end, he didn't want to talk).

Oh, and I went to Portugal for the European Cup, following the footballers' wives: going shopping, lounging around the pool and seeing Beckham's Posh acting the diva. I wrote a colour piece on that, and it went on Page 3!

The internet is an 'invaluable' source of information. 'I use it all the time. It's the first place I go to before I interview anyone. I check what's already been written on them while Google helps give me ideas. I find particularly useful fansites of the stars. Through them I can often find good people to talk to.'

She always tapes her interviews on a Dictaphone though rarely listens back over them, relying more on her written note. 'The tape is just there for back-up if they challenge something I've written.' And a copy of the Press Complaints Commission's Code of Conduct is always kept in her bag. 'I find it really useful. For instance, when you are doorstepping someone it lays down the parameters and helps you avoid harassment.' But on her age and salary Angella suddenly goes quiet. 'I'm not going to bloody tell you that.'

Angella has had an extremely varied career since studying English and History at Leicester University. She took the newspaper training course at City University, London, and then reported on a six-month programme funded by the European Commission in Brussels. After freelancing for Thames News and the BBC World Service and eighteen months on the *Slough Observer*, she did short spells on *The Times* and Robert Maxwell's ill-fated *London Daily News* before joining the *Guardian* in 1987.

Then in April 1996 she left for the Johannesburg *Weekly Mail and Guardian* and ended up covering brutal murders, rapes, prostitution, high politics and swinging sex in the suburbs. Her final post in Johannesburg, as columnist, was probably her most rewarding and enjoyable while in South Africa.

Crime is a burgeoning industry today in South Africa, growing faster even than the birth rate. And rape is a sort of national pastime for men. But I didn't do stupid things such as driving in the wrong area at the wrong time of night. I got to know the people in my neighbourhood. But after three years I felt my luck could be running out. Statistically it was all there ready to happen to me. So I thought: 'Time to go home.' And I felt I'd achieved everything I wanted journalistically.

Not long after returning to London, in September 2001, Angella secured her coveted post at the *Mail on Sunday*.

A WEEK IN THE LIFE OF ANGELLA JOHNSON

Sunday: to a school hall in Peckham, south London, to check out the controversial evangelical preacher Gilbert Deya, who is claiming the ability to create miracle babies – simply through touching women.

BBC radio had done a report on allegedly pregnant women being flown to Kenya where they had miraculously given birth. The DNA of only one baby had been tested and did not match those of the alleged parents. So there was a story here worth following up. I went to the school hall not expecting to see him. But in front of around 350 people (99 per cent black) there was Deya on the pulpit.

Angella starts to take down notes on bits of paper. 'It's more casual to do it that way. It's too obvious if you use a notebook.' While on the pulpit, Deya, amazingly, takes a call from a journalist on his mobile phone and proceeds to scream insults for at least an hour. 'You are the devil,' he shouts. 'Don't talk, just listen to me. Your country is filthy. The hand of God is upon you people in Britain. You are doomed.'

By this time, ushers in the hall have spotted Angella and urge her to go to the platform to explain herself. 'I decided to walk up to the edge of the stage. Gilbert Deya came over to me and grabbed me, calling me a "servant of satan" and "an enemy". And he said he had the power to destroy me. I started screaming at his "uncivilised behaviour" but I really wanted peace since I needed the interview. I left the stage and while money was being raised a woman and another pastor came up to me and apologised. In the end, I arranged to meet Deya for an interview the following day.' All that drama has taken up three hours. 'I thrive on all that excitement. It makes my adrenaline pump.'

Monday: to Deya's south London base in her Peugeot 206cc. 'He kept me waiting an hour. And when I was finally face to face he said how privileged I was and how he trusted me because I had a kind face. He apologised for the previous day but stressed I had visited his church without an invitation and that he had power of life and death blah blah.'

He then decides to play his 'trump card', introducing Edith Ezedom, a British woman who allegedly gave birth to two children (one of whom died) within a month in 2003 after having been touched by Deya. 'She told me: "Of course, I was surprised when the babies came so quickly but I believe it. God says all things are possible and Archbishop Deya is a very powerful servant of our Lord." She appeared rational and intelligent and stressed she was never asked to pay for her miracles.'

3.30 p.m.: reports to her Review section editor, Jim Gillespie. Begins writing feature.

Tuesday: continues writing. Checks facts with sources in Kenya, on the BBC website and with the Charity Commission.

Wednesday a.m: final checks on spelling and factual accuracy. Sends copy to Gillespie. (The 1,718-word feature duly appears under the headline 'You're a servant of Satan. You're in my holy empire. Here someone can die.')

I then spotted a short story in *The Times* about the first girlfriend of Freddie Mercury. Her name was Dr Rose Rose. I first checked the Electoral Roll, then the internet and directory enquiries. It wasn't difficult tracking her down. I was very friendly on the phone to her. She said she liked the sound of my voice and agreed to meet me.

Thursday: drives up to Dr Rose's terraced home in a quiet suburb of Sheffield. Until recently she was a lecturer in art theory at Sheffield University and had a passionate affair with Mercury between 1969 and 1970 after they met as graphic design students. 'I spent three hours with her. I let her talk on for quite a while; I joked with her; we had a cup of tea; I let her express her anxieties about being interviewed. All this helped make her feel more comfortable and happy to talk to me.'

Leaves after three hours. Rings through to the office, and they say the story is needed first thing the following day. 'So I booked into a local hotel and spent half the night writing.'

Friday: early morning: checks spelling and facts and then sends over. (The 1,690-word profile duly appears under the headline 'I was Freddie's first love, but I knew I'd lose him to a man'.) Drives back to London and checks in at the office.

Saturday: two hours in the gym. 'I need that. There's a lot of stress in this job.'

On the quirky qualities of the compact revolution

Profile ┆ Richard Garner, education editor
┆ the *Independent*

Richard Garner sits in front of his computer screen in the massive open-plan offices of the *Independent* in London's Docklands and muses on the contrasting styles of the two newspapers he has worked on over the last 14 years. 'Actually, it's much easier writing for the *Independent* than for the *Mirror*,' he says.

> I remember when I joined the *Indie* in March 2001. It was just before the annual conference of the National Union of Teachers and I wrote 700 words for a page lead. On the *Mirror* I rarely contemplated a story of that length. Here there's a more discursive style. And the shift to the compact size from the broadsheet has meant stories are more layout- and graphics-led than previously. The words I'm using haven't changed much. But I'm writing fewer typical hard news stories (with the five Ws in the intro section) and more stories with dropped intros and in a quirkier, lighter style.

Richard, 54, one of the longest-serving education specialists on Fleet Street, feels that with all this 'featurisation' the *Independent* is becoming more of a magazine than a newspaper. 'We may focus on seven or eight major topics in depth in one edition. And stories appear as packages with the main copy accompanied by sidebars, facts boxes and graphics.'

Unlike at the *Mirror*, where Richard was constantly aware that his copy could be spiked or cut to shreds by subeditors, 90 per cent of his reports at first made it at the *Independent*. 'I guess the story count has been reduced since we became a compact and so "second string" stories now tend to be spiked. So it can be a bit "hit and miss". Yet when a major report is published we can cover it in more depth than when we were broadsheet."

One of the aspects of his £67,000 job he particularly likes is the input he can make into the *Independent*'s editorials. 'At the *Mirror*, the editorials tended to be the monopoly of David Seymour. Here my views and analyses of educational issues can be fed into the editorials. And that's rewarding.'

It's also rewarding when his reporting can help people in difficult situations. Richard quotes the time he highlighted the plight of 30 teachers from Zimbabwe who were threatened with deportation once their contracts ran out. As a result, the Home Office gave them a six-month reprieve and, following the intervention of the NUT, the teachers were found alternative employment – some of them as classroom assistants.

In recent years, Garner has become a regular radio pundit on educational issues. Intriguingly, one of his first jobs after school in 1967 was as a disc jockey at a discotheque, even being auditioned for Radio 1. 'They thought I might have a good voice for late-night listening on Radio 2. I thought about it for a while but in the end realised as a career move it was the kiss of death.' Eventually he took the plunge, taking the journalism training course at Harlow and joining the *North London Press*, Islington, in 1970. It was his news editor on a later job at the *Camden Journal* who was to have a great impact on his journalistic thinking. 'He taught me that reporting was not simply about listening but campaigning on issues.'

His path towards becoming an education correspondent began in earnest in 1974 when he was appointed local government correspondent on the *Kent Evening Post*, Chatham, while four years later he became education specialist on the *Birmingham Evening Mail*. 'It was a right-wing tabloid with a definite slant on its political stories. They were obsessed with supposed Marxist infiltration of the local trade council. They were always going on about how teachers didn't work hard.' He was left devising various ingenious ways of subverting that bias. In 1980 he moved to the paper's London office as a general reporter and then to Rupert Murdoch's *Times Educational Supplement* where the following year he rose to become news editor. In 1990, to the amazement of many of his colleagues, he left to join the *Mirror* where over 11 years he built up an enormous reputation – breaking top stories and running hard-hitting campaigns.

A HOLIDAY IN THE LIFE OF RICHARD GARNER

Saturday: begins three-day holiday driving up to Wigan with wife and dogs Badger and TT (the Terrible Terrier) for surprise sixtieth-birthday party of brother-in-law. It's rather unfortunate. On the Monday, one of the biggest events of the education year, the publication of the report into the 14–19 curriculum and qualifications by a group headed by Mike Tomlinson, the former chief schools inspector, is expected.

Sunday 7.30 a.m.: Tomlinson's likely call for tougher marking at the top A grade at A level is the lead item on BBC news. Ten days previously Richard has written a story on these lines after a private chat with a head attending a conference. The news desk ring and ask for a piece, which Richard writes by hand and phones over. 'Tomlinson appeared likely to call for foreign languages to return to the centre of secondary schooling while the government was planning to make them only voluntary for children over 14. We on the *Independent* have long been running stories highlighting the need for compulsory languages, and so it was my natural intro angle.'

11.30 a.m.: sets off for holiday in Cornwall.

2 p.m.: while driving on the M5 Richard is rung by his news desk, who ask for a history of examination reform over the last 50 years. 'I did this all out of my own head and phoned it over from a service station.'

Richard realises that he has to be in London for the official launch of the report the following day. So his wife and dogs head for 'a cottage in deepest Cornwall' while he takes the train from Plymouth to Bristol. Arrives late evening and checks in hotel.

Monday 6.45 a.m.: train from Bristol to London. Arrives at press conference with just two minutes to spare.

4 p.m.: it becomes known that Prime Minister Tony Blair, due to speak at a meeting of the Confederation of British Industry in Birmingham that evening, is likely to back the continuation of GCSEs and A levels though not rule out entirely Tomlinson's proposals. So Richard writes 1,200 words, leading on Tomlinson's radical plans for a four-tier diploma, along with a 400-word analysis of the report's key points. Finishes at 5.30. Arrives at Paddington for 6.30 p.m. train with just five minutes to spare.

8.30 p.m.: on the train Richard is phoned by the news editor, who says PA have led on Blair not backing the diploma. Richard rings Tomlinson (who sounds to be relaxing in a pub judging by the background noise). 'He's quite relaxed about Blair's response and says he's simply "playing politics".'

11.15 p.m.: driving down a country lane, Richard is rung by his night news editor. The *Guardian* has led on Blair's failure to support Tomlinson. Can Richard rewrite his intro section mentioning Blair and fax it over? Richard replies: 'Actually, I can't. I'm in deepest Cornwall far away from the nearest fax and soon to be unreachable by mobile.' 'What the heck are you doing?' asks the news editor. 'I'm on holiday. And have been for the last three days – though you would never have guessed it!'

Promoting peace – the new tabloid way

Profile   *Peace News*

In late 2004 a new era began at *Peace News* (*PN*) when it shifted from being an A4 quarterly journal to a monthly tabloid newspaper. Says editor Ippy, sitting back in her tiny, chaotic office just round the corner from King's Cross station in central London:

> The web has changed what people want. The quarterly had done a valiant job but it was expensive to produce and not sufficiently news oriented. We've had very good feedback on our pilot newspaper with people thinking that with its emphasis on news and debate it will help place us at the centre of the broad peace and anti-war movement.

PN, she stresses, has aimed to provide a unique mix of news, hard news analysis and a more personal-based analysis as well as a 'safe place for the exploration of ideas' – and that recipe will remain in the new format.

Launched in the mid-1930s by the pacifist Peace Pledge Union (PPU) and backed over the years by luminaries such as Vera Brittain, Fenner Brockway and Bertrand Russell, Aldous Huxley, Eric Gill and Sybil Thorndike, PN's circulation peaked at forty thousand during the Second World War.

Then, in 1961, with the emergence of the civil rights movement in the United States and the Campaign for Nuclear Disarmament (CND) and direct anti-war

Figure 1.2 *Peace News* as quarterly journal and tabloid newspaper

action in Britain, *PN* broke its ties with the PPU but continued to promote its anti-militarist message. By 2004, around two thousand copies of the quarterly were being sold at £3 a time; some five thousand copies of the tabloid will sell at 50p each. The website, www.peacenews.info, already receives eight thousand to ten thousand hits every month.

Ippy argues that the mainstream media focus too much on people in authority and ultimately promote either despair or apathy. 'Take, for instance, the Palestine–Israeli conflict. People will watch the TV news every night and think: "What a mess – how can it be solved?" The news will feature, for instance, Sharon and Arafat's successors but who is talking to the people at the grass roots, say the women suffering in the refugee camps?' *PN*'s 2004 spring edition looked in detail at the work of non-violent activists in Israel and Palestine, drawing on the diverse experiences of grassroots organisations and committed academics – aiming to inspire political reflection and action. 'We sent hundreds of copies back to the region to try to support local campaigners.'

Ippy's involvement in the peace movement reaches back to the 1980s when she became a regular visitor to the women's camp at the Greenham Common US base. 'It proved to be a very good eye-opener introducing me to new ideas, new people and the advantages of working in a "women-only" environment outside the mainstream political structures.' During the Gulf conflict of 1991 she joined a non-stop vigil outside the Foreign and Commonwealth Office, in central London. 'I was arrested several times. We'd get a mixed reaction from the public. Some people brought us sandwiches. Others would shout at us. The media were either too intrusive; or they could be supportive – which was very pleasing.' Also during the 1990s, her activism took in anti-road-development protests and solidarity activities for women's, peace and refugee groups in the Balkans.

'It was not often realised that 90 per cent of the refugees were women. So on several trips to the region we'd take things women really wanted – like knickers, sanitary towels, paper, computers and cartridges for their offices.' Then after spells working for the Southampton-based Nuclear Information Service (a not-for-profit, independent information service promoting public awareness and fostering debate on nuclear disarmament and related safety and environmental issues), and promoting housing co-operatives in Brighton, Ippy was appointed, much to her surprise, *PN* editor in September 1999.

Perhaps surprisingly, Ippy does not define herself as a 'pacifist'. 'I think the pacifist ideal is a great one to aspire to. But I define myself very confidently as anti-militarist. I oppose war fundamentally as a way to resolve conflict.'

A MONTH IN THE LIFE OF IPPY

Week 1: working three days a week, this is the time for 'conceptualising work' and commissioning for the new edition. Leftovers from the previous issue to be tackled. For instance, copies will be sent out to contributors: most work for nothing but some photographers will be sent payments. Discussions with the promotions team of committed volunteers.

Week 2: largely devoted to company management business. Finances are checked: meetings held with the distribution teams. 'This is a relatively quiet week for me. But at least I know people are busy scribbling away at their articles.'

Week 3: contributors reminded of deadlines. Ippy begins subediting and type-setting all the copy and laying it out, proof-reading and last-minute fact-checking.

Week 4: the publication is completed and sent to the printers. Costs do not allow for proof copies, so there's no chance for making any last-minute corrections. 'It's a miracle more literals do not appear.'

2 Efficks, ethics or politics?

Mainstream journalists are often sceptical about the value of ethical debate. As media specialist Raymond Snoddy (1993) commented: 'It certainly sets the British press apart from newspapers in the US where on the whole the word "ethics" can be uttered without hoots of derision.' One journalism lecturer tells of when he invited a prominent Fleet Street editor to talk to his students about ethics. 'Efficks? What's that?' the editor asked, bemused, and proceeded to tell a string of stories about his life and times in the industry. Or as Kelvin MacKenzie, editor of the *Sun* in the 1980s, put it: 'Ethics is a place to the east of London where men wear white socks' (Hargreaves 2003: 211).

According to Ian Richards (2004: x–xi), similar attitudes predominate in Australia:

> many journalists give little if any consideration to ethical issues in their daily work. As a result, approaches to ethical dilemmas are often determined by individual decisions based on such immediate considerations as what was done last time, what a colleague suggests, what the editor wants, and what it is considered possible to get away with.

There are a number of reasons for this scepticism. Many journalists are profoundly idealistic, concerned about ethical issues and determined to improve standards. Yet the dominant attitude in the mainstream press prioritises 'getting the story' and the demands of the deadline above all else. Ethical and political concerns are secondary, if they are ever considered at all. Andrew Marr sums up this view when he suggests that the phrase 'responsible journalism' should be shunned (2004: 5): 'Responsible to whom? The state? Never. To "the people"? But which people, and of what views? To the readers? It is vanity to think you know them. Responsible, then to some general belief in truth and accuracy? Well, that would be nice.' Linked to this attitude usually is the belief that the best way to learn reporting is 'on the job'. Practical-based training is tolerated but theoretical studies are generally thought a waste of time.

More importantly, many journalists (in particular young ones) are deeply sceptical about the power they have as individuals to improve media standards. Newspapers seem too committed to entrenched routines and mythologies, too prone to stereotyping and crude sensationalising, too closely tied to the political establishment and to the rigours of surviving in a market-led economy. Most newspaper operations are hierarchically organised with power to those (usually white men) at the top. Many lower down the pecking order often see themselves as impotent (and largely dispensable) cogs in a much larger machine. There is much talk of press freedom but little of the journalists' freedom to influence the organisation for which they work.

Adding to this ethical malaise are the theatrical, unreal elements at the heart of the current debate. A major controversy developed during the 1990s over the invasions of the privacy of celebrities, randy royals and sports personalities. Yet these issues confront only a relative minority of journalists for a small part of their time. Far more significant political issues, such as the impact of advertisers or the role of the vast military–industrial complex on the coverage of wars, are marginalised. As John Wadham, director of human rights group Liberty, stressed: 'The press has been guilty of blatant intrusion into the private lives of citizens but it is not the worst offender. Our government has developed an almost obsessive desire to gather and control more and more data on its citizens and we need legislation to curb its excesses.'

The ethical tensions in the industry

Mainstream journalists' scepticism over standards is, in part, a consequence of the ethical contradictions within the newspaper industry. Its central position as a largely monopolistic industry in a profit-oriented economic system means that business and entertainment priorities dominate. News becomes, above all, a commodity to be sold. Yet journalists' rhetoric promotes notions of the public interest, the right to know, and the free press which are often in conflict with the priorities of the marketplace. Moreover, while journalists stress the importance of 'objectivity' and 'truth' (news being a mirror of reality), these notions conflict with the actual production of bias, myth and state propaganda by the press.

The ethics of everyday journalism

Journalists' widespread scepticism about ethics is strange given the importance of the job's moral and political dimensions. All journalists talk of news 'values'. Moreover, representations of good and bad, the just and the unjust or criminal predominate in the media (Cohen 1980). Read any red-top tabloid and you will see stories about 'evil' rapists, 'monsters' who attack old ladies, 'evil' mums who lead their children into prostitution. When Moors murderer Myra Hindley died in November 2002, Fleet Street almost in unison condemned her as 'evil'.

The 1991 Gulf conflict carried this reporting genre to its extreme with representations of President George Bush as 'good, pacific and heroic' engaged in a personal battle with President Saddam Hussein of Iraq, the 'evil, bully, Butcher, new Hitler of Baghdad'. During the NATO attacks on Serbia in 1999, President Slobodan Milosevic was also demonised as 'evil' and a 'new Hitler'. And in the run-up to the US–UK invasion of Iraq in 2003 and during the conflict, Saddam Hussein was predictably represented in the mainstream press as a 'monster' and 'global threat' (Keeble 1998b).

Jostein Gripsrud (1992) relates this moralising dimension of newspapers to the emotional excesses of the nineteenth-century morality play. Today it is the press (and mass media in general) which provide moral tales, stories that give lessons in and define what is good and bad, normal and abnormal.

General Council. Thus, the Press Council came into being in July 1963 – with twenty industry representatives and five lay members.

The first commission had predicted no significant trends towards further concentration of ownership. Events had proved it wrong. By 1962 the top three proprietors' slice of the national daily press had risen to 89 per cent, major monopolies were growing in the periodical press and only in local weeklies was concentration 'negligible'. To contain this trend it proposed a Press Amalgamations Court. Legislation in 1965 incorporated some elements of this idea with major takeovers having to be approved by the Secretary of State. Yet virtually all the acquisitions of newspaper companies by major press groups during the period 1965–99 were allowed.

The Younger Committee on Privacy was established in 1970 after a Private Member's bill seeking to introduce a general right of privacy was rejected by the Labour government. It considered a wide range of issues: for instance, how the right to know could conflict with the right to be protected from intrusive reporters; how reporting could cause personal suffering which might outweigh any claims of public interest. In the end it decided against the introduction of a right to privacy law.

A third Royal Commission (1974–7) reported with concern that three owners dominated the national daily and Sunday markets, while in the regions morning, evening and weekly papers were being owned by the same group. The commission was also critical of the performance of the Press Council, making twelve recommendations to transform its operating procedures. However, these were largely rejected and the council remained a weak body, lacking the confidence of both the managers and the NUJ (Robertson 1983).

Calcutt report into privacy and related matters

In 1989, following a spate of controversies over press intrusions into private grief, Margaret Thatcher's government authorised a committee to investigate the possible introduction of a privacy law. Chaired by David Calcutt, master of Magdalene College, Cambridge, the committee heard evidence from a wide range of people. For instance, the father of an *EastEnders* actor who had committed suicide complained of press harassment. In the end, the committee came out against a privacy law but recommended making physical intrusion an offence.

The industry, however, reacted quickly to the call to set up a self-regulatory Press Complaints Commission in place of the Press Council and so attempt to ward off legislation. The first of many versions of a Code of Practice was introduced and most of the national newspapers also appointed ombudsmen to consider readers' complaints. They were to prove to have only very limited influence.

Second Calcutt report on privacy and the press

In January 1993, Calcutt (by then Sir David) presented a second report focusing on press and privacy issues. The PCC was accused of being ineffective and too dominated by the industry. Calcutt singled out its handling of revelations contained in Andrew Morton's (1992) biography of Diana, Princess of Wales, various sex scandals (involving such prominent figures as Paddy Ashdown, leader of the Liberal Democrats, and David Mellor, National Heritage Minister and Chelsea supporter) and the *People*'s contemptuous treatment of the commission after it printed pictures of an infant royal running naked.

In response Calcutt proposed new offences carrying maximum fines of £5,000 for invasions of privacy and the use of surveillance and bugging devices in certain cases. In defence, journalists could claim the material was obtained for preventing, detecting or exposing crime or antisocial behaviour, or to prevent people being misled by some statement or action of the individual concerned. John Major's government responded positively and later in the year proposed the introduction of a privacy law. Yet it was determined not to apply the restrictions to the security services. As the *UK Press Gazette* of 6 September 1993 commented:

> The greatest invasion of privacy is carried out every day by the security services, with no control, no democratic authorisation and the most horrifying consequences for people's employment and lives. By comparison with them the press is a poodle.

The PCC responded to all this controversy by introducing new clauses to the code on bugging and the use of telephoto lenses, and a lay majority (though only of the great and the good) was created among its members. In addition it appointed Professor Robert Pinker, of the London School of Economics, as its special privacy commissioner.

How the privacy debate hit fever pitch

In November 1993, 'peeping Tom' photographs taken secretly of a reclining Princess Diana working out at a gym and published in the *Sunday Mirror* and the *Mirror* refuelled the privacy debate – though it continued to be focused narrowly on the problems faced by Britain's aristocracy and political elite. As John Tulloch (1998: 80) comments: 'The impression remains that the PCC, constructed out of a pact between the great and the good and the newspaper establishment, is most concerned to look after its own.'

A *Sunday Times* sting operation in July 1994 against two Conservative Members of Parliament (MPs), which revealed them accepting £1,000 from a journalist to ask questions in Parliament, provoked more controversy. The newspaper was originally backed by the PCC but predictably condemned in April 1995 by the Commons Privileges Committee (with its built-in Conservative majority) for 'falling substantially below the standards to be expected of legitimate journalism'. Then, surprisingly, in March 1996, the PCC reversed its decision, ruling that the newspaper did not first gather enough information since an issue of serious public interest was at stake.

In October 1994, the *Guardian* began its own long campaign to expose sleaze among Conservative MPs taking cash handouts in return for asking parliamentary questions. *Guardian* editor Peter Preston admitted that his reporters sent a 'cod fax' to the Ritz Hotel in Paris in the hunt for financial information about Cabinet minister (former journalist and great-nephew of *Daily Express* owner Lord Beaverbrook) Jonathan Aitken, using a mock-up of the House of Commons notepaper to protect the source. The privacy debate duly reached fever pitch (Leigh and Vulliamy 1997).

Preston was summoned to explain his use of the fax to Parliament's Sergeant-at-Arms and resigned from the PCC. Soon afterwards, Premier John Major set up a committee, chaired by Lord Nolan, which eventually drew up guidelines for the ethical behaviour of politicians and lobbyists. After being discovered lying over the payment of a bill at the Paris Ritz during a libel case against the *Guardian*, Aitken was duly jailed for 18 months in July 1999 (though in the end he served only 30 weeks) and the newspaper went on to win award after award for its fearless investigation.

The newly appointed PCC chairman, the Tory grandee Lord Wakeham, in early 1995 gave a strong warning to editors not to abuse the public-interest defence when facing complaints over invasions of privacy. Soon afterwards the PCC criticised the *News of the World* for publishing pictures, gained through the use of a long-lens camera, of yet another aristocrat, a frail-looking Countess Spencer, sister-in-law of the Princess of Wales, in the garden of a private health clinic. After her husband, Earl Spencer, complained, Professor Pinker contacted Rupert Murdoch, owner of the *News of the World*, who publicly reprimanded its editor, Piers Morgan. Murdoch described Morgan as 'a young man' who 'went over the top' in his coverage. The editor duly apologised – and went on to even greater fame as editor of the *Mirror* (Browne 1996).

Then, in July 1995, the government's long-awaited White Paper appeared – but it retreated from imposing any privacy legislation (Department of National Heritage 1995). Instead, it called for

- the PCC to pay compensation from an industry fund to victims of privacy intrusion
- a 'hotline' between the chairman and editors to head off breaches of the code
- non-industry members to sit on the PCC's code committee
- the code to be tightened to include a clearer definition of privacy.

Tory backbenchers greeted the announcement with jeers; the Labour Party expressed disappointment. Yet the privacy issue hit a new peak of intensity after the death of Princess Diana in Paris in a car crash on Sunday, 31 August 1997 (Hanstock 1999). Blame initially fell on the paparazzi following the royal Mercedes and on the press which had so mercilessly pursued the Princess (though it was generally acknowledged that she had exploited the press when it suited her). New guidelines on the use of paparazzi photographs were introduced; in revising the code, Lord Wakeham redefined 'a private place' as covering the interior of a church, a restaurant and other places 'where individuals might rightly be free from media attention'.

Privacy legislation: BY THE BACK DOOR?

While in opposition, the Labour Party had appeared largely sympathetic to calls for privacy legislation as a way of curbing press excesses. When in office, its tune changed. Soon after its May 1997 landslide victory, New Labour made it clear it was not planning to introduce privacy laws unless newspapers behaved in an 'intolerable fashion'. Journalists disguising themselves as doctors were given as an example of such behaviour.

Fears grew among prominent journalists that the European Convention on Human Rights, which the government was due to incorporate into British law, could introduce privacy legislation 'by the back door'. But, on 11 February 1998, Tony Blair pledged in the Commons that the government had no such intention. Article 8 of the convention, incorporated into British law in October 2000, states: 'Everybody has the right to respect for his private and family life, his home and his correspondence.'

But, 'balancing' this, Article 10 guarantees freedom of expression. Significantly, on 16 January 1998, the European Commission of Human Rights had ruled that Earl Spencer and his former wife had insufficient grounds for starting a case in court under the European Convention on Human Rights over the government's failure to protect them against press intrusions.

Then, in April 2000, the PCC condemned the *News of the World* in what Roy Greenslade, media commentator of the *Guardian*, described as a 'landmark' judgement on privacy. A typical kiss 'n' tell story by the former fiancé of *Coronation Street* actress Jacqueline Pirie was said to have breached clause 3 of the code: 'Everyone is entitled to his or her private and family life, home, health and correspondence.' As Greenslade (2000) concluded: 'In other words, the one-sided account by Pirie's ex-fiancé, even though its truth has not been disputed, was considered to have invaded her privacy.'

In recent years, Fleet Street has been ablaze with a series of privacy scandals (see Mayes 2002):

- In July 2001, Anna Ford asked High Court judge for judicial review of a PCC decision to reject her claim that the *Daily Mail* and *OK!* magazine had infringed her privacy by publishing secretly gained pictures of her in a bikini on a beach on holiday in Majorca. But Mr Justice Silber rejected her claim.

- In November 2001, Mr Justice Jack banned the *Sunday People* from 'exposing a married Premiership footballer who has two secret mistresses'. The judge controversially declared that all sexual relations should remain private. Then, in March 2002, Lord Chief Justice Woolf ruled that the judge was wrong to ban the newspaper from publishing interviews with a lapdancer and a teacher who had had affairs with married Premiership footballer Gary Flitcroft.

- In December 2001, publication of topless photographs of actress Amanda Holden taken while at a private holiday villa landed the *Daily Star* with £165,000 in an out-of-court settlement.

- In June 2003, radio DJ Sara Cox won £50,000 in a major out-of-court award after the *People* published pictures of her and husband nude while on honeymoon in the Seychelles. The newspaper was sued under section 8 of the Human Rights Act. The case first went to the PCC and an apology was printed in the next week's issue of the paper in October 2001. According to the editor and photographer concerned, she had yielded her right to privacy because she had posed for candid pictures in the past and given supposedly intimate interviews. But libel rules allow lawyers to take cases on a 'no win, no fee' basis and then charge 100 per cent uplift on fees if they win to make up for the risk of failure. Cox's lawyers claimed £275,000 in costs for fee uplift. And a group of top UK media organisations in September 2004 told Parliament that such rules were seriously threatening freedom of speech (Ponsford 2004b).

- The claim by supermodel Naomi Campbell for breach of privacy (when the *Mirror* revealed she was attending Narcotics Anonymous meetings) originally crashed despite her success in persuading the judge that she needed protection from intrusion. The trial was fought on confidentiality rather than privacy and Campbell won damages of only £3,500. In October 2002 the Appeal Court overturned the decision with the *Mirror* cleared of breaching the Data Protection Act when it published 'sensitive personal details' about her. Finally, just to prove the absurdly confusing state of the privacy legislation (and the way it is able to feed the pockets of overpaid lawyers), in May 2004 the Law Lords ruled 3–2 in favour of Campbell. Peter Hill, editor of the *Daily Express*, summed up the views of many: 'It's got nothing to do with freedom of the press or privacy. It's just a battle between two giant egos' (Morris 2004).

- In a case to delight the red-top tabloids, Hollywood superstars Catherine Zeta-Jones and Michael Douglas objected to unauthorised photographs of their wedding in *Hello!* after formal publicity arrangements had been agreed with *OK!* In November 2003, damages of £1,033,000-plus had to be paid for breach of commercial confidence to *OK!* which had lost huge sales as a result of the spoiler (Trkulja 2003). But after the stars' claim for invasion of privacy was rejected they received just £14,600 in damages – 'hardly enough to make it worth the bother of jetting in to the High Court and asking for £50,000 for personal distress' (Lamont 2004). Both sides (to the delight, this time, of the lawyers) were able to claim victory. *Hello!* indicated it would appeal against the costs as 'far too high'. And just to confuse everyone, in May 2005, the Court of Appeal overturned the £1m awarded to *OK!*. The lawyers smiled.

- In a less hyped but more significant case, senior policeman Brian Paddick won his legal battle in December 2003 against the *Mail on Sunday*. He claimed the paper invaded his privacy by revealing his gayness in two reports in March 2002. With the trial due to begin in February 2004, the newspaper agreed to apologise, contribute to the officer's legal costs and pay substantial damages. His lawyer, Tasmin Allen, claimed that the case proved her claimant had a right to privacy. But the newspaper claimed it had settled over libel – and not privacy.

- Then, in June 2004, the European Court of Human Rights ruled that photographs of Princess Caroline of Monaco and her children in a public place should not have been published since they invaded her privacy rights. The court overturned a German ruling in 1999 which said that as a public figure she had to accept being photographed in public. The rights of paparazzi photographers throughout Europe appeared threatened. But legal expert Dan Tench claimed the effects would be limited since many seemingly 'snatched' photographs of celebrities were taken with their permission while celebs would be reluctant to bring actions because of the relatively limited damages available (Ponsford and Slattery 2004a). Lawyers were waiting for the next instalment of the Great Privacy Saga, no doubt with glee.

Money matters: CHECKING OUT CHEQUEBOOK JOURNALISM

The Major government did threaten to intervene in the controversial area of 'chequebook journalism'. Following payments by newspapers to 19 witnesses in the Rosemary West multiple murders trial, the Lord Chancellor, Lord Mackay of Clashfern, in October 1996, proposed bringing in a criminal law to ban such payments. The PCC responded predictably by lauding the benefits of self-regulation and revising its code again to highlight the importance of full disclosure. The issue was even taken up by the Labour government in February 2000 when the Lord Chancellor, Lord Irvine, announced that the government was to review payments by the press to witnesses in criminal trials. Guy Black, PCC director, immediately responded by claiming that the issue had arisen only five times in the past fifty years so such legislation was unnecessary.

Earlier, a series of newspaper payments to criminals drew some intriguing rulings from the PCC. After two nurses, jailed in Saudi Arabia for murder, were released early, in May 1998, newspapers raced to dangle chequebooks in front of them. Deborah Parry was 'bought' by the *Express* and Lucille McLaughlan by the *Mirror*. Soon afterwards the PCC ruled that their stories were in the public interest. Payment controversies also erupted after *The Times* serialised Gitta Sereny's (1998) biography of child murderer Mary Bell (see Rozenberg 2004: 132–8) and after the *Daily Mail* paid £40,000 to the parents of au-pair Louise Woodward, convicted of the manslaughter of baby Matthew Eapen in Boston: again the PCC ruled that there were clear public-interest defences.

But the *Daily Telegraph* was censured by the PCC in July 1999 for paying Victoria Aitken about £1,000 for writing about her jailed father's plight since it could not be defended in the public interest. And in 2003 the *Guardian* was censured for paying £750 to a fellow prisoner of Jeffrey Archer.

The politics of sleaze reporting

An unprecedented number of political resignations occurred in the three years after John Major's election victory of 1992 and his launch of a 'Back to Basics' moral crusade, many of them following 'scandalous' revelations in the press. Such scandals were not confined to Britain. Hardly a country was unaffected as ruling elites bickered among themselves following the ending of the Cold War and the demise of the old Soviet enemy. In all, there were fourteen resignations on the grounds of scandal in Britain over the three years: about half the cases involved sexual activities and about half financial irregularities. All were men.

The *Independent on Sunday* (23 July 1995) claimed that a five-year period (1990–5) saw 34 Conservatives, one Liberal Democrat and four Labour scandals; of these, at least a quarter involved sex. Furthermore, a study of parliamentary reporting in the nationals between 1990 and 1995 found that 'scandal and personal misconduct' was the third most frequently reported topic, way ahead of major issues such as health (eighth), education (tenth), social services (thirty-fifth) and race (thirty-eighth) (Franklin 1997: 32).

Sleaze also dogged the Labour government. The breakdown of the marriage of the late Robin Cook, Foreign Secretary, and the failure of Peter Mandelson, Minister without Portfolio, to declare how a gift from Geoffrey Robinson, a Cabinet minister, had helped him purchase a London house (leading to the resignations of both Mandelson and Robinson) were among the most celebrated scandals to hit the headlines (Baston 2000: 192–209). And Mandelson was forced to resign for the second time on 24 January 2001 over his fatal refusal to be frank with the Prime Minister about his role in brokering a British passport for a £1 million donor to the Millennium Dome. But Prime Minister Blair was determined to rescue his friend (and member of the powerful though shadowy Bilderberg Group) from oblivion and so appointed him European Commissioner in July 2004 (a scandal of a kind, too, some would argue). And Home Secretary David Blunkett became embroiled in a scandal late in 2004 after his affair with Kimberly Quinn ended – and hit the headlines. He went on to resign – and take a few months' break from politics.

Sleaze engulfed the PCC, too, when its chairman Lord Wakeham was forced to resign in February 2002 after becoming embroiled in the Enron scandal. Privacy commissioner Professor Robert Pinker became the acting chair until the appointment of Sir Christopher Meyer, former ambassador to the USA, as chair in March 2002.

Underlying newspapers' coverage of sleaze lies the operation of consensual news values. As Hogan (1998) comments: 'The problem with the coverage of sleaze was how scandal of a predominantly sexual nature spread from Sunday tabloids to Sunday evening BBC and ITN news. By Monday the broadsheet press were covering the scandals.' Behind the formation of such a consensus, the political factors remain the most interesting and significant (Keeble 1998).

Now little distinguishes the three major parties in Britain. Tony Blair, the Labour leader, proclaimed himself a follower of Margaret Thatcher, mouthed Thatcherite rhetoric with consummate ease and dutifully followed Thatcherite politics (Hay 1999). The emergence of New Toryism as New Labour represents, in one respect, the death of (classical) politics. Peter Mair (2000) talks of the 'assault on partisan politics' and the 'depoliticised democracy'. In its place has emerged the politics of personality, of sexual scandal and sleaze. The Bill Clinton–Monica Lewinsky scandal represents the ultimate manifestation of this process in the United States. Newspapers no longer draw their central inspiration from politics but from the worlds of Hollywood, entertainment generally, television and sport.

To relate this coverage to the practicalities of the job, why not ask some journalists their views on the introduction of a privacy law? In June 2003, the Commons committee for culture, media and sport recommended that legislation should be introduced to 'clarify the protection that individuals can expect from unwarranted intrusion by anyone – not the press alone – into their private lives'. Following press disclosures about the marriage of David and Victoria Beckham, a *Guardian*–ICM poll in April 2004 found 69 per cent of voters would support a privacy law. And in October 2004 a poll conducted by Communicate Research for the *Independent* found that the introduction of a 'tightly defined privacy law with a clear public interest defence' would win the backing of 90 per cent of Labour MPs and 68 per cent of Conservatives (Burrell 2004b). Do your local journalists (on mainstream and non-mainstream media) agree? Have they ever used a bugging device in pursuit of a story? Or do they find ethical controversies largely irrelevant? Do newspapers in your area offer readers a right of reply?

Sex matters: COMBATING SEXISM

There are no easy answers to the many ethical dilemmas in journalism. Even when people agree on the importance of certain principles (such as anti-sexism, anti-racism, anti-militarism) differences may emerge over strategies for implementing them. While certain attitudes and routines predominate throughout the mainstream media, each newspaper still has its unique culture. What is possible at one will be impossible at another. Thus in tackling sexism within the industry there are many strategies available. For instance, once you have secured your first job, you may choose to lie low on ethical issues and wait until you have established your credibility before speaking out.

You may work on ethical or political issues through the National Union of Journalists. Your newspaper may routinely carry page-three-type images of women and glorify macho images of men. In this context, you may choose to work discreetly, raising issues in discussions with colleagues, using any freedom you have in choosing features and sources to tackle sexist assumptions. Some journalists even opt out of mainstream media for ethical reasons. For them, working in the mainstream involves too many ethical compromises. They may see racist, sexist and class biases too firmly entrenched. Constant confrontations over these issues can prove both exhausting and counter-productive. In contrast, they may find a culture away from the mainstream press more open to progressive ideas. Wherever you choose to work, a sense of humour and a willingness to subject your own views to searching criticism will always prove invaluable.

The questioning approach

Since ethical debate remains remote from the dominant journalists' culture, simply raising pertinent questions can become an important first step. Many ethical questions stem from the unjust distribution of power in society; they are, at root, political issues. The focus tends to fall on the 'oppressed' – women, children, elderly people, disabled people and ethnic minority groups. The dominant questions focus around how discrimination and stereotyping can be reduced. But is there not a danger here of focusing on these groups as victims (of oppression and consequent stereotyping) while the problem groups are really the oppressors – men, adults, the able-bodied, the dominant ethnic groups?

The question of sexism

The 1990s witnessed a few advances for women in the mainstream press (Sebba 1994). In May 1991, Eve Pollard became the first woman editor of the *Sunday Express* while, in April 1998, Rosie Boycott became the first woman editor of a broadsheet (the struggling *Independent on Sunday*) before moving on first to the editorship of the *Independent* and then – in April 1998 – of the *Express*. At the *Sunday Mirror*, editorial control in November 1996 was in the hands of three women: managing director Bridget Rowe, deputy managing director Pat Moore and acting editor Amanda Platell. This was the first time in Fleet Street history that an all-female executive triumvirate had held power on a national newspaper. And the 1990s Balkans conflicts saw the rise of women correspondents such as Maggie O'Kane (the *Guardian*) and Janine de Giovanni (*The Times*) (see Delano 2003).

In May 2000, Rebekah Wade, at 31, became editor of the *News of the World*, the world's biggest-selling English-language newspaper, and in the same month Rebecca Hardy, at 34, became the first woman editor of the *Scotsman*. In December 2002, Sly Bailey took over as head of Trinity Mirror. Then, in January 2003, Wade was appointed the first woman editor of the *Sun* in succession to David Yelland while in December of the same year Dawn Neeson became editor of the *Star* (though it remained one of the most sexist red-tops on Fleet Street).

At the local level, the *Diss Express* was staffed entirely by women. On 8 March 2000, to mark International Women's Day the *Western Mail* changed its name to the *Western Femail* and was edited by Pat English with Michelle Bower as head of content. As Noreen Taylor (2000) comments, male newspaper owners had 'realised that winning women readers and attracting female-targeted advertising is best achieved by promoting women'.

Attitudes have changed somewhat since 1964 when the *Daily Mail* headed the story 'British wife wins Nobel Prize' after Dorothy Crowfort Hodgkin became the first British woman to gain the honour. Yet research by the Women in Journalism (WiJ) pressure group published in 1996 revealed a 'pervasive and flexible strand of stereotyping through coverage of women in the news'. Newsrooms tended to be male-dominated and traditional sexist attitudes survived unscathed. WiJ concluded: 'It seems clear that sometimes news desks go on autopilot, trotting out clichés and stereo-types when, in fact, the woman in the story before them is unique.' A later report from WiJ, *Real Women: The Hidden Sex*, in November 1999 highlighted the sexist use of images of women to 'lift' pages.

Most political editors and lobby correspondents remain male. 'So,' according to Harriet Harman (2000), 'political news is reported in a way that appeals to and inter-ests men. Issues of particular concern to women are inevitably lower on the agenda. This reinforces the sense among women that politics is a male activity of no relevance to them.' Research has also shown the general bias in news reporting towards male sources (Allan 2004: 119–31). Margareta Melin-Higgins (1997) found that most of the female journalists she interviewed were concerned that the recruitment system was disadvantageous to women in an industry where an 'old-boys network loomed large'.

Concern of feminist critics focuses particularly on the coverage of sport. Women cricketers, footballers and golfers hardly get a look in. And often, when women do feature, their presence is heavily sexualised. From the early 1980s to the present day, coverage of sportswomen, such as the late Florence Griffith Joyner, Katarina Witt, Gabriela Sabatini, Mary Pierce, Anna Kournikova, Serena Williams and Maria Sharapova has tended to focus on their sexuality.

Take Lyndsay Clydesdale, in the *Mirror* of 9 July 2004. Sharapova, the Wimbledon 2004 winner, is described as a 'sexy smasher' who has both beauty and talent (as if they were mutually exclusive) and later on as a 'tennis babe' (thus predictably infan-tilising one of the world's top players). In a similar way, 34-year-old Kelly Holmes, double gold winner at the 2004 Olympics, was constantly described throughout the national press as 'our golden girl'.

An NUJ survey in 2004 found that more than half the union's gay, lesbian and transsexual members had suffered discrimination at work through having promotion refused, being verbally abused or bullied. Women journalists too often face ridicule from their male colleagues. Ginny Dougary (author of *Executive Tarts and Other Myths*) was criticised for being an 'ambitious girl reporter' (she was 38) after her revealing profile of Chancellor Norman Lamont was published in *The Times* magazine in September 1994. As Amanda Platell (1999: 144) comments on the institutionalised sexism in the press:

> it's about pigeonholing women journalists, denying equality of pay and conditions and opportunities, demeaning them and making assumptions about them. It's about a widespread and inherent belief by some men that women can't cut it, that news-papers are a man's world, that women are only good for one thing – 'features' – and that ritual humiliation is a way of keeping girls in their place.

All reporters should be aware of the major feminist theorists and campaigners such as Olympe de Gouges (1748–93), Mary Wollstonecraft (1759–97), Millicent Garrett Fawcett (1847–1929), Emmeline Pankhurst (1858–1929), Christabel Pankhurst

(1880–1958), Sylvia Pankhurst (1882–1960), Emma Goldman (1869–1940), Rosa Luxemburg (1871–1919), Simone de Beauvoir (1908–96), Andrea Dworkin (1946–2005), and contemporaries such as Kate Millet, Catherine MacKinnon, Angela Davis, Susan Faludi, Arundhati Roy, Joan Smith, Germaine Greer, Camille Paglia and Dale Spender (see http://www.marxists.org/reference/subject/philosophy/works/ot/spender.htm).

Try to combat the routine marginalisation of women's voices in the media. Reports and features, where possible, should reflect the gender (as well as the race, age and class) diversity of the society. Editors need to be convinced that women's issues should not be confined to special pages and soft features. Just as newspapers have defence and environment specialists, should they not have specialists producing news with a women's focus?

Men and sexism

All these issues 'problematise' women. Instead, let us focus on men (see MacKinnon 2003). To what extent are male roles stereotyped in the press with images glorifying macho firmness, violence, power, militarism, heroism and success? Do not reviewers have a responsibility to challenge such representations in films, plays and books? To what extent does the press encourage men to question their emotional unease, their career obsessions or their traditional roles away from the home and child-rearing? To what extent are men challenged over their responses to sexual violence towards women or to the sexual harassment of women in the workplace?

To add a further complexity to the debate, it can be argued that sexism sometimes works in favour of women. Women foreign correspondents often say the 'invisibility' of women in some cultures helps give them access to places where men would be banned or harassed (see Leslie 1999). Editors are sometimes said to favour women as profile writers since men are considered more likely to open up to a female interviewer.

Man-made language

The marginalisation of women in the press and the glorification of macho or laddish values do not usually come from any deliberate policy. They emerge within a political culture where certain attitudes are routinely adopted and certain questions are routinely eliminated. One area where sexism is most evident is in language. Very often the male bias of language can render women invisible (Spender 1980; Mills 1991). Or it can infantilise them. For instance, when the Labour victory of 1997 was accompanied by a large new influx of women MPs they were immediately dubbed (in sexist terms) 'Blair's babes'.

As Margaret Doyle stresses (1995: 4–5) in her seminal text on sexist language: 'The struggle for control of language has always been a political and highly charged one.' 'Political correctness' has become a useful label for ridiculing an opposing viewpoint and for discrediting 'the legitimate aspirations of different communities and their desire for a language that includes rather than excludes them'.

Challenging this bias is no easy task. Some newspaper style books avoid all mention of sexist language issues except in relation to the use of 'Ms', 'Miss' and 'Mrs'. Most newspapers now accept the use of 'Ms' where appropriate and avoid using 'he' when 'he or she' or 'they' (as a singular bisexual pronoun) is more accurate.

Phrases such as 'the common man' and the 'man in the street' are also widely avoided. Discussions over style book changes, then, provide opportunities to raise language issues. But style book revisions are often monopolised by an editorial elite. In certain situations it might be appropriate to work with your colleagues in the NUJ to confront sexist stereotyping in language. To assist such campaigns, the union has drawn up an *Equality Style Guide* suggesting words to be avoided and alternatives. Here are some examples:

businessman	business manager, executive, boss, business chief, head of firm
cameraman	photographer, camera operator
dustman	refuse collector
fireman/men	firefighter, fire services staff, fire crews
foreman	supervisor
forefathers	ancestors
gentleman's agreement	verbal agreement
ice cream man	ice cream seller
mankind	humanity, people
manpower	employers/workforce
newsman	journalist, reporter
nightwatchman	caretaker, security guard
old masters	classic art
policeman/men	police officer, police
rights of man	citizens'/people's rights
salesman/girl	assistant, shop worker, shop staff, representative, sales staff
spaceman	astronaut
stewardess/air hostess	airline staff, flight attendant, cabin crew
workmen	workers, workforce

Even where style books fail to acknowledge these issues, there is often a certain degree of stylistic freedom available to the reporter to use such language.

Race and anti-racism: NOT JUST A BLACK AND WHITE ISSUE

It could be argued that the British press is at its worst when engaging in racist, overtly xenophobic rhetoric. Attacks on 'scrounging asylum seekers', 'Arab rats', 'funny Frogs', 'boring Belgians' or 'lazy Irish' are commonplace in the patriotic pops (Searle 1989; Gordon and Rosenberg 1989). In March 2000, for instance, the *Sun* directed its venom at East European 'beggars' and 'Gypsy scroungers' yet failed to turn its attention to proprietor Rupert Murdoch, 'who has managed to avoid paying corporation tax in this country for years' (Wheen 2000).

In August 2001, the NUJ chapel at the *Express* and the *Star* significantly condemned proprietor Richard Desmond for the newspaper's 'hysterical and racist' campaign against asylum seekers. A report by the European Monitoring Centre on Racism and Xenophobia in May 2002 blamed the British mainstream media for using negative stereotypes of Muslims and portraying asylum seekers as 'terrorists' and 'the enemy within' following the September atrocities in the United States. In 2003, the human rights body Article 19 criticised reporting as 'characterised by the inaccurate and provocative use of language to describe those entering the country to seek asylum. 51 different labels were identified as making reference to individuals seeking refuge in Britain and included meaningless and derogatory terms such as "illegal refugee" and "asylum cheat"' (Article 19, 2003: 9). And in May 2004 a report by the Commission on British Muslims and Islamophobia blamed the media for promoting anti-Muslim attitudes.

Since racist oppression is historically rooted in Britain's imperial past, is it not inevitable that the press, operating essentially as the propaganda and ideological arm of the dominant economic system, should reflect this? As Simon Cottle argues (1999: 197): 'News values lead to the forefronting of images of ethnic minorities in terms of conflict, drama, controversy, violence and deviance. Such deep-seated qualities of "news" are professionally pursued as a matter of unconscious routine such is their contribution to a journalist's sense of what makes a "good" story.' Along with institutional racism goes the overt racism of some journalists and media proprietors. For instance, the *Sun*'s acting editor was recorded as saying: 'I'm not having pictures of darkies on the front page' (Hollingsworth 1990: 132). And, in April 2004, Richard Desmond, owner of the *Daily Express*, launched a tirade against Germans whom he accused of being Nazis as he goosestepped around a boardroom.

Ethnic minorities form 6.7 per cent of Britain's working population: 2.4 million out of 33 million. Yet a major report by Anthony Delano and John Henningham (1995), of the London College of Printing, concluded that fewer than 2 per cent of British press, radio and television journalists were black or ethnic while out of around four thousand national newspaper journalists only two or three dozen were black. A study by the Journalism Training Forum (linking various media training bodies) in 2002 similarly found just 2 per cent of journalists were from black or Asian backgrounds. And in October 2004 a report from the Society of Editors found just 28 ethnic journalists out of 634 on newspapers in ten major English towns and cities (Preston 2004b). As black *Guardian* journalist Gary Younge comments: 'Editors tend to hire in their own image and thus reinforce the status quo. Blacks aren't in the networks, it's as simple as that' (Keeble 2001: 74).

Editors tend to complain that they do not receive applications from ethnic minority communities and that journalism courses fail to recruit significantly from these groups. Moves to increase the number of black journalists through special training grants and other means clearly need to be supported. Too often newspaper coverage of ethnic minority groups and asylum seekers focuses on 'problems' such as 'riots', violence, crime, 'welfare scrounging' and drug abuse. Alongside this representation go media images of Muslim fanatics as mad and threatening global stability. The sensational coverage given to race issues feeds on people's fears and reinforces them.

Tackling racism

There are no easy answers. As Allan (2004: 168) comments: 'The ways in which racist presuppositions are implicated in the routinized practices of news production, from the news values in operation to "gut instincts" about source credibility, are often difficult to identify let alone reverse.' But there are some useful strategies. Language used uncritically can play a crucial role in perpetuating racism (van Dijk 1991). Thus be wary of using 'black' in a negative context. Should alternatives be found for blackspot (accident site) and blackleg (strike-breaker)? The NUJ has drawn up guidelines which are worth consulting for race reporting and for covering racist organisations.

Should newspapers ban coverage of racist parties? In 2004, the *Argus*, Brighton, banned the far right British National Party from its pages. Other newspapers argue it is important to expose the BNP's policies and campaign against them. Mainstream journalists certainly need to extend their range of contacts to incorporate ethnic minority groups. The *Washington Post*, for instance, has a diversity committee which reviews ethnic and racial composition of staff, a correspondent dedicated to race rela- tions issues, and a series of informal lunches where staff and the ombudsman meet to discuss the way the paper reports race issues. In London, scholarships are reserved for minority journalists at City University but all newspapers should develop strate- gies for recruiting, retaining and promoting ethnic-minority staff and consider the appointment of race relations specialists. Similarly, journalists need to be far more aware of the major religions of the world.

The *Leicester Mercury* has correspondents from the city's Asian communities who file news and pictures regularly. The Nottingham *Evening Post* has launched an ethnic awareness programme for all its editorial staff. The *Yorkshire Post* had an Asian columnist, Anila Baig, tackling such subjects as trips back to Pakistan and the cultural difficulties young Asians can encounter until she was snapped up (perhaps surpris- ingly) by the *Sun* after she was named Columnist of the Year in the 2004 Regional Press Awards (Moore 1999; Arnot 2004). Journalists need to be made aware of alter- native and ethnic-minority media (such as *Muslim News*, *Q News*, *Eastern Eye*, *Asian Times*, *Voice*, *New Nation*, the *Jewish Chronicle* and *Race and Class*), their different ethical standpoints and their opportunities for offering alternative careers away from mainstream stereotyping – and the anti-racist campaigns of journals such as *Socialist Worker*, *Searchlight, Peace News* and *New Left Review* (Keeble 2001: 71–83).

Handling disability: PEOPLE FIRST?

According to the leading campaigning body, the British Council of Disabled People (www.bcodp.org.uk), the disabled are people with impairments who are discriminated against by society. Government research suggests there are 8.6 million adults with disabilities in Britain (including 23,000 deaf people and people with impaired hearing), meaning that one in five people of working age are disabled. Yet they are too often marginalised, rendered invisible or stereotyped in the press and throughout the media. Scope (www.scope.org.uk), the organisation for people with cerebral palsy, in a survey of press coverage of disabled people, concluded: 'There remains an imbal- ance between the reality of people's lives, hopes and aspirations and the way they are written about. Too often stereotypes are used and false assumptions indulged.'

Covering people with disabilities poses a number of ethical issues for journalists which have been highlighted in a campaign 'People First' by the NUJ and the Campaign for Press and Broadcasting Freedom (with leaflets available for partially sighted people, in braille and on tape). The campaign suggests that, as a reporter, you should never assume that your audience is able-bodied. When advertising events (in listings, entertainment reviews, travel and eating-out features), newspapers have a responsibility to identify the provision for access by disabled people. Similarly, traditional news values which marginalise the concerns of people with disabilities and confine them to specialist columns and publications need to be challenged.

The campaign also raises some other pertinent questions. How often are the voices of disabled people represented in the press by 'able-bodied' experts? How much is coverage of disabled people over-sentimentalised? Too often, stereotypes of disability promote the idea that charity can solve their 'problems' while marginalising the view that political and economic changes are needed to end the discrimination they confront. Similarly, disabled people are often associated with being courageous, tragic victims, eternally cheerful, grateful, pathetic and asexual. How often is it recognised that they may be black, or lesbian or gay?

Language

As a number of style books point out, it is better to refer to 'disabled people' rather than 'the disabled', which depersonalises them and focuses entirely on their disability. Words such as 'cripple', 'deaf and dumb' and 'abnormal' should be avoided. Negative words and phrases should not be linked with disabilities as in 'lame duck', 'blind stupidity' and 'deaf to reason'. 'Physically challenged' is not generally accepted as a substitute for 'disabled'. Use 'wheelchair user' but not 'wheelchair bound'.

Avoiding the victim syndrome: HANDLING AIDS STORIES

Journalists face special ethical issues when compiling AIDS-related stories. Reporting of AIDS-related diseases in the early 1980s was minimal because those affected – gays, drug users and Africans – were already marginalised by the press. Since then coverage of AIDS-related stories has too often been either sensationalised, with the creation of 'moral panics' exploiting and perpetuating fears of the fatal condition, and of sexuality in general, or more recently marginalised. Not surprisingly, ignorance amongst the public about HIV is high, according to a survey published in December 2004 by Marie Stopes International (Boseley 2004a). Only 64 per cent knew that babies can be infected in the womb while 11 per cent thought you could get it from kissing and 5 per cent from eating with the same cutlery. Only 26 per cent thought behaviour by heterosexuals put them at high risk, even though the fastest rise around the world, including the UK, in recent years has been amongst heterosexuals. By 2004, HIV infection had become the fastest-growing serious health condition in the UK – and in many countries across the globe.

Some style books have identified areas where special care is needed. For instance, on reporting claims for an AIDS cure, the Reuters style book commented:

> If a story making dramatic claims for a cure for AIDS or cancer does not come from a reputable named source it must be checked with recognised medical experts before being issued (or spiked). If such a story is issued it should include whatever balancing or interpretative material is available from such authorities.

A leaflet produced by the NUJ and the Health Education Authority, *HIV and AIDS: A Guide for Journalists*, suggests that stories should not perpetuate myths that AIDS can be spread through casual contact such as kissing. It can be spread only through intimate sexual contact, by the sharing of needles by drug addicts, by blood transfusion or from mother to infant in pregnancy. Some reports about children with HIV, it says, have provoked anxieties among pupils and parents. Confidentiality about infection by either a child or adult should always be respected. No pressure should be put on people to reveal their identities. Even when names and addresses have been supplied by the police, these should be revealed only with the consent of those concerned.

The NUJ has also drawn up a useful guide for covering AIDS (acquired immune deficiency syndrome) stories. Instead of 'carrying AIDS' or 'AIDS carrier' or 'AIDS positive' (which confuses the two phases of being infected with HIV and having AIDS) it suggests 'people with HIV'. 'AIDS test' is to be avoided since the most commonly used test detects antibodies to HIV (human immunodeficiency virus). Someone who proves positive, and thus infected with HIV, does not necessarily go on to develop AIDS. A better phrase is 'HIV antibody test'. When the distinction is made clearly between HIV and AIDS, there is no need to use the term 'full-blown AIDS'. Nor is it possible to 'catch AIDS' like colds or flu. Better to say 'contract HIV'. People do not 'die of AIDS' but of cancers or pneumonia that develop because of a weakened immune system.

Many people with HIV express concern over the way the press has represented them as helpless victims. Reports should avoid phrases such as 'AIDS sufferer' or 'AIDS victim' since someone with AIDS can continue working for some time after diagnosis. Better to say 'person with AIDS'. Also avoid 'innocent victim' since this suggests that others are guilty. The style guide suggests avoiding the term 'high-risk groups' since there is risk behaviour rather than risk groups. In addition, the NUJ has drawn up a model, nine-point house agreement promoting employment protection for those infected with HIV or who have AIDS.

Censorship and self-censorship

It might seem strange to journalists on a small weekly to raise the issue of censorship. The problem at their newspaper might not be censorship but the opposite: finding enough material to fill the next edition. Proprietorial interference may be non existent. As for the advertisers, they might take up more space than is ideal but that is reality in a market-driven economy, isn't it? Yet, for all journalists, censorship issues are relevant. At the most basic level, the dominant news values prioritise certain sources and perspectives and marginalise or eliminate others. In a way, isn't that a form of censorship?

The impact of advertisers

The impact of advertisers on the press is enormous. Occasionally they will put pressure on editors to highlight favourable stories and downgrade or remove others. Freesheets, entirely dependent on advertisers, are particularly vulnerable to this. As Donald Trelford (2000), former editor of the *Observer*, commented: 'There are certainly some parts of newspapers, usually in consumer areas such as travel, motoring and property where the choice of subject and the editorial treatment dance to a tune set by the advertisement department.' Advertorials (features written by staff journalists but clearly labelled as advertisements) also show the impact of advertising on editorial strategies. But in general the pressure is far more subtle. Within the general economic environment, advertisers promote the values of materialism and consumerism as well as a conservative respect for the status quo.

Curran and Seaton (2003: 29–37) argue that the emergence of an advertisement-based newspaper industry in the late nineteenth century helped stifle the development of a radical press. Even as late as 1964, the Labour-backing *Daily Herald* closed with a readership far larger than that of *The Times* and the *Financial Times* combined. It had crucially failed to win the support of the advertisers.

The impact of proprietorial intervention:
THE MAXWELL FACTOR ET AL.

The film *Citizen Kane* captured all the mystique and romance that surround the media mogul in the cultural history of the West. Men such as the American media tycoon William Randolph Hearst, on whom Kane was based, and Northcliffe, Beaverbrook, Rothermere, Rowland, Murdoch and Maxwell have cultivated images which have made them seem almost larger than life: eccentric, egocentric, super-powerful, super-rich. There are many accounts of these proprietors interfering in the day-to-day operations of their newspapers.

Editorials have been written or rewritten, layouts have been altered. Partisan politics (largely right-wing and belligerent during crises and wars) have been promoted. Favoured journalists have risen through the ranks; others have been sacked or pressurised into leaving. The now-disgraced former proprietor of the *Telegraph*s, Lord Black, would write critically to the letters columns of his newspapers if he objected to a certain line. Newspapers end up being, not public watchdogs, but press lords' poodles (Bower 1988; Leapman 1983; Shawcross 1992). Fleet Street's history is often portrayed as a fascinating saga revolving around these figures (Wintour 1990).

Most serious has been the cumulative impact of these devout defenders of the free press on narrowing the consensus in British newspapers. Given the links between the major media throughout the UK, that censorship has seriously distorted news values, even in the provinces. Most national newspapers have plumped predictably, and often ferociously, for the Conservative Party, or more recently the newly respectable, right-wing and warmongering Labour Party.

In particular, the integration of the media barons' empires into the world of international finance and industry has given rise to a host of potential no-go areas for newspapers. Understandably, newspaper proprietors are reluctant to have reporters probing into their more murky activities. *Mirror* owner Robert Maxwell managed to keep the scandal of his pension-fund rip-off secret during his lifetime through a mixture of intimidation, a merciless use of the courts and libel laws, and exploiting journalists' desire for the quiet life (Greenslade 1992; Davies 1995).

Moreover, media moguls have inevitably promoted their own financial interests through their newspapers. Tiny Rowland's *Observer* campaigned against the Al Fayed family following their purchase of Harrods. Maxwell constantly publicised himself and his many 'charitable' and political activities. Murdoch has promoted his television, publishing and internet interests through his many outlets and opposed the

BBC at every opportunity. All the same, there is a danger of exaggerating the power of the proprietors. All have been or are colourful personalities. But virtually every industry today is led at local, national and international levels by a small group of companies. Media moguls are merely the newspaper manifestations of this trend: typical monopoly holders within advanced capitalism. Stressing their power serves to boost their egos while exonerating journalists from some of their worst excesses.

Big Brother?

Censorship by the state has served to create a climate of intimidation and 'emergency' at critical moments. But overt interventions by the state into the operations of newspapers have been the exceptions to the rule. Various other factors, such as the impact of advertisers, the role of the dominant news value system, proprietorial pressure, journalists' self-censorship and the growing number of repressive laws are more important in maintaining conformity and the mainstream press's propaganda role (Hillyard and Percy-Smith 1988).

The state has, in any case, interfered more with broadcasting than with the press, perhaps because the fervently right-wing owners of newspapers have been less independent of the government than the broadcasting companies have. One of the most notorious cases of the Conservative government slipping on a censorship banana skin followed its long-drawn-out, farcical and ultimately futile attempts to prevent publication of *Spycatcher* by a retired MI5 officer, Peter Wright (1987). In June 1986, the *Observer* and the *Guardian*, which had published some of Wright's allegations of sedition by the secret service in advance of publication, were served with injunctions.

Then the short-lived *News on Sunday*, the *Sunday Times* and the *Independent* were each fined £50,000 for having intended to prejudice legal proceedings in the original case through publishing information from the book (in fact, so boring nobody would have bothered to read it had not the government tried to ban it). Eventually these fines were set aside on appeal. Similarly injunctions against the *Observer* and the *Guardian* were set aside and the Law Lords ruled that, in view of the worldwide publication, national security could in no way be damaged by publication in the UK (Stone 2002: 229–36).

More recently the Labour government proved itself equally heavy-handed and authoritarian in its response to various revelations by a disgruntled MI5 officer, David Shayler, in the *Mail on Sunday* in August 1997. Among his allegations, Shayler claimed that the security services had files on various members of the Labour government. Injunctions were served on the British news media from airing any more of his allegations and again in August 1998 after Shayler threatened to disclose details of a 1996 plot by MI6 to assassinate President Muammar Gadafi of Libya. But the *Guardian* cleverly got round this injunction by reproducing a *New York Times* report on the Gadafi plot. Shayler was jailed in Paris pending extradition to Britain to face charges under the Official Secrets Act. Then, in November 1998, he was surprisingly released from jail – after the French judge argued that extradition could not go ahead since his revelations had been political – and began his life on the run (Hollingsworth and Fielding 1999).

When, in February 2000, Shayler and the *Mail on Sunday* were sued by the government for breaches of confidence and of contract and Shayler sent to the media names of two intelligence officers involved in the Gadafi plot, newspapers obeyed instructions not to publish. Yet still the government continued its harassment of the media and went to the High Court demanding that the *Guardian* and the *Observer* hand over material sent them by Shayler. The judge's final rejection of the police's demands in July 2000 was hailed as a 'ringing endorsement of freedom-of-expression'. Then, in October 2000, concerns of freedom-of-information campaigners mounted again after a High Court judge found *Punch* magazine guilty of contempt for publishing an article by Shayler on the IRA's bombing campaign – even though he found no evidence it had damaged national security.

Shayler was finally given a six-month jail sentence in 2002 under the Official Secrets Act 1989 forbidding security and intelligence officers from disclosing anything about their activities without official approval. He was denied any public-interest defence.

The wrong arm of the law

David Northmore (1990) has calculated that there are well over a hundred laws prohibiting disclosure of information. He concludes, along with many other commentators, that Britain is the most secretive state in the so-called developed world (see also Ponting 1990 and Harcup 2004: 22). In 1994, the Guild of Editors listed forty-six laws restricting disclosure of information of particular relevance to journalists, including the Trade Union Reform and Employment Rights Act 1993 and Young Persons Act 1993. Moreover, the Criminal Procedures and Investigations Act 1996 gave the courts even more powers to impose reporting restrictions. According to the Cancer Act 1939, it is even an offence to advertise an offer to treat anyone for cancer, a disease that claims around 120,000 deaths each year in the UK – though claims by alternative therapists about their cancer treatments in features articles present no problems under the Act (Alway 2004).

Privatised utilities (such as gas, water and electricity), once accountable to Parliament, have been criticised even by the Confederation of British Industry for their lack of accountability and openness in decision-making. There are an estimated 6,424 quasi-autonomous non-governmental organisations (quangos) in Britain responsible for £63 billion of taxpayers' money, yet there is no legal obligation on them to disclose information (see Chapter 9). Employee contracts often contain restrictive 'gagging' clauses (Johnson 1996).

In 1989, the secret state was further strengthened with a new Official Secrets Act (OSA). The 1911 OSA had proved notorious, particularly after civil servant Sarah Tisdall was jailed in 1983 for leaking to the *Guardian* government plans for the timing of the arrival of cruise missiles in England. National security seemed hardly threatened by the disclosure. Then came the acquittal of top civil servant Clive Ponting, charged under Section 2(1) of the Act after he leaked information showing the government had misled the House of Commons on the sinking of the Argentine ship *General Belgrano* during the Falklands conflict.

The 1911 legislation, rushed through Parliament during a manufactured scare about Britain being infiltrated by German spies (Stafford 1988: 8–9), was proving an embarrassment to the government and the 1989 Act was introduced to sort out the mess. In an Orwellian piece of doublethink, the Home Secretary, Douglas Hurd, claimed the Act represented 'a substantial, unprecedented thrust in the direction of greater openness'. The opposite is nearer the truth. The Act covers five main areas: law enforcement, information supplied in confidence by foreign governments, international relations, defence, and security and intelligence. The publishing of leaks on any of these is banned. Journalists are denied a public-interest defence; nor can they claim in defence that no harm had resulted to national security through their disclosures.

After a disgruntled former officer, Richard Tomlinson, sent a synopsis of a book about his four years in MI6 to a publisher in Australia, he was jailed for six months in December 1997. He became the first MI6 officer to be prosecuted for secrets offences since George Blake, thirty-six years earlier. As the secret state's powers steadily mounted, in 1993 the Intelligence Services Act allowed MI6, with the permission of the Foreign Secretary, to commit acts abroad which, if carried out in Britain, would be illegal. It also created the Intelligence and Security Committee, which meets in secret to overview the security services' activities. Apart from France, virtually every other western country has independent oversight of intelligence agencies.

In 1996 the Security Service Act extended MI5's functions to 'act in support of the prevention and detection of crime' while the Labour government continued its moves to extend the secret state, allowing intelligence services and other government agencies to conduct covert surveillance including bugging phones and property. The government proceeded, somewhat reluctantly, to introduce Freedom of Information (FoI) legislation, but its critics claimed that it would be more protective of law enforcers than the law in any other country with a FoI Act.

Good news appeared to come with a landmark decision on 20 December 1996 by the High Court, which ruled that a blanket ban by the government a year earlier on journalists interviewing prison inmates was illegal and an unjustified restriction of freedom of speech. The ruling came after freelance journalist Bob Woffinden and BBC Wales reporter Karen Voisey refused to sign undertakings not to publish material obtained during visits to two prisoners whose life sentences for murder they were investigating as possible cases of miscarriages of justice. The appeal court renewed the ban. But this decision was finally overruled by the Law Lords on 8 July 1999.

As another exercise, ask journalists to what extent the 'culture of secrecy' impedes them in their work. How many say they enjoy freedom to write whatever they want? Given that the links between the security services and mainstream media have always been close, how many of them have been invited by MI5 or MI6 to work for them as paid agents?

See *Statewatch* magazine, PO Box 1516, London N16 0EW; tel: 020-8802 1882; fax: 020-8880 1727; email: office@statewatch.org; website: http://www.statewatch. org. See also literature produced by the anti-censorship body Article 19, 33 Islington High Street, London N1 9HL; tel: 020-7278 9292; fax: 020-7713 1356; email: info@article19.org; website: http://www.article19.org. For a global view see *Index on Censorship*, 33 Islington High Street, London N1 9LH; tel: 020-7278 2313; fax: 020-7278 1878; email: contact@indexoncensorship.org; website: http://www. indexonline.org. Amnesty has a special network campaigning for imprisoned journalists. Contact Natalie Smith 020-7417 6365; email: activism@amnesty.org.uk; website: http://www.amnesty.org.uk/journos.

Principled or pointless: CODES OF CONDUCT

Journalists work under many constraints, from proprietors, advertisers, laws and so on. One way in which journalists have regulated their own activities, with the aim of improving ethical standards, is through codes of conduct.

Starting the ball rolling: THE NUJ

One of the most enduring is the National Union of Journalists' code drawn up in the late 1930s (accessible at http://www.nuj.org). In February 1998, the NUJ agreed to an amendment to the code to outlaw misrepresenting news through digital manipulation of photographs. The new clause prohibits use of manipulated photographs unless they are labelled with an internationally recognised symbol within the image area. The thirteen-clause code relies on generalised statements of high principle. On the one hand this has clear benefits. As Nigel Harris (1992: 67) argues, detailed sets of regulations foster a 'loophole-seeking attitude of mind'. And Chris Frost, Professor of Journalism at Liverpool John Moores University and chair of the NUJ Ethics Council, comments (2000: 98): 'A short code has the advantage of being easier for journalists to remember and use. They are able to measure directly their performance against the principles contained in the code and quickly realise when they are straying from the straight and narrow.'

On the other hand, the code incorporates principles broken every day all over the country by NUJ members. What is the point of having them if they are not backed up by any penalties? As Bill Norris (2000: 325) argues: 'Every story is different and every reporter is driven by the compulsion to get the story and get it first. To imagine that he or she is going to consult the union's code of ethics while struggling to meet a deadline is to live in cloud-cuckoo land.' Attempts to impose the code through a disciplinary procedure and, since 1986, an NUJ ethics council have proved difficult, but the union has set up an ethics hotline to advise those taking difficult decisions.

The Press Complaints Commission's Code of Practice

Following stern warnings from the first Calcutt committee that the press should clean up its act or face statutory regulation, the PCC drew up a detailed Code of Practice (accessible at http://www.pcc.org.uk). Since then it has been amended more than 30 times, according to its chair Sir Christopher Meyer (2004). A new controversy blows up and so new changes are made to the code. For instance, after statutory threats emerged over bugging and the use of telephoto lenses, the code was amended appropriately. After the death of Princess Diana, the sections on intrusion and privacy were substantially rewritten; definitions of private property and public-interest defence have both been altered (Frost 2000: 99). In May 2004, in the first major review of the code for six years, the interception of text messages by journalists was outlawed in the code. It followed a *News of the World* report of an alleged affair between footballer David Beckham and Rebecca Loos which centred on the publication of text messages between the pair. But it failed to take up calls from the NUJ for a 'conscience clause' to protect journalists when editors or proprietors force them to breach the code (Ponsford 2004c).

The move to greater detail in the code marks a shift towards the American tradition where codes of conduct can cover a wide range of categories such as conflicts of interests, special privileges enjoyed by journalists (such as freebies), plagiarism and the use of shocking pictures (Goodwin 1994). Many mainstream journalists argue that the PCC's Code has had a positive impact on standards, particularly since the death of Princess Diana. Moreover, the commission claims it is no industry poodle since ten of its 17 members have no connection with the press (while the other seven are senior editors).

But critics have accused the PCC of being a toothless watchdog, a cosy gathering of 'the great and the good' too concerned to preserve the interests of the elite and incapable of halting the 'dumbing down' of the press. As Mike Jempson, of Media-Wise Trust (www.presswise.org.uk), which backs those with complaints and aims to raise standards in journalism, argues: 'All the signs are that the PCC has created a sort of *cordon sanitaire* around the press and woe betide anybody who tries to upset the applecart.'

As an exercise you might interview (or simply talk to) journalists about their views on codes of conduct. Are they aware of their existence? What impact do they have on their work? Do a survey of newspapers in your region and see how many incorporate the PCC Code into their style books.

Some more ethical websites

- www.cfoi.org.uk Campaign for Freedom of Information.
- www.cpbf.org.uk Campaign for Press and Broadcasting Freedom (its journal *Free Press* is available at www.freepress.org.uk).
- www.ethicalspace.org.uk journal of the Institute of Communication Ethics.
- www.uta.fi/ethicnet University of Tampere site carries comprehensive list of European journalists' codes of ethics.
- www.globalethics.org.uk site of the Institute for Global Ethics.
- www.hrw.org Human Rights Watch's site.
- www.iwpr.net award-winning site of Institute for War and Peace Reporting.
- www.ifj.org site of International Federation of Journalists which, along with the NUJ and MediaWise, has produced a leaflet 'The Media and Suicide' providing guidance on this sensitive topic.
- www.mediachannel.org US-based site critical of mainstream reporting.
- www.mentalhealth.org site of the Mental Health Foundation, which has produced a practical guide for journalists, *Mental Health in the Media*.
- www.mindout.net site of Mind Out for Mental Health, promoting positive attitudes and behaviour surrounding mental health. Has produced *Mindshift: A Guide to Open-minded Media Coverage of Mental Health*.
- www.minorityrights.org Minority Rights Group.
- www.poynter.com US-based media ethics institute.
- www.presscouncils.org Professor Claude-Jean Bertrand's site drawing together codes of ethics from around the world.
- www.transcend.org a peace and development network site with a special section on peace journalism.

3 Sourcing the news

At the heart of journalism lies the source. Becoming a journalist to a great extent means developing sources. As a journalist you need to know a lot – where to go for information, whom to ask. For career development, contacts are crucial.

The contacts book

One of the most treasured possessions of any journalist is their contacts book in which sources' phone and mobile numbers, addresses, fax and pager numbers, email and website details are listed. David Conley (2002: 164) describes the contacts books as the 'reporter's bible'. 'It is a reporter's lifeline to the community; a bridge to news stories.' To be safe, journalists should keep a duplicate in a secure place since the loss or theft of a sole contacts book can be disastrous. Many journalists have contacts on a computer file as a further back-up or use personal digital assistants which, at best, can combine the functions of contacts book, notepad and word processor.

Reporters investigating sensitive issues (national security, spying, the arms or drugs trade, share dealings) tend to keep details of important, exclusive sources in their heads. Police have been known to raid the homes and computers of journalists involved in sensitive areas and thus every step should be taken to preserve the anonymity of such contacts.

The importance of the phone to the journalist means that one of the most vital sources is the telephone directory (online or offline). You are researching a story on Islam. Just go to the directory and see which local and national organisations are listed (and try Muslim at the same time). Telephone directories are also a source for feature ideas. Diamond cutters, chimney sweeps, feminist car repairs, fallout shelters or robots may be listed and worth a follow-up.

Sourcing: GENERAL COMMENTS

Immediacy and newsiness

Sourcing conventions help provide the news dimension of many stories. An issue may be long-running but new information or opinion from a source will bring it into the news. The state of the national economy is an issue of constant concern. The Chancellor of the Exchequer warning of further 'inevitable' bankruptcies over the next year becomes news, just as the release of a report by a group of Cambridge University economists highlighting the plight of small businesses is newsworthy.

Elitism and hierarchy

Media research suggests that journalists use a remarkably limited range of sources (McQuail 1992: 112–59; Manning 2001: 139). The components of the hierarchy will differ from newspaper to newspaper. Television soap stars and showbiz celebrities feature far more in the national tabloids than in the broadsheets, for instance, yet there exists a remarkable consensus over news values and sourcing routines throughout the mainstream press. Some sources will be prominent, others marginalised or generally covered in a negative way. Elitism is particularly evident in foreign reporting. Moreover, this consensus over news sourcing is reinforced by the growing centralisation and secrecy of government and the ever-narrowing consensus between the three major political parties.

At the local level, councils, Members of Parliament and of the European Parliament, courts, police, fire brigade, ambulance service, hospitals, local industries and their representative bodies, trade unions and trades councils, and the local football and cricket clubs are also important sources. Schools and colleges, churches, local clubs and societies, army, naval and air force bases, local branches of national pressure groups and charities are secondary sources. In rural areas important sources may include village postal workers, publicans and hotel keepers, agricultural merchants, livestock auctioneers, countryside rangers or wardens. In coastal areas they include coastguards, harbour officials and lifeboat station personnel.

Significantly, many local journalists marginalise a wide range of sources loosely termed 'alternative'. These might include representatives of religions other than Christian, ethnic minority groups, members and representatives of political parties other than the dominant three; feminist, lesbian and gay groups; pacifist, environmental and animal rights campaigning groups.

Journalists' sourcing routines tend to reflect the distribution of power in society; representatives of leading institutions and public services dominate, having easier access to the press. Representatives of 'alternative' bodies are either marginalised or eliminated from the local and national press, which reinforces their relative powerlessness in society. Women and ethnic minorities are marginalised by the political system just as they are marginalised in the press (Allan 2004: 119–70).

Professional routines: on- and off-diary sources

Sources are often defined according to their relation to journalistic routines of news gathering. Thus, on-diary routine sources will include on a national newspaper the government, Parliament and select committees, the major political parties, the Confederation of British Industry (CBI), Church of England Synod meetings, prominent court cases, press conferences arranged by prominent bodies such as campaigning groups (Amnesty International), companies, the police, trade unions and charities.

At the same time a system of 'calls' institutionalises this sourcing routine. The news editor, news desk member or specialist correspondent will contact by phone at regular intervals (as often as every hour) such bodies as the police, ambulance service or fire brigade to check on any breaking news. Such bodies are increasingly providing taped news updates so local reporters will often 'call in' for chats to help personalise the contacts.

Similarly a local reporter will meet at regular intervals locally important people (such as vicars, business leaders, prominent campaigners and trade unionists) for informal chats from which news angles may or may not emerge. Bob Franklin and David Murphy (1991), in a study of 865 stories in the local press, found that local and regional government, voluntary organisations, the courts, police and business accounted for 66.7 per cent of the total. Such groups and individuals are described as on-diary sources since details of their activities are listed in diaries traditionally in book form supplemented by dated files but increasingly now on screens.

Representation

Linked to journalists' sourcing routines are certain notions about representation. Sources other than celebrities in their own right tend to assume significance for a journalist when they can be shown representing not just their personal views but also those of a larger group or institution. Thus, usually accompanying the name of a source is their title or other description. Ms X may have believed Tony Blair ought to have resigned from the premiership over the invasion of Iraq in 2003. But her views will mostly be of interest to a journalist if they can be shown to represent a larger group such as the local Labour Party, of which she is the treasurer.

Journalists are sometimes tempted, because of sourcing conventions, to invent a title when none exists. During the early 1980s when the Greenham Common women were protesting outside the US airbase near Newbury, journalists often represented the relatively few people they quoted as 'spokeswomen' for the camp. In fact, the women sought to challenge traditional hierarchical notions of representation. Each woman spoke for herself. The group did not have representatives as such. By describing them as 'spokeswomen' journalists were failing to understand or respect an important political dimension of their struggle.

Credibility and authority

Accompanying journalists' sourcing routines and linked closely to views about representation are notions relating to credibility and authority. The views of party politicians tend to be prominent in the national and local press because they are seen as having been democratically elected to represent certain widely held views. Along with that representative element go authority and credibility.

Ms A may have very strong views about abortion. But on what authority does she speak and how credible are those views? Those short titles or descriptive phrases accompanying the name of the person quoted answer that kind of question. Ms B might be described as having 'launched a campaign against abortion at her parish church'. This immediately identifies her commitment to the cause and her authority as a source. Similarly when someone is described as 'an eye-witness to a road accident', their authority is established (though they may be mistaken and must not be seen to allocate blame). Inclusion of such details immediately 'hardens' the story. In the same way, the presence of 'ordinary people' (without any title or representative function) 'softens' the story.

Bias and neutrality

Reporters use sources to distance themselves from the issues explored. Rather than express their views on a subject, reporters use sources to present a range of views over which they can appear to remain objective and neutral. The title or descriptive phrase accompanying the quoted person clarifies the bias. But this is the bias of the source, not of the reporter. Sourcing routines also reinforce notions of balance. A campaigning group accuses a local authority of inadequate provision. It is the responsibility of the reporter to contact the authority to balance the report with their response to the allegations. But such a process eliminates a range of other views. Indeed, many media theorists question journalists' notion of balance and locate the construction of the notion of objectivity historically (Schudson 1978; Tumber 1999: 285–392). Considering the highly selective process of news gathering, the financial, political and legal pressures on newspapers and the absence of any neutral language, they argue that objectivity is unattainable and a myth.

Experts

Experts are often sought by journalists as sources. They play a crucial role since authority and independence are associated with their views. Journalists often use experts such as academics, think-tank members and pressure-group campaigners (sometimes even fellow reporters) to provide background information, which is not necessarily used in copy, and ideas for future, more newsy contacts. But they can also use them more subtly to add extra weight to a view they (or their proprietors) wish to promote. The *Sun,* for instance, often quotes psychiatric 'experts' on the alleged insanity or otherwise of people in the news (such as 'madman' Saddam Hussein and Tony Benn of the 'loony left'). But experts can be wrong.

Professional status

Journalists enjoying close contact with people at the top of the sourcing hierarchy tend to have a high professional status. On a national broadsheet, the parliamentary correspondent enjoys high status just as the posting as a foreign correspondent (with all the contacts with presidents and other VIPs this will involve) ranks as a journalistic top job. At the local level, the journalist whose everyday contacts are councillors enjoys high status; the journalist dealing with the Women's Institute reports or the children's page is usually low on the professional ladder.

As Bob Franklin (1994: 19–20) comments: 'Journalists are conscious of being sited in a finely graduated hierarchy which influences their access to politicians. . . . Acknowledging and exploiting to the full the advantages which their position in the hierarchy bestows is a precondition for journalistic advancement.'

Journalists' reputations can be built on the ability to extract good quotes from sources. 'Did you get any good quotes?' is often asked by colleagues when they return from an assignment.

Professionalism as a construct generally implies a certain objectivity and neutrality towards sources. In reality this is difficult to maintain. Many argue that journalists often get too close to their sources. Journalists' regular contact with elite sources means they are often accused of disseminating a range of conflicting elite perspectives. Journalists tend to be part of the same social milieu as the political elite, they speak the same language and often come from similar social and educational backgrounds.

Press poachers: THE MEDIA AS A SOURCE

All journalists spend some considerable time each day going through the media. They have to know what is going on, what is being covered and more particularly what is not being covered. They become 'media junkies'. As US broadcaster Dan Rather warns: 'Be careful. Journalism is more addictive than crack cocaine' (Burrell 2004c). Whatever your feelings about the heavies or the popular press, it is important to read (in hard copy or on the internet) as many papers as possible. You may despise the red-tops for their blatant racism and sexism but they have the power to set the national news agenda and need to be watched. Similarly, you may find the heavies tedious and long-winded but (while their omissions are often more significant than their contents) they carry masses of important national and international news which might even spark ideas for follow-ups.

Don't concentrate all the time on the nationals and your mainstream locals. They are just one (though the most powerful) ingredient of a diverse range of journals available. Even if you do not belong to these groups yourself, look at the lively ethnic minority press (*New Nation*, *Voice*, *Caribbean Times*, *Asian Times*, *Eastern Eye*), the religious press (*Q News*, the *Jewish Chronicle*, the *Methodist Recorder*, the *Catholic Herald*, the *Church Times*), the left press (*Tribune*, *Socialist Worker*, *Socialist Resistance*, the *Morning Star*, *News Line*, *Lobster*, *Peace News*) or the gay media (*Gay Times; www. uk.gaytimes.com*). For contact details see the invaluable *Media Guide/Directory* series which is updated every year (London: Guardian Books). It is worth looking at these alternative publications (in hard copy or online versions) for a number of reasons:

- They often carry articles by specialists raising issues and perpectives marginalised in the mainstream press and which can be followed up.
- The listings of meetings, conferences, demonstrations, vigils and visits to the UK by potentially newsworthy figures can be followed up.
- Journalists on them are useful contacts and their journals could provide outlets for freelance work (if your contract permits).
- They can prove rewarding places for student work attachments.

Newspapers published outside England and easily accessible via the internet, such as the *Scotsman*, the *Glasgow Herald* and the *Irish Independent*, should not be ignored. The *International Herald Tribune*, carrying a compilation of reports from the *New York Times* and published on 26 sites around the world every day, is essential reading for anyone wanting an insight into elite opinion in the United States. See *Mother Jones* (www.motherjones.org) or *Z Magazine* (www.zmag.org) for more dissident perspectives. Most journalists will either speak or want to speak a second language and follow the press in that country. Comparisons with foreign newspapers on elements such as editorial bias, content, use of pictures, design and questions of taste can all throw up interesting insights into the UK press.

The journalist's own newspaper often provides a source for news. Letters to the editor can provide the basis for a follow-up (but should not be converted into interviews) while an advert asking for sources on a particular topic can often produce good results. Similarly newsworthy letters in other newspapers or magazines can be followed up. National and local newspapers sponsor charity or sporting events or run campaigns which can also provide colourful, exclusive coverage.

Cuttings

Most newspapers have their own cuttings library (mostly online now), which is a crucial resource. Journalists also create their own filing system. For a freelance without regular access to a cuttings library, it is an essential. Most journalists, especially free-lances, develop specialist areas and tidy filing of cuttings, magazines, internet print-outs, photocopies, notes from books and internet sources, and jottings of feature ideas can prove enormously useful and time-saving during research. But reporters can get details and quotes wrong. Unless cuttings are treated critically, there are dangers of reporters repeating each other's errors. In its March 1992 report, the PCC criticised journalists' over-reliance on cuttings: 'Cuttings are an essential part of newspaper research but too many journalists now seem to act in the belief that to copy from 10 old stories is better than to write a new one with confirmation by proper fresh enquiry.'

Follow-ups

The follow-up of an item in the news is a constant feature of newspaper coverage. As controversy emerges in the national press, a local paper will 'do a follow-up' carrying the views of relevant local people and providing local information on the issue. Similarly, a report in a local paper, say about an educational controversy consid-ered sufficiently sensational, unusual or with wider implications, will be followed up by a national with new sources and new information.

Newspapers routinely tape selected radio and television news programmes, build up stories from interviews on these media and perhaps do follow-ups on others. A great deal of the coverage in the Sunday heavies comprises follow-ups on the main stories of the previous week. On Mondays (following the relatively dead news day of Sunday) nationals are in the habit of carrying reports on interviews given by promi-nent politicians on weekend television and radio programmes (McNair 2000: 100–2). Investigations by Sunday newspapers can be followed up by the national press. Sometimes a reporter will 'lift' a story from another newspaper, rewording it slightly, perhaps adding only a few original pars.

Columnists on both national and local newspapers often base some comment on an event or opinion highlighted in a national. Journalists will also habitually use other reporters as sources. Sometimes a specialist in the field will be contacted by other reporters new to the area for contacts and ideas. It is a matter for the indi-vidual journalist how much they co-operate with such requests. The issue is compli-cated when the questions come from a friend or colleague on a competing paper. Some journalists say no to all such requests. Others supply basic information and contacts and keep to themselves special sources gained only after considerable effort.

Journalists are often used as 'hard sources' for media-related sources. Often in for-eign stories the views of local journalists are considered informed and authoritative.

Reinforcing the consensus

As competition intensifies between newspapers, pressures to conform to the domi-nant news agenda grow. Rather than feeling confident and pursuing their own news values, newspapers constantly look over their shoulder to see what their competitors are up to. Consequently, the range of views and experience expressed narrows and newspapers become increasingly predictable (Herman and Chomsky 1994). The media's over-reliance on the media also promotes a passive form of journalism.

Investigative reporter Tom Bower (1992) has spoken of the 'culture of inactivity'. Reporting becomes a reactive activity, requiring little imagination and courage. Office-based, it becomes a glorified form of clerking. Former editor of the *Independent* and BBC political editor Andrew Marr agrees. He writes (2004: 98): 'Stories about ordinary life in Britain are being pushed aside by stories that are easier to write in the office – stories about new products, new consumer trends – and about brief celebrities. A deadly idleness has gripped journalism.'

Disinformation dangers

Histories of the secret services show the extent to which newspapers are used for misinformation, disinformation and propaganda purposes (Pilger 1998: 492–9; Bloch and Fitzgerald 1983: 134–41; Keeble 2004a). As Roy Greenslade, former editor of the *Mirror*, commented: 'Most tabloid newspapers – or even newspapers in general – are playthings of MI5. You are the recipient of the sting' (quoted in Milne 1995: 262). For instance, a contrived story alleging various atrocities by a certain anti-US movement may be planted in a foreign newspaper, perhaps financially backed by the secret service. It may then be picked up by the major international news agencies. That first report provides the authenticity and credibility for the ensuing coverage.

Media used to combat censorship

Sometimes journalists send copy unsuitable for their own newspaper to another outlet (say *Private Eye*). Media in one country can be used to break through censorship regulations in another. In 1986 the Israeli anti-nuclear campaigner Mordechai Vanunu used the *Sunday Times* to reveal details of the secret Israeli nuclear programme which lay hidden behind a rigid censorship regime. (He was later captured by Mossad, the Israeli secret service, sentenced to 18 years in jail and finally released only in 2004. Then, in November 2004, Vanunu was re-arrested by Israeli soldiers 'on suspicion of passing classified information to unauthorised parties'.)

During the lead-up to the Gulf conflict of 1991, after details of the 'allied' strategy were stolen from a Defence Ministry official's car, a D-Notice banning newspapers from reporting the event was issued by a special government committee. News of it leaked to an Irish paper. Thus it became public knowledge and London-based papers went ahead and carried their own reports. National security did not appear to be seriously damaged.

On and off the record

On the record

The basis for any good contact between a journalist and a source is trust. When that trust is broken, the source is lost. Most news is given on the record. A press release is issued; someone talks to you on the telephone or face to face or over the email; you report a conference. All this information and opinion you gain on the record.

Off the record

An off-the-record briefing is completely different. Information is given but because of its sensitive nature should not be reported. If the off-the-record undertaking is broken, trust is lost. At the same time, such an undertaking leaves the journalist free to try to acquire the same information from another source who might be prepared to go on the record. Public meetings are on the record. If someone says during one, 'Oh, incidentally, that comment was off the record', you have no obligation to treat it as such. Similarly, private conversations are on the record unless otherwise established. Though it is tempting for students to submit copy to their lecturers drawn from off-the-record interviews (with the interviewee presuming no publication is intended) they will be indulging in an unreal form of journalism – which should be avoided.

Probably the most famous off-the-record source was Deep Throat, who fed information to the *Washington Post*'s Watergate duo, Carl Bernstein and Bob Woodward. In April 2003, their papers (which included 250 spiral notebooks, tapes, transcripts, scribbled jottings, internal memos, and notes on discussions with editor Ben Bradlee) were sold for $5 million (£3.2 million). But, significantly, the identity of Deep Throat remained secret – until Mark Felt, the FBI's No. 2, revealed himself to be the source in May 2005.

Unattributable or background comments

Halfway between off-the-record and on-the-record comments lie unattributed or 'for background only' comments. Reports can carry these quotes but attribution is deliberately vague to conceal identities. During the 1992 saga of the Prince Charles and Princess Diana split such phrases as 'sources close to Buckingham Palace' or 'sources close to the Princess' were prominent. By 2004, the use of anonymous, unattributed quotes was running out of control in Fleet Street, dominating the reporting of politics, journalism and 'human interest' gossip around celebrities. For instance, most of the over-hyped spat between the Blairites and Brownites in the government was reported via unattributed sources such as 'a senior Labour backbencher', 'a senior Cabinet minister', 'a veteran Labour MP' and so on. In December 2004, coverage of the 'nannygate' scandal surrounding the affair of Home Secretary David Blunkett was saturated in quotes from 'friends of Kimberly Quinn', 'the Blunkett camp', 'informed sources' and so on. How can the reader trust that all of this is not simply made up? Similarly much of the reporting of the 'war on terror' since the 9/11 atrocities in the United States has been based on anonymous (and competing) intelligence sources.

The reasons for all this secret sourcing are clear. As newspaper sales dip, editors' demands for exclusives feed the process, blurring the distinctions between fact and fiction. So too is the growth of the secret state with intelligence moving to the centre of power in Blair's cabal. As the power of the intelligence services advances (both in Britain and the US) and Fleet Street hacks' links to the spooks deepen, so the culture of anonymous sourcing will spread.

Yet off-the-record unattributed briefings can potentially benefit both the source and the journalist. The reporter can be informed on complicated details of which they may have no specialist knowledge and will learn of the source's bias. Sources often speak more openly at these meetings. And, for the source, the briefing provides an opportunity to impress their perspectives on the journalist. As Rodney Tiffen (1989: 112) comments:

> covert manoeuvres are commonly deployed to shape interpretations of public events, of success and failure, of intentions and portents. In complex or technical devel-

opments, briefings can highlight the 'essential meaning' of the details, to provide what journalists will welcome as a short-cut through the maze, but by doing so affording the briefer convenient scope for convenient selectivity. The meaning of opinion polls and some election results, of economic reports and indicators, of international agreements often pass into the news after the filters of briefings.

Dominant groups, individuals and institutions have the power and access to the press to organise such briefings and the chance to attempt to influence the news agenda. Weaker groups and individuals have much-reduced opportunities for such manoeuvring. Campaigning journalist John Pilger (1996) offers this advice: 'Beware all background briefings, especially from politicians. Indeed, try to avoid, where possible, all contact with politicians. That way you find out more about them.'

Fact, fiction or faction?

Unattributed and anonymous comments can also blur the distinction between fact and fiction. For instance, the *Sunday Express* ran an exclusive in 2000 headlined 'Isabella: the blonde tipped to be Prince William's wife'. It was pure fantasy. It started with a jokey story in the December 1999 *Tatler* about Isabella Anstruther-Gough-Calthorpe 'tipped to be a fairytale princess'. *GQ* and the Edinburgh University student paper followed up the prediction. By the time the *Sunday Express* carried it, a jokey 'tip' had become a 'fact' supported by anonymous sources: 'Royal insiders say the 19-year-old blonde has formed a close bond' with the Prince, it reported. In fact, Isabella and the Prince had never met. Similarly most national newspapers faithfully reproduced the warnings by Prime Minister Tony Blair and the intelligence services about Iraq's weapons of mass destruction before the invasion in 2003: they were all lies (Miller 2004).

Keeping it confidential

There are other occasions when journalists will legitimately want to protect the identity of a source. For instance:

*   Given the high unemployment figures, people are reluctant to criticise their employers for fear of the consequences. Nurses may not dare to speak out on the impact of the financial cutbacks on the health service – some who have spoken to the press have been intimidated. Teachers may be reluctant to put their names to protests over the radical education changes of recent years. Journalists should respect this reserve and not try to tease out names simply to harden their story.
*   Interviews with people who talk about intimate aspects of their lives such as sexual problems, illnesses and domestic violence are often carried with fictitious names. Relevant places, ages and descriptions are either changed or omitted. The newspaper ought to indicate this style at the start of the article. If it is left until the end, the reader may feel cheated. Thus, the *East Anglian Daily Times* (7 April 2000) began a story about child sexual abuse: 'Rebecca (not her real name) and her sister Lizzie . . .'
*   When an investigative journalist has acquired information without disclosing their professional identity, the newspaper does not then normally carry the sources' names. For instance, Esther Oxford (1992) explored the world of rent-a-male agencies which

provide women with escort and sexual services. She contacted the agencies and described her experiences. Clearly, she could not take her notebook. All quotes and place descriptions had to be written from memory. But the paper left until the end the short disclaimer: 'The names of the men have been changed.'

Leaking in the public interest

According to Rodney Tiffen (1989: 96–7), a leak can be broadly defined as the unauthorised release of confidential information:

> However, this umbrella covers many variations – that release may come from a dissident but also from someone in authority seeking political advantage, that confidentiality ranges from the very sensitive to the innocuous, from what was intended to be forever secret to the about-to-be-announced.

Leaks and the use of anonymous quotations by compliant journalists can be manipulated to launch 'trial balloons' or 'fly a kite'. Government officials may release proposals anonymously through leaks to test responses. If an outcry emerges, the government can denounce the plans they drew up, though only reporters pledged to confidentiality will know this. Leaking can lead to institutionalised lying.

Leaks by brave whistleblowers can also be used to expose corruption – as auditor Paul van Buitenen found at the European Commission in 1998 (but he was sacked for his pains). In 2003, Katherine Gun was sacked from the top-secret government eavesdropping centre, GCHQ, after leaking to the *Observer* details of a US 'dirty tricks' operation to win UN Security Council support for the use of force in Iraq. The government controversially dropped her prosecution under the Official Secrets Act in February 2004 after it was put under pressure to reveal the legal advice that took Britain to war. Gun (2004) went on to help form the Truth-Telling Coalition to support those engaged in public-spirited whistleblowing (www.truthtellingproject.org).

Leaks can also be used to discredit opponents. Histories of the Harold Wilson administration (Leigh 1989; Dorril and Ramsay 1991; Porter 1992: 210–27) show the extent to which secret service leaks to sympathetic journalists in national newspapers were used systematically to smear the Prime Minister and some of his close associates before his unexpected resignation in 1976. Because of the aura and glamour surrounding secrecy, information drawn from such sources can be overvalued, with an accompanying devaluation of information drawn from other sources. The desire to gain exclusives through privileged access to secret sources can lead to a critical dependency between source and journalist. The lure of the 'exposé' can also make a reporter more reluctant to explore alternative perspectives.

Editors' guidelines

Following the publication of the Hutton Report into the events surrounding the alleged suicide of arms expert Dr David Kelly, on 30 January 2004 the *Guardian*'s editor, Alan Rusbridger, issued new guidelines to staff on the use of anonymous sources. BBC Today's Andrew Gilligan had sparked a massive controversy (and ultimately the Hutton inquiry) after using a secret source to back a claim the government had 'sexed up' WMD allegations against Iraq against the wishes of the intelligence services. Not surprisingly, Rusbridger advised staff to use anonymous sources sparingly and to avoid using unattributed pejorative quotes – unless in exceptional circumstances. Yet on that day alone in the *Guardian* there were 31 cases of the use of anonymous quotes.

In the United States, attribution rules tend to be tighter than in Britain. Guidelines provided by the editor of the *Cincinnati Enquirer* (Greenslade 1995) to his staff included:

• The identities of all sources must be verified and confidentially disclosed to the editor.

• Misleading information about the true identity of a source may not be used in a story, even to 'throw off' suspicion.

• Information supplied by an unnamed source should be verified independently or confirmed by at least one other source. An exception may be made for individuals who are sole possessors of the information or whose integrity is unassailable.

• The motive of an anonymous source should be fully examined to prevent [journalists] being used unwittingly to grind someone's axe.

• Information attributed to an anonymous source must be factual and important to the story. Peripheral information or a 'good quote' aren't good enough reasons for anonymity.

Hoaxes

Journalists' over-reliance on unattributed sources can make them vulnerable to hoaxes. Some hoaxers, such as Rocky Ryan and Joe Flynn, make a profession of fooling the press. On 17 May 1992, the *Independent on Sunday* revealed that 'one of Fleet Street's most prolific sources of information', particularly about the aviation business, was a conman. He claimed to be a highly placed source within British Airways. He was nothing of the sort. One of the most famous hoaxes of all was when the *Sunday Times* printed what it believed to be the diaries of Adolf Hitler. This was only after they were sold to *Stern* magazine by three German businessmen for £2.5 million and Sir Hugh Trevor-Roper, author of *The Last Days of Hitler*, said that he believed they were genuine.

In November 1996, Stuart Higgins, editor of the *Sun*, fell victim to an elaborate hoax involving a video that supposedly showed Princess Diana cavorting with a lover. In May 2004, the *News of the World* paid model Lucie Clark £6,000 to reveal that *EastEnders* actor Chris Parker was a 'superstud'. It was all lies, promoted by the actor (see *Private Eye*, 12–25 November 2004: 3). And after the US–UK forces occupied Iraq, in April 2003, the warmongering *Daily Telegraph* ran a report claiming that George Galloway MP was in the secret pay of Iraqi President Saddam Hussein. But the documents discovered in the Iraqi foreign ministry on which the claims were based were all forgeries and so, on 2 December 2004, the *Telegraph* was forced to pay damages of £150,000. The newspaper had rushed into print and taken no steps to verify the claims.

Local papers are by no means no-go areas for hoaxes. New sources, particularly in controversial areas, should be routinely checked and their views and information corroborated by another reliable source. Journalists should be particularly wary of hoaxes just before 1 April and in letters, emails and on the internet. For instance,

Kaycee Nicole narrated her brave struggle against leukaemia in a widely reported daily online diary for two years. In 2001, it was revealed to be an elaborate hoax by 40-year-old Kansas housewife Debbie Swenson (see http://www.museumofhoaxes.com/kaycee.html).

Lobby changes: A SIGNIFICANT SHIFT IN THE SECRET STATE?

One of the most famous institutional manifestations of the briefings session is the parliamentary lobby. Every day on which the House of Commons sits, Downing Street gives two briefings to accredited lobby correspondents, of which there are around 210 men and 30 women (out of 312 correspondents based at Westminster). The first meeting is at Downing Street at 11 a.m.; the second in the House of Commons at 4 p.m. In addition there are Friday briefings for Sunday journalists, a briefing on Thursdays by the Leader of the House on the following week's business and a weekly Opposition briefing. There are also briefings by ministers or their mouthpieces to groups and individual lobby journalists.

The lobby was launched in 1884 – just five years before the first Official Secrets Act became law. All lobby members were pledged to secrecy, never attaching a name to any information. Instead, phrases such as 'sources close to Downing Street' or 'government sources' or 'members close to the Labour leadership' were used. As Michael Cockerell, Peter Hennessy and David Walker say in their study of the lobby (1984: 34):

> The paradox was that as Britain was moving towards a democracy by extending the vote to men of all classes (women still had 40 years to wait) mechanisms were being created to frustrate popular participation in government and to control, channel and even manufacture the political news.

Over the years, the lobby has raised enormous passions, pro and anti (see also Chapter 9). For a number of years while Bernard Ingham was Margaret Thatcher's press secretary until October 1991, three high-minded newspapers – the newly launched *Independent*, the *Guardian* and the *Scotsman* – together with *The Economist*, withdrew from the system. Ingham used the lobby for blatant disinformation campaigns on political issues and against individuals both inside and outside the cabinet (R. Harris 1990). His immediate successors did not adopt similar tactics, and the decision by Christopher Meyer in 1995 to allow off-the-record briefings to be attributed to Downing Street marked the beginnings of changes which were to transform the operations of the lobby.

Finally Alastair Campbell, Tony Blair's press secretary (or spin doctor in the jargon), on 13 March 2000, ruled that he could be named as the source of his briefings (rather than the 'Prime Minister's official spokesman'). During the previous month, the twice-daily briefings for journalists were put on the Downing Street website, so allowing anyone to gain access to the discussions just hours after they had finished.

What are we to make of these seemingly radical changes? Was a new spirit of openness racing through the corridors of Westminster? Or was it more an attempt by the government to bypass media 'spin' and communicate directly with the electorate via the internet? Soon after Campbell's announcement, Fleet Street heavies printed verbatim versions of a lobby briefing, and Fleet Street began mourning the death of the lobby. 'If local reporters in Darlington can access the Downing Street line, what's so special about being in the lobby,' said one lobby correspondent (McCann 2000).

Most of the important business is still being conducted behind the scenes in informal, bilateral contacts between journalist and politicians. As former lobby corre-spondent Andrew Pierce (2000) commented: 'Ministers, their special advisers and senior Labour Party workers are still being wined by political journalists in fashion-able restaurants within the shadow of Big Ben.' In April 2004, proposals to introduce daily televised lobby briefings in a review of government communications chaired by Bob Phillis, chief executive of Guardian Media Group, were welcomed by Number 10. But there were concerns that such briefings would be dominated by journalists sympathetic to the Blair clique with few opportunities for provincial reporters.

Perhaps the UK was heading towards adopting the American system in which televised press conference and a detailed Freedom of Information Act existed along-side the most secret of government machines. Hellinger and Judd (1991: 190–1) speak of the 'covert presidency': 'There now exists a recognizable pattern of hidden powers, a covert presidency, that rests on centralising presidential direction of personnel, budgets and information, on the manipulation of the media and on the expanding use of "national security" to control the political agenda.'

Controversies over confidentiality

Non-attributable briefings are vital to the journalist on many occasions and the Code of Conduct (clause 7) of the NUJ calls for journalists to preserve the confiden-tiality of sources. Yet the journalists' right to this confidentiality is not enshrined in law (as it is in most other European countries and the USA) and under Section 10 of the Contempt of Court Act 1981 courts have the right to demand that journalists reveal sources if 'disclosure is necessary in the interests of justice or national security or for the prevention of disorder or crime'. As legal expert Dan Tench advises: 'A journalist about to publish an article which reveals official secrets would be prudent to consider destroying all material which would lead to the identity of a source' (2004).

In 1984 the *Guardian*, under pressure from the courts, handed over material that helped reveal that civil servant Sarah Tisdall had leaked information about the delivery of cruise missiles to Greenham Common. Tisdall was jailed. Then Jeremy Warner, of the *Independent*, was ordered in 1988 to disclose the source of a story on insider dealings and shady takeover bids in the City. He refused and was ordered to pay a £20,000 fine and £100,000 costs in the High Court. His paper paid up for him and received good publicity in the process. He later commented: 'I quite enjoyed it, to tell you the truth. It's a great thing for a young journalist to become a *cause célèbre*' (Lashmar 2000).

In 1990, William Goodwin, a trainee reporter on a weekly trade magazine, the *Engineer*, was fined £5,000 for contempt after refusing to hand over notes of a phone call which revealed confidential information about a computer company's financial affairs. He thus escaped becoming the fourth journalist in the twentieth century in Britain to be jailed for contempt. In 1963, Brendon Mulholland, a *Daily Mail* reporter, and Reginald Foster, of the *Daily Sketch*, were sentenced to six months and three months respectively in Brixton jail for refusing to disclose sources in the Vassall spy tribunal presided over by Viscount Radcliffe. In 1971, Bernard Falk refused to tell the court whether one of two Provisional IRA men he interviewed for the BBC was a man subsequently charged with membership, and went to prison for his pains.

However, pressure on the government to enshrine in law a journalist's right to protect the identity of sources intensified after Goodwin took his case to the European Commission of Human Rights. In September 1993, the commission ruled that Goodwin's case was admissible and called on the government to negotiate a 'friendly settlement'. Three years later, the European Court of Human Rights ruled that Goodwin had been right to protect his sources. But still the Lord Chancellor refused to change the Contempt of Court Act.

Earlier, Dani Garavelli, then chief reporter for the *Journal*, Newcastle, was threatened under the contempt law for refusing to name a source after being subpoenaed to give evidence to a police disciplinary hearing. Her 20-month battle ended in 1996 when a High Court ruled against the attempt by two chief constables to jail her. A judge's decision to throw out a Norfolk Police application for the *Eastern Daily Press* and reporter Adrian Galvin, who was backed by the NUJ, to name a source was lauded as a 'landmark judgment' by editor Peter Franzen. Judge Michael Hyman ruled: 'There is undoubtedly a very formidable interest in a journalist being able to protect his sources.'

In September 1999, Ed Moloney, northern editor of the Dublin-based *Sunday Tribune*, faced imprisonment for refusing to hand over notes (dating back ten years) of interviews with a loyalist accused of murdering a Catholic solicitor. Moloney's ordeal ended the following month when Belfast High Court overturned an order by Antrim Crown Court that he should hand over the notes. Then, in April 2000, the *Express* overturned a High Court ruling that it had to reveal the source from which financial reporter Rachel Baird obtained confidential documents about a High Court action involving Sir Elton John.

The Prevention of Terrorism Act has also been used by the state in an attempt to intimidate journalists into revealing confidential sources. Thus, in 1988 the BBC was forced to hand over footage of the mobbing of two soldiers who ran into a funeral procession in Belfast. Following a *Dispatches* programme, *The Committee*, by the independent company Box Productions in 1991, alleging collusion between loyalist death squads and members of the security forces in Northern Ireland, Channel 4 was committed for contempt for refusing to reveal its source and fined £75,000.

Subsequently a researcher on the programme, Ben Hamilton, was charged with perjury by the Royal Ulster Constabulary. Though the charge was suddenly dropped in November 1992, the police retained all items seized from Hamilton. They included his personal computer, all disks, newspaper cuttings and notes of telephone calls and meetings with other journalists interested in the programme. Another journalist involved in the programme received death threats and was forced to leave his home and live incognito at a secret address.

New terrorism legislation also provoked serious concerns among civil rights campaigners and journalists. The Terrorism Act 2000 extended the definition of terrorism to mean: 'The use of serious violence against persons or property or the threat to use such violence, to intimidate or coerce a government, the public or any section of the public for political, religious of ideological ends'. Journalists covering direct action could be caught by clause 18, carrying a five-year sentence for failure to report information received professionally which could lead to a terrorist act (Zobel 2000). Moreover, the Anti-Terrorism, Crime and Security Act 2001 gave the police alarming new powers of surveillance (see www.liberty-human-rights.org.uk).

Extra threats

In recent years a number of new threats have emerged to undermine journalists' attempts to keep sources confidential. According to the Police and Criminal Evidence Act (PACE) 1984 a police officer investigating a 'serious offence' can obtain an order requiring the journalist to hand over evidence deemed useful to the court. This can include unpublished notes and photographs. The first major controversy emerged just eight months after PACE passed into law. The *Bristol Evening News* was ordered to hand over film following a drug bust: it refused and lost the case, and the police took away 264 pictures and negatives. Following violent demonstrations outside the premises of Rupert Murdoch's News International in Wapping, east London, in early 1987, the *Independent*, the *Mail on Sunday* and the *Observer,* two television companies and four freelance photographers appealed against an order requiring them to hand over pictures.

On 23 May 1988, Mr Justice Alliot ruled that the pictures should be surrendered on the ground that this would not undermine the freedom and independence of the press. All complied except the four freelance photographers who had earlier taken the unprecedented step of sending their materials, via the NUJ, to the International Federation of Journalists in Brussels. In October 1988, the contempt charges against the freelances were thrown out because they were considered no longer to be owners of the material or to possess it.

Following the poll tax riots of 31 March 1990 the police applied under PACE for access to 'all transmitted, published and/or unpublished cine film, video tape, still photographs and negatives of the demonstration and subsequent disturbances which was obtained with a view to being of a newsworthy interest'. Some national newspapers complied. Again, the NUJ moved quickly, sending prints and negatives out of the UK. An attempt by the police to force the media to hand over photographs and journalists' notes taken during the riots in the City of London in June 1999 was thrown out by a judge on 2 July 1999.

Managing the new information monster:
THE INTERNET

Over recent years the internet has become a vast, almost unmanageable source of information for journalists. Conceived in the USA in the late 1980s, the web was being accessed by millions worldwide by 2004, with search engine Google able to access more than 8,000,000,000 sites (the vast majority worthless to journalists). In Britain, the latest official figures indicated that while 99 per cent of homes had a television only 44 per cent had internet access.

The *Daily Telegraph* (http://www.telegraph.co.uk) was the first Fleet Street paper to go online – on 15 November 1994 when the word 'internet' was not even included in the *Shorter Oxford English Dictionary*. By 2004, virtually all national, local and alternative newspapers had gone online (some of them also providing audio and video); the *Guardian*'s sites, for instance (http://www.guardianunlimited.co.uk) contained an archive of stories going back to 1 September 1998 and were recording more than 100 million page impressions in June 2004 (up from ten million five years previously), made by about nine million individuals ('unique users' in the net jargon). Of these users, about 4.3 million were Americans (MacArthur 2004).

Freelances were routinely submitting copy via email while journalists on the smallest of weeklies were surfing the web for sources, using it for interviews and downloading information from databases. Participation in newsgroups was providing access to expert and committed voices around the world. Many reporters were adding their email addresses at the end of their stories encouraging reader feedback from Britain and around the globe. Online supplements and features mushroomed. Dot.com start-ups were providing thousands of new jobs for journalists brave enough to quit the traditional media. Journalists were writing personal blogs and posting early drafts of stories on the web for reader feedback before finally publishing them. As Dan Gillmor, of the *San Jose Mercury News*, argues, the 'news as lecture' model is giving way to 'news as conversation or seminar'.

Certain weblogs, such as Belle de Jour's 'blog of a London call girl', were hitting the headlines. And blogs were becoming so familiar that novelists were imitating them. *An Opening Act of Unspeakable Evil*, for instance, by Canadian Jim Munroe takes the form of a blog composed by a woman concerned her flatmate is demonic.

But, according to Ben Rooney (2004), launch editor of the *electronic telegraph*, the internet's impact on mainstream newspapers has been virtually nil. 'With the exception of a few links at the bottom of stories and, every now and then, a report *à la* Hutton being posted in its entirety online, what has changed?'

Is the deadline dying?

Certainly 24-hour online publishing is revolutionising journalistic practices. Most print journalists would recoil in horror at the notion of the death of the deadline. But that is what an online medium does: it eliminates the fixed news deadline (Wallace 1996). Stories are updated as and when required. This means that the shelf life of the news content is greatly extended, allowing journalists to offer more in-depth information, to craft stories more carefully, to tease out relevant links and provide supporting data.

But as Wayne Ellwood (1996) argued: 'Computerisation is at the core of the slimmed-down, re-engineered workplace that free-market boasters claim is necessary to survive the lean-and-mean global competition of the 1990s. Even factory jobs that have been relocated to the Third World are being automated quickly.' John Naughton, internet specialist on the *Observer* and author of the seminal *A Brief History of the Future: The Origins of the Internet* (London: Orion, second edition 2000) reminded his readers (4 July 1999):

> It is a relatively 'clean' industry – but it also produces serious environmental pollution and needs unconscionable amounts of water. It enables us to do wonderful things but also polarises society into those who are wired and those who are not. It creates 'virtual communities' while wiping out industries which once supported real ones. And the gadgets it sells are often not assembled by hi-tech robots but by sweated labour.

Since anyone with a web browser can access almost any site, even the smallest of publishers can register their sites with search engines and directories and achieve instantly a worldwide audience. That is the theory at least. In practice, the web has come to be dominated by big US-based multinationals. Some 85 per cent of the revenue from internet businesses goes to American firms, which hold 95 per cent of the stock-market value of internet properties.

US sites are increasingly globalising their activities: Yahoo!, for instance, has operations in 20 countries including Brazil, China, Denmark, Japan, Korea, Mexico, Norway, Singapore and Taiwan. Just four companies account for half of all web surfing: Yahoo, Microsoft, AOL Time Warner and Napster and their various online properties and applications. As investigative reporter John Pilger (1996) argued: 'Beware celebrating technology until you find out who controls it. The internet is brilliant, but its most fervid bedfellows are the American government and a cluster of multi-national companies whose message posting is outstripping all others.' And the technology is hardly robust, being under constant threat from viruses (such as the MyDoom outbreak which infected millions of emails in January 2004).

Moreover, the internet is accelerating the process by which English is becoming the dominant global language, helping eradicate one language every two weeks, according to Andrew Dalby (2002: ix). Significantly, some 80 per cent of all the information stored in electronic retrieval systems is in English, thus providing the US and the UK with the 'soft power' (alongside the military 'hard power') to influence the views and actions of people and countries across the globe (see http: debatebase.org/details.asp?topicID=268).

Universities are now wired up to the web, offering student journalists every opportunity to surf the information superhighway – for nothing. All journalism programmes now contain units on producing for the internet. Yet, as Theodore Roszak (1996) argues: 'If computer literacy does not include material on what computers can't do and shouldn't do, it is advertising, not education.'

Some useful sites for harassed hacks

Most journalists will bookmark their favourite sites for easy access. Here are a few which you should find useful (but remember: sites can come and go):

- http://www.192.com telephone directory inquiries, electoral rolls, maps, addresses and a 'people finder'
- http://www.acronymfinder.com invaluable resource
- http://www.ananova.com PA News Centre (UK)
- http://www.anti-spin.com site campaigning against 'the flood of propaganda'
- www.bigfoot.com offers a useful list of email addresses
- www.britannica.com online version of the encyclopaedia
- http://catalogue.bl.uk the British Library's catalogue online
- http://www.cia.gov/cia/publications/factbook/ CIA's factbook provides comprehensive collection of country profiles: but beware the bias
- http://www.cpj.org US-based Committee to Protect Journalists campaigning on behalf of harassed or killed journalists worldwide
- http://dictionary.com with a Thesaurus as well
- www.gnn.gov.uk/ for government news (both local and national)
- http://www.infobel.com/teldir.com for the world's phone books
- http://media-solicitors.co.uk invaluable site introducing laws which have a direct relevance to journalists
- http://www.onelook.com more than 5 million words in more than 900 online dictionaries are indexed by this search engine.

- http://www.disinfo.com Disinformation is a US-based site providing stories on government surveillance, counterculture and links to alternative news sources
- www.drudgereport.com the alternative gossip site that broke the Clinton–Lewinsky scandal
- www.globalreview.btinternet.co.uk Jim Brennan's look at journalism around the world
- www.holdthefrontpage.com provides links to many local newspapers and a useful sections on training, campaigning
- www.NewsDesk-UK.com a massive resource for journalists set up by Vincent Kelly and Alan Bott
- http://ojr.org *Online Journalism Review* (with a strong US bias)
- www.pressgazette.co.uk the trade magazine's important news and comment site
- www.quoteland.com a quotation search engine
- www.facsnet.org Randy Reddick's site provides advice to journalists
- www.statistics.gov.uk/ national statistics online
- www.thesaurus.com *Roget's Thesaurus*
- http://www.uk.multimap.com a street guide to Britain
- http://upmystreet.com provides local house price figures, crime statistics, school performance data, council and other data
- http://www.mediainfo.co.uk/willings/pressguide.htm *Willings Press Guide* carrying contact details of all print media in the UK
- www.worldemail.com provides a world email directory

Taking the slog out of searching

Without search engines, journalists would find tracking down information nearly impossible. Search engines do all the hard work, trawling through web information, indexing it and providing access to sites through keyword searches (Milner 2000). After emailing, using search engines is the second most popular activity on the internet, with an estimated 550 million searches daily (Reece 2004). Phil Bradley, at www.philb.com, lists 2,086 search engines in 216 countries, territories and regions while the website www.searchenginecolossus.com offers links to search engines in 196 countries and 59 territories across the world.

Most of the early search engines, such as AltaVista (now able to search audio and video clips), Metacrawler and Webcrawler were US-based. But in recent years a large number of UK-specific portals have emerged, building big businesses on the advertising revenue (see www.searchenginesgalore.com). Bradley lists 135 search engines for the UK alone.

The most popular include Google (http://www.google.co.uk), Yahoo! (http://uk.yahoo.com), Microsoft (http://search.msn.com), Lycos (http://www.lycos.co.uk), Excite (http://www.excite.co.uk), Ask Jeeves (http://www.ask.co.uk), Infoseek (http://www.go.com) and Northern Light (www.northernlight.com) (Teather 2004). Hotbot (http://hotbot.com) is a US-based engine providing advanced searching facilities.

There are countless specialist sites worth checking out (see http://www.search enginewatch.com). For instance, www.switchboard.com provides access to millions of individual and business telephone numbers and email addresses.

And did you know that you can use Google as a calculator? (Milstein and Dornfest 2004). Simply enter 3 + 3 and the right answer will appear. For multiplication use the (*) like this: 3*3. For division, use the slash (/) like this: 10/2. It can also perform conversions, from kilometres to miles and so on (see www.googleguide.com/calculator.html). Google also operates as a dictionary. Simply type 'define' into the search box followed by your word (say 'sedulous') and the definition will appear, drawn from the websites Google tracks.

The joy (and pain) of email

As internet expert Milverton Wallace stresses (2004), the internet mainly serves as a medium of conversation: 'The best-supported services on the internet (apart from porn web sites) are newsgroups, mailing lists, message boards, chat rooms, weblogs, and other collaborative networks. In other words, verbally rich spaces in which billions of conversations take place every day.'

With more than thirty years of development, email is one of the most sophisticated tools for reporters. Journalists are increasingly using it to file copy, engage in discussions with readers, receive press releases, search information and interview sources. According to Bill Thompson of the *Guardian*, it is easy to get people to reply to email:

> The medium is fresh enough for most people and many of the barriers we have put up to block unwanted contact have not yet been developed for email. It may be impossible to reach the chief executive by phone but an email may well get a response; a researcher may be travelling but will probably be checking email daily.

Thompson also stresses the limitations of email. 'An email "conversation" is more like an epistolary novel than a live interview and while it does allow some space for reflection, the outcome cannot be compared to a real interview.' Mike Ward (2002: 90) warns: 'You can spend hours looking for a person's email address when two phone calls might put you in touch more quickly – one to check his or her company's phone number, the second to make the call. Do not become email obsessed.'

But Jane Dorner (2000: 32) comments: 'Using email to interview forces you to be more prepared by formulating questions in advance. It's less intrusive, allowing you to ask your questions at any hour of the day without bothering anyone. It's also cheaper than picking up the phone every time you need to check a point.' 'Real-time chat' via email allows immediate follow-up questions and answers and approaches the informality of traditional interviews (Metzler 1997: 137).

There are specific skills in email interviewing. For instance, do not bombard your source initially with a long list of questions. State your background, intentions and target publication, and ask for permission first. Then ask a few questions perhaps following up with a few more. But there are serious downsides to the email explosion. They constitute yet another form of communication for the journalist to cope with, thus adding to the demands and stresses of the job. Viruses that can wreak havoc on computer systems often arrive via email. Always remember it is relatively easy to snoop on emails, as secret services and certain managements are only too well aware. Even deleted files can be retrieved.

Chatting on the web: EMAIL DISCUSSION LISTS

Randy Reddick and Elliot King argue that reading or participating in a discussion list can be extremely useful to the journalist (1997: 94–5): 'It puts reporters in contact with people who generally know a lot about a specific topic. The reporter can then follow up with those people, ask where more information can be found or ask who would be a good source to interview.' The principle of the discussion list is simple: an individual sends a message to a specific address for a particular discussion list and that message is automatically distributed to all subscribers. The address of the list distribution software is known as a Listserv.

Indiana University has produced a database of thousands of discussion lists as http://listuniverse.com while a visit to Yahoo! or AltaVista can often reveal information about a relevant mailing list. Regular newsletters are also sent through email. Particularly useful for journalists is Free Pint (http://www.freepint.co.uk) which is sent to subscribers regularly and provides tips and tricks on finding useful information on the internet.

Some ethical issues

Since internet technology has developed at such a rapid pace over recent years it is not surprising that journalists have found it difficult to establish the precise implications for their working routines and ethics. No clear rules have emerged. Issues relating to copyrights on internet material, for instance, remain unresolved. Journalist Andrew Bibby advises web users to include a copyright notice on every item. His reads:

> Copyright held by Andrew Bibby. Use for commercial purposes prohibited without prior written permission from the copyright holder. This text has been placed here as a facility for internet users and downloading is permitted for purposes of private, non-commercial research. The text must not be modified nor this copyright notice removed.

Certainly the temptations towards plagiarism are growing with the internet explosion. Ian Mayes (2000), readers' editor at the *Guardian*, comments: 'Over-reliance on cuttings and now, even more to the point, the ease of electronically cutting and pasting from the internet, may be not simply attractive options, but the only options open to hard-pressed journalists in certain circumstances.' Other issues surround journalists' involvement in discussion groups. When investigating sensitive and dangerous issues, journalists may be justified in seeking anonymity of gathering background information. But Randy Reddick and Elliot King (1997: 219) argue:

> Journalists should always identify themselves as such if they plan to use information from discussion lists. In most cases, journalists have the ethical obligation to allow people to choose to go on-the-record or not. To lurk in a discussion list,

then quote people who did not know that what they wrote would be used in a different context is as deceptive as posing or going undercover to report a story.

Though the Americans have developed the concept of 'precision journalism' in relation to the web, journalists have still to be specially careful in assessing the value of material drawn from the internet. Robert Kiley (1999) advises internet users to check always that the information is current: 'A well organised web page will state when it was first written and last updated.' See if there is a named author. If so, then search an appropriate database for their previous publications. 'If there is no identifed author the information should be treated with caution.' Who is funding the site? The owner should be clearly displayed along with details of any sponsorship or advertising. Researchers at the Poynter Institute, in St Petersburg, USA, have published guidelines for online research (http://www.poynter.org), and these guidelines are also available at www.journalismnet.com and http://powerreporting.com (though with a strong US bias).

The legal position on internet content remains confused. In theory, online media discussion groups could face problems if they carried material considered defamatory, grossly indecent or offensive, with the website providers subject to a civil action for defamation or charged under the Telecommunications Act 1984. In November 1999, the Lord Chancellor's department had a website closed down because material posted on it criticised five judges. Then, in March 2000, Demon Internet paid Lawrence Godfrey, a university lecturer and physicist, £15,000 plus legal fees of around £250,000 in an out-of-court settlement after he was the subject of an allegedly libellous bulletin board posting. Soon afterwards British internet service providers (ISPs) closed two websites – a gay one called Outcast and another devoted (fittingly) to opposing censorship. Concerns were also raised in October 2004 after Rackspace, a US company with offices in London, handed over to the FBI computer equipment used by the radical alternative network Indymedia (http://indymedia.org) to run and host websites (see Empson 2004). As a result Indymedia's coverage of the European Social Forum was temporarily halted.

Certainly journalists should be aware that publication online raises the prospect of being sued in any country where the report is downloaded. And court reports archived on websites are another problem area since they lose the legally privileged status of being a contemporaneous report (Ponsford and Slattery 2004b).

Fears that the libertarian view of the internet as a medium immune to censorship is merely a myth seemed justified after Giles Wilson, a BBC journalist, compiled a spoof web page ridiculing a colleague and found most ISPs would pull it in the face of any complaint. As John Naughton commented in the *Observer*: 'ISPs are run by businesses whose main interest is making money, not defending free speech.' To confuse the issue further, in May 2000, a US Supreme Court ruling gave ISPs full protection against libellous or obscene messages sent out over the web, putting them on the same legal footing as telephone companies. Journalists' investigative work and promises of confidentiality appeared also threatened by the Regulation of Investigatory Powers Act 2000 (see Chapter 9). As a result, the contents and details of emails and telephone calls became accessible to a wide range of government agencies, police officers and even low-grade council officials.

Moreover, a report by Privacy International and the GreenNet Educational Trust (2003: 7) found censorship of the internet 'commonplace' in most regions of the world:

It is clear that in most countries over the past two years there has been an acceleration of efforts to either close down or inhibit the internet. In some countries, for example in China and Burma, the level of control is such that the internet has relatively little value as a medium for organised free speech, and its use could well create additional dangers at a personal level for activists.

The web and the revival of the alternative media

Atton (2002: 80–102) identifies the upsurge in the alternative media in the 1990s within the context of the revival of 'alternative public sphere' in anti-establishment political and social movements. With Tony Blair's New Labour governments adopting anti-trade-union and anti-human-rights policies, radical activists, disillusioned with mainstream politics and media, have become increasingly vocal. And environmental protesters, anti-fascists, squatters, anarchists, peace campaigners, anti-globalisation activists, radical feminists and gays have all used alternative media (magazines, newsletters and websites) creatively to promote debate and solidarity.

Now, in fact, anyone with a PC or a laptop can become a 'journalist'. Inevitably, with the rapid rise of the bloggers, e-zines, campaigning community websites, personal web pages and alternative or leftist internet sites, mainstream journalists' notions of professionalism (built around the protection and promotion of specialised skills and ethical standards) are coming under increasing challenge (see Wroe 2003). In 2000 there were only 130,000 blog sites; by 2004 there were around 10 million (Hargrave 2004). As Jim Hall argues (2001: 53), the roles journalists assigned to themselves in the nineteenth century 'as gatekeeper, agenda-setter and news filter, are all placed at risk when its primary sources become readily available to its audiences'. At the same time, emailers and bloggers are placing the media's performances under intense critical scrutiny. Tony Harcup (2004: 146) highlights the way in which the 'empowering' of internet users 'blurs the boundaries between journalist and audience'.

Yet the mainstream press need not react defensively: they could learn a lot from the alternative media in terms of ethical standards, sourcing routines (reflecting better, for instance, the ethnic diversity of the country) and democratic organisational structures (Atton 2003). Mike Ward (2002: 25) acknowledges that interactivity can be unsettling for mainstream journalists. But he stresses: 'It challenges the whole premise of the journalists as a "gatekeeper" and information provider. It also raises all sorts of issues about accuracy, veracity and perspective of that information and reportage. Yet some online journalists are embracing the opportunity.'

Reasons for optimism

The internet has provided the state with extraordinarily powerful new means to watch over its people. As Paul Todd and Jonathan Bloch comment (2003: 35): 'For the populations of advanced industrialised countries in particular, the 21st century is an age of surveillance unparalleled in history.' And in the media field the same extremely powerful corporations dominate both online and offline. But there is also an alternative current in the rapid development of the internet which is providing a new, international space for dissident views.

Significantly Manuel Castells (1997: 358) highlights the potential of the internet to build oppositional social movements within what he describes as 'post-industrial capitalism'. Thus, 'communes of resistance', such as the Zapatistas in Mexico and the global feminist movement, are able to exploit the internet to promote 'people's horizontal communication' and to challenge society's dominant voices. And investigative journalist John Pilger comments (2004a: xxviii):

> My own view is that the immediate future lies with the emerging 'samidzat', the word for the 'unofficial' media during the late Soviet period. Given the current technology, the potential is huge. On the worldwide web, the best 'alternative' websites are already read by an audience of millions.

Sites such as www.medialens.com (critical media monitoring), www.coldtype.net and www.counterpoint.org (leftist investigative sites), www.eclipse.com (anti-war analysis), www.indymedia.org (international journalism from the grassroots), www.privacyinternational.org (the website of the human rights campaigning body Privacy International) are just a few of the many which are challenging the myths, stereotypes and propaganda of the mainstream media. Thus, for those concerned with the promotion of human rights and progressive ideas in general through the media, there are reasons for optimism.

4 The art of interviewing

The dynamics of every interview are different. They may be short or long, in a pub, an airport lounge or a sauna. Rex Reed once interviewed singer Bette Midler while she was sitting on a toilet in a gay bathhouse (Silvester 1994: 30). They may be friendly or (occasionally) confrontational. They may be about someone's sex life or about high matters of state. Many interviews are unpredictable. Sometimes an interview can change your life. This happened to Fenner Brockway (1986), the late Labour peer, peace activist and journalist, who was 'converted' to socialism following his interview with Keir Hardie.

How, then, to write about such imponderables? One of the most eminent Fleet Street interviewers, Lynn Barber, of the *Observer* and formerly of *Penthouse*, the *Independent on Sunday* and the *Sunday Times*, admitted: 'I've made various attempts at instituting a system for organising interviews but have come to the conclusion that, in journalism, panic is the system.'

Here, then, are a few tips to help you traverse the fascinating territory of the interview. The best way to learn is to go out and do it. But always go about your journalism with a critical hat on. Watch colleagues, see interviewers on television, listen to them on the radio. Notice how they can differ in their techniques. Seek all the time to improve what you are doing.

Why interview?

An interview is intentional conversation. But, as a journalistic convention, it has to be seen in its historical context. It is easy to imagine the interview as a 'natural', unproblematic activity. Christopher Silvester (1994: 4–48) shows, however, in his seminal history that the interview, as a journalistic technique, had to be invented. In fact, the interview between Horace Greeley, editor of the *New York Tribune*, and Brigham Young, the leader of the Mormon Church, in 1859, lays claim to being 'the first full-fledged interview with a celebrity, much of it in the question and answer format familiar to modern readers', as Silvester (1994: 4) comments. According to Jean K. Chalaby (1998: 127), the practice of interviewing spread to England in the 1880s, largely pioneered by W.T. Stead, the editor of the *Pall Mall Gazette*.

Journalists should always be aware of the interview's specific purposes: they may be seeking exclusive, new information or confirming established facts; they may be providing opinion or evidence of someone's state of mind. They may be investigating a subject and seeking to expose a lie or a wrongdoing. Observing closely the work or home environment in which the interview takes place can help provide extra details to the picture of the subject being drawn by the journalist. For the source, the interview has a purpose too: they are seeking to convey an opinion or information, hide a secret, or merely articulate their mood. But beware:

- The source may be confused, yet afraid to admit this.
- They may be afraid to speak their true opinion; they could lose their job or face social or professional isolation.
- The source may be lying, conveying misinformation, propaganda or seeking revenge.
- They may be intimidated by the presence of a reporter and so not express their true feelings.
- The source may be flattered by the interest of the journalist and be more extrovert and 'colourful' than they normally are.
- They may forget or hide important details.
- They may be speaking in a foreign language and so unable to express what they mean.
- They may be making fun of the whole process of interviewing.
- The reporter's personality and bias, even their body language, are likely to affect the relationship with the source and the kinds of responses solicited. A reporter may be afraid of their source (for instance, if he is a Balkan warlord) or defer to someone they consider famous or powerful. A different reporter might draw different answers. Someone may respond more openly to a woman reporter, another may feel more relaxed with an older man. Research has shown that interviews by black and white people draw different kinds of responses.

But remember: relax. Studs (Louis) Terkel, the celebrated American interviewer, had this modest explanation for why people so easily opened up to him: 'I'm inept. I'm known as the man with the tape recorder but I'm inept. Often I press the wrong button. So people aren't in awe – they see this guy who's having trouble with a tape recorder' (Burkeman 2002).

The quickie or grabbed interview

Many interviews are short. You may be covering a parliamentary select committee and want to follow up something said. You have time to ask just a few questions. You have a clear idea of your angle and need extra information and/or quotes to support it. You go to the MP, pen and notebook in hand (tape recorders are not permitted in the House of Commons). There are just a few minutes before the MP is off on other business.

Vox pop

This is not about interviewing Madonna or Robbie Williams. It is the jargon term for the short interviews that journalists have with people on a given subject (vox pop is derived from the Latin for 'voice of the people'). Do you think a law should be introduced to restrain the press from invading people's privacy? That sort of thing. Local papers love vox pops: accompanied by mug shots of those quoted, it provides lively, easy-to-display, 'human interest' copy. Newspapers often build up a story around a series of short quotes drawn from street interviews (a photographer accompanying the reporter to provide mug shots for the story) or ring-arounds. A subject is identified and there follows a list of people with direct quotes attached to them. Or a vox pop can constitute part of a feature. The main story can dwell on the news, background and important details. A series of quotes highlights a range of views in an easy-to-read format. Sally Adams gives this advice on out-of-doors vox pops (2001: 11):

> The best way to find people likely to talk is to look for the journalistic equivalent of a captive audience: people who are already standing still, waiting for a bus, for instance, or in a queue to get into a club. Shopping centres and street markets can be productive areas.

Also be aware of the ethical issues involved: how important is it to reflect ethnic, age and gender diversities and range of viewpoints in your selection?

Doorstepping and ambush interviews

Occasionally journalists wait outside people's homes in the hope of gaining an interview. This 'doorstepping' technique is used particularly to gain access to celebrities. It can be abused, with the journalistic 'rat-pack' intimidating sources with their constant presence. Similarly a journalist might suddenly swoop on a source to ask them questions. The 'ambush' technique should be used only when all other means of gaining access have been exhausted and when the issues are serious enough to warrant such treatment. It is most commonly used by television investigative reporters, the ambush itself providing dramatic footage.

Phoney journalism

Speed is the essence of journalism, and the phone and email provide the easiest and quickest ways of contacting a source. But as Christopher Browne (1996) comments:

> The speed and frequency of deadlines means that instead of meeting their sources face to face an increasing number of today's reporters and correspondents rely on mobile and standard telephones, faxes, pagers, teleprinters and computers to get their stories. This creates an artificial barrier between the newsmen [sic] and the news leading to errors, misunderstandings and reports that lack the inimitable freshness of human contact.

The advice is clear: whenever you have an opportunity to see a source face to face, take it. If you are to develop that source, you will need to meet them.

Phone interviews tend to be shorter than face-to-face contacts. Reporters have to be clear about the questions they are to put and the information they need. There is little time for waffle. Profiles are rarely conducted by phone: the contact between reporter and source is too superficial and impersonal. At the same time, reporters conducting phone interviews have to be extra-sensitive to the nuances of speech: a hesitancy, an abruptness, a quivering in the voice all carry meanings which the reporter should be quick to note or respond to.

A reporter should also try to confront the impersonality of the phone and respond emotionally to the conversation. Facial and arm gestures can all help; if you are stressing a point, move your hands about; if jokes are made, laugh. Standing up can help provide extra confidence when making a particularly difficult call. Some journalists lodge a phone on their shoulder and type up the conversation at the same time. Not only can this practice lead to repetitive strain injury (RSI), but it can also be intimidating to the source and the reporter may have to return to note-taking with a pen if no other solution is possible.

Interview phobia

It is common for people new to journalism to find first contact with sources difficult. It is a challenge to ask a stranger questions (maybe in a foreign language) and maintain a coherent conversation while taking a note. Some find the 'distance' provided by the phone reassuring; others find face-to-face interviewing less intimidating. If you are not at ease on the phone, you are not alone. According to Dr Guy Fielding, a communications specialist, 2.5 million people in Britain suffer telephone phobia (Rowlands 1993).

In your first few months of reporting it is a good idea to join up with a colleague during assignments. While journalism is an individualistic job, it can succeed only through people working in a team. Joint reporting in no way conflicts with journalistic norms. One of the most famous scoops, the exposé of the 1972 Watergate break-in, was the result of a joint effort by Carl Bernstein and Bob Woodward of the *Washington Post*. Investigative reporters often work in pairs or in threesomes. It is safer, and while one asks the questions the other/s can observe reactions and the environment closely (K. Williams 1998; Spark 1999; De Burgh 2000).

If you are alone on an assignment in those early months, or at any other time, it is fine to ask someone to slow down in their talking. Don't hesitate to ask the interviewee to spell out a difficult word, to repeat a strong quote or important information. Figures, names and titles are worth particular attention. Don't hesitate to ring back to check or extract new information. That merely reflects painstaking efficiency rather than incompetence.

Phone tip-offs

Sometimes journalists are rung at their homes or offices with some news. The journalist has no time to prepare questions. They have to think quickly. Information drawn from an unknown source in this way has to be checked and the source's contact details sought so they can be rung back if necessary.

The role of PROs

If you are contacting pressure groups, political parties or professional bodies, you are likely to come into contact with their public relations officer (PRO). It is important to establish good relations with this person. They can be a vital source for background information and sometimes good for a quote. They can provide contact numbers for other sources and help in setting up meetings and interpreters if deaf people or foreign-language speakers are being interviewed.

But PROs expect a certain amount of background knowledge from reporters. A local government PRO would not expect to have to explain the intricacies of the council tax to an enquiring reporter. Official spokespersons are generally not referred to by name. They are described as 'a spokeswoman for such-and-such body'. They might also refer you to someone else in the organisation with specialist knowledge and responsibility in the area you are investigating.

In case of intimidation

Some people may feel intimidated by a phone call from a journalist. It might be their first contact with this awesome and seemingly powerful institution, the press, so capable of destroying reputations. You may decide to give them time to think about their responses. You could give them a few basic questions which they can respond to when you ring back in say twenty minutes. You have established some trust and they may be more inclined to respond to other questions. If the source is a racist attacking Pakistani or gypsy homes in your area you will adopt a different approach. As so often in reporting, political and ethical issues merge.

Arranging a face-to-face

Be polite, stay relaxed and sound efficient. It is important straight away to establish the likely length of the interview. The source is likely to have their own diary of engagements to complete. PROs often organise the meetings for celebrities, and minor skirmishes are likely over arranging the time and place of the interview. Negotiating the time-length is important since it provides a shorthand indication of the probable depth of the questioning.

Most interviews aiming to extract specific information can last for around half an hour; for a profile of any depth at least three-quarters of an hour is required, though they can last up to three hours (with a follow-up phone conversation as well). Lynn Barber (1999: 198) says that she refuses to do any profile interview for less than an hour. Ginny Dougary, of *The Times*, says she spent two hours with Michael Portillo for her award-winning interview in which he revealed his gay past – and followed it up with a telephone conversation.

Give a brief indication of the purpose of the interview (whether for a profile, as part of a feature or an investigation) and, in general terms, the kind of questions to be put. Identify clearly the newspaper you are working for and, if you are a freelance, the target publication you are aiming at. In some cases a subject will be interviewed by a group of reporters. In that case, it is a good idea to spell out briefly how your approach is intended to be different. Indicate if you are to be accompanied by a photographer or (where relevant) an interpreter.

Fixing time and place

There are several potential locations:

- *Your territory* (newspaper office if you are a staff writer; your home or office if you are a freelance; college if you are a student). This is rarely adopted by reporters; offices lack the privacy and relative calm needed for interviews and can appear intimidating to members of the public.

- *Their territory* (home, particularly likely if the person is unemployed, office or shop floor). Journalists often visit the source's home when writing a profile. People tend to feel relaxed there and talk most freely. The home is an expression of their personality: the source might wish to display it. The reporter can certainly use their observations of it and the source's behaviour within it to provide colour in their copy.

- The reporter might also visit the home when the source considers it too sensitive to hold the interview at their workplace. Visiting homes is not without its problems. The source is extending their hand to the reporter, inviting them into their private territory. The reporter can find it more difficult criticising the source after developing this kind of contact. Investigative reporter Nick Davies advises reporters not to park outside their source's home. 'If they are prompted to look out of the window they will make decisions about you before you introduce yourself.' The source's office is a common site for an interview (factory shopfloor workers are rarely profiled given current news values). The environment can be made relatively free from distractions, and relevant information and documents will be at hand.

- *Neutral territory* (a pub or restaurant): useful sites when you are building up contacts. Their informality promotes fruitful contact. The source is being 'entertained' and that helps the conversation flow. The journalist will always go with a specific intention but the informality allows time for digressions, small talk, gossip and jokes. All this helps in the development of the relationship. The journalist can express their own knowledge of and views about the subjects discussed and that, too, helps trust develop.

Reassuring the source

Sometimes a source will need reassuring that they are not opening themselves to attack by agreeing to be interviewed. Members of progressive groups such as peace activists, feminists, trade unionists, gays, lesbians and anti-capitalists have been pilloried in the media, and their fears are understandable. Even in today's supposedly democratic Britain, a large number of people are afraid or unwilling to express their views to the media. In these situations it is important to explain whom you are writing for, what you hope to extract from the interview. Edward Jay Friedlander and John Lee advise (2004: 146): 'If you detect reluctance on the part of the subject, try to find out what's bothering the potential interviewee. If the problem is something you can correct, correct it. For example, if the subject is concerned about the kind of story you intend to write, send a sample of a previous story you've written.'

Never speak to someone on the basis that you are writing for one media outlet which they are happy with and then send the copy elsewhere without consulting them. Student journalists might win a difficult interview on the understanding it is not for publication. This makes for unreal journalism (since it is only credible in the context of a target publication) and so should generally be avoided. Certainly the student should resist the temptation to betray the trust and send the copy off to a newspaper.

Submitting questions in advance

Someone might speak to you only on condition that they see a list of questions beforehand. Many politicians and showbiz celebrities are now adopting this line. It is a practice which, in general, should be challenged. Journalists can end up clerical poodles pandering to the whims of the famous. But it is wrong to call for a blanket ban on this request for questions.

A journalist may be aware of the interviewee's views; they are more important as a source of information. Since speed is the essence in journalism, the source might plead ignorance and essential information may go missing. They might need to do some research, consult colleagues before answering. At least the sending of questions gives them time. They cannot plead ignorance during the face-to-face interview.

It might be legitimate when a crucial source is sought and no other way appears possible to agree to send a list of questions. You may even suggest it. At least some response is gained and there is the possibility the source will be impressed by your questions and invite you in for a face-to-face.

An interviewee might first promise half an hour of their time but then running through the previously submitted and impressive questions might easily last for an hour and a half. At the opposite end of the scale from the media-shy person is the self-publicist. Every newspaper office will be harassed by someone desperate for coverage. Reporters need to be on their guard against this kind of person.

Preparing for an in-depth interview

Preparation is essential (Coleman 1993). If you are well informed, you are more likely to extract new and interesting information and be sensitive to the source's bias. Read the cuttings, do the research, check the internet (particularly fan sites if you are to cover a celebrity), talk to friends and colleagues about the subjects likely to be raised. An uninformed reporter becomes the pawn in the hand of the source, who can lie, hide crucial information, misinform – or steer the conversation away from tricky subjects. Celebrity interviewer Ginny Dougary says that she prepares for an interview 'like a military campaign'. To help prepare asking difficult questions she psychs herself up with deep breathing, wears smart clothes and makes absolutely sure her tapes are working.

Most professions have their own stock of jargon and a bewildering array of acronyms with which the reporter should have some familiarity. But sources used to handling the press have different expectations of journalists. The specialist is assumed to have more knowledge than the generalist and cub reporter. Never be afraid to express ignorance. Better to clarify a point than flounder or carry mistakes in your copy.

The question of questions

Journalists differ on the extent to which they prepare specific questions. To avoid 'drying up', some argue it is best to write down most of the crucial questions in a logical order and tick them off as the interview proceeds. Many find this can impede free-flowing conversation. Talk moves too fast usually to allow this 'ticking off'. If the detailed list of questions is used, it should be on a separate sheet of paper and not buried in a notebook.

In any case, interviews can often move in unpredictable directions making it absurd to stick to any pre-planned outline. Another approach is to think through the interview beforehand listing detailed questions in order. The act of writing helps the memory. For the interview, three or four vital headings are listed and around this skeleton the flesh of the interview can be spread.

Dress sense

A journalist should be conscious of the messages put out by their dress. Informal dress will be appropriate on some occasions such as when interviewing members of progressive campaigning groups or think-tanks, formal dress when meeting white-collar professionals or politicians. A journalist will always have at the back of their mind: 'If I dressed differently, would the source be more open to me and trusting?'

Preliminary courtesies

First contact is crucial. The reporter should be calm and relaxed, polite but assertive. The greeting should be pleasant with a firm handshake and some eye-to-eye contact. The reporter might need to make clear again the purpose of the interview (though during some investigations the real purpose might be hidden).

If the interview is for some reason off-the-record or unattributable, this needs to be established. Politicians and most PROs will be aware of the attribution conventions of newspapers. Many people are not. They may begin to answer questions and then try to designate them as off the record. A journalist should not be willing to permit that kind of arrangement automatically. A source may say something on the record which, in print, could damage them or someone else unnecessarily. In this case the journalist will operate self-censorship.

If you are planning to use a tape recorder or a Dictaphone, make sure this is fine with the source, who might choose to set up their own taping device, after all. You might not wish to bring out your notebook until you have relaxed into the conversation and passed the preliminary courtesies. The notebook should never be over-prominent.

The actual interview: GENERAL POINTS

Note-taking

In your first weeks as a reporter you may find it difficult keeping a conversation going while making notes at the same time. Don't feel self-conscious about that. You may even say: 'That's an important point. Would you mind repeating that?' Selecting the useful information and quotes becomes an art. Sometimes all the notes will be used, usually just a part of them. The writer, confident in their powers of memory, might add more details or comments they remember but did not take down. This has to be handled carefully, particularly if the views are contentious and potentially libellous. Without any notes or tape recording, the journalist has little defence in court.

Presenting your personality

Dennis Barker (1998), former media correspondent and columnist on the *Guardian*, argues that journalists should ask 'questions which the Man on the Clapham Omnibus would ask if he were there' and should not follow their own agenda. But it is impossible to deny your personality in the meeting. The selection and bias of your questions, your manner and your dress will carry the stamp of your personality. The extent to which your personality more overtly intrudes on the interview will differ according to the circumstances.

In most interviews where the focus is on extracting views and information, the reporter's intervention is likely to be limited. An exchange of views and a joke or two are useful for varying the mood and helping conversation flow. In profile interviews your own personality can come more and more to the fore. Someone confronted with a reporter who is nothing more than a blank sheet of a personality merely uttering concise questions can hardly convey their own.

But you should never come to dominate a meeting. Your views and experiences are of secondary importance and should be revealed only to entice more out of your subject. Displaying some of your knowledge on the subject can also impress the interviewee and help build up trust. Never show off. And don't be too familiar: it is rarely appropriate to address your source by their first name.

Pacing the interview

Most journalistic training manuals advise reporters to begin always with the non-threatening questions establishing basic information and views. This helps to create trust after which more sensitive questions can be raised. In practice, reporters respond in many different ways to the shifting dynamics of the interview. Some suggest it is best to throw in a difficult question near the start. As Lynn Barber (1991) comments: 'The subject's relief at having survived it so quickly and painlessly may pay dividends for the rest of the interview.'

Yet there is always the danger that the interviewee may call a stop to the conversation early on if this strategy fails. Barber (see Reeves 2002) says that at the start of interviews she makes the point of stressing the interviewee's right to refuse: 'Please don't be offended by my questions. If you don't want to answer them, just shake your head and I won't even put no comment.' Questions should be concise. But the interview is not likely to be all questions. It may be fruitful to exchange ideas. Formulate a mix of open-ended questions and specific questions, avoiding those which give a yes/no answer.

Active listening

Most interviewers stress that active listening is one of the most crucial skills. Journalists can often be surprised at how open and talkative people are when profiled. Their vanity may be flattered. Here is someone taking an interest in them; however fleeting, a little fame is assured by the coverage. In some respects the press (and the media in general) has taken over the role of the Church as being the site of the confessional, where personal secrets are revealed. Every day the press carries the revelation of some secret: the secret of so-and-so's sex life; the leak of secret divisions in the Cabinet; a secret arms sale.

Paradoxically, this is happening in a society where government and industry are becoming increasingly secretive and remote from democratic accountability. Given the willingness to talk, the journalist's role is to listen intelligently and help the conversation along with concise, clearly focused questions.

The flexible approach

Reporters should be relaxed and flexible, ready to abandon their list of questions and follow up more interesting ideas as they emerge. They should always be clear about what they want from an interview. It is dangerous to go into an interview with a vague brief hoping that something will come out of it. It rarely does; the reporter will end up with a lot of waffle. In contrast, continual evasive responses to key questions suggest to the reporter they are on to something important. There is a place for unstructured chat, say over a meal, between journalist and source. Contacts are being maintained and maybe something of interest will emerge. But chat is very different from an interview.

Power games people play

The distribution of power in many communication processes is complex and fluctuating. A source may seek to exploit the reporter to transmit their views, their misinformation or their propaganda. The reporter exploits the source as a 'quote giver' or 'information giver'. In this light, interviews can be seen as a contest. The journalist must be aware as far as possible of the dynamics of the interview and try to be in control, determining the flow. The interviewee should never take over. If they do, by rambling on some irrelevant point, for instance, the journalist should reassert their authority with a pointed question.

Body talk

Eye contact is important, but continuous contact is likely to appear intimidating. During profile interviews, other aspects of body language and non-verbal communication, such as sighs, shrugs, silences, coughs or shrugging of shoulders, will be closely observed by the reporter. Interviewing children (having gained their parents' consent) poses special problems for the journalist. For instance, getting eye contact with them often involves crouching down (Hughes and McCrum 1998). Also be aware of your own body language: is it helping to put the subject at ease?

Dealing with the difficult ones

The hostile interviewee

An interviewee may be hostile for a number of reasons. They may have a poor opinion of the press in general or have been criticised in the past. They may feel threatened or insulted by a particular line of questioning. They may simply dislike the sound of your voice or the colour of your jacket. As a result, you may have to reassure them about the standards you and your newspaper follow, and that you understand their sensitivity about a particular issue.

Whatever happens, keep cool. Never argue with an interviewee. Try to steer the conversation towards calmer waters. If the source is particularly important and reacts nervously to your questions, you may agree to show them the copy before publication. Lynn Barber (1999: 197) says 'the best interview ever' was Lillian Ross's profile of Hemingway. Ross sent him the article before publication: he asked for one deletion, which she made. Sometimes the source might walk out on you. That is their privilege.

The over-hasty interviewee

This is the person who says: 'I don't have time to talk to you.' A good response is to say something like: 'I won't take up much of your time but this is an important matter and I want to get it right.' Be sympathetic and straight to the point. They should thaw.

The silent interviewee

You don't seem to be going anywhere. They answer in dull, monosyllabic tones. Give them time to warm up, open-ended questions and lots of encouraging head-nods. If all else fails, fall silent and see what happens.

The 'no comment'

As veteran investigative journalist Phillip Knightley (1998) advises, never take 'no' for an answer. If the source is particularly important, be persistent but don't harass them. If they continue to say 'no comment', you could tell them this looks bad in print. Stress that you don't want to write a one-sided story and that you need their comments, perhaps to correct inaccuracies. Ask why they cannot comment. Someone may try to delay you until the following day. Suggest the story is going to print and will be unbalanced without their quotes.

The dodger

They may claim ignorance of some major detail but be simply trying to avoid controversy. You need to be well briefed to cope. They claim to have been absent from a crucial meeting. 'Ah, but I have looked at the minutes of the meeting and noticed you were present.' That sort of comment should jog their memory.

The waffler

They may habitually be a raconteur and stray away from the main conversational issues. Or they may be trying to evade a delicate issue. Don't let them take command of the conversation. Keep it focused.

Ending the interview

- Sometimes it is worth asking: 'Is there anything else you wish to mention?'
- Appropriate courtesies should be made: thanks for time and so on.
- Arrangements for checking and future contact (perhaps also by a photographer) can be made. If you have interviewed them at their office, it might be useful to have their home number and email details.
- An interviewee might ask to see copy before it is published. You will then have to deal with that issue.

After the interview

This is another crucial period. You might need to ring or email back to clarify some points. They might well contact you again. Often, after profile interviews, it is courteous to write back thanking them for their time. Also try to transcribe the tape and compile your article as soon as possible after the event. If you wait, you are more likely to forget details, distort others and find your notes incomprehensible. When the interview is part of a feature investigation, it should similarly be written up as soon as possible and ideas for new interviews and issues to examine should be noted.

Direct quotes

These are best reserved for expressions of opinion. For instance: 'She said: "Tony Blair has already proved himself to be the best Prime Minister of the century."' Direct quotes add newsy elements to stories and provide colour, immediacy, authenticity and the crucial human dimension to copy, hence their prominence. They can add humour. Quotes also help personalise the news. It is always better to have an individual express a view than an impersonal institutional voice. Instead of 'the National Union of Teachers claimed', say 'a spokeswoman for the NUT claimed'. When using a press release, a phone call or email may be necessary to add this detail.

Lengths of direct quotes will vary. But take any book of quotations and see how short the majority are. Some of the most famous are a matter of a few words. Just as the heavies use longer sentences than the pops, so their quotes tend to be longer. But do people speak in shorter sentences to tabloid journalists?

It is a vexed question among journalists as to how much freedom they have to edit a direct quote. Most will agree that such phrases as 'you know', 'like I said' and 'er, er' slipped into conversation can easily be cut. Beyond that, some argue that a direct quote should never be changed. However, there is a case for editing when someone speaks ungrammatically. Nothing is served by leaving in an ungrammatical phrase other than showing that the source is stupid. Thus, particular care should be given when quoting people for whom English is not their first language. Nonsense is worth quoting when the subject of the piece requires it. For instance, newspapers have focused on the ungrammatical language used by a series of prominent US politicians (Reaganspeak, Haigspeak, Bushspeak), often in off-the-cuff remarks to journalists. Peculiar speech mannerisms and dialect can be quoted to convey the source's typical speech patterns. This has to be done sensitively, mostly in features.

Particular kinds of cliché, jargon and rhetoric do not make good quotes. Thus 'The President said: "This historic meeting of the world's leading industrial states has achieved a lot and we have reason to be proud of what we have done this weekend."' 'She was "very pleased" with the takings from the raffle for handicapped children.' These are examples of clichés and rhetoric which can be easily cut.

Reported speech

The conventions of reported speech are simple. Following verbs such as 'said', 'informed', 'claimed', 'warned', 'demanded', 'alleged', 'hinted', 'added', the tense of the verb in reported speech takes one step into the past.

Direct speech	*Reported speech*
am/are/is	was/were
shall	should
will	would
may	might
was/were	had been
have been	had been
must	had to
could	could have

'Aneurin Bevan said: "I read the newspaper avidly. It is my one form of continuous fiction"' is using the direct quote. In reported speech it becomes: 'Aneurin Bevan said he read the newspaper avidly. It was his one form of continuous fiction ' It is wrong to say: 'Aneurin Bevan said he reads the newspaper avidly. It is his one form of continuous fiction.'

Thus 'He said: "The trade union movement has been crippled by the Tories' punitive legislation and has little support from the Blair government"' becomes: 'He said the trade union movement had been crippled by the Tories' punitive legislation and had little support from the Blair government.'

Pronouns are affected by reported-speech conventions. 'She said: "We may decide to emigrate to Iceland"' becomes: 'She said they might decide to emigrate to Iceland.' 'She told the council "Your attempts at promoting equal opportunities in this county are pathetic"' becomes: 'She told the council its attempts at promoting equal opportunities in the county were pathetic.'

Adverbs and time-related adjectives and nouns are also affected. Thus 'He said: "We shall all meet here soon to plan next week's agenda"' becomes: 'He said they should all meet there soon to plan the following week's agenda.' For a longer exposition of reported-speech rules, see Aitchison (1988) and Hicks (1998: 53–4).

Note the use of reported speech in this article in the *Morning Star* of 10 November 2004:

A lesbian couple who wed in Canada can seek to have their union legally recognised in Ireland, Irish High Court Justice Minister Liam McKechnie ruled yesterday.

> Mr McKechnie said that lawyers representing Ann Louise Gilligan and Katherine Zappone had presented an arguable case that merited a full hearing, which is likely to take place next year.
>
> He predicted that the case would have profound consequences for predominantly Catholic Ireland.

- In the first par, following 'can seek', 'ruled' is used (following the convention for intros) instead of the reported speech 'could seek' to maintain immediacy.
- In par two, after verb 'said' notice reported speech 'had presented'. But 'is likely' is used (rather than 'was likely') since this was not said by McKechnie but information inserted by the reporter.
- In par three, after 'predicted' note 'would have' ('will have' would be wrong).

Beware of making reported speech, say in a press release, into direct speech. A release that says: 'Former President Nelson Mandela accused the South African government of continuing to suppress black rights' cannot be changed into: 'Nelson Mandela said: "The South African government is continuing to suppress black rights."' There is no proof that he said those words. The indirect speech might have been the paraphrase of a longer sentence or a combination of sentences.

Reported speech within a direct quote cannot be converted into direct speech. Thus 'He said he would ask his wife if he should resign tomorrow' cannot become: 'He asked his wife: "Should I resign tomorrow?"'

Most reports of speeches will combine direct and indirect speech. A report concentrating too heavily on indirect speech will lack immediacy and colour; a report almost exclusively in direct quotation conveys the impression that the journalist has surrendered their role of selection and interpretation to the source.

Partial quotes

These are used to highlight particular words in sentences. Thus, the *Yorkshire Post* reported (14 July 2003): 'Services aimed at tackling drug addiction in parts of Yorkshire are at "complete meltdown", it was claimed last night.' Journalists use partial quotes sparingly. They are most commonly used in intros but become confusing if used throughout a story.

Quotation dangers

Two or more people rarely speak in unison. When reporting a public meeting it is strange to have two people identified with the same direct quote. Thus: '"The BBC should be privatised immediately," two Conservative councillors urged yesterday' is wrong. People can agree on an issue and be linked to a direct quote without any problem. Thus it is perfectly feasible to say: 'The BBC should be privatised immediately, two Conservative councillors urged yesterday.'

Be careful not to distort reports by over-selective quoting. Someone may devote part of a speech to conveying the pros of an issue, the other part to the cons. One side of the argument may be highlighted; it is irresponsible to eliminate all reference to the other side.

Journalists can let their imagination take over when quoting. The Press Complaints Commission has gone so far as to censure journalists for too frequently resorting to invention in the use of quotes. One of the most famous instances was the *Sun*'s invented interview with the wife of a Falklands war 'hero' killed in battle. (The woman journalist involved went on to edit a national newspaper.)

A variation on the invention theme is the 'words in the mouth' technique. When an interviewee remains unresponsive, the journalist is tempted to feed them quotes. They may ask the interviewee: 'Do you think this scheme for Blackpool transport is outrageous and should never have been backed?' When the hesitant interviewee replies: 'Er, yes', the journalist is able to report: 'She said she thought the transport scheme for Blackpool was outrageous and should never have been backed.' Such a technique should be used sparingly.

But former *Sunday Mirror* reporter Wendsley Clarkson (1990) tells of when he met ex-Beatle Paul McCartney in his car with his wife alongside him as he drove out of his country estate. Merely on the basis of a few grunts of the 'Yep, sure do' variety, Clarkson invented an 'exclusive'.

Along with invention can go exaggeration and sensationalism. Two residents are quoted as being opposed to plans for a shopping complex on a school sports site. The story reads: 'Residents are protesting etc.' The report gives a false picture of the strength of opposition for the sake of journalistic hyperbole. If one of the residents was a spokesperson for the residents, then you could intro: 'Residents are protesting etc.' When opposing views are expressed, 'rows' have not necessarily broken out, nor have 'wars', nor is one side necessarily 'up in arms'. Disputes at churches need not always be dubbed 'unholy rows'.

There is a danger of placing direct quote marks around a phrase and not making clear the source. Such 'hanging' quotes confuse. Always make the attribution of any quote clear. And be careful not to run two sections of a direct quote together when they were separated by sentences. End the first sentence with inverted commas. Begin the next sentences with, say: 'She added: "Etc. . . ."'

Quotes punctuation

Lynne Truss's surprise global bestseller *Eats, Shoots & Leaves* (2003) usefully, and humorously, highlights the importance of correct punctuation to good prose (see also King 2000). Most newspapers adopt the following style. They will say:

She added: 'I intend to vote for the Raving Loony Party.'

Notice the colon followed by a space, then inverted commas and a capital letter. Some papers use double inverted commas (single within double), others do the reverse. At the end of the sentence the full stop is followed by the inverted commas. Variations on those models are considered wrong. Avoid:

She said, 'I intend to vote for the Raving Loony Party'.

and

She said that 'I intend to vote for the Raving Loony Party.'

When a partial quote is used the punctuation should fall outside the quote marks. Thus:

He described the US-led attacks on Iraq as 'necessary to remove the evil Saddam'.

The rail strike is 'outrageous', according to Prime Minister Tony Blair.

If double quotes are used, single quotes are used for quotes within quotes. Thus:

He said: "The US–UK attacks on Baghdad are best seen as a 'barbaric slaughter' of innocent Iraqi civilians."

First words in partial quotes are not capitalised. Thus: 'Barbara Tuchman said war was the "Unfolding of miscalculations"' is wrong. It should read:

Barbara Tuchman said war was the 'unfolding of miscalculations'.

Square brackets are used in direct quotations around words inserted by the journalist to make the meaning clear. Thus:

He [President Clinton] quite obviously backed the bombing of Iraq to deflect attention from the controversy surrounding his affair with Monica Lewinsky.

Interestingly, American newspapers place square brackets around copy from agencies (such as Reuters or Agence France Presse) which is inserted into stories by staff reporters.

Put an ellipsis (. . .) in a direct quote to indicate irrelevant words are missing. Used more than once it looks as if the reporter is struggling with a poor note or indulging in over-zealous editing. Simpler to change the quote into indirect speech and remove the offending dots.

Attribution verbs

'Said' is most commonly used to convey attribution. It is short and neutral, and for these reasons is rapidly read over. To use 'said' on every occasion would be dull, and words such as 'replied', 'commented', 'pointed out', 'protested', 'warned', 'indicated', 'explained', 'added', 'hinted', 'revealed', 'claimed' and 'alleged', which have specific meanings, are used, always carefully. They are most often placed in intros where they convey extra emphasis and drama. They should never be used simply to provide colour in news stories, though more flexibility is possible in features.

'Claimed' should be used only for controversial statements of alleged fact when there is some reasonable doubt over them. When evidence is undisputed the use of 'claim' throws up unnecessary doubts. When a newspaper reports: 'In its report which follows a detailed review of the operation of the 1976 Race Relations Act, the commission claims ethnic minorities continue to suffer high levels of discrimination and disadvantage', it is using 'claims' in a subtly racist way to dispute the fact of widespread discrimination.

'Admitted' should be used only when a source is confessing to an error, a failing, a limitation, charge or crime. Thus, the *Lincolnshire Echo* (20 October 2004) reported on a magistrates' court case in which a man was accused of hurling abuse at a police officer:

> Bourke (40), of Gibson Close, Branston, admitted being drunk and disorderly on 18 October.

'Added' should be used only after a source has already been quoted. It is wrong to introduce a new source with the words: 'She added: "Etc. . ."'

'Revealed' should be used only when significant new information is being relayed. 'Stated' is archaic and generally avoided. 'Quipped', 'joked' and 'chuckled' are clichés and best avoided or confined to light features and diary pieces.

An effective way of conveying attribution is to use the phrase 'according to . . .' It is most commonly used in intros, as here from the *Hull Daily Mail* (23 June 2004):

> Fake identification is openly for sale on the internet, according to a study out today. An investigation uncovered bogus proof of age, national ID and employee cards on offer from UK-based companies.

Getting the quotes down: RECORDING TECHNIQUES

Shorthand

One of the essential skills of the journalist is recording notes effectively. The National Council for the Training of Journalists requires 100 words per minute (wpm) from successful candidates. Many training courses devote considerable time to shorthand and most provincial newspapers will require good shorthand from applicants. The two most popular systems with journalists are Pitmans and Teeline, the latter invented primarily with trainee journalists in mind.

During the nineteenth century the emergence of shorthand as a special journalistic technique (with novelist Charles Dickens demonstrating particular skills) helped in the development of the notion of 'professionalism'. As Anthony Smith (1978) argues: 'It meant that a man could specialise in observing or hearing and recording with precision . . . it gave the reporter an aura of neutrality as he stood between event and reader.'

Today there is a paradox that the higher up the greasy pole of journalistic success you go, the less likely you are to find shorthand competence. Not all Fleet Street writers possess it. Very few other journalistic cultures give shorthand the kind of importance that British provincial newspapers attach to it. Yet it is important for all aspiring journalists to do shorthand to at least 100 words a minute. Nobody regrets the effort put into the learning. For certain jobs, such as covering Parliament, select committees, courts and coroners' courts where tapes are banned, and council meetings, good shorthand is essential. If reporters had better recording techniques, fewer errors would crop up and the habit of inventing quotes and facts would diminish.

Personal shorthands

The most commonly used abbreviation system is Astbury's, and you may want to develop your own based on the idea of cutting out vowels. 'Between' becomes 'btwn', 'against' 'agst' and so on. A new shorthand system, AgiliWriting (with a special 13,000-word dictionary), has been invented by Anne Gresham; she describes it as 'ezy t rd, ezy t wrt and ezy t lrn'. The outstanding feature is that it is accompanied by a computer program allowing the writer to type in shorthand copy and transfer it into longhand. (For more information: 76 Hadley Road, Barnet, Hertfordshire EN5 5QR; 020 8447 1011; http://www.shorthand.co.uk.) Thus, it is possible that in the near future journalists will attend press conferences with their laptop computers, type notes in shorthand form, then send them via a modem to the office for conversion into longhand.

Selective note-taking

Acquiring the skills of selective note-taking is crucial. It is not essential to record everything said. Over-detailed note-taking prevents profitable contact in interviews. The best shorthand writers are not necessarily the best writers. The good journalist knows when something of interest is being said. Their ears prick up and all attention is paid to getting down those facts, those views, that feeling. If you are not certain you have the quote correct, either double check or paraphrase the general meaning (if you are clear about that) and put it in reported speech. David Spark (1999: 47) offers this additional advice: 'If you are in the habit of adorning your notes with comments about the people you are speaking to give up the habit. In court, a rude comment can be construed as showing your evidence-gathering was malicious, not even-handed. In a libel case, malice invalidates a defence of fair comment or a claim to privilege.'

Memory

In some cases, journalists don't take down notes at all. During a risky investigation a journalist may keep their identity hidden. At a particularly sensitive interview a journalist may consider the presence of a notebook impedes conversation and over-formalises the meeting. A source may be prepared to talk but find the notebook intimidating. On these occasions the reporter has to rely on memory. Only those with a good memory should adopt this approach.

Tidiness

Reporters usually use easy-to-handle notebooks that slip easily into pockets and whose pages flip over quickly. Notes should never be made on odd sheets of paper. These can be easily mislaid. A tidy system of keeping used notebooks is essential since back-referencing is sometimes needed. When complaints are made to newspapers over coverage, easy access to the relevant note is essential. The Press Complaints Commission has warned newspapers over their increasing habit of losing important notes. When complaints were made, newspapers had little ground on which to base a defence.

Note-taking from written sources

- For developing background knowledge of people, events and issues, written sources are vital.
- For research in libraries (with CD-ROM, cuttings, the internet and other written sources) you may work with a quiet laptop or more usually with pen and paper.

Always make clear the title of the book or article, full name of author, publisher, place and year of publication. These details are usually in small type on the imprint page, before the contents list. It is also advisable to identify the page number as you note the document. This can be important if you go on to write a project or book on the subject. Many journalists work on books in their spare time or on sabbaticals. So it is a useful habit to develop.

• Make clear the distinction between a direct quote from a work and a paraphrase. To lift someone's words directly and not attribute them can lead to allegations of plagiarism.

• Learn to use books, reports, articles and website features selectively. You will rarely read from beginning to end. There is not the time. Sometimes you will rapid-read a work and take detailed notes of the conclusions or recommendations. There may be a vital book or article which is worth reading three times to digest. Use book indexes to go straight to the material you need. Look at the bibliographies for other useful sources.

Tapes: pros and cons

Many journalists are relying increasingly on tape recorders or Dictaphones. Prices range from around £30 up to £200 and beyond. They are small and unobtrusive, and few people are intimidated by their presence. If a source challenges a reporter over a quote, nothing is better at ending the controversy than a tape providing the evidence. But courts are aware that tapes can be tampered with. Alastair Brett, a lawyer at Times Newspapers, advises: 'Tape everything you can, every word you utter or is uttered to you.' After a solicitor complained that a *Sunday Times* reporter had 'grossly misled' him, the newspaper was able to show that the whole conversation had been taped and was able to prove otherwise (Spark 1999: 45).

You should inform your source that you are using a tape. Some newspapers have phones set aside for taping while a few journalists have devices on their phones at home. Taping always requires careful handling. Never rely entirely on a tape. You may lose it or may have forgotten to press the vital 'on' switch. The battery may run low; the microphone may pick up unwanted noises. If you put it on the centre of a table during a panel discussion, it might not register the voices at the end of the table. Always take a back-up note. The dangers of having a tape erased were highlighted in the case of Jason Connery versus the *Sun* in 1992 when the newspaper's defence failed after a tape that promised to provide crucial evidence was 'lost'. The only record remaining was a transcript of the conversation which the judge said had been 'embellished, added to and altered' (Leyland 1998).

For copy needed quickly, tape recorders can be a positive nuisance. There is not time to wade through the tape to find the relevant quotes and information. Tapes are best used for features and profiles when you have time to note and digest their contents. Journalists very rarely transcribe all the tape. Take down the most important sections as soon as possible after the interview, then return to it for a more thorough run-through when writing up your story.

Bugging

Bugging devices are available at relatively low prices: a study in 2000 by the campaigning body Privacy International found that 200,000 bugs are sold quite legally in Britain every year (see, for instance, www.spy-equipment.co.uk and www.spy phones.biz). Managements use them to snoop on staff – and a few journalists use them during investigations. Investigative reporter Gerry Brown (1995a) highlights the fact that bugging is illegal under the Interception of Communications Act 1985. But recording your own end of a two-way telephone conversation is legal (see also Brown 1995b). He says:

> Quite simply, newspaper reporters who tap people's phones are already breaking the law. I've been doing sneaky investigations for the tabloids for 20-odd years and I've never tapped a phone or been asked by a newspaper to tap a phone. What I do is monitor and record phone calls. The difference is simple. When you hook up to a phone line and listen in to two people without either of them being aware you're eavesdropping, then that's tapping and you're breaking the law. But if you or your contacts are simply recording your own end of a two-way conversation, that's monitoring.
>
> Hide a radio microphone in a room and crouch behind the bushes in the garden to snoop on what's being said, and that's bugging, an offence under Section 1, the Wireless Telegraphy Act 1949. But if you are in the room yourself with the microphone running to a micro-tape recorder stuffed down your underpants, again, perfectly legal.

The PCC Code of Practice advises against bugging bar exceptional cases. However, the use of bugging by the state and its secret services and by industrial spies is far more widespread (Wingfield 1984; Campbell and Connor 1986).

The law is currently confused on scanners. Possession is not illegal: they can be bought for around £300 in the high street. People use them for listening to citizens' band radio and the weather report from ship to shore. There is even a UK scanning directory listing such sensitive frequencies as airport security, US Air Force bomb disposal units and defence tactical communications. But it is illegal to listen in to official or private conversations, and mobile phones are particularly vulnerable to scanning.

5 Learning the language of news

The language of news today is the product of centuries of linguistic evolution. It is not a 'natural' form of writing. It is a particular discourse with its own rhythms, tones, words and phrases (van Dijk 1988; Fowler 1991). It has to be learnt.

Kiss and tell

Many young reporters from academic backgrounds where writing essays 2,000 words long may be the norm find writing news difficult. Compose a story of 300 words and every word has to count. The sense of news values has to be sharp, and that comes only with practice. 'Kiss (*keep it short and simple*) and tell' could be the journalist's motto. Complex sentences overloaded with long subordinate clauses should be avoided. Short, precise sentences are best. As the left-wing novelist and journalist George Orwell (1984 [1957]: 151–2) advised:

> A scrupulous writer, in every sentence that he writes, will ask himself at least four questions, thus: What am I trying to say? What words will express it? What image or idiom will make it clearer? Is this image fresh enough to have an effect? And he will probably ask himself two more: Could I put it more shortly? Have I said anything that is avoidably ugly?

You don't need to count words all the time. But think in terms of a maximum of around 32–5 for a news sentence. The tabloids and many local and ethnic minority papers have around 16–20 maximum limit. Take these three examples.

First, these opening pars from a report in the *Asian Post* (www.theasianpost.co.uk) of 4–10 July 2003 have 13, 17 and 21 words.

A motion of no-confidence against the speaker of Pakistan's National Assembly has failed.

The opposition tabled a motion after Speaker Chaudhry Amir Hussain backed sweeping powers for President Pervez Musharraf.

> But in the end, radical Islamic and mainstream secular opposition parties boycotted a process they initiated and the motion was rejected.

Second, these pars from the *Daily Star* (www.dailystar.co.uk) of 19 July 2004 have 13, 19 and 10 words.

> Police and firemen staged Britain's biggest mock-up of a nerve gas attack yesterday.
> Nearly 2,000 rescuers swooped on the National Exhibition Centre at Birmingham in the exercise to test real doomsday procedures.
> But it took nearly three hours to 'decontaminate' pretend victims.

Third, these from the *Socialist Worker* (www.socialistworker.co.uk) of 23 October 2004 have 26, 9, 18 and 20.

> Tony Blair has made a secret deal with George Bush to site US missiles in Britain as part of the US's 'Son of Star Wars' programme. The deal was revealed by the *Independent on Sunday*.
> Bush has pledged to spend £5.5 billion a year erecting a missile defence around the US if re-elected.
> The British government has given an agreement 'in principle' to siting US interceptor missiles at RAF Fylingdales base in Yorkshire.

Economic base of economical writing

Many factors lie behind the creation of this concise news language. The arrival of the telegraph and telegram during the nineteenth century put a clear cost on elaborate language. With the competition today between advertisers and editorial for space in newspapers, every reported word involves a cost. Economic language helps provide economies in production. Speed is the essence of newspapers. Sentence structure and page design are influenced by the need to help readers move through the newspaper quickly. As the speed of everyday life increases, the average concentration span narrows. Sentences become shorter; headlines end up just a few 'punchy' words.

Acronyms of mass deception

Acronyms proliferate. In the lead-up to the US–UK invasion of Iraq in 2003, WMD (weapons of mass destruction) were at the centre of the controversy (though later proved to be non-existent). Words made from acronyms become standards ('yuppie', 'yummie', 'AIDS'). Phrases that compress complex meaning into a few words are everywhere ('the silent majority', the 'new world order'). Newspaper design also influences language and sentence lengths. As Fred Fedler (1989: 28) comments:

> Newspapers are printed in small type, with narrow columns, on cheap paper. Long paragraphs – large, gray blocks of type – discourage readers. So reporters divide stories into bite-size chunks that are easy to read. Also, the white space left at the ends of paragraphs helps brighten each page.

Boil it down

Never use two or three words when one will do. As Matthew Arnold put it succintly: 'Have something to say and say it as clearly as you can. That is the only secret to style' (see Humphrys 2004a: xiii). Words and phrases such as 'in order to' (use simply 'to'), 'at the present time' ('now'), 'in the region of' ('about'), 'despite the fact that' ('even though'), 'in view of the fact that' ('because'), 'on the subject of training' ('on training') and 'strike action' ('strike') are all cuttable. Prefer short to long words: 'about' rather than 'approximately', 'show' rather than 'demonstrate', 'after' rather than 'following'. Avoid the over-wordiness of adjectives and adverbs: 'totally destroyed', 'root cause', 'important essential', 'past history', 'invited guest', 'best ever', 'broad daylight', 'close proximity', 'considerable difficulty', 'initial beginning', 'final outcome'. 'Very', 'quite' and 'rather' are meaningless modifiers, eminently cuttable. Beware unnecessary prepositions as in 'divided up', 'circled around', 'fell down', 'raise up', 'revert back' (Humphrys 2004b). Try not to repeat a word in the same sentence or any striking words close together unless a specific effect is intended.

The word 'that' can often be cut, as in: 'He admitted that he was guilty of stealing a pen from the office.' Also be careful when using the small word 'of'. Usually you can make a phrase more precise. 'In the northern part of Iraq' is better written 'in northern Iraq'. Use language precisely. Don't confuse decimate/destroy, less/fewer, luxurious/luxuriant, affect/effect, it is/its. Ian Mayes, the *Guardian*'s readers' editor, is constantly having to highlight errors over 'homophones': words pronounced in the same way but differing in meaning or spelling or both – as in bear and bare, sort/sought, diffusing/defusing, censor/censure, rites/rights, yoke/yolk, draws/drawers. Generally try to avoid using 'thing'. It is vague and ugly. (For useful sections on wasteful and commonly misused words and redundancies, see Bagnall 1993: 4–11.)

Be active

Rather than 'A meeting will be held by TUC leaders next week to discuss the government's new privatisation strategy' it is better to say 'TUC leaders will meet next week to discuss the government's new privatisation strategy'.

Fun with puns

Puns are extremely important in newspapers. They play with language and its many-faceted meanings. Some can be forced. But their contrivance is part of their appeal. A certain wit is needed to construct them just as they can convey a certain humour (Fiske 1989). Puns feature particularly in the pops. Their humour contributes to their overall hedonistic appeal. For instance, the *News of the World* (*NoW*) (5 September 2004) carried this (highly contrived) headline 'Nell's wed over heels!' and (along-side 'exclusive' pictures of the happy, half-naked couple cuddling on a beach) followed it with this intro:

> Do you take this woman Nell McAndrew to have and to hold? It shore looks like it. For the lucky guy planting a sizzling kiss on beach beauty Nell is getting married to her this Christmas.

The heavies are more likely to reserve puns for soft news stories and headlines. But many of the parliamentary sketch writers, such as Matthew Parris of *The Times*, can build their copy on a simple pun idea.

Clichés: AVOID THEM LIKE THE PLAGUE

Clichés for Fleet Street columnist Keith Waterhouse (1991) count as his number 1 sin among his 'seven deadly sins' of writing. There are thousands of clichés and they come in many guises. For instance, there are alliterative phrases such as 'safe and sound', 'slow but sure', 'chop and change', 'share and share alike', 'petticoat protest', 'followed in the footsteps', 'few and far between'. They appear as meaningless, over-dramatic adjectives such as in 'driving rain', 'miraculous escape', 'tragic accident', 'brutal murder', 'coveted title', 'sudden death', 'horrific injuries', 'sweeping reforms', 'heated argument', 'proud parents', 'bare minimum', 'shock/major/hard-hitting report', 'mercy mission'. There are metaphors gone stale with overuse: 'blanket of snow', 'pillar of strength', 'tower of strength', 'tip of the iceberg', 'sweep under the rug', 'local boy made good'. Some single words such as 'fairytale', 'viable', 'ongoing', 'crisis', 'situation', 'scandal', 'tragedy', 'disaster', 'fury', 'fuming', 'angry', 'shock', 'outrage' amount to clichés.

Amongst those listed by John Humphrys (2004a: 230) are 'on hold', 'up for grabs', 'calm before the storm', 'explore every avenue' and 'conspicuous by its absence'.

One of journalism's biggest clichés is 'exclusive', which is constantly devalued through overuse. The *News of the World* of 5 September 2004 had 13 news 'exclusives' and five in its sports section. The *Daily Star*, of 19 July 2004, carried four 'exclusives' on its front page alone (alongside a massive, predictable picture of a pouting Jordan). On 5 December, the *People* carried 16 'exclusives' in its main section and another nine in its sports section. Investigative reporter Phillip Knightley (1998: 44) argues that newspapers, in any case, give 'exclusives' the importance they don't deserve. 'Scoops are a journalist's way of assessing his or her colleagues and of interest only to journalists.'

Celebrating heroism in a post-heroic era

Newspapers clearly live on clichés. For instance, every day the popular press, in these post-heroic times (when machines and technology have taken the place of humans in so many fields – scientific exploration and warfare to name but two), re-create clichéd images of heroism. During the Gulf conflict of 1991 the press was full of images of 'Top Gun heroes'; the British hostages (sudden 'victims' caught up in the drama of history) were all transformed into 'heroes'. In the *Sun* of 13 November 1999, a child suffering from leukaemia was described as a 'brave angel'. The Bradford *Telegraph and Argus* won a Newspaper Society award in 2000 for its campaign to honour local 'heroes'. Throughout Fleet Street and the local media, all the British medal-winners at the Athens 2004 Olympics were celebrated as national 'heroes'. When Paula Radcliffe broke down in the marathon, the *Mirror*'s front page splash of 23 August read: 'Tears of a hero'.

The mindless militarisation of language

One of the most prominent clichés revolves around metaphors of violence and warfare. 'Hit out at', '(bitter) battle', 'under siege', 'fight', 'massacre', 'blast', 'axe', 'mount a defence' are everywhere. There are many factors behind this militarisation of language. It reflects the militarisation of culture with the enormous expenditure on the weapons of war and the industrial importance of the arms trade. In addition, there is a high social status enjoyed by the military, the ever-presence of war toys, violent computer games and the media's glorification of violence and macho 'firmness'. Just as the culture is brutalised, so is the language of news.

Many stories are built around the drama of conflict, and warfare is an obvious metaphor for this. Moreover, as the media are driven to extremes to capture attention, constantly 'bombarding' readers with sensationalised trivia, so the language of violence is used to carry out this 'bombardment'. Politics and sport are the two areas most afflicted by this form of cliché. Thus, on 16 February 2004, the *Independent* reported under the headline 'Kerry takes war to Bush as candidates gather pace': Senator John Kerry was raising his defences against attacks from the Bush White House this weekend. On 19 June 2004, the *Sun* reported under the headline 'Croat war': 'Croatia's plans for Monday's crucial clash with England have been rocked by a war of words'. 'Beef war', 'trade war', 'banana war', 'Spice wars', 'tabloid wars' are all common clichés. On 1 July 2004, the *Lincoln Target* reported a gardener battling it out in 'the war of the roses'.

To simplify the historical record and highlight its confrontational dimension, the press often resorts to categorising. Doves and hawks, hardliners, loony/soft/cuddly/hard left, unilateralists and multilateralists, militants, extremists, moderates, realists, pragmatists and reformers are constantly 'doing battle' in the press.

Euphemisms: HOW JOB CUTS BECOME RATIONALISATION

Journalists stress their commitment to writing plain English, and so it is not surprising that euphemisms (bland expressions) are considered out. Thus never write so-and-so 'passed away' or 'slipped away calmly' – they died. Philip Howard (1984) describes euphemism as the 'British linguistic vice': they are part of the air we breathe. It is impossible for journalists to avoid them. Thus, instead of the emotive-sounding 'slump' we have the euphemistic, abstract Latinism of 'recession'. In business, 'rationalisation' and 'restructuring' mean job cuts. Hospitals often describe people seriously hurt as 'comfortable'. The 'spikes' for the tramps of Orwell's day are now the (equally appalling) 'rehabilitation centres' for down-and-outs.

'Wars' today are no longer declared. Bombings of cities are described as 'humanitarian'. People are no longer killed in them (except 'by mistake'). 'Targets' are hit by 'precise', 'clean', 'surgical' missiles. A whole lexicon of euphemistic nukespeak, such as 'independent nuclear deterrent', 'flexible response', 'collateral damage' (for civilian deaths) and 'strategic sufficiency', has emerged to acclimatise our minds to the unspeakable horror of the nuclear holocaust (Aubrey 1982; Chilton 1985). In his spirited critique of 'junk language', broadcaster John Humphrys reports (2004a: 124) journalist Bernard Levin as believing all euphemisms are lies. 'He admired the writer Marghanita Laski, who translated "simple, inexpensive gowns for the fuller figure" into "nasty, cheap dresses for fat old women".'

Jargon: GETTING RID OF GOBBLEDEGOOK

One of the biggest challenges young journalists face is to cast aside the academic trappings of their background and the jargon that accompanies it. Each social grouping (local authorities, education, the military, law, computers, librarians, Trotskyists, Conservatives) has its own in-language/jargon and acronyms as a communication aid and 'shorthand'. Academics, with their often mind-numbing abstractions, are in no way peculiar. General Norman Schwarzkopf contributed this piece of military nonsense during the 1991 Gulf conflict: 'It's not yet possible to get clear BDA in this area of KTO. The continued presence of Triple A means a constant risk of allied personnel becoming KIA or WIA.' With jargon such as this, language becomes a kind of fetish not serving as a communication tool but reinforcing the group's special identity – and excluding uninitiated outsiders. And Donald Rumsfeld, the American Defence Secretary during the attack on Iraq in 2003, uttered this mumbo-jumbo classic (see Humphrys 2004a: 214):

> Reports that say something hasn't happened are always interesting to me because, as we know, there are known knowns: there are things we know. We also know there are known unknowns, that is to say we know there are some things that we do not know. But there are also unknown unknowns – the ones we don't know we don't know.

The reporter's task, often, is to learn rapidly the jargon of a group and translate it into terms comprehensible to a mass readership. It's not easy, particularly when spoken at speed. Journalism has its own jargon (see Glossary). Many of the clichés of journalism (journalese), such as 'probe', 'axe', 'boost', 'jibe', 'shock' and 'blast', all have a currency which bears no relation to their use in conversation. Martin Conboy (2003: 47) highlights the popular press's constant use of such words as 'jobless', 'hunks', 'fellas', 'the Beeb', 'shocker', 'pervert', 'plonker', 'stunna', 'beauty', 'fiend', 'groper', 'nut' and 'love cheat'. And he suggests this process 'constitutes a narrowing of cultural and linguistic reference. It is cultural compression, a set of allusions to the way the world works. One might say that in its compressed style of debate any rational political debate has imploded'.

Times: THEY ARE A-CHANGIN'

One way to examine the newspaper language of today is to see how *The Times*'s style has changed over the years, just as it will, no doubt, change in the future. The following story (on p. 100) was published on 1 January 1855. Joseph Sturge (1793–1859), the leading source in the report, played an important part in the fight to abolish slavery. He was also a member of a deputation from the Society of Friends (Quakers) which went to Russia in 1854 to carry their protest against the Crimean War to the Tsar.

Notice how the language is influenced by the news sense applied. 'Spoke . . . on the subject of war' is too generalised and carries no dramatic weight according to today's news values. The second sentence fails to carry a verb, merely listing the

The 'Friends' on the War

THREE NOTABLE members of the Peace Society, and of the Society of Friends, spoke at a Christmas meeting of workmen in Gloucester, on Thursday night, on the subject of the war. Mr. Joseph Sturge, one of the deputation from the Society of Friends to the Czar, Mr. S. Bowly, the peace and temperance advocate, and Mr. T. M. Sturge, of Gloucester.

Mr Joseph Sturge, after alluding to his mission to St Petersburg, with the view of bringing about a termination of hostilities, expressed his firm belief, notwithstanding all that had been said against the Emperor of Russia, or whatever might be the evils existing in his Government, that there was no man in Europe who more earnestly desired a return of peace than that monarch, provided it could be done consistently with what he regarded as the honour of his country.

He also alluded to certain accusations which had been made against him in a letter that had been published, he having been accused of a desire to promote the war because it kept up the price of grain, and, in another part of the same letter, he said he was charged with wishing to put an end to the war, simply because it interfered with his trade.

Providence had, however, placed him in such a position that personally he should not feel the effect of the war further than now being unable to obtain grain from where he could formerly procure it; but he was unable to give employment to as many men as formerly, and he feared matters in this respect would grow worse.

At the present time when wheat was, in England, worth about 10s a bushel, whereas in Russia it could be bought for 2s; and thus, as a pecuniary question, it was desirable that the war should be terminated, apart from higher ground of the Christian duty of putting an end to such fearful scenes of bloodshed as were now taking place in the Crimea. He did not wish to say on whom the blame of the war rested, but he was desirous that each of his friends would use his influence to promote peace, should an opportunity of so doing present itself.

Mr Thomas Sturge recalled to mind the horrors of the wars of the French empire during which period it was computed by the most credible historians that 5,000,000 human beings were slaughtered. During the seven years of the Wellington campaigns 70,000 British lives were destroyed; and at the battle of Waterloo, where there were under 40,000 British engaged, no less than between 800 and 900 officers, and upwards of 10,000 soldiers, were destroyed. And he was of the opinion that if the war in the Crimea continued there would be an equal loss of life.

'three notable members' of the first sentence. Current newspaper style would be stricter on the coverage of the names. Mr Joseph Sturge carries the necessary first name while Bowly and the other Sturge are given only their initials. Today this would be considered an unfortunate disturbance of style. The repetition of Society of Friends is unnecessary.

The second par is a monster by modern standards – 80 words with five subordinate clauses. There is an over-expansive, literary feel to the par. 'Alluding to', 'with the view of bringing about a termination' and 'notwithstanding' today have an archaic air.

The third par is also long – 67 words with repetitions of 'war', 'letter' and the awkward 'accusations'/'accused'. As well as being cluttered with subordinate phrases, it has such unnecessary embellishing words as 'certain' and 'simply' and phrases such as 'a letter that had been published' (better to say 'published letter') and 'to put an end to the war' (better to say 'to end the war'). The letter is contradictory (and probably drew laughter from the audience) so hardly worth reporting.

The fourth par has 59 words – still long by today's standards. The next sentence has 63 words. The following two are short in comparison: 38 and 32. The final two are 41 and 21. Notice how the explicit words 'slaughtered' and 'destroyed' are used to describe deaths in battle: there's none of the euphemistic 'collateral damage' jargon of today that aims to hide the horror of warfare. It is also interesting to see that, though the report covers a speech, there are no direct quotes, probably because of the reporter's lack of a confident note (and with no shorthand).

Converted into the news language of today, the report would read something like:

The Russian Emperor urgently desires peace in the Crimea, Joseph Sturge, who has just returned from a meeting with the Tsar, said on Thursday.

But any peace for the Tsar had to preserve the honour of Russia, he told a meeting of workers in Gloucester.

Mr Sturge, who met the Tsar in St Petersburg on a peace mission for the Society of Friends, said the war had interfered with his buying of grain and he had been forced to lay off some workers.

In England, wheat cost 10s a bushel against 2s in Russia. So it was not only his Christian duty to seek an end to the bloodshed but such a move was needed for financial reasons.

No side could be blamed for the war, and he urged everyone to do their best to promote peace.

Thomas Sturge, also of the Peace Society, said 5m people had been slaughtered during the wars of the French empire. Some 70,000 Britons had died during the seven years of the Wellington campaigns while at the battle of Waterloo between 800 and 900 British officers and 10,000 soldiers had been killed.

He feared there would be an equal loss of life if the Crimean War continued.

This *Times* report (18 January 1940) (see p. 102) shows how language and sentence structure were becoming shorter, though the copy still lacked the directness of journalism today.

Of the first five sentences, four begin with subordinate clauses. Newspapers now adopt the opposite style, starting with the main clause except occasionally for variety. Sentence lengths are still long: the first six have 43, 37, 31, 44, 17, 79 words.

The first par opens without any impact on a subordinate clause about the weather. If the Russians have been driven back, the phrases 'are still active' and 'are distinguishing themselves' are redundant. The second sentence focuses on the communiqué 'stating' rather than on the more dramatic 'routing' of the enemy. The next par also reflects the passive, low-key coverage. Rather than the active '400 planes attack' it says 'attacks were made with 400 machines'. Similarly, instead of 'civilians have suffered greatly' it says more passively 'the sufferings of the civilian population have been great'. The next sentence repeats the point about the winter coldness made at the start.

Note the bias of the coverage. The Finns, fighting the Nazis, are represented as heroic and the sufferings of innocent civilians are highlighted. In contrast, the enemy

FINLAND was invaded by Russia in November 1939, and in spite of heroic resistance was compelled to surrender in March 1940.

FINNS' NEW SUCCESS
UNEQUAL STRUGGLE IN THE AIR

From Our Special Correspondent

Helsinki, Jan. 17

ALTHOUGH THE weather is the coldest for 35 years, the Finnish ski patrols are still active and are distinguishing themselves in the Salla area, where the Russians have been driven back some 12 miles, and are still retreating, pressed by Finnish troops. Today's communiqué states that there was patrol activity north-east of Lake Ladoga between forces of similar strength, in which the Finnish troops routed an enemy company, which lost 70 killed, two tanks, and about 100 rifles.

While the strictly military results of the Russian air raids have been comparatively small, even when attacks were made with 400 machines, the sufferings of the civilian population have been great. Although most of the houses in the provincial towns are still standing, bomb explosions have smashed thousands of windows over wide areas, so that each day more and more houses become uninhabitable in this Arctic winter with temperatures which are exceptional even for Finland.

In the village of Ryttyla, where there are no military objectives, Soviet airmen machine-gunned a funeral procession.

The size of Finland is such that it is impossible to keep the whole of it, or even the most densely populated southern and central districts, adequately supplied with anti-aircraft guns and bomb-proof cellars; but considering that even now Finnish airmen, with rather slow machines, have been able to bring down a good number of enemy aircraft is evidence that a sufficient force of quick, modern fighters is the best means of checking and ending the attacks on civilians. The need for aircraft from abroad is at present the most urgent and decisive issue, the Finns declare.

One example will show the spirit in which the nation is meeting the horrors of air warfare. In a large industrial centre, where there have been frequent air raids, the management of a certain factory asked the employees whether they would be willing to continue to work during air-raid alarms to save time and increase the output of this important factory. The men were offered an extension of their summer holidays in exchange. They answered that they agreed to work during the raids, but would not accept the reward offered them. "We are doing this," they said, "because the Russians must be defeated."

Soviets are portrayed as ruthless warriors, even machine-gunning a funeral procession. Coverage of the Soviets was to change dramatically once they changed sides following the Nazi invasion of their country.

In 2003, Britain was again at war, backing the US-led attacks on Iraq. Notice how the language and sentence structure have changed. Focusing on the first pars of this 861-word report of 28 March 2003, see how much shorter, in general, the sentences are than in the previous examples: 20, 25, 24, 22, 17, 48, 28, 25, 19.

US paratroopers send Saddam a dramatic message

Catherine Philp in Harir

THE long-awaited northern front was finally opened yesterday after US troops parachuted into Kurdish-controlled northern Iraq under cover of night. They were the first of thousands expected here in the coming days to launch a ground assault towards the key cities of Kirkuk and Mosul.

About 1,000 American paratroopers were dropped into the tiny Harir airfield in an operation marking the beginning of a new phase in the war. The troops spent yesterday preparing the airfield for the arrival of thousands of reinforcements accompanied by light artillery, tanks and armoured vehicles.

"We're ready to give Saddam Hussein another front to worry about," an American special forces commander said.

Along with several hundred special forces soldiers already in the area and thousands of Kurdish fighters under their command, the force's task will be to punch through an estimated 100,000 Iraqi troops stationed along the heavily fortified "green line" separating the northern Kurdish enclave from the rest of Iraq.

There was a dramatic escalation in airstrikes along the green line in preparation for a ground invasion by a force much smaller and lighter than was originally envisaged.

At Chamchamal, on the road to Kirkuk, Iraqi troops fled their frontline bunkers after two days of intensive bombing, pulling back more than ten miles. Huge explosions were seen on the high ridge at Kalak, where the road to Mosul runs under Iraqi guns.

Commanders hope that the opening of the northern front will alleviate pressure on forces in the south. While the northern force's first job will be to secure oilfields around Kirkuk and Mosul, they will also be well placed to march southwards to encircle Baghdad.

The Pentagon had hoped to open a northern front at the same time as the assault from the south, but Turkey balked at allowing 62,000 troops from the US Army 4th Infantry Division to launch an invasion from its soil.

That forced the US to opt for a lighter, smaller force drawn from the army's 173rd Airborne Brigade, based in Vicenza, Italy.

Commanders said that they had decided on a parachute landing for speed and to circumvent difficult weather and ground conditions, but also for its theatrical value. "It sends a dramatic message to the whole region that the Americans are here," the special forces commander said.

Warplanes circled overhead to provide cover for the landing as bombing raids were stepped up on Iraqi positions and artillery to the south. Helicopters accompanied the airdrop, swooping in to land on the small airstrip.

Cargo planes dropped several light Humvee vehicles on to the airfield, which landed with a thud in the deep mud. Paratroopers spent much of the next morning retrieving them from the swampy field as others dug trenches and built defensive positions.

One paratrooper was caked from head to foot in mud from his marshy landing. "It's cold but it's good to be here," he said. "The peshmerga were excited to see us."

The Kurdish fighters turned out in their hundreds to guard the airfield and welcome their new allies.

A few soldiers suffered minor injuries on landing but commanders said there were no serious casualties. One soldier assembling a machinegun at the edge of the field fingered a badly swollen lip from where he had fallen on rocks. Villagers assembled at the top of the hill the next morning. "I wanted to run down and welcome them but the peshmerga wouldn't let me," Hassan Ali said. "We are very happy they are here. We have waited a long time. Now Saddam will be gone soon."

Others, however, fretted that the presence of US forces might put them in danger.

"I'm worried that Saddam will try to bomb them and hit us instead," Ahmed, another villager, said.

28th March 2003

Precise language and structure

Most sentences begin with the main clause, the language precise and dramatic. The opening par sets the main news theme (the opening of the northern front) with the second par expanding on this point and providing figures of troop numbers. Adjectives and adverbs are used only sparingly in broadsheet/compact hard news; different criteria apply in the red-top tabloids. Here only 'long-awaited' and 'finally' stand out at the start (articulating the views and sentiments of the western elites determined on 'regime change'). 'Tiny', in the second par, provides striking detail, contrasting with enormity of the military machine being assembled by the US.

Language, propaganda and the impact of dominant sources

The language of the news is profoundly influenced by the language, biases, jargon, tones and rhythms of the sources quoted. Notice how the warring, colloquial rhetoric of the American special forces commander takes over par three and appears again in par 10. And see how the jargon of the military (militaryspeak) such as 'punch through', 'intensive bombing', 'pulling back', 'opening up the northern front' and 'stepped up bombing raid' is unproblematically appropriated by the journalist in her supposedly 'objective' report.

Language tone and contrasts in human interest bias

The tone is mainly dramatic rather than emotional and sensational. The main early focus is on the activities of the US troops and the commander's quotes. Predictably, he represents the 'enemy' as 'Saddam Hussein'. This hyper-demonisation of the President of Iraq (beginning during the 1990–91 crisis and continuing to this day) by the military, politicians and mainstream media has served to simplify an enormously complex situation and direct blame on the one man (thus clearing the West of responsibility for any ensuing atrocities).

Similarly, NATO leaders throughout the Kosovo war of 1999 constantly referred in their propaganda to the President of Serbia, Slobodan Milosevic, as Hitler and to the Serbs as Nazis. At the same time, the roles of US–UK imperialism and militarism, of the International Monetary Fund (IMF) and World Bank strategies to destabilise the Balkans, of Croatian and German nationalism in provoking the conflict were marginalised (Chomsky 1999; Chossudovsky 1998; Keeble 1999).

Even the two 'villagers' quoted later on in Philp's report focus on 'Saddam' as their 'enemy', thus reinforcing (and in a subtle way legitimising) the military's rhetoric by giving it the appearance of 'common sense'. Other quotes support the positive tone of the piece: a paratrooper stresses how 'it's good to be here' with the peshmerga 'excited' to see their advance while Ali says they are 'very happy'. Yet all around them innocent Iraqis are being slaughtered. 'Bombing raids' are reported but no consideration is given to the human consequences: the deaths, the trauma, the homes and hospitals destroyed. In this way, the unthinkable horror becomes normal. As Edward Herman wrote in his landmark essay 'The Banality of Evil', 'Doing terrible things in an organised and systematic way rests on "normalisation"... It is the function of the experts and the mainstream media to normalise the unthinkable for the general public' (see Pilger 2004b).

Significantly during the Gulf war of 1991 and the Kosovo war of 1999 outrage was expressed in the press only once: over the BBC's coverage of the US attack on the al-Ameriyya shelter in Baghdad, which killed more than a thousand women and children (Keeble 1997: 166–73). But consider the outrage that would be expressed if a long-range Serbian or Iraqi missile landed on Tony Blair's home.

Notice also Philp's use of descriptive colour and the close attention to eye-witness detail, as in: 'One paratrooper was caked from head to foot in mud from his marshy landing' and 'One soldier assembling a machinegun at the edge of the field fingered a badly swollen lip from where he had fallen on rocks'. In this way the reporter is adopting a typical war-story narrative style that serves essentially to celebrate the heroism of 'our' men at war.

Language and the simplification process

The language of news also seeks to simplify events, to make the complex dynamics of history intelligible. Here the personalisation of news and the narrative style (pitting 'good' Americans and Kurds against 'bad' Saddam and Iraqis) are part of this process.

News language is concrete and non-abstract

On a more fundamental level there is simply not the space to explore the complexities and abstractions of historical factors. News language, as here, is concrete, dwelling on 'facts', colour, quotes and narrative, and very rarely abstract.

Word play

One of the most fascinating features of journalism is the way it records society's complex language shifts and at the same time creates new words (neologisms) and new meanings (see Dent 2004; Beal 2004: 14–34). Many hundreds of new words are recorded and invented every year in newspapers and magazines. For instance, the close political links between President Bill Clinton and his wife, Hillary, gave birth to the word 'Billary'. 'Lunch box' came to describe male genitals; paparazzi who pursued celebrities round-the-clock became known as 'stalkerazzi'. The list of new words in the *Concise Oxford Dictionary* of 2004 included threequel (a second sequel), sex up, pole dancing and speed dating (Ezard 2004). Lake Superior State University, Michigan, has been compiling (with appropriate humour) since 1976 a list of new words which it claims should be 'banished from the Queen's English for mis-use, over-use and general uselessness'. It's worth exploring at www.lssu.ed/banished (see Merritt 2003).

Many new words emerge from play with well-known prefixes or suffixes. Thus the 'Euro' prefix may provoke 'Euro-wimp' or 'Euro-chic'. The suffix 'mania' has given birth to 'Gorbymania' and 'Spicemania'. The suffix 'ite' has provoked 'Trotskyite', 'Thatcherite' and 'Blairite' (but 'Howard-ite' for a follower of the Conservative leader is distinctly absent from the dictionary). Following Watergate, there has been a flood of 'gates': 'Mirrorgate', 'bananagate', 'Zippergate', 'Shaylergate', Janet Jackson's 'Nipplegate' and so on.

Just as George Orwell coined the words 'doublespeak' and 'newspeak', so they have spawned endless variations: 'nukespeak', 'massacrespeak', 'quangospeak', 'Reagan-speak'. The 1990s saw a new breed of neologism emerge alongside the internet explosion. Virtually any noun could be preceded by an 'e', 'dotcom' or 'cyber': so, for instance, 'email', 'e-commerce', 'e-university', 'e-tailers', 'dotcom economy', 'dotcom advertising', 'cyber-players', 'cyber-verse'. A special e-commerce jargon (or cyber-slang) emerged including 'buzzword compliant' (meaning literate in the latest inter-netspeak), 'incubators' (companies hatching dotcom start-ups) and 'bizzdev' (business development stage of an internet start-up).

Trade names

There is a long list of registered trade names which journalists can easily mistake for generic terms. For instance, it is tempting to think that Hoover is a general and accepted word for vacuum cleaner, but, whenever it is used, the first letter must be capped. Other such trade names include: Aspirin, Aspro, Autocue, Band-Aid, Biro, Burberry, Calor, Catseye (road studs), Dettol, Dictaphone, Duffel, Dunlopillo, Fibreglas (note one 's'), Gillette, Horlicks, Jacuzzi, Jiffy, Kleenex, Lego, Marmite, Martini, Meccano, Plasticine, Polaroid, Portakabin, Scotchtape, Sellotape, Tampax tampons (the two words should always be used together and with a lower case 't' for tampons), Tannoy, Thermos, Vaseline, Yellow Pages.

Doing it in style?

All newspapers have a view about good house style. This is outlined in a document called the style book (occasionally editorial handbook or sheet) though it is increasingly carried on screen. It will tend to focus on such elements as spellings (Peking or Beijing?), punctuation, abbreviations, the use of capitals, titles, Americanisms to avoid, the handling of quotations. Ethical issues, such as the handling of anonymous quotes or AIDS, can also be covered. That is the theory. The reality is very different. As Keith Waterhouse notes, style books are unfortunately 'often peppered with the random idiosyncrasies of editors and proprietors past and present'. Moreover, there is an enormous variation in approaches to house style throughout the industry. Some newspapers even manage to survive without a formalised style book.

The *Guardian*, in contrast, has made its style book, following debates with readers, available on its website (www.guardian.co.uk). On 'Direct speech' it comments: 'People we write about are allowed to speak in their own, not necessarily the *Guardian*'s style, but be sensitive: do not, for example, expose someone to ridicule for dialect or grammatical errors.' Under a section on 'Disability' it suggests that 'wheelchair-bound' and 'in a wheelchair' should be avoided: better 'wheelchair user'. Rather than 'backward', 'retarded' or 'slow', say 'person with a learning disability'. Under 'Gender issues' it says: 'Phrases such as career girl or career woman are outdated (more women have careers than men) and patronising (there is no male equivalent).' It also recommends special care in handling mental health issues. Terms to avoid because they stereotype and stigmatise include 'victim of', 'suffering from', just as 'a person with' is preferable to 'a person suffering from'. Under 'Clichés to avoid', it includes 'boost (massive or otherwise)', 'dropdead gorgeous', 'luvvies' and 'politically correct'. Other newspapers, such as *The Times* (www.timeonline.co.uk) and the *Independent* (www. independent.co.uk) have published their style books while Keith Waterhouse's *The Mirror's Way with Words* (1981) is a lively critique of the tabloid's style.

While the subeditors are usually regarded as the ultimate 'guardians' of style, staff reporters, freelances and student journalists should always be aware of the importance of following style and the journalistic disciplines involved. If there is no house style covering an issue, then make one yourself. Thus, if in copy you use 'jail' on first mention it should be similarly spelled throughout. If you spell the President of Libya 'Col. Gadafi' at first mention it should not later change to 'Col. Khadafi' or 'Col. Qaddafi'. And so on.

Presentation of copy

It is vital that all copy, whether for your college, newspaper or freelance outlet, is immaculately tidy and follows basic rules. Untidy copy is simply spiked (thrown away). Freelances should particularly bear this in mind. Copy layout rules differ slightly from paper to paper but the essential principles remain the same throughout the industry. Copy is written on screen, transferred to subeditors working on screen and appears in 'hard' form only when printed out in the newspaper. When 'hard' copy is presented (say by freelances, accompanying a computer disk or email attachment), it is always typed in a standard font such as Times New Roman on one side of a white A4 sheet. Handwritten copy is never accepted unless from a big Fleet Street 'name' who can get away with such archaic eccentricity.

All freelances should work on Macs or PCs. And, while conventions on copy layout have relaxed considerably in recent years with the emergence of electronically transmitted copy, it is still worth bearing in mind these points.

Byline

Use the 'header' facility on your Word program to put on the top left-hand side of the first page your name. Unless otherwise stated, this will be the name on any byline accompanying the story. Then comes an oblique stroke followed by the name of the publication.

Dateline

In the centre goes the date of publication, not the date of writing. This is particularly important for weeklies or monthlies. When using words such as 'yesterday' or 'tomorrow' it is advisable to put the day in parentheses afterwards to avoid confusion.

Catchline

At the top right-hand corner goes the catchline. This will usually be one word that clearly identifies the story. Page one of a story about David Shayler will be catch-lined 'Shayler 1', page two automatically 'Shayler 2' and so on. Avoid using such words as 'kill', 'dead', 'report', 'story', 'must', 'spike', 'flush', 'splash', 'header' or 'leader' which have specific meanings in newspaper jargon (see Glossary for other words to avoid). When covering a crash, council meeting or fire, don't use the obvious catchlines such as 'crash', 'council' or 'fire'. Similar events may be covered by other journalists and, to avoid duplication, words identifying the story's uniqueness should be used.

Copy

Your copy will begin some way down the first folio (page). Copy typed on news-paper computers will be formatted appropriately but freelances should normally present their copy with double-spaced lines. Leave wide margins on both sides of the copy and clear spaces at the top and bottom of the page. Never hyphenate words between lines. Never let a sentence run from one folio to another.

At the foot of each folio except the last (in the 'footer' facility) should be 'more' or 'mf' (short for 'more follows'), usually centred. The story finishes with 'end'. Bylines, publication, date of publication and catchline will be produced at the top of each folio. Normally no large space is needed between the headers and copy on the second and any subsequent pages.

Copy should always be carefully checked before submission. Never delete the file of your story on disk. Copy can be lost or mislaid. Sometimes you might need to refer back to a previous story. If you send a disk through the post, always make a copy. Whenever there is an unusual spelling, such as 'Smythe' instead of 'Smith' or a name with possible variations such as 'Dennis' or 'Denis', 'Maryline' or 'Marilyn' put 'correct' in square brackets afterwards. The sub should then delete it. Convoluted foreign names should be treated similarly to make clear to the sub that you are aware of the spelling issue and confirming its correctness. The sub should double-check anyway.

If submitting copy as a freelance, it is usually advisable to attach a covering letter, reminding the editor of any necessary background to the commission, the payment agreed and add daytime details, address and phone number along with home details. In some cases, a brief outline of your special credentials for writing the story might be appropriate. A word count is also invaluable to editors. If you are including photographs, remind the editor of payment agreed for these – and any expenses, too.

6 News reporting

Beyond the five Ws

For the purpose of simplicity, let us say that hard news is the reporting of issues or events in the past or about to happen. It is largely based on selected details and quotations in direct or indirect speech. Hard news begins with the most striking details and thereafter information progressively declines in importance. Some background details may be needed to make the news intelligible but description, analysis, comment and the subjective 'I' of the reporter are either excluded or included only briefly. Hard news has the highest status in newspapers and tends to fill front pages. But Anne Sebba (Allan 1999: 130) is critical of the emphasis on hard news. 'Writing about numbers of planes shot down and military hardware is the "soft" option male journalists often go for because it is easier and less taxing to one's emotional being.' Hard news differs from a range of newspaper genres which have emerged over the last couple of centuries (see Pöttker 2003) which include the following:

- *Soft news*: the news element is still strong and prominent at or near the opening but is treated in a lighter way. Largely based on factual detail and quotations, the writing is more flexible and there is likely to be more description and comment. The tone, established in the intro section, might be witty or ironic. The separation of hard and soft news emerged in the second half of the nineteenth century: the first, linked to notions of accuracy, objectivity, neutrality, was for conveying information; the second was more an entertainment genre.

- *News feature*: usually longer than a straight news story. The news angle is prominent though not necessarily in the opening par and quotations are again important. It can contain description, comment, analysis, background historical detail, eye-witness reporting and wider or deeper coverage of the issues and range of sources.

- *Timeless feature*: no specific news angle, the special interest is provided by the subject or sources. For example, a feature could explore youths' experiences of coming out as gay.

- *Backgrounder/preview/curtain-raiser news story or feature*: emphasis is not so much on the news but on explaining the news or setting the scene for an event about to happen. It might focus on historical background and/or seek to explain a range of issues and personalities involved. A *retrospective* is a similar feature looking back at an event.

- *Colour feature*: an article of feature length concentrating on description, eye-witness reporting, quotations and the build-up of factual details. It can also contain historical background material, and need not have a strong news angle.

- *Eye-witness news feature*: based on reporter's observations of newsy event, it can incorporate descriptions, conversations, interviews, analysis, comment, jokes. The 'I' of the reporter might also be present.

- *Participatory feature*: in which the reporter engages in an activity (such as joining a circus for a month) and describes the experience.

- *Sketch*: opinionated, colourful, light piece usually associated with Parliament, for example Michael White in the *Guardian*, Matthew Parris in *The Times*, Quentin Letts, formerly of the *Daily Telegraph*, in the *Daily Mail*.

- *Opinion piece/personal/think piece*: emphasis on the journalist conveying their views and experiences usually in an idiosyncratic, colourful, controversial fashion. Journalists with regular slots are known as columnists.

- *Diary items*: short, light-hearted, opinionated, gossipy news items are generally grouped together under a single byline.

- *Profile* (sometimes labelled *interview*): description of people usually based on interviews with them and sometimes with their friends, critics, relations or work colleagues. A news dimension is often prominent. Jet planes, hotels, shops, Father Christmas and not just celebrities can be profiled. *Obituaries* are profiles appearing after the death of the subject, though often prepared beforehand.

- *Vox pop*: collection of quotes on topical issues, usually accompanied by mug shots of sources (and it is important to be race- or gender- or age-sensitive over the selection).

- *Reviews*: descriptions and assessments of works of art, television programmes, exhibitions, books, theatre shows, CDs, rock gigs and so on.

- *Lifestyle features*: including advice columns (such as on health or education matters, slimming, gardening, do-it-yourself, computer problems), shopping features, fashion, travel.

- *Editorials*: commentary reflecting the institutional voice of the newspaper. Usually carried in a larger font than that of the basic body text and without a byline. They can be written by the editor, but most newspapers have editorial writing specialists.

- *Graphics-driven feature:* here the emphasis is on the graphics, with the text playing a supportive role.

- *News and feature packages*: stories in a range of genres are increasingly being 'packaged' together. Thus a main investigative piece, say, will be accompanied by short profiles of the leading players, a 'fact box' outlining the chronology of events, an opinionated, bylined piece on a particular issue and a graphic (produced by the artist with input from the subeditor and the reporter). In the *Observer* of 28 November 2004, Jo Revill's long news feature on cancer (the 'Big C') was accompanied by an eight-point fact box, another tinted box outlining the 'Six stages of cancer', a profile of a woman who had both her breasts removed after doctors had discovered a lump, and another box listing useful websites.

Going straight to the point

The intro

The intro (known in the US as the lead or the nose and in France as the *attaque*) is the most important par since it has to draw the reader into the story by creating a sense of urgency and exciting their interest. It should highlight the main theme or angle of the story and set the tone. When a reader surveys a newspaper page, there are a few major foci for attention: pictures, headlines, intros and picture captions. Their grammatical style and content set the tone and character of the whole paper. Choosing the best angle (news peg in the US) is one of the biggest challenges for a journalist. Reporters often find that once the opening angle has been 'bashed out', the rest 'writes itself'. A good intro also helps the subeditor to think of a suitable headline quickly.

The famous five Ws

'Who', 'what', 'where', 'when' and 'why' are the famous five intro Ws. In addition, some stories have a 'how' element. But the intro should not seek to answer all of those questions, it would be overloaded with words. Usually the intro defines the news angle by selecting two or three of these questions. The rest of the story may go on to answer some of the others.

Journalists tend to feel most at home with the 'who', 'what', 'where', 'when' and 'how' of events coverage. The 'why' factors (the causal linkages) are often complex – and can be missed out, handled superficially or stereotypically. Liz Curtis (1984: 107), in studying the coverage of Ireland, comments:

> The British media's emphasis on 'factual' reporting of incidents, concentrating on 'who what where and when' and leaving out background and significance, appears to be objective and straightforward but is, in fact, very misleading. This type of reporting provides the audience with details of age, sex, type of incident, injuries, location and time of day. But such information says nothing about the causes of the incident making violence appear as random as a natural disaster or accident.

Take this story from the *Rutland and Stamford Mercury* (27 June 2003):

> Thieves fled empty-handed after breaking into a newsagents in Welton Road, Oakham.

Who: Thieves
What: fled
How: empty-handed
When: after breaking into a newsagent's
Where: in Welton Road, Oakham

Here is an intro from the *Scunthorpe Telegraph* (11 July 2003):

> Two people were killed today when a bomb tore through an office block in Karachi, Pakistan.

Who: Two people
What: were killed
When: today when a bomb tore through an office block
Where: in Karachi, Pakistan

Here is an intro from the *Caribbean Times* (2 April 2004):

> One of the FBI's Ten Most Wanted fugitives was shot dead by Jamaican police in Lilliput, St James last week.

Who: One of the FBI's Ten Most Wanted fugitives
What: was shot dead
How: by Jamaican police
Where: in Lilliput, St James
When: last week.

Main clause

Most news begins with the main clause as in these three examples. This is because the 'who' and the 'what' tend to be the most important. Readers don't want to wade through dull details, background or comment before arriving at the main point. Thus, the *Cambridge Evening News* (11 July 2003) did not report:

> Following the declaration of victory in Iraq by President Bush on 1 May 2003, hostilities between the occupying forces and Iraqi fighters have continued with mounting casualties on both sides. And journalists have increasingly fallen victim to the killers. Last Saturday a former Cambridge University student was gunned down in Baghdad. And today his friends paid tribute to him.

Instead, the newspaper went straight to the main, newsy angle:

> Friends have today paid tribute to a former Cambridge University student who was gunned down in Iraq.

People

News often tends to focus on the human angle. Thus, if you were a news agency reporter covering the IRA attack on the Conservative Party conference in 1984 it would have been poor to write:

> The Grand Hotel, Brighton, was rocked today by a Provisional IRA bomb attack during the Conservative Party conference, but Mrs Thatcher escaped unhurt.

The focus needed to be on the fate of the Prime Minister. The angle could not wait until the end of the first sentence:

> Premier Mrs Thatcher narrowly escaped an assassination attempt today after the Provisional IRA bombed the Grand Hotel, Brighton, where she was staying for the annual Conservative Party conference.

Given the choice between the structural damage to a hotel and the fate of the Prime Minister, the second provides the better angle.

Descriptions and titles

People in the news are always accompanied by a title or a description. The reader needs to know on what authority or on what basis they are speaking. Thus, the *Lincolnshire Echo* (20 October 2004), under a headline 'Free money advice for hard-up tenants', reports on North Kesteven District Council's director of housing, planning and community services, Clive Redshaw, while another source, Yvonne Robinson, is described as 'money adviser for the Citizen's Advice Bureau' immediately after the first mention of her name. People with long titles provide problems for intros. They can clutter them up with words. For instance, 'Mr Doug McAvoy, former general secretary of the National Union of Teachers, yesterday claimed'. One way round this problem is to use a phrase such as: 'The former leader of a teachers' union yesterday claimed'. Then in the next par or sentence you may give the name or title.

The description of the person in the news does not have to be a formal title such as secretary, MP, councillor or director. It can be looser, for instance, 'of the Green Party' or 'who witnessed the rail crash'. And newspapers often delay mention of names to avoid cluttering up the intro. Thus, the *Daily Express* (17 July 2003) carried this intro:

> A vicar who claimed he was suffering from stress has dumped his parishioners and run off with his married Sunday school teacher.

The name and age follow in the next par.

> Worried churchgoers were concerned that Canon Robert Oakes, 55, had been 'overdoing things' in recent weeks.

Timing

News is rooted in time, the more up-to-date the better. Thus the 'when' element ('yesterday', 'last night', 'earlier today', 'next week') is crucial in many hard news intros. This emphasis on newsiness is commercially driven. The hotter the news, the more sellable it is. But intros hardly ever begin with the basic 'when' words such as 'last night'. Occasionally, when the timing is significant, it should be highlighted, as here from the *Guardian* of 25 October 2004:

> And finally, after 50 matches, 542 days and claims of invincibility, Arsenal have been beaten in the Premiership.

Or here in the *Rutland and Stamford Mercury* (26 November 2004):

> After nearly three years as the Inspector for Stamford, Bourne and The Deepings, Mick Howells is saying goodbye to his patch.

Usually is it not necessary to be precise over the 'when' in the intro. Do not say: 'Mrs Gandhi, the Indian Prime Minister, was assassinated by Sikh bodyguards at 2.59 am today.' Sufficient to report 'earlier today'. The precise detail can be added later.

Another popular way of conveying news urgency is used here in the *Independent* (25 October 2004):

> The battle-battered brass helmet of the general who led the Heavy Brigade cavalry to a little-known victory in the Crimean War hours before the disastrous Charge of the Light Brigade, has been handed over to the state.

This eliminates the specific 'when' element from the first sentence. It can be carried later in the story. But weeklies often eliminate specific 'when' references since phrases such as 'last Wednesday' and 'early last week' reduce the news impact.

Where

Local papers will often include the 'where' element prominently in the intro since it stresses the local angle. Thus the *Belper News* (19 October 2004) had this among numerous examples:

> A Belper town councillor has said it is essential the town retains a learning centre.

National papers may sometimes delay mention of the 'where' to add an element of vagueness and encourage everyone from all over the country to read on, as here in the *Daily Star* (19 July 2004):

> An unlucky trucker got the shock of his life when he jumped out of his lorry to confront another driver – and came face-to-face with Lennox Lewis.

Only in par 4 is the 'where' element ('on the outskirts of London') revealed.

Most foreign stories carry the 'where' prominently, as here in the *Socialist Worker* (23 October 2004):

> US Guards subjected detainees at the Guantanamo Bay prison camp to torture, ex-workers at the camp have admitted. In interviews for the *New York Times* military guards, intelligence agents and others revealed the horrific treatment dished out to detainees.

Brevity

As the chapter on language identified, intros should be written as concisely as possible. The maximum number of words you should be thinking about for the first sentence is 30, though intros in broadsheets will tend to be longer than in the populars and local papers. The average wordage in the seven stories on the broadsheet *Guardian*'s first two news pages was 30; in the red-top tabloid *Daily Star*, the average in the eight stories on the first two pages was 20, and in the local weekly *Haverhill Echo* its eight stories averaged 22, while the figure for the black weekly the *Voice*'s seven stories was 25. Here is the intro in the *Daily Star* (9 October 2004) with just 23 words:

> British hostage Ken Bigley has been ruthlessly executed by bloodthirsty killers after they ignored pleas from around the world to spare his life.

In comparison, the *Guardian* intro for the same story was somewhat overloaded with 47 words:

> Ken Bigley, the Briton whose caged and shackled image was broadcast around the world pleading for his life, and whose ordeal cast a pall over Downing Street and the conference season as his family begged directly to Tony Blair for help, has been murdered by his kidnappers.

Brightness

While always remaining true to the style of your publication, be as bright as possible. Try to use active verbs and strong nouns. Take this intro from the *Nottingham and Long Eaton Topper* (22 December 1999): 'Revellers', 'splash out', 'big way', 'snub' and 'celebrations' all carry impact.

> Revellers across Nottingham are all set to splash out on Christmas in a big way – and snub turn of the century celebrations.

Popular tabloids tend to heighten the sensational, emotional content by adding adjectives and adverbs. Take this par from the *Daily Mail* (18 August 2004):

> The disastrous floods that smashed through beautiful Boscastle miraculously claimed not a single life.

'Disastrous' and 'beautiful' are adjectives – and 'miraculously' an adverb – aiming to add impact to the intro. But broadsheets/compacts also use adjectives and adverbs to dramatise copy. Here is how the *Observer* (23 November 2003) began its story:

> Children as young as five are taking knives into school as dramatic new figures reveal that police are being called into classrooms at least three times a week to seize dangerous weapons.

'As young as five', 'dramatic new figures', 'reveal' and 'dangerous' all add to the impact.

Quotations

Lively and controversial comments provide material for many intros. But hard news hardly ever begins with direct quotes. There is a 'softness' about a direct quote which is felt more appropriate to 'soft' news, news features or profiles. Such a convention is not universal. In France, hard news stories commonly begin with direct quotes, as here in *Libération* (12 November 2004):

> « *Une enquête officielle sur les causes de la mort et une autopsie* », c'est ce qu'a reclamé hier soir sur Al-Jazira le médecin personnel de Yasser Arafat.

Notice, too, how French newspapers often highlight direct quotations by using the italic, sloping typeface. There is no such convention in Britain or the US. The quotes convention is also broken in the UK from time to time. Here, for instance, is the *Socialist Worker* (20 November 2004) opening its report on the US assault on Fallujah, Iraq:

> 'We have liberated the city of Fallujah,' crowed General John Abizaid of US Central Command last Sunday.
>   Fallujah, a city of 300,000 people, had been cut off from the world for six days, and subjected to a massive bombardment and invasion.

Now look at this intro from the *Independent* (25 February 2004):

> The Government has 'turned the corner' on asylum, Downing Street said yesterday after it was revealed that the number of people claiming refuge in Britain tumbled last year by almost 35,000.

The reporter did not say: '"We have turned the corner." These were the words of a Downing Street spokesman yesterday after it was revealed the numbers claiming refuge in Britain dropped last year by almost 35,000.' Such copy separating the quote from its source would be too disjointed.

Direct quotes are often reserved for a second or third par which makes a strong back-up to the intro, expanding on the opening theme. Sometimes individual words or short phrases have inverted commas around them without being attributed. This happens usually when colourful or significant words or phrases conveying opinion which the inverted commas imply will be later attributed. Inclusion of the attribution in the intro would overload it. For instance, the Bournemouth *Daily Echo* (23 October 2004) reported:

> A sales adviser who attacked two young men in Ferndown has been given 'one last chance' to change his ways.

Later on in the report, these three highlighted words are attributed to Recorder Peter Wright.

Sometimes, quote marks are placed around single words or phrases in intros to highlight them, as in the *Sunday Times* (24 October 2004):

> The decision to send Black Watch troops into Iraq's "triangle of death" followed requests by British military chiefs to take over a US-controlled area.

Attribution

Opinion is nearly always attributed clearly in the intro par. Thus, the *Dorset Echo* (25 October 2004) reported:

> Rises in fees and charges may be used to plug a £1 million council budget shortfall in Weymouth and Portland, borough councillors have warned.

Concise attribution (such as 'it emerged today' or 'it was reported yesterday') can also give a newsy angle to a report of an event in the past, as in this *Independent* intro (29 November 2004):

> The British government was given details of an alleged plot to overthrow the government of Equatorial Guinea, including the names of mercenaries and the expected date of the attack months in advance, it was reported yesterday.

Clear attribution is particularly important when covering allegations and counter-allegations in court cases. Thus the *Lincolnshire Echo* (20 October 2004) reported:

> A police officer who approached a drunken man to check on his welfare was met with verbal abuse, a court heard.

Casualty figures following disasters usually need to be clearly attributed, as here in the *Morning Star* (26 October 2004):

> Rescuers have found more bodies in a coal mine in central China, raising the death toll from a gas explosion to 86, with no sign of survivors among 62 missing miners, the government said yesterday.

Tenses

A news update on the *Jewish Telegraph* site (www.jta.org) on 26 October 2004 reported:

> The era of infighting within the Russian Jewish community is over, the incoming president of the Russian Jewish Congress said.

Normally with such words as 'warned', 'said', 'declared' or 'criticised', the accompanying clauses follow the rules of reported speech and move back one tense into the past. An intro is one place where these rules are often ignored. This gives an extra sense of urgency to the report. Similarly headlines and picture captions are usually in the present tense though they report on past events. The future tense can also be used, as here in the *Daily Telegraph* (21 November 1999):

> Four out of 10 councils in England are failing to inspect old people's homes in their area regularly, the Government will disclose this week.

Some errors to avoid

Questions

Hard news intros do not normally start with questions, just as question marks do not normally occur in hard news headlines. Intros are for informing readers, not interrogating them. Occasionally questions can open features and 'soft' news stories.

The 'There is/was' cliché

Avoid beginning stories 'There was' or 'There is' or 'There will be'. This is dead copy delaying the appearance of the real news. So don't report 'There was a riot in Bow, East London, last night in which four policemen and two youths were injured.' Better to say: 'Two youths and four policemen were injured in riots in Bow, East London, last night.' The *Independent* reported on 10 November 2004:

> There was something familiar in the reports from Fallujah yesterday. Just as during the invasion of Iraq, last year, television pictures provided drama but little hard information. Nobody was sure how the American assault was going.

But, significantly, it's labeled an 'analysis' piece and so is not hard news.

Label intros

Label intros are drab sentences showing no news sense. A good intro will do more than say 'a meeting was held', 'a speech was given'. 'Vladimir Putin, President of Russia, gave a long speech at the United Nations in New York yesterday covering issues as diverse as the threat to the rain forests and nuclear disarmament.' A better angle would be more specific: 'President Putin of Russia yesterday called on the world community to introduce a 50 per cent arms trade tax to fight poverty in the Third World. In a wide-ranging 50-minute speech to the United Nations in New York, he said . . .'

Present participles

Intro sentences starting with the present participle are to be avoided: 'Referring to humanitarian crisis in Kurdistan, Noam Chomsky' or 'Criticising the government for "monumental ineptitude", Michael Howard'. Better to say: 'A humanitarian crisis is engulfing Kurdistan, Noam Chomsky warned' and 'The government was accused of "monumental ineptitude" by Michael Howard'.

Unidentified pronouns

Opening with a subordinate clause is particularly poor when there is an unidentified pronoun, as in 'With what his colleagues described as a clarion call to the party, John Kerry'.

Negatives

There is always a way to avoid using negatives. For instance, instead of 'The Foreign Office would today neither confirm nor deny that two British pilots had been released by North Korea', say: 'The North Koreans are reported to have freed two British pilots but the Foreign Office was non-committal.'

Numerals

Sentences never begin with numerals. Don't say: '11 people were injured after a bus collided with two stray pigs in Bognor Regis last night.' Instead: 'Eleven people were. . . .' One way round the problem is to avoid precise figures and say 'More than . . .' or 'Fewer than . . .' as *Peace News* (October 2004) reported:

> More than 200 people travelled to Belmarsh prison on 3 October to protest at Britain's own version of Guantanamo Bay. Inside, eleven men remain imprisoned without trial under the 2001 'anti-terrorism law'.

Varieties of hard news intros

Some of the 68 – and more – varieties of intro include the following.

Clothesline intro

So-called because everything hangs on it. For instance: 'Lady Godiva rode naked through the streets of Coventry today in an attempt to cut taxes.' This contains the six basic ingredients: 'who', 'what', 'where', 'when', 'why' and 'how'.

Immediate identification intro

Used where the person concerned is so important or newsworthy that their presence is a main part of the story. For instance: 'Mr Blair made a sponsored jump from a plane at RAF Brize Norton today and wrecked a three-ton truck after his parachute failed to open.' It would be wrong to say 'A three-ton truck was wrecked after a parachute failed to open after a daring sponsored jump from a plane at RAF Brize Norton today.'

Delayed identification intro

Used where the person involved is not inherently newsworthy but has become so because of what he or she has done or said. Thus a 'brief' in the *Guardian* (25 October 2004) reported:

> A Briton who completed his 12,000 mile, eight-month journey from Exeter to Shanghai by bicycle yesterday said he was thinking of cycling all the way back again. Edward Genochio, 27, began his trip in March.

Summary intro

This is used when the reporter, faced with a number of competing angles, none of which stands out, settles for a generalised intro. Thus:

> Former US President Jimmy Carter presented a revolutionary package of disarmament proposals to a historic session of the United Nations General Assembly yesterday.

Single element intro

This contrasts with the summary intro and is used when one angle is particularly strong and needs highlighting. Thus:

> President Chirac of France called the arms race 'a crime against humanity which must be halted' at a meeting of the United Nations General Assembly yesterday.

Bullet or staccato intro

This is used where the main point can be covered very briefly. For instance, the *Independent* (10 November 2004) reported:

> Dubliners are in shock: Bewley's is closing the city's two most favourite cafes, for decades iconic fixtures of its social and cultural life.

Personalised intro

Generally news excludes the 'I' of the journalist. It suggests too much subjectivity. The personalised intro subverts that convention and places the 'I' (or 'we') at the centre of the action. The journalist's actions or witnessing an event carries its own newsworthiness. Thus when *Daily Mirror* journalist Ryan Parry secretly worked as a footman at Buckingham Palace to expose a 'shocking royal security scandal', he reported (19 November 2003):

> The horse-drawn carriage came to a halt outside the Grand Entrance to Buckingham Palace. I jumped off, opened the heavy carriage door and lowered the blue-carpeted steps.
>
> It was a grand occasion for the occupants – they were about to have an audience with Her Majesty the Queen.
>
> Moments earlier I had stood proudly on the rear of the black and gold carriage as hundreds of tourists and royal watchers saw our convoy clatter up The Mall.

Or, here, James Hilder reported in *The Times* (10 November 2004) on the US assault on Fallujah, Iraq:

> The green video screen in the back of the Bradley fighting vehicle is the ultimate in reality television, and that is how we watched the battle of Fallujah unfold as our 30-tonne steel beast advanced into the district of Jolan, the rebels' bastion, in the small hours of yesterday morning.

Comment intro

News often has the appearance of objectivity when, in fact, it is the journalist commenting. For instance, the *Daily Express* (17 July 2003) reported:

> Women graduates will have to spend half their working lives paying off their student debts if Labour ploughs ahead with its hated top-up fees.

Here 'ploughs ahead' and 'hated' convey the newspaper's opposition to the scheme.
    The *Socialist Worker* (10 July 2004) had this overtly biased news story:

> Blair's five-year plan for education will haunt ordinary parents and schoolchildren for generations to come.
>   He wants to drive another nail into the coffin of comprehensive education.

His education secretary, Charles Clarke, is announcing the creation of around 500 independent schools with even greater freedom from state control.

Punning intro

This is found particularly in the red tops and some local newspapers (see also Chapter 5). It provides brightness, humour and a playful, hedonistic dimension to the copy. Thus the *Daily Star* (19 July 2004) reported in a soap 'exclusive':

Corrie hairdresser Sarah Platt won't be cutting it long – because she'll get the chop almost as soon as she starts.

The *Sunday Mirror* (24 October 2004) ran this intro:

Paul Gascoigne really has gone bananas . . . by dating Bananarama star Sara Dallin.

And the *Sun* (not to be outdone) had this opening par (26 October 2004):

Prince Philip sported a nasty eye yesterday – leaving everyone asking: Who filled him in?

The plug intro

Newspapers often like to publicise their own investigations in intros; as the *Observer* (31 October 2004) reported:

An *Observer* investigation in the United States has uncovered widespread allegations of electoral abuse, many of them going uninvestigated despite complaints of what would appear to be criminal attempts to manipulate voter lists.

And the *Sun* did it this way (26 October 2004):

Full astonishing details of Old Trafford's pizza-chucking tunnel bust-up can be revealed by the *Sun* today.

Softening the news: INTROS

'Softened' news stories have the news element at or near the opening. But the news is treated more colourfully and some of the 'rules' of hard news reporting outlined above are broken to provide a 'softer' feel to the copy.

Direct quotation

Starting with a direct quote softens the story, as here from the *Socialist Worker* (10 July 2004):

'Choice is the political buzzword this week, but up until Respect was formed voters had no real choice.

> 'We offer that choice and the reception we are getting is brilliant.'
> This is how Respect candidate Yvonne Ridley described the parliamentary by-election campaign in the Leicester South constituency as around 200 Respect supporters mobilised over the weekend.

Questions

Beginning with a question also softens the impact of a story, or adds variety, as here in the *Guardian* (19 October 2004):

> Is it for the US elections or the Iraqi elections? That was the question buzzing around the Labour backbenches yesterday in the wake of defence secretary Geoff Hoon's Commons statement effectively confirming that British troops will be sent to "backfill" for US forces while they mount a full frontal assault on Fallujah.

Delayed-drop intro

Delaying the main angle (also known as the 'buried lead') is difficult to achieve and needs to be handled with caution (see Conley 2002: 82). But as the 'featurisation' and 'magazinification' of news proceeds it is likely become a more prominent style in both national and local newspapers. It works by arousing the reader's sense of curiosity and will fail if the reader is not curious to know how it all ends. It is best used when something unusual or eccentric is being reported and the reader is kept in suspense before being let into the secret. Here, from the *Guardian* (15 November 1999), a colourful human interest section precedes the news, which comes in par 3.

> He wore sandals without socks which was a daring thing to do in Wigan at the time.
> He also sported a cape, goatee beard and long hair, and he painted hundreds of canvases (including a portrait of Mary Whitehouse with five breasts) in an eccentric artistic life dominated by twin passions: alcohol and his mother.
> Almost 300 of the paintings of James Lawrence Isherwood, some wild and brilliant, others dark and sombre, went on sale at the weekend in the function suite at Wigan town hall, with prices ranging from £75 to £1,200.

Here, in the *Independent* (25 October 2004), the main news (the massacre of 49 soldiers) is delayed slightly to contrast the Iraqis' hopes with their tragic end.

> They were a group of unarmed army recruits, young Iraqis who had volunteered to help build a force capable of providing their country with security when the international troops had returned home.
> But, to the insurgents, they were seen as traitors working hand-in-hand with the hated powers of occupation. And so, they were massacred, 49 of them, in one of the most brutal acts of violence in the current rebellion.

Offbeat intro

A variant of the delayed-drop intro, it creates interest and surprise by highlighting an unexpected, obscure aspect of an event or a person. Here, the *Independent* (4 April 2000) focused on the seventieth-birthday celebrations of former Chancellor Kohl:

At the inn where Margaret Thatcher had her first encounter with stuffed pig's stomach, a few regulars came together last night to toast their illustrious absent friend. Helmut Kohl had been due to celebrate his 70th birthday at the Deidersheimer Hof, but the home town feast was cancelled at short notice. Early in the morning Mr and Mrs Kohl were driven away in a black Mercedes, destination unknown.

Eye-witness human interest

Here is an example from *The Times* (8 November 1999):

Dancing girls, bands and a crowd of several thousand surrounded the Accra airport's tarmac as the Queen, beginning a 48-hour state visit to Ghana, stepped into the cool evening air last night and one of the warmest and noisiest welcomes she has received on a foreign tour for some time.

She even took a brief, unscripted walk along the front of the crowd, safely corralled behind a stout barrier, to acknowledge the cheers and flag waving.

Picture link-up

Intros can also refer to a photograph alongside, with the story becoming a sort of extended caption. As here in the *Sun* (26 October 2004), in a centre spread featuring stills from Eric Prydz's chart-topping DVD:

These sensational scenes have now been at No 1 for five weeks . . . oh, and so has some pop single or other that goes with them.

Sex angle

Not surprisingly, newspapers (and the tabloids in particular) will take any opportunity to highlight the sexy elements of any soft, human interest, news story. Thus the *Daily Star* (9 October 2004) manages to mix sex, reality TV gossip and the fascination with celebrities' astronomically high earnings in this intro:

Sleazy senorita Rebecca Loos will rake in £1 million plus after her saucy antics on The Farm.

Keep it flowing, keep it clear: STRUCTURING THE NEWS STORY

News stories, whether of five or thirty-five pars, are formed through the linking of thematic sections. The reader progresses through them in order of importance, except on those few occasions when the punch line is delayed for dramatic reasons. The journalist's news sense comes into operation not only for the intro but also throughout the story. Who is the most important person to quote? Who is the next most important person? What details should be highlighted and which left to the end or eliminated?

How much background information is required and where is it best included? All these questions are answered according to a set of news values held by the reporter.

Structure

Speed is the essence of news reading just as it is of news gathering. Information should flow logically and easily through copy, the structure being so refined that it is invisible to the reader. Only when a story is badly organised with confusing chronology, say, or jumbled-up quotes, does the reader become aware of any structure.

Opening section

Intro pars tend to highlight the news angle. Second and third pars can expand on intro angles giving extra information. There is an urgency about hard copy which should be maintained throughout the story but particularly in the opening pars. Unnecessary background information, comment and description should not be allowed to delay the dramatic flow of the copy. Take these opening pars from the *Evesham Journal* (www.thisisevesham.co.uk) of 21 October 2004:

TV Alan praises work of railway

TV celebrity Alan Titchmarsh paid tribute to volunteers at the Gloucestershire Warwickshire Railway as he helped to launch a new locomotive on the line.

The Black Prince has been given to the GWR by wildlife artist and railway enthusiast David Shepherd, who also came to Toddington Station on Monday.

Hundreds of people lined the platform to watch the train, one of the last steam locomotives built by British Railways, arrive amid puffs of steam.

Speaking as he sprayed the locomotive's boiler with champagne in the service of rededication, Mr Titchmarsh said: 'We need people like David and all the enthusiasts on this railway.

'True heroes are often left unsung – but I hope today they are being well and truly sung because this is a wonderful line run by some great people. We all need the pleasure they provide.'

He added despite a lifelong fascination with steam trains, Monday had been the first chance he had ever had to take the controls of a locomotive. 'I can hardly tell you what a thrill this has been for me,' he said.

Mr Shepherd said he was delighted to be handing the engine over to the GWR. 'It is a fantastic line for an engine like this.'

The intro summarises the main angle (and notice how the national newspaper obsession with celebrities is matched so often in the local press). The next par follows up concisely giving extra details about the Black Prince locomotive and the dateline (Monday). The third par maintains the dramatic flow by providing concisely written colour and specific details of those attending. Pars four, five and six carry striking quotes supporting the main theme from the main source. Par seven has a (somewhat gushing) quote from the other celebrity involved.

Later sections: the inverted pyramids concept

Traditional analysis of news stories stresses the notion of the inverted pyramid with the most important elements at the top and the least important (often defined as background) briefly at the bottom (Pöttker 2003). This notion is useful for stories based in the main on one source. For the vast majority it oversimplifies the writing process. News values operate throughout the individual sections while background can occur anywhere in a news story. Sometimes when a story is unintelligible without background information, it will occur high up.

News stories are never neutral or objective. An overall 'frame of understanding' influences the choice of content, sources, language and quotes used. Within this context, they are usually made up from a mix of quotes (in direct and indirect speech), factual details, background information and occasionally brief analysis. Each of these elements usually makes up a separate thematic section. News values are applied to each section: the most important comes first, the least important last. Thus, instead of a single inverted pyramid it is more useful to think of a series of inverted pyramids within an overall inverted pyramid (see Figure 6.1).

Thematic structure

Each section will tend to begin with its main subject and most newsy elements associated with it. This could be the most important quote (in direct or indirect speech) or detail. Take, for instance, this report from the *Bolton News* website (posted 25 October 2004):

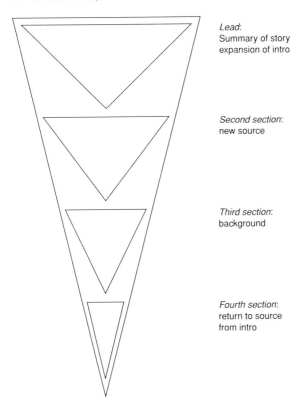

Lead:
Summary of story
expansion of intro

Second section:
new source

Third section:
background

Fourth section:
return to source
from intro

Figure 6.1 The inverted pyramids concept

7 Planning for the unforeseen

Covering transport accidents, fires, demonstrations and human interest stories

Reports of transport accidents and fires feature regularly in local papers. A survey by Durrants press cuttings agency found that during 1997 accidents and disasters secured more newspaper coverage than any other subject. They beat sport into second place, with the economy and crime in third position. Indeed, while journalists stress the 'newness' of the news, sociologists often highlight its 'endless repetitiveness' (Rock 1988). Yet, in fact, accidents fortunately remain extremely rare. According to an editorial in the *Guardian* (8 November 2004), between 1992 and 2001 (the latest period for which figures were available) on average there were three deaths a year per billion passenger kilometres involving cars compared with only 0.4 deaths on the railways. Air transport remained by far the safest, with just 0.01 deaths per billion passenger kilometres.

The more serious the consequences of any accident, the more prominent will be the coverage. Nationals are likely to cover accidents and fires only if they involve a serious loss of life (and thus amount to disasters) or if some celebrity is involved. Journalists will only rarely witness an accident. News comes through tip-offs from the public or more usually from routine calls by reporters to police, hospitals and fire services. In contrast, a major fire might be witnessed by reporters.

Readers relate ambivalently to the coverage. They are drawn in, somewhat voyeuristically, to the tragedy, the human suffering, the drama of any rescue attempt. They are relieved they are not involved. At the same time they are repelled by the event's awfulness, the terrible unpredictability of 'fate' that strikes down one person and leaves another (the reader, for instance) unscathed.

Coverage of transport accidents and fires (as well as of natural disasters) falls within a dominant genre which presents news as a series of disconnected 'bad' events and individuals as victims of forces beyond their control. Ideological, economic, cultural and religious factors are more difficult to identify and report, though their historical impact is considerable. An accident, in contrast, can be reported as an isolated event with a beginning and an end. Coverage can slot easily within the dominant routines of journalistic research. The accumulation of details is always important in accident reports. Yet research suggests readers remember little of it. Instead, the coverage contributes to the representation of a powerful, ever-present symbolic world of tragedy, suffering and potential heroism (Bird and Dardenne 1988). Moreover, reports of accidents and disasters reflect the anglocentric bias of the dominant media.

For instance, on 24 May 2004, the *Guardian* reported that 200 passengers were feared drowned after a river ferry capsized in Bangladesh. There were just 26 words in the story, which appeared at the foot of page 12.

Details to stress

The human interest angle

The most important focus for any report will tend to be on the consequences to human life. The impact on property or means of transport is secondary to this. Thus it is wrong to intro: 'An engineering factory was gutted by a fire in Birmingham yesterday (Monday) in which four employees were seriously injured and two died.' Better to say: 'Two engineering workers died and four were seriously injured in a fire which gutted a Birmingham factory yesterday (Monday).' Similarly, in an accident coverage it would be poor to intro: 'A Rolls-Royce driven by a Cardiff man was seriously damaged in an accident with an Austin Maestro in Doncaster yesterday (Thursday).'

In reporting the huge earthquake in Japan, the *Guardian* (25 October 2004) significantly introed:

> Thousands of people were facing a second night in emergency shelters or out in the open yesterday after the deadliest earthquake to strike Japan in nine years left at least 21 people dead and more than 1,800 injured.

On the day after the 11 September 2001 atrocities in the United States, *The Times* reported:

> Terrorists laid waste to the citadels of American capitalism and defence yesterday with co-ordinated attacks that destroyed the World Trade Center in New York and struck the Pentagon in Washington, killing thousands and spreading fear and chaos across America.

And, following the Reading level-crossing accident, the *Independent on Sunday* (7 November 2004) reported:

> Up to nine people were reported killed and as many as 150 injured after a high-speed train collided with a vehicle thought to be a car at a level crossing near Reading in Berkshire last night.

Be specific

Hospitals are usually well prepared to deal with media inquiries following fires and accidents. Spokespersons are available (either in face-to-face or phone interviews) to provide regular bulletins on the conditions of any casualties. Go for specific details. Thus, rather than 'Many people were injured after a fire swept through a night club in Bognor Regis last night (Friday)' it is better to report: 'Twelve people were admitted to hospital with serious burns after fire swept through a Bognor Regis night club last night (Friday).'

In fast-breaking fire and accident stories, hospital and ambulance authorities are often unclear about the exact number of casualties. A fire breaks out in a hotel: twelve people are pronounced dead at the scene or in hospital and three others are unaccounted for. In this case it is possible to say: 'At least 15 people were feared dead after fire swept through a hotel overlooking Margate promenade yesterday (Monday).'

Controversial guidelines issued by the Association of Chief Police Officers (ACPO) in May 1999 indicated that, following the Data Protection Act, victims and witnesses of road crashes or other accidents were entitled not to have personal details released without their permission. An ACPO survey in June 2000 revealed that thirty-one forces (70.5 per cent) were implementing the guidelines or had similar policies. But journalists throughout the UK challenged them. Sometimes details of work status are provided or can be gathered from friends or relatives. In accident reports it is important in local papers to identify where the accident happened and at what time. The number and types of vehicles need to be identified. The ages of accident victims are usually carried prominently.

Use the past tense

In covering fires and disasters, there is a temptation to use the present tense to convey the drama. For instance: 'Seven people are feared to have died in a fire which gutted a factory in Huddersfield earlier today (Friday). Ten fire appliances are at the scene trying to bring the flames under control.' But by the time the paper appears (and almost certainly by the time the reader sees the copy) the situation is likely to have changed. The fire may well have been contained. All details have to go into the past tense. 'Seven people were feared dead after a fire gutted a factory in Huddersfield today (Friday).' Take this report from the *Daily Express* (27 October 2004):

We knotted hotel sheets to escape flames of death: Britons tell of holiday inferno ordeal
By Polly Dunbar

Holidaymakers Ian and Sandra Bloom made a dramatic escape from a blazing hotel in Italy by knotting sheets together and jumping out of a window.

The teachers had to lower themselves to safety because there was no other way of escaping the blaze which killed two Italians.

They desperately tied two bedsheets together to make an improvised rope as their second-floor room filled with smoke and the fire raged in the corridor outside.

They then attached the sheets to bars at the top of the 30ft-high window so they could climb down.

But the sheets were not long enough to reach the ground and Mrs Bloom fell the last 15ft on to a gravel path, cracking two vertebrae and badly bruising her ankles.

She was last night due to be airlifted back to Britain, where she will have to spend a month flat on her back in hospital and three months in a body cast.

Mr Bloom, 53[,] headmaster of Downham Market High School, Norfolk, and his wife, who teaches English at King Edward VII School in King's Lynn, had checked into the Green Farm hotel near Pisa just six hours before the fire started.

Mother of two Mrs Bloom, 50, said from her hospital bed in Pisa: 'I'm just so grateful to be alive. It was very traumatic. There was so much smoke and even now I can still taste smoke in my mouth.

We knotted hotel sheets to escape flames of death

Pictures: FABIO MUZZI & ALBANPIX.COM

SCENE OF DESTRUCTION: Firemen inspect damage in the wrecked reception area

Britons tell of holiday inferno ordeal

By **Polly Dunbar**

HOLIDAYMAKERS Ian and Sandra Bloom made a dramatic escape from a blazing hotel in Italy by knotting sheets together and jumping out of a window.

The teachers had to lower themselves to safety because there was no other way of escaping the blaze which killed two Italians.

They desperately tied two bedsheets together to make an improvised rope as their second-floor room filled with smoke and the fire raged in the corridor outside.

They then attached the sheets to bars at the top of the 30ft-high window so that they could climb down.

But the sheets were not long enough to reach the ground and Mrs Bloom fell the last 15ft on to a gravel path, cracking two vertebrae and badly bruising her ankles.

She was last night due to be airlifted back to Britain, where she will have to

Suffocate

spend a month flat on her back in hospital and three months in a body cast.

Mr Bloom, 53 headmaster of Downham Market High School, Norfolk, and his wife, who teaches English at King Edward VII School in King's Lynn, had checked into the Green Farm hotel near Pisa just six hours before the fire started.

Mother-of-two Mrs Bloom, 50, said from her hospital bed in Pisa: "I'm just so grateful to be alive. It was very traumatic. There was so much smoke and even now I can still taste smoke in my mouth.

"We had just gone to bed when I heard a lot of strange popping noises which I know now were the windows along the corridor smashing because of the heat. Ian opened the door to see what was happening and as soon as he did a load of smoke

came in and engulfed the place. It was thick, dense, choking smoke, there was so much of it I think we were lucky we didn't die then from suffocation.

"Ian grabbed some sheets and knotted them together and we threw them out of the window and used them to climb down.

"It was like something out of a film but I'm a lot shorter than Ian and the sheets weren't quite long enough so I had to jump the last 15ft and landed heavily."

"I am in agony and have been told I will need a back support for at least three months because I have cracked some vertebrae in my spine.

Mrs Bloom's daughter, Caroline Colwill, 24, of Shotley Gate, near Ipswich, Suffolk, said: "It was so hot that my mum's waterproof jacket melted on the door where it was hanging.

"My stepfather tried to throw the double bed mattress out of the window to break their fall but it was too big to get out.

Mrs Bloom added: "The couple who died were along the corridor from us and that's what really hits you. We were so lucky."

30ft

LUCKY TO BE ALIVE: The sheets, left, that saved teachers Ian and Sandra Bloom, right

'We had just gone to bed when I heard a lot of strange popping noises which I now know were the windows along the corridor smashing because of the heat. Ian opened the door to see what was happening and as soon as he did a load of smoke came in and engulfed the place. It was thick, dense, choking smoke, there was so much of it I think we were lucky we didn't die then from suffocation.

'Ian grabbed some sheets and knotted them together and we threw them out of the window and used them to climb down.

'It was like something out of a film but I'm a lot shorter than Ian and the sheets weren't quite long enough so I had to jump the last 15ft and landed heavily.

'I am in agony and have been told I will need back support for at least three months because I have cracked some vertebrae in my spine.'

Mrs Bloom's daughter, Caroline Colwill, 24, of Shotley Gate, near Ipswich, Suffolk, said: 'It was so hot that my mum's waterproof jacket melted on the door where it was hanging.

'My stepfather tried to throw the double bed mattress out of the window to break their fall but it was too big to get out.'

Mrs Bloom added: 'The couple who died were along the corridor from us and that's what really hits you. We were so lucky.'

Drama

The report focuses conventionally and concisely on the dramatic escape. The chronology of the drama (knotting the bedsheets, the escape through the window, the final, dangerous 15 ft leap) is clear throughout. Notice how the dateline is obscured because it is probably some distance in the past: 'last night' is delayed until par 6 – and there it is referring to Mrs Bloom being airlifted, not to the drama.

Highlight any uniqueness

Reports of fires and accidents should aim to highlight any uniqueness or special aspect of the tragedy. Holidays fund the enormous global tourist industry and are traditionally times of pleasure and relaxation. Here the holiday has been transformed into a nightmare – and that contrast provides the urgency to the copy. Significantly out of 35 pages of news and features in the *Daily Express* that day only two have a foreign focus. One reports the £225 billion cost of the US 'war on terror'. The other is our Pisa fire where the focus is on the British holidaymakers and so is not strictly 'foreign'. Two people have died in the blaze. But they are Italians and, according to conventional UK journalistic news conventions, they do not carry the importance of the Brits. So they are confined to the end of the second par and left unnamed.

The causes

Normally, after a tragedy like a fire, one of the first questions to be asked is why it happened. Thus the 'why' element will often be prominent in fire stories and sourced to an appropriate authority. For instance, the Torquay *Herald Express* (17 March 2004) introed on the police suspicion of arson and highlighted a 'why' element:

> Detectives are probing the blaze which left two adults and two teenagers needing treatment for inhaling smoke which filled their four-storey home in Pennsylvania Road, Ellacombe. It appears an accelerant, possibly a flammable liquid, was poured through the letterbox of the property.

Even if the authorities have no explanation at the time of going to press, this is still worth carrying: 'Police were unable to determine the cause of the blaze.' Be careful if the police refuse to confirm or deny rumours that arson took place. They may say: 'We have heard rumours that the fire was started deliberately. At the moment we have no evidence to support that theory. At the same time we are not ruling out the possibility.' You may afterwards look at your note and see 'We have no evidence to support the arson theory'. But the police spokesperson went on to qualify that statement. It would be possible to intro strongly on 'Two elderly women died in a fire in Burnley yesterday (Monday). Afterwards police refused to rule out the possibility of arson.'

Similarly, in transport accidents, one of the major issues to be addressed high up in the story is why it happened. Theories over the immediate causes of the tragedy can be explored (failure of warning lights at the crossing, for instance) but no individuals should be identifiable in the criticisms. Newspapers tend to marginalise the deeper social and economic factors behind many accidents. As Wendy Moore (1999) stresses, accidents are the biggest killers of children today. Government figures indicate that around 500 youngsters die in accidents (mainly as pedestrians, in fires and in the home) every year, but children of poorer families are eight times more likely to be killed by a car, and fifteen times more likely to die in a fire, than children from better-off families. 'The reason for such inequality is a lethal combination of more dangerous living conditions and fewer safeguards.'

Be careful not to over-hype any information for dramatic effect. The *Guardian*, for instance, described the Ladbroke Grove (near Paddington) crash of 1999 in which thirty-one people died as 'the worst rail disaster in 50 years'. It wasn't: a crash at Harrow and Wealdstone in 1952 claimed 112 lives. And be extra-sensitive about the language you use. Following the Ladbroke Grove crash, in which many died from burns, the *Guardian* said the disaster would 'rightly ignite the smouldering debate [about safety]'. Some readers found that 'crass'.

In the *Daily Express* story, above, there is no attempt to explore the 'why' dimension, possibly because of the difficulties in accessing the firefighters and police by telephone from London (and any associated language problems). Is this not a small (but telling) example of the way in which newspapers' failure to invest in foreign staff has an impact on the quality of copy?

The leading sources

Police

The police examine the causes of the blaze, the time of outbreak and how it was discovered; they often provide details of casualties. The police can issue appeals for witnesses (providing contact name and telephone number). After accidents, the police are often able to describe the incident, perhaps on the evidence provided by street surveillance videos (though journalists should be aware of the implications for civil rights posed by those videos). Following rail accidents, British Transport Police deal with media queries.

Be careful not to impute blame to a particular driver after a road crash. Better to say: 'The cars were in a collision' rather than 'Car A collided with car B' or even worse 'Car A hit car B'. Under provisions of new Youth Justice and Criminal Evidence legislation, the media are unable to print the names of young persons alleged to be involved in offences, such as under-aged driving, before court proceedings. Some newspapers have opposed these plans, with *The News*, Portsmouth, going so far as to publish the names and photographs of three schoolboys involved in a motorway death crash.

Ambulance services

Ambulance services provide details of the number of ambulances (sometimes helicopter ambulances) and paramedics sent to the scene, and the number of people taken to hospital or treated at the scene and sent home.

Hospitals

Hospitals give casualty details, condition of those in hospitals, kinds of injuries suffered; numbers of those in intensive care; numbers pronounced dead. It is important to avoid such clichés as 'fighting for her life'. Better to say 'in a critical condition'. Remember injuries are not 'received' but 'suffered' or 'sustained'. 'Lacerations' and 'contusions' are medical jargon words to avoid. Instead, use 'cuts' and 'bruises' respectively. Skulls can be 'fractured' but bones are 'broken'.

Relations, friends, colleagues and fellow trade unionists

Relatives of victims can provide details of funerals. After disasters they often lead campaigns and petitions for changes in safety provisions and the law. For instance, after the October 1999 Ladbroke Grove rail crash, relatives of the victims featured prominently at a *Mirror*-backed demonstration in London calling for the installation of a new train safety system. Depending on the time available before your deadline, you may be able to follow up friends and relatives of anyone killed in an accident for their tributes. Particular sensitivity will be required for these assignments, known as 'death knocks' (Tulloch 2004).

Journalists have sometimes refused to conduct such interviews – and been sacked as a result. In December 1999, for instance, Ian Bailey, a reporter on the *Stoke Sentinel*, who refused his editor's order to seek an interview with a football manager after his son's suicide, lost his claim for unfair dismissal (Keeble 2001: 59). Others have simply lied or found an excuse not to do the news desk's wishes. Colleagues and fellow trade unionists are sometimes interviewed. For instance, following the Berkshire level crossing train crash in November 2004, the *Morning Star* carried a tribute to the train driver who died from the acting general secretary of ASLEF (www.aslef.org.uk), Keith Norman. The Rail, Maritime and Transport Union (www.rmt.org.uk) also has members in the transport sector and will be worth contacting.

Fire service

Firefighters can supply details of number of appliances at the scene and give accounts of any rescue operation and specific difficulties (practical and psychological) encountered. They might also conduct their own investigations into causes, and provide warnings and advice to avoid a repeat of the tragedy. Avoid using 'firemen' (they may be women). The *Guardian*'s style guide says simply: 'firefighter: not fireman'. Other style books suggest 'fire service spokesman' or 'spokeswoman'. Because of firefighters' crucial roles in saving lives, plans to close stations can provide a focus for local newspaper campaigns – such as that conducted by the *East Anglian Daily Times* in 1999: 'Hands off Sudbury Fire Station' ran the slogan, supported by news stories and editorials.

Survivors, eye-witnesses and neighbours

In the *Daily Express* report, the comments of the survivor carried at length convey all the horror of the event. But it is strange that there are no comments from the husband who, presumably, escaped unhurt. And the evidence of the daughter towards the end comes as a surprise. How does she know this? Why is she left speaking for her stepfather?

Members of the public often provide dramatic accounts of how people reacted and, in cases of fires, how buildings and contents were affected. Thus, the Torquay *Herald Express* (17 March 2004) quoted eye-witness Emma Timbs:

> 'I woke up to this crackling sound and looked out of the window. It was then that I saw the fire. The flames were outside the front door, coming from the cat flap.
>
> 'I went over the road and kept on banging on the door until I heard voices and I knew they were awake. Just a little while later the fire brigade arrived.'

But be careful not to blame the fire or accident on any person. Formal inquiries are held to determine that. Eye-witnesses can be mistaken. You may visit the scene of the fire or accident, perhaps accompanied by a photographer or video journalist, which may prove harrowing. Be sensitive to the feelings of anyone involved in the tragedy and any eye-witnesses. They may not be prepared to talk. Photographing them may be unnecessarily intruding on their private grief. However, some might want to talk since it could help to release their anxiety.

Owners of property

Following fires, owners are sometimes able to provide an estimated cost of the damage and details of whether the property was insured. There can often be special 'human interest' dimensions to the tragedy worth highlighting. For instance, the *East Anglian Daily Times* (7 April 2000) carried this quote after a fire: 'One of my hobbies has been collecting cricket memorabilia, which includes more than 500 club ties, and if I had lost them I would have been very upset.'

Motoring organisations and rail companies

The Automobile Association (AA) (www.theaa.com) provides details about the impact of accidents on traffic flows. Rail companies provide information about the impact of accidents on train timetables. The Health and Safety Executive (www.hse.gov.uk) conducts investigations after accidents and provides reports on transport safety (though, in 2004, the Labour government announced plans radically to reduce its powers) while rail users' consultative committees are on hand to comment about punctuality and general efficiency. Network Rail (www.networkrail.co.uk), which took over from Railtrack in 2002, will report on the maintenance (or otherwise) of the line.

Meteorological Office

This is usually carried as the Met Office: many serious accidents happen in poor weather. The Met Office (www.met-office.gov.uk) provides necessary background and can forecast warnings.

Campaigners

Campaigning groups, such as the Safe Trains Action Group, may well call for increased investment into transport safety following an accident or for stricter seat-belt rules. Rail passenger councils and regional committees have been set up by Parliament to look after train users' interests (www.railpassengers.org.uk) and may well be worth contacting.

Follow-ups

Follow-ups are often possible. In the week following the Ladbroke Grove rail disaster on 5 October 1999, the *Guardian* carried 40,000 words explaining what happened, looking at the apparent causes, trying to provide a political context and exploring some of the ethical issues raised by the media's coverage (Mayes 1999). Casualty lists may change over time and need updating. Emergency services may be criticised for their alleged inefficiency or praised for the speed of their reaction. Coroners' inquiries and sometimes public or local authority inquiries are held to determine the truth. In cases of suspected arson police investigations will need to be followed closely. Calls may come for safety improvements at junctions, at notorious accident spots or to planes. Political parties (often keen to stress the impact of underfunding of public services) and campaigning groups are good sources here.

The emotional trauma of accident and fire victims and of those who witness them generally goes unrecognised, not only by the media but also by health professionals and their families and friends. A feature could highlight their plight and the ways they are overcoming it. For example, Headway, the Brain Injury Association (formerly known as the National Head Injuries Association) has more than a hundred branches and groups around Britain helping accident victims (contact: 0115-924 0800; media@headway.org.uk).

Dealing with demos: COVERING MARCHES

Press and political strategies increasingly overlap. Though demonstrations were held long before our mass media age, their media dimension is now crucial. People carry banners with simple slogans, they wear eccentric costumes, they chant, they play music, they choose routes often heavy with symbolism, they distribute leaflets and they attract prominent speakers. They do all this for political reasons. But they also do it hoping to attract media attention. A demonstration serves many purposes. For the participants and organisers, it represents a public statement of solidarity for a cause. When people are angry or concerned they may demonstrate. It is as if the more traditional avenues for debate and political action – the smoke-filled committee room, media, Parliament, the protest meeting – are incapable of containing the feelings involved. They then break out on to the streets.

Demonstrations and vigils are regular occurrences in London and, not surprisingly, the vast majority are ignored by Fleet Street. Even well-attended ones (with numbers in the thousands) often suffer the same fate or are marginalised in various ways. Coverage of a political march may be confined to an aesthetically pleasing picture or over-personalised with stress on the presence or speech of a 'celebrity'. The tone and prominence of coverage is often influenced by the attitude of the newspaper to the event. The massive Campaign for Nuclear Disarmament (CND) demos during the early 1980s received largely negative coverage because of the papers' almost universal opposition to unilateral nuclear disarmament. In contrast, the London march in support of the miners following the Conservative government's sudden announcement of pit closures in 1992 and the pro-hunt Countryside Alliance march of September 2003 were given generally positive, front-page coverage.

A demo at which violence breaks out is almost always given negative coverage, even though the violence may involve only a tiny fraction of the participants and last for a matter of minutes and may even have been started by the police (Halloran et al. 1970). Sometimes newspapers (bizarrely) intro on the absence of violence: 'The CND demo in London passed off peacefully yesterday with the only problems coming to police in the form of massive traffic jams.' When violence breaks out, the blame is often explicitly or implicitly put on the demonstrators. Criticisms of police over-reactions (such as during the 1 May 2000 anti-capitalist demo in London) tend to be marginalised. Sometimes a demonstration can be covered neutrally in the news columns but is attacked or supported in features and/or editorial comments. For local papers a demonstration (even the peaceful variety) can usually provide good copy. Advances are often compiled outlining the plans of the organisers and the police.

Guidelines for demo reporting

It is important to report the numbers of people involved. There can often be significant differences between figures given by the organisers and by the police. Figures should always be attributed. Sources might also have views about the numbers attending. They may be delighted at the turn-out or disappointed and blame the weather. Do not take the word of an organiser that the demo is, say, the biggest ever in the town. Claims like that need to be carefully checked. If a demo includes a march, indicate its route. Observe the responses of passers-by.

Police in Britain, as in France, Luxembourg and the Netherlands, have introduced voluntary identity card schemes for journalists, and possession can sometimes help when covering dramatic events such as riots, disaster and demos (Frost 2000: 49). It is always worth joining the march. Chants and slogans can often provide useful 'eye-witness' colour. In his report on the 1 May 2000 anti-capitalist demo in London, the *Guardian*'s John Vidal carried this exchange:

> 'What is happening?' asked a Japanese mother, feeding grain to the pigeons. 'Don't worry ma'am,' said one man. 'We're just overthrowing the state.' 'I see,' replied the woman.

In some cases it is not advisable to identify yourself as a journalist. Some reporters and photographers have been attacked by demonstrators suspicious of the bias of most newspapers. The compliance of some editors with police demands for incriminating photographs following demo violence (see p. 65) has not helped protect journalists on such assignments.

Participants may be drawn from a variety of groups, local and national. These are worth identifying. Prominent participants, not necessarily speakers, can also be identified. Demos usually end with rallies at which speeches are given. Coverage will depend on space available. Local papers, operating as 'journals of record', will often cover as many speeches as possible in order of news value. Responses of audience to speeches (applause, jeers, heckling, for example) are worth carrying to convey eye-witness colour.

Background details are often essential. For instance, when the demo is part of a nationwide or European-wide series of protests, that needs to be mentioned to place the local action within its proper context. If violence breaks out, or if arrests are made, be careful not to sensationalise these elements. Try to convey any conflicting views on causes of violence from police, organisers, participants and eye-witnesses. Police throughout Europe are increasingly detaining and even attacking journalists covering demonstrations. During the demonstrations at the G8 summit in Genoa in July 2001 undercover *Sunday Times* reporter John Elliott was beaten up by police despite protests in Italian that he was a British journalist. As Andrew Wasley (2000) wrote:

> Since environmental activists first resorted to direct action at the Twyford Down anti-bypass siege in 1992–93 protests have attracted media attention like never before. With this, however, there has been an alarming increase in the number of journalists reportedly assaulted, harried and even arrested by the police at such events.
>
> Those covering road protests, hunt sabotage and action against genetically modified crops claim to have been targeted most frequently. Some say they have been arrested as many as seven times, others that they have been beaten by the police, their houses raided and equipment seized. All say their press card credentials have been systematically ignored, in spite of a police-operated PIN number identification scheme.

Some journalists argue that all this represents a deliberate and organised attempt on the part of the police to intimidate campaign-sympathetic reporters and to 'manage' the news. The situation is further complicated by reports that private detectives pose as freelance reporters and photographers at demos to gather information.

The importance of risk-assessment

At the same time, demonstrators are becoming increasingly hostile to journalists. Journalists, for instance, came under attack during the 1 May 2000 anti-capitalist demo in London and at the July 2001 Genoa demo – by black-hooded rioters. You should always assess the risks involved before covering any story – but in particular potentially dangerous investigative assignments and demos. Newspapers and training courses in general have been slow to acknowledge the importance of such training. But in 2000, the Rory Peck Trust (www.rorypecktrust.org) along with CNN, BBC News, ITN, the *Guardian* and the *Financial Times* launched an initiative to provide safety training to freelances working in hostile environments. The organisation Reporters Sans Frontières (5 rue Geoffroy-Marie, 75009 Paris) has also produced a useful *Survival Manual for Journalists* on dangerous assignments.

It might be more appropriate to cover a demo from a vantage point, high above the demonstrators; if you decide to walk with the protesters, it might be sensible to be accompanied by a colleague and with a mobile phone to keep in regular contact with your news desk. Always be aware of 'get-out' routes in case violence breaks out and protesters are pinned into a confined space by the police. Chris Frost advises (2002: 66): 'Avoid getting caught in the middle. Talk to people at the edge first so that you have enough material to do a basic story yet can slip away easily. Always keep your eye on an escape route to a safe area and ensure it remains clear. You should bear in mind any police instructions and only ignore them if you think you will be safe doing so.' And as the safety manual *Danger: Journalists at Work* (International Federation of Journalists, Boulevard Charlemagne, 1 Bte 5, 1041 Brussels, Belgium) stresses: 'No story is worth your life. You are more important than the story. If you are threatened, get out fast.'

All journalists covering dangerous assignments, in particular freelances, should either be aware of or organise their insurance cover. After particularly harassing assignments journalists may suffer Post Traumatic Stress Syndrome. Chris Cramer (2000), a BBC journalist who was caught up in the London Iranian Embassy siege of 1980, commented: 'I was back at work the day after the siege ended. With hindsight, I should have accepted the offers for psychiatric help, as many of my fellow hostages did, and maybe saved myself years of stress and anxiety.' To help journalists deal with stress, particularly in war zones and disaster areas, the Dart Centre Europe for Journalism and Trauma has set up a UK branch. For details see www.dartcentre.org/europe. And in 2003 the Frontline Club (www.thefrontlineclub.com) was formed to support journalists, camera operators and photographers who risk their lives in the course of their work.

Reporters covering demonstrations should be aware of the 24 January 1997 High Court judgement. This ruled that, under the offence of trespassory assembly aimed at curbing road protests, police can ban groups of twenty or more meeting in a particular area if they fear 'serious disruption to the life of the community', even if the meeting is non-obstructive and non-violent. The ruling related to the cases of two people who were the first to be convicted of trespassory assembly under the controversial Criminal Justice Act 1994 after taking part in a peaceful demonstration at Stonehenge in 1995.

Journalists covering marches should also be aware of the provisions of the Public Order Act 1986. This gave the police unprecedented new powers. Organisers must give police seven days' notice unless it is not reasonably practical to do so. Police can impose conditions on a march or ban it. Moreover it becomes an offence if the date, time and route differ from that notified to police. Road blocks are now routinely used by the police to stop people from attending major demonstrations. More than three hundred thousand, were estimated to have been stopped by police road blocks during the coal dispute of 1984–5. Peace campaigners and travellers aiming to hold their traditional midsummer festival at Stonehenge have also faced road blocks (Hillyard and Percy-Smith 1988).

Take the opening pars of Tony Rennell's report in the *Sunday Mirror* (16 February 2003):

LISTEN TO US

THE PEOPLE'S MARCH: A TIDE OF PROTEST – BRITAIN SAYS NO TO WAR **by Tony Rennell**

The little girl clutched her home-made cardboard placard coloured in with crayons. It was in the shape of a school crossing sign and had one word on it – 'STOP'.

It said all you needed to know about yesterday's mass anti-war march through London.

On a crisp winter's day, the girl and her parents were among the estimated two million who tramped the time-honoured route to make their voices heard. It is an awesome feeling when the people take over the streets of the capital.

In years gone by, governments were always wary of what they called The Mob. Governments should still be frightened, very frightened. Not by thoughts of violence . . . but by the sheer power of numbers.

To be there felt like history in the making.

The day began with blue skies but was soon overcast – a greyness that fitted the generally sombre mood.

In public gardens along the way and in Hyde Park, where the march ended in a huge rally, a sprinkling of snowdrops and crocuses heralded a spring that, if these protests fail, some British servicemen may never live to see.

While it was true that militants, anarchists, anti-capitalists and anti-Americans – what one weary PC called 'the great unwashed' – were out in force, the heart and mind of the protest was ordinary people.

Worried mums and dads of all ages, all races and religions. Not traitors or cowards. Not faint-hearts. But people who had come to express a genuine feeling they cannot ignore – that the Prime Minister is wrong.

You should have been there, Mr Blair. If you had, you would have witnessed London's biggest-ever demonstration. With organisers claiming two million protesters, it dwarfed the 100,000 at the 1990 Poll Tax march and the 400,000 of last year's Countryside march.

Dozens of causes were represented. The professionally-produced placards of the protest groups with their fierce messages – 'Blair and Bush – Wanted for Murder' – contrasted with cobbled-together banners. 'Notts County supporters say Make Love Not War', said one.

'Make tea, not war,' proclaimed another, over a picture of the Prime Minister with a gun in his hand and a teapot on his head.

- *Tony Rennell is the co-author with John Nichol of* The Last Escape, *the story of the demobilisation of Allied prisoners of war in Germany 1944–45.*

Analysis

Overall comment

It is impossible to consider this eye-witness report without reference to the vigorous opposition being voiced by the *Daily Mirror* and *Sunday Mirror* as the 2003 US–UK invasion of Iraq loomed. Public opinion polls at the time showed massive disquiet over the prospect of military action and significantly Fleet Street's pro-war consensus for the US–UK attacks on Serbia in 1999 and the invasion of Afghanistan in 2001 had broken down by early 2003. The *Guardian* and the *Independent*s were also expressing opposition to the invasion plans while the *Mail*s were critical of the rush to 'regime change'. Yet still most of Fleet Street backed the Blair government, giving prominent coverage to intelligence service misinformation about Iraq's alleged 'weapons of mass destruction'. All of Rupert Murdoch's 175 newspapers around the globe editorially backed the invasion and so it was perhaps not surprising that the *Mirror* (engaged in a fierce circulation contest with the *Sun*) took the opposite line. Significantly, when the conflict erupted and the *Mirror*s were inundated with letters opposing their stance, the editor, Piers Morgan, took the opportunity to soften the paper's opposition and it quickly reverted to its celebrity/scandal obsessions. Indeed, the ambivalent support even in this report appears to anticipate that shift.

Section 1: A study in contrasts: a little girl in a massive demo

Par 1: The reporter reports simply what he sees. And the eye-witness voice as always carries an implicit message: 'Because I record what I see it must be true.' Here he highlights one tiny human interest element but it captures so concisely all the fervent anti-war sentiment driving the newspaper's coverage of the Iraqi invasion plans. The focus on the 'little girl' with her 'home-made cardboard placard' implicitly contrasts an image of 'innocence' with the massive power of the US–UK military machine being challenged in the demonstration. And the par ends with one short dramatic word, the capital letters adding extra weight and urgency.

Par 2: The what (mass anti-war march) and the where (London) are clarified in this concise, summary par.

Par 3: There is colour ('a crisp winter's day', 'tramped') mixed with fact (the estimated two million). And the reporter reproduces uncritically the organisers' estimate of numbers reinforcing his expression of solidarity with the marchers. (In contrast, the pro-invasion *Daily Telegraph* quoted the police estimate of one million; the *Mail on Sunday* quoted one million five hundred thousand.) This is overtly biased reporting. But he still maintains a certain distance from the event. Rather than speak with the 'I' voice and say: 'I feel a sense of awe as I join the people in taking over the streets of the capital,' he says 'It is an awesome feeling when the people take over . . .'

Par 4: The reporter reinforces his alignment with the marchers against the government dwelling on 'the sheer power of numbers' (compared to the frightening power of the military machine).

Par 5: Notice how the short sentences convey the dramatic intensity. This sentence is something of a cliché and would have been stronger if it had been made clear this was the largest political demonstration in the history of the country. Notice, too, how the reporter is still reluctant to use the 'I' voice.

numbers of human interest stories. The human interest bias can often end up representing people's biographies as being untouched by the social, political, economic dynamics of history. Newspapers are said to provide the first draft of history. But it is often a distorted, elitist history. Exaggerating the power of a few individuals serves to eliminate so many other people and their struggles from the historical record.

Alongside this elitist dimension of the human interest story runs a significant 'democratic' element. The dramas, hopes, fears, tragedies of 'ordinary' people feature every day in such stories – just as the press's tendency to seek to bring the powerful down to size (through scandals and revelations) promotes this 'democratic', 'subversive' dimension. The front-page lead story (splash) of the *Bury Free Press* (7 April 2000) is typical of the genre. Under the big headline 'Please end this misery' that carries an urgent, compassionate and campaigning tone, the report by Mark Baxter opens:

> A Bury St Edmunds man is desperately waiting for life-saving surgery after two operations were cancelled.
>
> Ray Orr, 58, has a brain aneurysm which could rupture at any time, killing or permanently disabling him.
>
> Addenbrooke's Hospital in Cambridge has cancelled the operation twice, and now Mr Orr is hoping he does not lose the chance of surgery on April 19.

A picture of a smiling Mr Orr being embraced by his loving wife provides extra impact to the story.

Analysis of 'Elton makes a wish come true':
KENT MESSENGER (30 DECEMBER 1999)

Elton makes a wish come true

A DREAM CAME true for one of Elton John's youngest fans when he performed at **Leeds Castle in September.**

Minutes before the superstar stepped out on stage in front of 14,000 people he met seven-year-old Lorna Harvey and her family backstage.

Lorna, who went blind as a baby, was given the chance to meet Sir Elton when her parents, of Orchard Way, Horsmonden, contacted his management company to ask for tickets.

Her father, Paul Harvey, said: 'It was a nice thing to achieve. It also restores your faith in the celebrity world to find that they do pay attention to other people's situa-

tions. It came from the heart, which was great.'

It was the second time the family had trekked to Leeds Castle, after Sir Elton's earlier July dates had to be cancelled so that the singer could have a pacemaker fitted.

But Lorna didn't mind. She was thrilled to meet Sir Elton and take her presents of signed CDs, T-shirts and hats. Mr Harvey said: 'He was a nice guy and very friendly although he was distracted by the fact that he was about to go on stage. He was very open. I asked him how he was and he said he was doing okay and was still playing tennis. I offered him a game but he didn't reply.'

This article is highlighted as particularly interesting in an end-of-year compilation. Indeed, it carries many the ingredients of a fine local story: a multimillionaire celebrity visits the area and meets a blind child. There is a touching story here and the chance for some colourful quotes. The media are increasingly fascinated by the world of celebrities; yet it is essentially unreal: their lifestyle, their wealth, their fame so removed from the daily lives of 'ordinary' folk. Hence our ambivalence towards it (so subtly exploited by the media): on the one hand we succumb to its seductive appeal; on the other hand we are offended by its superficiality and outrageous wealth in a world of mass poverty. Here Lorna has a 'dream come true' entering, however fleetingly, the dream world of super-celebrity.

- *Par 1*: the 19-word opening par stresses the local angle but delays mention of Lorna's name until par 2 to help keep it concise. 'A dream came true' is a cliché, of course, but it works fine here.
- *Par 2*: clever coverage. The par flows logically on from the intro, embellishing it and adding necessary details and colour. 'Minutes before the superstar stepped out' carries narrative interest while the reference to the 14,000 spectators helps stress the uniqueness (and newsworthiness) of Sir Elton's attention to 7-year-old Lorna.
- *Par 3*: background details and local angle stressed with home address.
- *Par 4*: important direct quote from the father focusing on the drama of the meeting between the 'ordinary' family and the superstar. Significantly, the father expresses in one short sentence the archetypal ambivalence. His 'faith' in celebrity had foundered (perhaps as a result of so many tabloid sleaze exposés) but Sir Elton's charitable act had 'restored' it. The quote is snappy and supports the overall positive tone.
- *Par 5*: more background, conveying the determination of the family as well as the suffering of the superstar (they are human after all). 'It was the second time' is a useful transitional phrase linking with the previous par.
- *Par 6*: 'But Lorna didn't mind' is another excellent transitional, linking phrase bringing the focus back to Lorna. The father's final quote again captures the ambivalence. Sir Elton is a 'nice guy' but when Mr Harvey suggests they meet for a game of tennis, he doesn't reply. After all, the 'ordinary' and 'celebrity' worlds can meet for fleeting photo-opportunities such as this (which place the celebrity in the best possible light); but more than that is simply not possible. The two worlds are separated by an invisible wall.

Sexploitation of the human interest

Sex sells. At least that's what press proprietors believe. So day after day stories about sex fill pages of newspapers. Extra-marital affairs, prostitutes, sex-changes, bedroom secrets, ministerial and royal 'scandals', love-children of Catholic bishops, randy vicars, presidential passions, 'kinky' schoolgirls, full-frontal nudity on TV, Hollywood starlets who do or don't (strip for the cameras or in a West End show); how to do it; where to do – the list of subjects seems endless.

The sex lives of virtually everyone, from former FBI chiefs through media celebrities to truck drivers, seem fair game for the press. Nor is this sex obsession confined to the pops. The 'heavies' are equally interested – though in more discreet ways, of course. Serialisation of biographies will usually focus on the bits about sex; photographs accompanying reviews of plays or operas in which nudity occurs will be far more explicit than anything in the pops. *Independent on Sunday* columnist and feminist Joan Smith comments:

> The tabloids treat sex as something which has to be discussed in a kind of grown-up baby language – bonk, shag, boobs and so on – while the broadsheets invented high-minded motives for what is essentially voyeurism. Both approaches are predicated on the unspoken assumption that sex is taboo, not to be spoken about. They leave us without a language to talk comfortably about desire.

On one level this sex obsession of the press is all escapist, titillatory trash. Significantly, when Rupert Murdoch bought the *News of the World* in 1969 and his mother expressed unease at his association with the scandal sheet, he explained that the poor Brits had to have such entertainment as their lives were so wretched (Shawcross 1992). But what distinguishes a lot of the sex coverage is its humorous tone. It is rather like grown-ups giggling with embarrassment over a taboo subject. John Fiske (1992) takes a different approach and argues that this witty approach carries a 'subversive' agenda critical of the elite and the hypocrisies of those who presume to be our moral guardians.

The pops are, indeed, virulent supporters of the status quo, usually rushing to support right-wing parties, whether Conservative or New Labour, by all means (fair or foul) at election times and other critical moments. At the same time they subtly tap some of the anti-establishment feelings held by many people. This tone of 'subversive laughter' is peculiar to many of the tabloids and accounts for much of their popularity. A lot of their contrived humour is built on downright lies, sexism and racism. But, in a complex way, people want to be lied to, to be seduced into a fantasy world while at the same time seeing through the lies. Ask someone why they read a paper like the *Sun* and they may well say: 'It is a laugh, isn't it?' That humour, that blend of fact and fiction, leads to a curious, mass-selling product.

Analysis of 'Virginie's Secret': *MIRROR* (23 FEBRUARY 2000) JENNY JOHNSTON

> Chic Virginie Ledoyen strolls along the shore after turning her back on Hollywood's hottest heart-throb.
>
> The French actress who filmed a passionate love scene with Leonardo DiCaprio in The Beach, has revealed that he left her cold.
>
> While waves lapped at their sun-bronzed bodies and their lips met in a salty kiss, 23-year-old Virginie had only one man on her mind.
>
> It definitely wasn't baby-faced Leo, 25. She could barely wait to rush home to her 40-year-old boyfriend, movie technician Louis Saint Calbre.
>
> Louis, who shares a flat with her in Paris, is tall and dark with manly Latin looks. And he's the sort of partner Virginie prefers – mature.
>
> She rolls her eyes in astonishment at the thought that she might have been sexually attracted by the pale young American.

'Leo and I got on very well as friends,' she says. 'He is very funny and very intelligent, but he did nothing to me on a romantic level. I suppose he is quite good-looking but Leonardo is really not the kind of guy I go for.

'When we did our love scene, I got no physical pleasure from it.

'Sure I kissed Leonardo, but it did nothing for me. I was pretty unimpressed, if you must know.

'We had to repeat the scene a dozen times and it was hard work, but certainly not a turn-on.

'All I can remember is the taste of the salt because we were kissing in the sea and the water kept getting into our mouths.'

Leonardo modestly agrees that he failed to make the ocean roar for his co-star as they filmed in Thailand.

'She simply wasn't interested in me,' he confirms. 'The fact that I was a Hollywood star meant nothing to her, and rightly so. She's a very sophisticated European lady.'

Virginie has dated Louis for three years. She has also been closely linked to Paris lawyer Thierry Meunier, 40.

A friend said yesterday: 'She ended her last affair with Meunier before she started the next one with Saint Calbre.'

'The one thing both men have in common is that they are both much older than she is and both dote on her.'

Virginie herself seems wise beyond her years. Indeed she is already a show-business veteran.

She appeared in a TV commercial at the age of three and made her first movie when she was nine.

At 16 she saved enough money to leave home and buy her own flat. Her beauty also won her a modelling contract with the cosmetics giant L'Oreal.

Featuring in 15 French films made her a big name in her own country. Now the phenomenal success of The Beach has opened the door to Hollywood's riches. Yet she is in no rush.

'It's true that since Leonardo, the film offers have been rolling in,' she concedes.

'But I intend to choose my films carefully so I don't get typecast as just the pretty French girl in a short skirt. I am a tough person and want tough intelligent roles.'

The Beach's British director Danny Boyle predicts a great future for Virginie, not least because of the way she coped with DiCaprio.

Danny recalls: 'While other actresses might have been overwhelmed at sharing a lead role with the world's number one film star, she always remained cool and detached.'

Since the emergence of the *Sun*'s topless 'pin-up' in the early 1970s, page three in the tabloids has always been associated with titillation. Here, the *Mirror* blindly follows that convention, presenting a picture of long-legged 'chic' Virginie Ledoyen striding down a beach – arms outstretched, tantalisingly, towards us, the readers. Her hair hangs wet and dishevelled; sand clings to her swimsuit and legs; she smiles warmly (though her eyes are merely dark splodges). This is an image of a beautiful, active, playful, assertive woman.

The story has all the typical tabloid ingredients: sex, film stars, gossip, secrets revealed, Hollywood hype. Yet at its core lies an archetypal non-event: a manufactured kiss between Ledoyen and Leonardo DiCaprio on the set of the latest Hollywood blockbuster *The Beach*. So often the media create heroes – and then soon afterwards mock and debunk them. Here, in that same style, DiCaprio, 'Hollywood's hottest heart throb', is 'revealed' as sexually cold. And beneath the appearance of sexual permissiveness, lies the assertion of a conventional moral code that prioritises commitment either in marriage, or here, in a long-standing relationship. In the end there emerges a fascinating tension – between the unreality of the central event (the film's 'passionate scene' which was not even passionate) and the conventions of journalism (the narrative structure, sourcing, 'balance') which are ultimately striving to represent a real world.

There are five thematic sections:

Section 1: pars 1–11: 'mature' Virginie (her name tantalisingly close to 'virgin') finds DiCaprio cold in the sex scene on the set and is not turned on by him; she pines only for her current 'man' (intriguingly carrying the name 'Saint').

Section 2: pars 12–13: Leonardo's views.

Section 3: pars 14–16: Virginie and the men in her life.

Section 4: pars 17–22: biographical background to Virginie, stressing her 'maturity'.

Section 5: pars 23–end: comments of Danny Boyle on Virginie reinforcing theme of 'maturity'.

- *Par 1*: just 15 words, the piece constantly plays on contrasts: here Virginie turns her back on Leonardo – but strides towards us. The alliteration in 'Hollywood's hottest heart-throb' adds extras emphasis at the end of the par.

- *Par 2*: again just 22 words – the contrast between the 'passionate love scene' and Virginie being left 'cold'.

- *Par 3*: here the central theme contrasting the 'maturity' of Virginie's 'man' (Louis Saint Calbre) and Virginie herself and their steady relationship with boy Leo (who symbolises illicit, immature sex) emerges. 'While waves lapped at their sun-bronzed bodies and their lips met in a salty kiss' has the feel of a Mills & Boon romance – but this romantic mood is quickly shattered.

- *Par 4*: Leo's immaturity is confirmed by his looks: he's 'baby-faced' while, in contrast, Virginie's conventional credentials are confirmed: she can barely (a contrived pun) wait to rush home to her man. Similarly the two small inset pictures (to the left of Virginie) contrast Louis's 'true love' with the 'faked love' of DiCaprio.

- *Par 5*: Louis's maturity is reaffirmed.

- *Par 6*: DiCaprio well and truly debunked: he's described simply as a 'pale young American', not at all sexually attractive.

- *Pars 7–11*: the long direct quote seeks to add a note of authenticity to the story (for if she is being reported accurately, then the story must be real). First there is the contrast between friends and lovers (which they never became). The emphasis all the time is on the sex ('love scene', 'physical pleasure', 'kissed Leonardo', 'kissing in the sea') but the paradox is that none of it was a 'turn on'.

- *Pars 12–13*: Leonardo confirms the central line of the story (and so it must be true, real, it seems to be arguing again) and describes Virginie as 'a very sophisticated European lady'. The phrase 'failed to make the ocean roar' continues the 'sea' and 'beach' themes.

- *Pars 14–17*: Virginie has also been linked to a Paris lawyer. A 'friend' is needed to reaffirm her moral credentials.

- *Pars 18–22*: brief biography reaffirms her 'maturity': she is already a film 'veteran'. The direct quote adds a feeling of authenticity and immediacy.

- *Pars 23–4*: after the story has dwelt on the past, Danny Boyle now predicts a 'great future' for Virginie. Above all he praises her for resisting the sexual allure of the heart-throb; amidst all the potential sexual heat of the beach she remained 'cool'.

the other end of the country may talk to you and reveal a wonderful story you would otherwise have missed. Afterwards you will follow it up.

'Dullness', in any case, is a subjective notion. What is dull to you may be fascinating to someone else. One of the many challenges for a journalist is to report the 'dull' in an interesting way. Many public meetings contain informal discussion rather than set-piece speeches. Often a more 'feature-ish' approach is suited to this event where you may incorporate some comment and descriptive elements. While the meeting itself may not produce hard copy, a talk with one or more of the participants afterwards might.

After the meeting

Many meetings covered in the press are never attended by the reporter. The spread of 'phone journalism' (and increasingly email journalism) means they are often simply 'picked up'. A journalist will contact either one or more people present for their account of the decisions made and for their views on any possible consequences. They may follow up a press release. Or a reporter may compile a retrospective, looking back at the meeting or conference, or write an opinionated feature on the meeting and its implications.

Events or pseudo-events: COVERING PRESS CONFERENCES

Press conferences often provide important sources of news for journalists. They are useful for both the organisers and the journalist. For the organisation it marks an attempt to influence the news agenda. Journalists will be given a chance to look in depth at issues from the perspective of the organisation and to meet some of their important representatives. For the journalist, the event can provide the basis for a news report, for gathering background information, for developing contacts. Organisations tend to send out press conference details three or four weeks in advance. If the news editor considers it possibly worth attending, details will be noted in the diary for the day. Any accompanying literature, for instance, contact numbers and names, will be filed. If there is likely to be a photo-opportunity ('pic op') linked to the event, the picture desk will be notified. Organisations often contact the newspaper again by telephone a few days before the event as a reminder. They can also send a press release (embargoed until after the likely end of the conference) giving an account of the event as if it had already occurred but not enough information to discourage journalists from attending.

When you arrive at the conference venue you are usually asked to add your name and that of your newspaper (or to indicate freelance) to a list. You may be given an agenda and a badge to identify yourself when meeting others afterwards. Transcripts of one or more of the speeches to be made and other background information on the organisation and relevant issues may be provided. It is important to compare the transcript with the actual speech. Occasionally small changes appear and there can be a story behind those alterations. For instance, there may have been a last-minute compromise to delete or amend some controversial statements or proposals. Equally, non-scripted asides can provide the most interesting quotes and angles.

It is important to establish, soon after arriving, the names, spellings and titles of the people on any panel. Contributions can often move rapidly among the speakers and, without notes giving attributions to the various quotes clearly, writing a story afterwards can prove nightmarish. When a striking, intro-worthy quote or fact emerges, ring or star it to help identification later on. Conferences usually begin on time or just five minutes late, so it is important to arrive on time. In any case, it reflects badly on your paper if you arrive late.

An organisation may spend most of the conference on an issue it considers important but which the journalist may regard as only marginally newsworthy. For instance, an organisation may use the press conference to spell out its '14-point charter for green consumerism'. A passing comment by a speaker may be more newsworthy. A prominent environmentalist may claim that a BBC documentary the previous night had 'seriously misrepresented the environmentalists' case' and that her organisation was planning to protest to the corporation. That angle may then dominate the intro with reference to the 14-point plan coming later or eliminated altogether.

Question of questions

It is often important to raise questions, particularly if you think later opportunities will be denied you. Perhaps an important source has indicated they will have to leave immediately after their contribution. Sometimes journalists, as a pack, co-ordinate on a series of questions to extract particularly complex and sensitive information. David Conley reports (2002: 67): 'When President Nixon refused to answer a Watergate-based question during a media conference, he pointed to another reporter whom he invited to pose a question. The reporter did: "Would you please answer the previous question?"'

Sometimes reporters will swap around ideas for angles and quotes afterwards. When questions are asked out loud, it becomes difficult for the journalist to identify an 'exclusive' angle. Press conferences can promote a culture in which conformist, consensual news reporting is accepted too uncritically.

On many occasions, the most important part of the press conference for the reporter is during the informal questioning afterwards. This provides the chance for following up individual angles and delving into an issue more deeply. It provides the reporter with a chance to check details, quotes and spellings. Never feel embarrassed to ask for clarification of a complicated point. Better to get it right than botched up. Ideas for further follow-ups and contacts can emerge from these informal meetings. In addition to the speakers, other people from the organisation often attend who can provide useful sources of information.

Different circumstances will demand different strategies on handling the notebook or Dictaphone during this informal period. Sometimes you will approach with your notebook and pen clearly visible. At other times it will be more appropriate to chat on in a relaxed way perhaps with a drink in one hand but aiming to remember everything said and only after a time bringing out your notebook or Dictaphone (if at all).

Stage-management and manipulation

All press conferences should be treated carefully. Sociologists have called them the archetypal 'pseudo' news event (Boorstin 1962). It is not a 'real' event like a football match, a car accident or a court case. It is artificially contrived, aimed at gaining publicity. It has no status other than in relation to the media coverage it is seeking. An organisation calling one has a message to sell. It has gone to the trouble of sending out the details to the press, maybe booking a room, laying on drinks (and sometimes a meal) for journalists. It expects something in return. Namely publicity and preferably good publicity.

There is a danger that journalists will be used as glorified PR officers for the organisation. Press conferences are attempts to stage-manage the news. Since they are tightly managed affairs you should be thinking all the time: what are they trying to tell me and, more importantly, what are they trying to prevent me from knowing? The experience of the Australian war correspondent Wilfred Burchett is pertinent here (Kiernan 1986; Pilger 2004a: 10–25). At the end of the Second World War, following the bombing of Hiroshima and Nagasaki, 600 Allied journalists covered the official Japanese surrender aboard the battleship *Missouri*. Only Burchett subverted the dominant news values and went, with great difficulty and courage, to Hiroshima. From there, he filed one of the most famous scoops of all time. His description of the devastation of the Japanese city after the nuclear bombing and the suffering and dying of people from radiation sickness was carried in the *Daily Express* of 5 September 1945 under the headline: 'The atomic plague: I write this as a warning to the world'. His reporting of radiation sickness was to be ferociously denied by the Allies for years afterwards. But he was right about radiation sickness – and right to report it (Burchett 1981 and 1983).

Reporting reports

Reports constitute an important source for news stories and features. They can appear in book or leaflet form, as press releases, in specialist journal articles or in the agenda papers or minutes of meetings. Their value comes from the deep research which normally underpins them. Reports from such bodies as Shelter, the International Institute for Strategic Studies, Amnesty International, the Joseph Rowntree Foundation, Low Pay Unit, Child Poverty Action Group, Oxfam and other prominent charities provide a body of 'authoritative' details which journalists can use as the basis for their articles. Reports with a national focus will also provide opportunities for local follow-ups. They will usually argue a case or come to conclusions which can lead to recommendations for action. These provide good copy. The reporter will aim to highlight the most important finding, conclusion or recommendation from the report in the intro and attribute it clearly to the source.

For instance, the *Guardian* (25 October 2004) reported:

> Daffodils, cod, Christmas trees and the Highlands' ski resorts could have become victims of global warming by 2050 according to an energy efficiency report today.
>
> Warmer weather will, instead, introduce vineyards to Scotland, stingrays and more types of sharks to our coastal waters as well as termites, scorpions and mosquitoes carrying West Nile virus and dengue fever, the study – Forecasting the Future – says.

The *Daily Star* (3 November 2004) reported:

> A record number of young single women are buying their homes.
>
> More and more of them are modelling their lives on film character Bridget Jones.

> Research by the Halifax shows that single women now take out 23% of mortgages – compared with under 10% in 1983.

Conventional reporting routines are followed. Both reports highlight the most interesting/newsy element in the report. In the *Guardian*, there is a clear attribution to 'an energy efficiency report'. To avoid overloading the intro with details, the story delays mention of the precise title until the second par.

The *Star* leaves the main angle in the intro unattributed (implicitly recognising it as 'fact'), naming the source, the Halifax, only in the third par. The second par aims to 'lift' the copy with the reference to the famous film character Bridget Jones (at the same time providing the opportunity to carry a picture of Renée Zellweger alongside the story).

Press conferences

Press conferences may accompany the publishing of reports. These provide journalists with the chance to 'humanise' their coverage, presenting views through the voices of spokespeople as well as the impersonal report. Background details can also be established. When press conferences are not held, reporters often ring up the writers for comments. In all cases they might contact others for follow-up responses. Publication details should always accompany reports, but normally they don't in the mainstream press (though websites may provide useful links to the publishers).

Reactions to reports

Reactions are usually worth following up and can provide lively intro copy, as in this *Daily Telegraph* story (3 December 2004) on the pre-budget report of Chancellor Gordon Brown:

> Scientists criticised the Chancellor's report for neglecting the crisis in university science.

Or again in the same issue:

> Film financiers yesterday warned the government's new tax arrangements would have a devastating effect on the British film industry.

In his *Independent* report (30 November 2004), science editor Steve Connor delayed the main response angle until par 2:

> A study of genetically modified crops has found no evidence to suggest they are harmful to the countryside, fuelling the debate about the environmental effects of the technology.
>
> Environmentalists were quick to dispute the research, published yesterday and jointly funded by the biotechnology industry and the government.

Analysis of 'Jackpot winners are moaning lott':

DAILY STAR (15 NOVEMBER 1999)

Jackpot winners are moaning lott

By Thomas Harding

ONLY HALF those who win massive National Lottery prizes are happy, a survey revealed yesterday.

A study of millionaires found the win has made them fat slobs who quit work just to stay at home. Lottery operator Camelot released the findings as the game celebrates its fifth birthday this week with a £20 million superdraw on Saturday.

The findings show that 75 per cent of millionaire winners quit their jobs but very few take up new hobbies and can't be bothered to go to health clubs, despite having heaps of dough and spare time to spend it in.

A third of winners have piled on pounds of weight as well as in the bank and their lives are so dull that 91 per cent still play the weekly lottery. And only four out of ten stump up cash for charities.

The Mori survey of 249 players, which included 111 who scooped more than £1 million, also shows blokes give away more cash than women.

Just 55 per cent of winners were 'happy' since hitting the jackpot. Almost 10 per cent of marriages have broken down. Best friends still remain pals with winners, with men giving money, on average, £170,000 to three mates and women just giving to one pal, averaging £60,000.

Scots and Northerners were the most generous, followed by Midlanders and then Southerners who gave away a measly £17,000 to pals. But one unnamed winner has given away £3 million. Half of £2 million winners remain in their original homes, but those who do move want to distance themselves from their former lives by buying country mansions.

Since its launch five years ago the lottery has created 866 millionaires and raised £7.5 billion for good causes.

One player scooped the £6,240,358 jackpot on Saturday with the numbers 7, 10, 21, 28, 29 and 39. The bonus ball was 2.

There is little punning in the copy, surprisingly so. The headline attempts a pun (though it is an exceptionally contrived one). The sentence lengths are typical of a red-top tabloid in being generally short: 15 words, 20, 22, 41, 31, 11, 23, 12, 9, 26, 21, 8, 26, 19, 18, 5. Very few sentences carry subordinate clauses.

The language is (typically for a red-top tabloid) often based on slang and vernacular: such as 'fat slobs', 'can't be bothered', 'heaps of dough', 'stump up cash', 'blokes', 'pal', 'mates', 'measly'. (Other tabloid variants are 'yobs', 'brutes', 'thugs' for 'soccer hooligans'; 'cops' for 'police officers'; 'boozing' for 'drinking beer'; 'aggro' for 'commotion'; 'boss' for 'manager'; 'blasted' for 'criticised'; 'mum' for 'mother'; 'cock-up' for 'mistake'; 'our boys' for 'British soldiers'.)

- *Par 1*: a bit of journalistic licence here. Most of us, who have not won the lottery, secretly want to know that winning a million cannot automatically bring happiness (whatever that may be). We want to be reassured that our lifestyles are OK. Later in the copy, it is said that 55 per cent of winners feel 'happier'. In other words, more than half. But that is not what the reporter wants us to be told. And so he has averaged the figure down and begun with the qualifying word 'only'. Notice the clear attribution phrase 'a survey revealed yesterday' following news reporting conventions.

- *Par 2*: focuses on the striking 'fat slobs' angle and then gives background on the survey (accompanying the fifth anniversary of the Lottery's launch).
- *Par 3–4*: the 'fat slobs' angle is revealed as weak and unnecessarily contrived. Only a third 'have piled on weight' so it was wrong to exaggerate this statistic. Better to have cut the 'fat slobs' sentence and replaced it with par 4, which provides the precise details. This par also contains the text's only pun ('piled on pounds of weight as well as in the bank'), though it is rather contrived.
- *Par 5*: clear focus on precise details. Then shifts to the 'charity' angle, concentrating first on the gender distinctions. This is developed at the end of the next par (with men giving on average £170,000 to three friends and women giving £60,000 to one). But ideally these details should have followed immediately after the reference to this in par 5 and not been separated.
- *Par 6*: the evidence to support the intro finally appears. 'Just' aims to deflate that figure as well as usefully drawing the number away from the start of the par.
- *Par 7*: focus on regional differences in the charity stakes – particularly interesting for a newspaper with national circulation.
- *Par 8*: background details. Unnecessary repetition of five years; we were told about the 'fifth birthday' in par 2.
- *Par 9*: wrap up providing Saturday's results.

Covering speeches

A speech constitutes a perfect event for news coverage: it has a tidy beginning, middle and end. A chosen speech will usually provide some copy so attendance makes economic sense. A complex and controversial issue may be usefully simplified through the voice of one person. The war in Kosovo in 1999 had its roots deep within the military–industrial complex of the US and the UK and in the local animosities which followed the break-up of the former Yugoslav republic. A report of a speech on the conflict by a celebrity, peace campaigner or politician provided a focus for news coverage, reducing the complexities to a comprehensible event rooted in the 'now' of news.

Many covered speeches are not attended by the press. Publicity departments (of political parties, companies, campaigning organisations and the government, for example) distribute a regular supply of press releases (increasingly through email and over the internet) giving verbatim or edited accounts of speeches. A journalist attending a speech will often, then, attempt to incorporate some 'eye-witness' element to indicate their presence. They may report the responses of the audience or the mood of the speaker. They may place a Dictaphone close to the speaker but this should never be entirely relied on. Problems can follow. Always back up with a written note, perhaps starring quotes which stand out as particularly newsy, interesting and maybe even worth following up.

A report will tend to combine reported speech with direct quotes, these being reserved for the most colourful expressions of opinion. As the story progresses, extracts from the speech will decrease in news value; brief background details, comment, analysis and colour will be slotted in where relevant. Take these opening pars from a page lead in the *Scunthorpe Telegraph* (30 November 2004):

> The Chief Constable of Humberside Police believes major issues still surround the sharing of specialist child protection information – almost a year after Soham murderer Ian Huntley's conviction.
>
> In a speech to be delivered in London today to leading figures in child protection, David Westwood was to say more needs to be done to prevent another similar killer slipping through the net.

The newspaper has received an advance press release (clearly without an embargo) on the Chief Constable's speech and decided to run the account before the event. It comes from an elite source and focuses on an issue of major interest to the media: law and order and the protection of children. The intro focuses concisely on the most newsworthy claim, attributes it clearly to the Chief Constable and then, in the next par, follows with the 'where' ('in London' before 'leading figures in child protection') and the 'when' ('today'). Only the 'was to say' appears somewhat convoluted.

Take this page lead in the *Guardian* (1 December 2004):

> **Brown to offer a vision of Britain's destiny**
> **Patriotism and need to plug skills gaps will be keynotes**
> Patrick Wintour, chief political correspondent
>
> Gordon Brown yesterday promised that tomorrow's pre-budget report will offer a 'patriotic vision of Britain's future', but also address the country's weaknesses – 'the need to invest long-term in science, enterprise and education'.
>
> Mr Brown said: 'The theme of the pre-budget report will be that the next decade can be a British decade.'
>
> In a speech that sought to head off claims that he is a covert Eurosceptic, the chancellor said it was vital to understand that British values and history involve 'being outward looking, internationalist and pro-European as a country of aspiration and ambition'.
>
> Such an understanding was 'the way to solve the vexed question of Europe for our generation'.
>
> He proposed a new Institute and Forum for Britishness, to create a shared national purpose and identity and prepare Britain for the challenges of global competition.
>
> Politicians, academics and journalists would join forces in 'examining the forces at work in shaping the future of Britain'.
>
> 'Britain's success and destiny depends upon understanding and building upon our historic strengths: our stability, our openness to the world, our scientific creativity, our world-class universities – and then understanding and addressing our weaknesses: the need to invest long-term in science, enterprise, education and in the potential of every young person and adult.
>
> 'So at the heart of the pre-budget report is a patriotic vision of Britain's future as a country.'

The chancellor aims to bring a new urgency to the debate by focusing on the threat to an unreformed Europe of the rise of India and China.

The tone of Mr Brown's remarks will be watched closely by pro-Europeans who have been calling on him to give a more upbeat account of the region's economic story.

A recent meeting between the chancellor and the board of the Britain in Europe group ended in acrimony amid claims that the chancellor was more interested in knocking Europe than reforming it.

In a pamphlet this week Roger Liddle, assistant to the new EU trade commissioner, Peter Mandelson, argues that European productivity at least matches US performance, and in some cases exceeds it.

This is a contrast to the chancellor's oft-repeated claim that Europe is falling behind.

Mr Liddle argues that European productivity on a per hour basis is better than America's, adding that this 'is an important corrective to the absurdities of the claims that the EU is a basket case in comparison with the rest of the world'.

Mr Mandelson recently caused waves in the Treasury when he warned against gloating over comparisons.

However, in a Policy Network pamphlet on economic reform in Europe, Mr Liddle warns that the European social model may no longer be sustainable, and proposes a series of changes to make the union deregulate and become more competitive.

In his statement tomorrow Mr Brown will develop his plans to boost British productivity, including greater help for science and innovation and a nationwide extension of employment training pilots.

He has already published five reports alongside his annual budgets analysing aspects of the productivity problem. Critics such as the TUC claim that he has made too much of the way in which the US outstrips the EU.

Some economists have used OECD evidence to challenge the Treasury's claim, which was based on Office of National Statistics figures showing Britain recently closed the productivity gap with Germany in terms of output per worker.

Interestingly, it's an eclectic report combining hard news, comment, background details and analysis, drawing evidence from a separate pamphlet and from speeches both 'yesterday' and 'tomorrow'.

Analysis

Thematic section 1: Brown's speech – Pars 1–8

- *Par 1*: Dual-angled intro: 'patriotic vision' and 'need to address weaknesses'. With 33 words, somewhat convoluted and awkward, the dash after 'weaknesses' seriously damaging the flow of the text.
- *Par 2*: simple direct quote reinforcing 'patriotic' theme of intro (but nowhere is the 'where' indicated).
- *Par 3*: an interpretative section ('sought to head off claims that he is a covert Eurosceptic') adds colour but at 42 words the par appears overloaded again.

12 *The Guardian* Wednesday December 1 2004

Policy and politics

Brown to offer a vision of Britain's destiny

Patriotism and need to plug skills gaps will be keynotes

Patrick Wintour
Chief political correspondent

Gordon Brown yesterday promised that tomorrow's pre-budget report will offer a "patriotic vision of Britain's future", but also address the country's weaknesses — "the need to invest long-term in science, enterprise and education".

Mr Brown said: "The theme of the pre-budget report will be that the next decade can be a British decade."

In a speech that sought to head off claims that he is a covert Eurosceptic, the chancellor said it was vital to understand that British values and history involve "being outward looking, internationalist and pro-European as a country of aspiration and ambition".

Such an understanding was "the way to solve the the vexed question of Europe for our generation".

He proposed a new Institute and Forum for Britishness, to create a shared national purpose and identity and prepare Britain for the challenges of global competition.

Politicians, academics and journalists would join forces in "examining the forces at work in shaping the future of Britain".

"Britain's success and destiny depends upon understanding and building upon our historic strengths: our stability, our openness to the world, our scientific creativity, and then understanding and addressing our weaknesses: the need to invest long-term in science, enterprise, education and in the potential of every young person and adult.

"So at the heart of the pre-budget report is a patriotic vision of Britain's future as a country."

The chancellor aims to bring a new urgency to the debate by focusing on the threat to an unreformed Europe of the rise of India and China.

The tone of Mr Brown's remarks will be watched closely by pro-Europeans who have been calling on him to give a more upbeat account of the region's economic story.

A recent meeting between the chancellor and the board of the Britain in Europe group ended in acrimony amid claims that the chancellor was more interested in knocking Europe than reforming it.

In a pamphlet this week Roger Liddle, assistant to the new EU trade commissioner, Peter Mandelson, argues that European productivity at least matches US performance, and in some cases exceeds it.

This is a contrast to the chancellor's oft-repeated claim that Europe is falling behind.

Mr Liddle argues that European productivity on a per hour basis is better than America's, adding that this "is an important corrective to the absurdities of the claims that the EU is a basket case in comparison with the rest of the world".

Mr Mandelson recently caused waves in the Treasury when he warned against gloating over comparisons.

However, in a Policy Network pamphlet on economic reform in Europe, Mr Liddle warns that the European social model may no longer be sustainable, and proposes a series of changes to make the union deregulate and become more competitive.

In his statement tomorrow Mr Brown will develop his plans to boost British productivity, including greater help for science and innovation and a nationwide extension of employment training pilots.

He has already published five reports alongside his annual budgets analysing aspects of the productivity problem. Critics such as the TUC claim that he has made too much of the way in which the US outstrips the EU.

Some economists have used OECD evidence to challenge the Treasury's claim, which was based on Office of National Statistics figures showing Britain recently closed the productivity gap with Germany in terms of output per worker.

guardian.co.uk/eu

- *Par 4*: good use of reported speech 'was' before concise partial quote and punctuation at end spot on.
- *Par 5*: new strong angle (Institute and Forum for Britishness) adds impetus to the copy.
- *Par 6*: another sentence mixing reported speech ('would join') and partial quote.
- *Par 7*: 53 words, so far too long. Needed to break down into a mix of short direct quote(s), reported speech and partial quotes.
- *Par 8*: another reinforcement of the 'patriotic vision' angle of the intro, so unnecessary.

Thematic section 2: Pars 9–16: the European dimension

- *Pars 9* and *10*: more interpretative sentences focusing for the first time on the European dimension.
- *Par 11*: background on the European controversy

- *Pars 12–16*: sub-section focuses on the contrasting views on Europe of Liddle and Mandelson. Fleet Street throughout this period, in the absence of any credible opposition from the Conservative Party, took every opportunity to highlight disagreements amongst the New Labour elite as a way of brightening up the news. Significantly, *The Times*, in its pre-budget coverage on the same day, led on the (over-hyped) spat between Brown and Blair, based on claims in a book written by journalist Robert Peston.

Thematic section 3: Pars 17–19: final wrap-up looking ahead to tomorrow's budget statement and at some critics of the Treasury line.

- *Par 17*: focus on main points of budget statement, clearly drawn from leak. Early stress on the 'when' ('tomorrow'). Reference to 'British productivity' returns to 'patriotic' theme that has run through the piece.
- *Par 18*: background details and TUC response (covered, significantly, very superficially and buried in copy).
- *Par 19*: criticisms of 'some economists' remain rather vague.

Local newspapers sometimes follow up speeches made in private meetings. For instance, the *Newark Advertiser* (24 December 1999) led on a story about the Conservative prospective candidate, Patrick Mercer, calling for a review of the medical benefits of cannabis. He had made the comments first during a debate at the Minster School, Southwell; reporter James Kelly later interviewed Mercer, giving him the space to expand on his argument.

All in the eye of the beholder: EYE-WITNESS REPORTING

Journalists are the observers of history (Inglis 2002). When the Berlin Wall falls, they are there describing the tumultuous events. When the Americans invade Grenada (in 1983) and ban journalists from the island, the brave ones take to boats in an attempt to evade the censorship regime and see the attacks at first hand. More mundanely, a local journalist attends a football match and reports what he or she sees. The 'eye-witness' dimension (also known as 'direct observation') is one of the crucial distinguishing features of journalism. But it can become a cliché, with the eye-witness journalist failing to explore the deeper underlying factors behind the events.

Reporters cannot possibly witness all the events they report. They have to rely on others for accounts. Editorial cutbacks of recent years have further reduced the eye-witness element in the news. Meetings, for instance, are often no longer attended but 'picked up' afterwards or handled on the basis of press releases. But when reporters are present at significant events that witnessing can be used to dramatic effect, providing an immediacy, a 'human interest' and an appearance of authenticity to copy. Even a straight report of a meeting can be enlivened by the inclusion of an eye-witness element such as descriptions of participants' appearance, accounts of questions from the floor and responses from the audience. Take these opening pars by sketch writer Matthew Parris in *The Times*:

Analysis of 'Portillo hunting party targets early birds': *THE TIMES* (24 NOVEMBER 1999)

HALF PAST SEVEN in the morning is no time to be out on the streets of Kensington and Chelsea. The first grey light was lifting over the smart rooftops, Entry-phone gates and magnolia trees as your shivering sketchwriter awaited the arrival of Michael Portillo's campaigning hit-squad for a dawn blitz on Holland Park Tube Station. Will these Portillo desperados stop at nothing?

By 7.45 – Outrage still abed – eager Tories were mustered, assembling piles of blue leaflets, bearing smiling snapshots of the great man and anchoring little flotillas of blue balloons to their sleeves. The youngest of these strange creatures sported only stubble on his head. "Shaved it for charity," he confessed. "Last week I was bald." The biggest Portillista wore a green waxed-cotton coat and curious felt hat. "Trilby or what?" I asked.

"I go shooting in it."

But his quarry today were unfeathered: the voters. And these birds were shy. Until El Numero Uno arrived, no commuter had been successfully apprehended.

'He's coming', hissed an excited Portillista. Down the pavement from Notting Hill steamed a lone Portillo, at a cracking pace. "Morning everyone," he growled sternly in his big Daddy Bear voice, readying himself to press the flesh by the station door. I slunk behind to overhear. Portillo has a massive neck. People kept slipping by, unapprehended.

Commuters were mostly a mixture of Filipino maidservants (baffled by Portillo's outstretched hand), hungover construction workers hiding beneath hard hats and the occasional expensive Suit, coat and scarf (who invariably turned out to be a Member of the Kensington and Chelsea Conservative Association already). 'Where are you going,' boomed the Candidate at a group of little boys in school uniforms. They gave him a withering glance.

• *Par 1*: present tense used in first sentence to convey immediacy. But then the device is suddenly dropped ('was lifting') for no apparent reason. News is rooted in time and here Parris begins firmly by stating the precise time. Perhaps he betrays his privileged social position (and that of his readers whose sympathies he is trying to capture) by stressing immediately the 'ordeal' involved in getting up so early. For many (such as the 'construction workers' and 'Filipino maidservants' he notices later on) it is the normal time to be out in the streets. Then precise observations ('grey light . . . over the smart rooftops, Entry-phone gates and magnolia trees') set the scene. Again, Parris makes an appeal for his readers' sympathies addressing us intimately as 'your shivering sketchwriter'. And then comes the news angle: Michael Portillo, just elected as Tory candidate after a period in the political wilderness (and later to be William Hague's deputy), is due to join a group of Tory supporters campaigning outside a Tube station. But Parris (somewhat unimaginatively) fixes on the biggest cliché of all (relating to war and violence) and describes the Tory group as a 'hit squad' preparing for a 'dawn blitz'. There is an ironic, humorous tone here and throughout, but at root there is no biting political critique; it is all too friendly. Irony becomes a part of a strategy to help distance the writer from his sources. But it appears inauthentic and over-contrived. Parris (a former Tory MP) is like a court jester to Parliament and politicians: making fun of them, mocking them sometimes, but (with the mass media closely linked through economic ties to the dominant elite) always from a safe, insider position. Finally he calls the Tory faithful 'Portillo desperados'.

- *Par 2*: there is almost a poetic feel to this text focusing on precise observations: 'abed', 'eager Tories', 'mustered', 'assembling', 'bearing smiling snapshots', 'anchoring little flotillas' is language untypical of traditional news coverage. Repetition of 'blue' stresses the Toryism of the event while 'great man' continues the ironic tone of the intro. His eye then focuses, in typical journalistic fashion, on the unusual: a man with just stubble on his head. 'Strange creatures' continues the leg-pulling tone, but how come he knew this chap to be the youngest? Did Parris ask him his age? If he did, why didn't he include it? Perhaps it was a piece of journalistic licence, aiming simply to brighten up still further the copy with a superlative. The short and snappy sentences in the dialogue add to its humour and impact. Then, striving hard for literary effect, he invents the word 'Portillista' (to mean a female supporter of Portillo). Again, the dialogue helps convey the eccentricity of those present which the writer is at pains to stress.

- *Par 3*: short, sharp quote varies the rhythm of the piece – and thus its overall interest. As his eye shifts, so does the rhythm of the text.

- *Par 4*: to help the text flow, the copy builds on the shooting reference in the previous par (with 'quarry', 'unfeathered', 'birds'). The cognoscenti will know that Portillo's father is Spanish – and the Spanish theme (begun with 'Portillista') continues with El Numero Uno, while 'apprehended' attempts ironically to compare the campaigning Tories to over-eager police officers. He mocks their lack of success.

- *Par 5*: the over-contrived 'literary' feel to this text emerges with the use of 'hissed' here (and later on 'growled sternly'). A simple 'said' would have been inadequate: just as is later 'shaking hands'. It has to be 'press the flesh'. Similarly there is a deliberate emphasis on alliteration with 'Portillista', 'pavement', 'Portillo', 'pace'. And notice how most nouns have to be accompanied by adjectives. Portillo is transformed into 'Daddy Bear' (since bears growl) but that theme is neither anticipated nor developed. Our intrepid reporter slinks (bear-fashion) behind the great man and notices the thickness of his neck. That's an unusual observation which works well here. The mocking of the Tories' canvassing failures continues.

- *Par 6*: observations on the kinds of folk around early in the morning (even the Suits turn out to be Tory faithfuls). Again an over-contrived emphasis on alliteration with 'hungover construction workers hiding beneath hard hats'. 'Boomed' aims to mock the great man for his pretensions (as does the capitalising of Candidate). The contempt shown him by the 'little boys' mirrors the contempt felt by the writer. But how authentic is that contempt?

9 Powerful information

Reporting national and local government

John Turner

Politics is about power, and information is power. Journalists are part of the information business and are crucial in a political process which involves the exercise of this potent force. People with power, whether Cabinet ministers, senior civil servants or chief executives of local councils, have a vested interest, not only in protecting their own power but also in obscuring the extent of their authority in the first place. The journalist occupies a pivotal position between those who make and implement important decisions and those who are often forced to comply with such decisions. Any democratic system depends on people being well informed and educated about politics by a media which give a full and accurate account of news, encompassing a wide and varied range of political opinions.

The media in general have a large and growing significance on politics. However, there is unclear evidence regarding the nature and extent of this influence. The political impact of the media, and the press in particular, is difficult to assess for various reasons:

- It is difficult to isolate the effect of the media from other influences such as family, education, work and economic circumstances.

- There is a complex myriad of mutually influencing factors which complicate the relationship between newspaper and reader. The political impact of a paper will depend less on what is being read than on who is doing the reading and their level of knowledge and experience about politics in general.

- The media are fragmented, with television, radio and the national press having different effects compared with local coverage. A direct relationship between any media's influence on a political issue is therefore confused.

- Similar messages are received and interpreted in different ways by different people; hence a claim that the media are being used for propaganda purposes cannot be verified because one cannot be sure of the effect intended.

Before turning to aspects of local and national politics, it is important briefly to outline three ways in which the impact of the media has been assessed.

- *Agenda-setting and primary definers*: here the media are accused less of telling people what to believe than of providing a more pervasive influence on what people think about and how they make judgements about different issues. Agenda-setting involves a constant interaction between a newspaper and its readers. Newspapers also tend to take on board sources of information which control and establish initial definitions of particular issues. As such, a great deal of news coverage reflects the interpretations initially created by official sources.

- *Reinforcement and hegemony*: here the media are not so much creating attitudes as involved in strengthening and reinforcing existing beliefs and prejudices. This can be linked to the notion of hegemony whereby consent is sought for those ways of making sense of the world which fit with the perspective of those in power

- *Independent effects*: there is a growing view that the media have a more direct and independent effect on beliefs and behaviour. Again evidence for such a view remains controversial. New media technologies have as much of an influence on attitudes and behaviour as the uses to which they are put.

Newton (1986) has pointed to a paradox in the media's impact on political aware-ness. Whereas political information is delivered faster to more people, nevertheless the mass tabloids contain only a little political content, and what they report is person-alised, trivialised, sensationalised and biased. Consequently, a large proportion of the public is provided with restricted news and knowledge of current affairs. This contra-diction has been discussed by Seymour-Ure (1974) in his distinction of levels of readership between a mass public and informed political public. An information gap has been created with a small, well-educated public who use the media to become better informed and a mass public who mainly read gossip columns and sports pages and are therefore more readily influenced by biased news.

Local papers do not work in a vacuum. They are as much a part of the political system and process as anyone, and journalists working for them have assumptions about the way in which the political system operates. There is far less of a division between local and national politics today. Local government has increasingly become simply an arm of central administration and, as in the case of education policy, it is difficult to disentangle separate national and local agendas. Equally, there is nothing inherently local about local newspapers. Much of what is considered to be national news is local in nature and source. Indeed, Britain's tradition of a domin-ant national press has imposed a kind of artificial parochialism on the local press which has led to a number of criticisms about the rather narrow way in which local papers have covered local politics. The homogeneous and national nature of the British political system and political culture must not be underestimated in this respect. They have had an important effect on the way in which politics is reported by the local press.

The British political system

Previous studies of the British political system have pointed to its strong civic culture, supported by a stable and cohesive system of politics (Almond and Verba 1963; Rose 1965). Power in Britain is centralised and, according to the traditional view, is concen-trated in the Cabinet in Parliament and Whitehall, supported by political conventions, the cohesiveness of political parties, Treasury control, ministerial responsibility and the Crown prerogative. This strong and cohesive model of British government has been accentuated by a period of prime ministerial dominance, without the safeguards of accountability which might be imposed by a Bill of Rights or Freedom of Information Act. Before considering aspects of these institutions it is important to consider the underpinning nature of Britain's political culture.

The culture of deference

Deference and tradition

People in Britain have a remarkably deferential attitude towards the dominant political institutions. An appeal to tradition is used as a way of defending many of the institutions which have become a stable part of the political system. The monarchy, the House of Lords, the dominant role of the Prime Minister and pervasive secrecy are the ingredients of a political culture which has not been up-ended by revolution or war. Leigh (1980) has referred to the system as a huge mountain with abandoned monuments, with some still powerful and others forgotten. An example is the system granting special rights and powers to the monarch – known as the royal prerogative. It is no longer abused by monarchical power but has been transferred to the hands of the Prime Minister and executive. Before MPs protested in 1993, the government considered denying Parliament the right to vote on the Maastricht Treaty. The Prime Minister's press office attempted to argue that under the Crown prerogative such treaties did not need the vote of Parliament but could be ratified by the PM on behalf of the Crown.

Political participation

Such deference has made Britain a relatively law-abiding country. There is a general respect for authority and the law which complements a low level of political participation. Many social scientists were surprised that there were not greater social disturbances as a result of mass unemployment in the 1980s. Participation in voting at general elections has fallen in recent years. In 2001 only 59.4 per cent turned out to vote, a fall of 12 per cent on the 1997 general election. Local election turnout has fallen to around 30 per cent. Added to this, only about 5 per cent are members of a political party, with only about 2 per cent becoming party activists.

Centralisation and concentration of power

In Britain's unitary system of government decision-making power has been highly concentrated and centralised. Parliament, government, the administration, law courts, major companies and the BBC are all based in central London. Given the lack of a written constitution, save European law which Britain has had to sign up to as a member of the EU, Britain has failed to develop any notion of federal-style government. Therefore, local government does not have the type of autonomy and independent powers which states have in the United States or Germany. Local government is controlled from the centre, reinforced by party politics, which is similarly controlled from the centre. However, since 1997 we have seen the emergence of a Scottish Parliament, a Welsh Assembly and a mayoral government in London and other large cities and boroughs. These innovations have increased, rather than assuaged, further demands for regional government in Britain.

Politics at the periphery

There has always been a tension between local government's administrative and political roles. Central government of whatever party has always safeguarded its powers to change politics at the periphery and determine the nature of service delivery. This has involved the abolition of significant parts of the local government system, such as the Greater London Council (GLC) and metropolitan authorities; the reorganisation of the local taxation system, the reform of the management and operation of councils and the type of services which they can and cannot deliver. In 1986 the Widdicombe report warned of the increasing politicisation of local government which led to an unprecedented period of reorganisation. This process of permanent revolution has continued more recently under New Labour.

Supranational politics

The 25-state European Union now has a fundamental influence on the politics of Britain. After joining the then European Community in 1973, Britain signed in 1986 the Single European Act, which established an integrated single market 'without frontiers'. For federalists and those who wanted to see a political dimension to these economic reforms, further political integration became an important part of the European agenda. In 1991 the Maastricht Treaty was signed establishing a three-pillar structure including, first, the old European Community which would establish a single currency, second, a common foreign and security policy, and, third, policing and immigration control. Britain initially obtained opt-outs from monetary union and the Social Chapter, although Tony Blair has now accepted the latter. Britain's entry to the single currency, the Euro (which was established in 1999), remains highly controversial, with all parties divided on the issue.

Clearly the EU has moved towards greater interdependence and integration. Federalists especially want greater powers for the European Parliament and a more executive role for the Commission, alongside greater judicial authority for the European Court. In 2004, the EU was enlarged by the accession of 10 countries including some ex-communist states in eastern Europe (such as Estonia, Hungary and Poland) and Cyprus and Malta. Moreover, the development of the single currency will make Europe an ever-present issue in British party politics (John Turner 2000). Most recently, controversy has centred on a proposed new European Constitution designed to reorganise all existing treaties. New elements introduced include a Charter of Fundamental Rights, a President of the European Council, a European Foreign Minister and greater integration of policy in the areas of defence and policing. The British government was proposing to hold a referendum on the new constitution after the 2005 general election.

Quango state

In recent years there has been a tendency to distance areas of administration from direct political control and public accountability. This quasi-government operates in a no man's land, occupying an increasingly crowded territory between central and local government. Quangos include public, private or voluntary organisations, or combinations of all of them. In Britain, examples include the Independent Television Commission, set up as a statutory body by Parliament; the BBC, established by Royal

Charter; the Higher Education Funding Council, set up by the Treasury; and the National Consumers' Council, a non-profit-making company.

A key issue for these bodies is the degree to which they are accountable to the public or to the political process of election. A further problem with the growth in quangos has been the process of patronage and the process of appointment to such bodies by ministers. Many posts involve some financial benefit, and a large proportion of them have been filled by appointees supportive of the government. The *Guardian* (11 April 1996) reported that the chairman of the London Ports Authority received a payment of £4,000 a day for 12 days' work a year. In 1996 the Nolan Committee on Standards in Public Life recommended that there should be an end to payments for those sitting on public bodies (Nolan 1996).

Privatisation

The process of privatisation has seen public utilities which were formerly nationalized industries sold off to the private sector. These private companies, like British Telecom, British Gas and the electricity and water companies, are now huge monopolies which have been able to make very large profits for their senior managers and shareholders. In a number of cases the problem of delivering public services in an efficient and cost-effective way has raised issues of accountability. The water companies, for example, have been criticised for failing to deliver services in Yorkshire, and British Gas executives were criticised for paying themselves large increases in salary. In all these cases it has been difficult for politicians to regulate the activities of these bodies. Regulatory bodies such as OFWAT and OFGAS have been powerless to interfere with their activities. New Labour has continued to extol the virtues of the private sector over the public sector, going ahead with the privatisation of air traffic control and rejecting completely any suggestion of the renationalisation of the railways following the train crashes at Ladbroke Grove (1999), Hatfield (2000) and Potters Bar (2002).

Secrecy

Linked to this centralisation of power is the secrecy which pervades British politics and the patronising assumption that the government knows best. Britain's culture of secrecy is buttressed by harsh libel laws, weak rights of access to official information, the Official Secrets Act and the D-Notice system (according to which national newspaper editors agree voluntarily to censor sensitive information on the advice of the Ministry of Defence). Freedom of information legislation gives fewer rights to official information than those enjoyed by people in the US, Australia, Canada, New Zealand or the Irish Republic. More rights were given under the last Conservative government's open government code. New clauses introduced by Jack Straw, the Home Secretary, explicitly ban the public from access to documents on policy-making. A 'catch-all' clause prevents disclosure on any matter which might reveal ministerial disagreements over policy. The clause applies to government, Parliament and all public bodies.

For local government a new cabinet system allows councillors to take decisions about education, social services and planning in much greater secrecy. People lose their right to know compared with the previous system which required councils to take decisions at open meetings of the full council or its committees. Anti-terrorism legislation goes one step further in putting journalists in danger of arrest if they cover the activities of campaigning groups such as pro-hunt activists, road protesters, animal liberationist or environmentalist groups. For example, Greenpeace can be targeted when taking action against genetically modified (GM) crops. The Regulation of Investigatory Powers Act 2000 also threatens journalists' sources and confidential information. The state is now able to intercept email and telephone calls across private networks 'in the interests of the economic well-being of the United Kingdom'.

Party politics

Since the 1880s Britain has been dominated by political parties, and politics is still organised around a two-party system. In the 1980s some 80 per cent of people still identified with one of the two main parties and just over 50 per cent of the electorate voted for them in the 1997 general election. In 2001 this figure fell to just 43 per cent. Parties control the political agenda through professional party machines and discipline, while party managers, through the Whips, dominate in Parliament.

The emphasis on *laissez-faire*

Britain has a strong state and free economy. There is active state intervention to ensure law and order and social control, but little to ensure full employment and increased social justice. In the past decade the trend since 1945 towards collectivism and corporatism has been halted and the Keynesian rationale for state intervention has been undermined by free-market philosophies

Language and symbols of politics

The use of particular forms of language defines political identities and reassures supporters. On the right, terms such as 'freedom of choice', 'patriotism', 'individuality', 'efficiency' are used. The left is labelled 'extremist', 'communist', 'red' and 'unpatriotic'. For the left, terms such as 'equality', 'socialism', 'class' and 'the state' are used, and the right is labelled as 'uncaring', 'capitalist', 'fascist' and 'selfish'. Such terms have tended to highlight differences between the parties which have not in policy terms existed.

Consensus

Despite the radical policy shifts of Margaret Thatcher there has been a high level of agreement on the main areas of policy in British politics. Over a range of policies, like foreign affairs (Iraq and Bosnia), Northern Ireland, race relations, there has been agreement between the parties, with governments being prepared to negotiate and compromise with pressure groups. Significantly, once elected in May 1997, Gordon Brown made an economic commitment to stay within the spending guidelines of the previous Conservative government. Yet, the consensus appeared to be breaking down with the US–UK invasion of Iraq provoking massive dissent as an estimated 2 million people took to the streets of London in protest on 15 February 2003.

Authoritarian populism

A more populist politics under Thatcher in the 1980s placed a new emphasis on self-reliance, individualism, market economics, curbing trade union immunities and

encouraging private enterprise. There was also a more vigorous attack on many traditional institutions in the name of the market and efficiency. The civil service, health
service and law profession were all targeted. Thatcher attacked important elements
of the postwar consensus and was prepared to go beyond Parliament and the Cabinet
by direct appeals to the electorate.

The shape of local government

Local government has two principal roles in the British political system. First, there
is a political role as democratically elected bodies representing local people and giving
legitimacy to local political demands and interests. Second, there is an administrative role in implementing policy, including the delivery of services, which have often
already been determined by central government. There has always been a potential
conflict between these roles and there were a number of reasons over the past 20
years why the political relationship between central and local government became
more adversarial.

- *Partisanship*: local government has become increasingly politicised with parties
  in local government prepared to challenge the policies of central government and
  build up a power base in their own locality.
- *Polarisation*: there was increasing conflict between the right-wing policies of the
  Thatcher governments and many, especially urban, local authorities run by Labour
  groups who saw themselves as a last bastion of opposition during the eighteen
  years when the party nationally remained out of power.
- *Breaking the consensus*: the Thatcher governments in the 1980s proposed a radical
  shake-up in the ways that local government operated, generally attacking them as
  inefficient, over-staffed and undemocratic.
- *Economic cuts*: a major reason for these attacks on local authorities in the 1980s
  was that central government wanted to cut local government spending and their
  ability to raise taxes (the rates, poll tax, council tax). Local government spends
  over £75 billion a year, 80 per cent of which comes from the central Exchequer,
  and it employs over 2 million people.

Partly because of these factors local government underwent a constant process of
change in the 1980s. There were important changes to structure, including in 1985
the abolition of the GLC and the six metropolitan authorities in Tyne and Wear,
South Yorkshire, West Yorkshire, Merseyside, Greater Manchester and the West
Midlands. These were seen as key Labour-controlled authorities which had the
ability to challenge the policies of central government at this time. Just before
the 1997 general election there was yet another overhaul of the local government
system in the non-metropolitan areas of England and throughout Scotland and
Wales. In Scotland the old two-tier system of regions (or counties) and districts was
replaced with a system of all-purpose unitary councils. In England reforms were more
limited, with the two-tier system being mainly retained in thirty-four of the thirty-
nine existing counties. Avon, Cleveland, Humberside and Berkshire are now no longer
part of the local government map, and some thirty-five unitary authorities were established, such as Milton Keynes, Nottingham, Southampton and Leicester, which now
run all local services (see Figure 9.1).

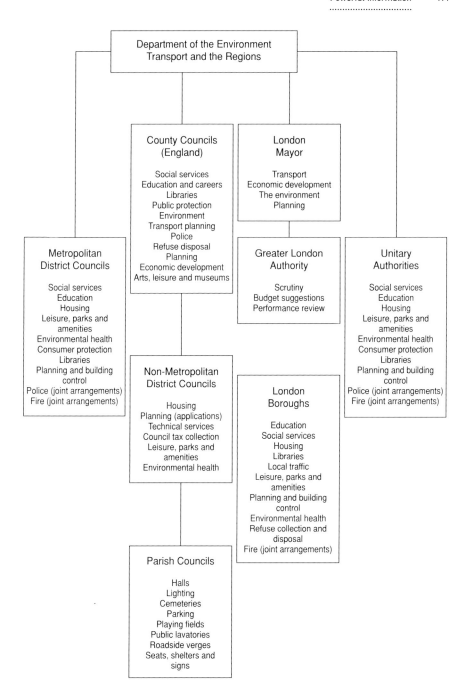

Figure 9.1 Local government in England and Wales

78 per cent of people voted against the proposed assembly. This has meant the government has all but abandoned its regional assembly programme.

'Best value' and the abolition of compulsory competitive tendering

New Labour's ambivalence towards local councils can be seen in its consumerist 'best value' regime designed to set performance indicators and improve the quality of services. Local authorities now face regular inspections from a unit of 400 staff based in the Audit Commission, created at a cost of £40 million. Councils will draw up local performance plans and central government has powers to intervene to remedy clear performance failure (Boyne 1999). In the 2002 White Paper, *Strong Local Leadership – Quality Public Services*, the government claimed to offer councils 'earned autonomy'. It established a new assessment for policy delivering, rating councils as high-performing (excellent), striving (good), coasting (fair) and poor-performing (weak).

New ethical procedures

Labour announced a new 'ethical framework' for English councils in March 1999 in the wake of a much-publicised fraud in Doncaster council where councillors had been imprisoned for expenses fraud and planning corruption, so highlighting the financial rewards allocated to committee chairpersons.

In response to the Nolan report on local government standards of conduct, a new independent standards board has been proposed to investigate all allegations that a council's code of conduct has been breached. Each council is required to keep a register of members' interests and a standards committee to oversee it. There will be regional standards boards and an appeals system to the national standards board.

Reinvigorating local democracy

In local elections in May 2000 turnout was around 30 per cent and only 33.6 per cent for the new form of London government. This followed the European parliamentary elections in June 1999 when only 23 per cent went to the polls. Indeed, the 1997 general election saw the lowest turnout since the Second World War, with only 40 per cent of younger people bothering to vote.

To remedy such low public interest in elections – what some have called the rise of 'sod them politics' – the Labour government aimed to stimulate greater participation, more frequent elections to ensure accountability and innovations in electoral procedures. Gordon Brown, the Chancellor, has spoken of restoring 'civic patriotism'. It is intended to stimulate greater participation by giving local authorities a duty to consult the public over local performance plans, including the public assessment of beacon councils and best value services. It is also envisaged that there will be a greater use of non-binding referendums by local councils on issues of local controversy such as forms of council organisation and planning.

Labour has suggested there should be more frequent local government elections – in two-tier structures, half the county and half the district councillors being elected each year. In unitary councils a third of councillors should be elected each year.

The government also wants to encourage experiments in new forms of voting to increase turnout. This involves the introduction of electronic voting, including the use of the internet, mobile polling stations, entire elections by postal ballot and polling in supermarkets and shopping centres. The government is also looking at rolling registration to include people who have recently moved into a new local authority area. In 2004, there were experiments using all postal votes in local and European Parliamentary elections. There was a slight increase in voting in these pilot areas. However, there were a number of allegations of fraud. The Electoral Commission now opposes all-postal voting for the UK (www.electoralcommission.org.uk). In the future the government wants to consider the introduction of proportional representation across all local elections. Other methods for increasing the vote have included a tour of sheltered housing by a polling van which achieved a 44 per cent poll of elderly residents. In Watford, customers at the Asda supermarket had a polling station open between Friday and Sunday to increase turnout.

New forms of political structure

Labour planned important legislation regarding the role of the committee system in local government. It sees the old system as failing to provide decisive leadership and accountability as well as being too time-consuming. Legislation was delayed in the House of Lords, where it was argued councils should have the discretion either to set up a new cabinet system or retain the old committee system (see Figure 9.2). Councils such as Hammersmith and Fulham, Lewisham, Cardiff and Buckinghamshire were quick to move to a new system (Leach 1999).

Blair has been greatly influenced by the US mayoral system, and the government initiated three models of reform:

- a directly elected mayor with a cabinet selected from among the councillors
- a cabinet with a leader
- a directly elected mayor with a council manager.

In each case local referendums were held. There are, however, important criticisms of the new cabinet style of local government. First, where there is one strong party dominating this will affect the composition of the cabinet and relegate any opposition councillors to the role of backbenchers. Second, backbenchers will have limited powers to check the cabinet and gain access to key policy papers, especially where partisan politics dominates. Third, cabinets may lead to even greater secrecy and unaccountability. Cardiff's new civic cabinet arranged a £58,500 pay package for the lord mayor and council leader without wider council discussion and public accountability (Jones and Stewart 1998).

The first experiment in this new form of local government was the election of a London mayor and a Greater London Authority (GLA). This involved using a supplementary vote system (SV), with the GLA elected by an additional member system (AMS). Under these new systems councils are required to establish scrutiny committees of backbenchers to review and question the executive's decisions and performance. In general local councils have preferred the cabinet system to the mayoral system, although the mayoral system is now being discussed in relation to other large cities such as Liverpool, Manchester and Birmingham.

The powers of the new London mayor include responsibility for transport, economic development, the environment and planning, with a new Police Authority

Full council meeting

This is often the least interesting meeting to attend as a journalist. The parties have already agreed their positions on policy and the meeting is devoted to ratifying decisions and reports made by the committees.

The full council is chaired by the (lord) mayor or chairperson (chair). They sit at the front of a semicircle of desks, with party leaders, deputy leaders and the committee chairs sitting in the front rows. The mayor is often joined by a chief officer while other officers usually sit in the back rows of the chamber. The council clerk is in administrative charge of procedure and an important person to cultivate if you are a reporter. Journalists may occupy a table outside this semicircle or be given a special place in the public gallery. Reporters should ensure they know the names of the principal speakers – the leaders, committee chairs and opposition speakers – though the clerk is normally available to help with names after the meeting.

Full council procedures

Councils have set procedures for dealing with points of order and votes. The council meeting will have an *agenda* which will outline matters to be discussed and indicate parts of the meeting open to the public and those parts when the public and press will be excluded. The full council meeting usually begins with the *approval of the minutes* of the last full council meeting. The mayor reports back on any matters arising and outlines any relevant correspondence, changes in the membership of the council or petitions from the public. Petitions from council-house residents or from parents of under-fives about the provision of services may be heard directly from the public in the council chamber itself.

The rest of the full council meeting is mainly taken up with the approval of committee minutes and reports arising from meetings which have been held since the last full council. Committee minutes are received, adopted and then approved by the full council. The committee chair may present the report and explain any details. There are four courses of action which the full meeting may decide:

- It may automatically accept items in the minutes which are *resolved* items. This is when the full council has already given delegated powers to the committee to decide on issues on its behalf.
- The meeting can *approve recommendations* made by the committee. The opposition may move that a recommendation should not be accepted and, in this case, there may be a debate and vote. Each recommendation is dealt with in turn, some meetings choosing to take them in blocks. It is important for the journalist to follow the proceedings carefully, making a note of the item number or the page reference given by the mayor.
- A *recommendation* may be amended, in which case there may be a vote.
- The meeting can ask the committee to look at the item again. In this case the matter is referred back to the committee.

Councillors do have the opportunity to ask the committee chair questions, and may give *written notice* where they require detail and further explanation.

The newsroom will be given three days' notice of the meeting and will be sent copies of the relevant minutes. Reporters need to read through these papers for items which may form the basis of a news story.

Committees

Most of the council's work is done in committees and subcommittees. Each is a microcosm of the full council, with the majority party taking most of the seats in the committee. Some councils have a tradition of allowing the opposition to chair some committees although, in the main, the dominant party takes all the chairs. Journalists are allowed to attend committee meetings, although their access to subcommittees may be restricted.

Committee work is detailed and greatly informed by officers. Heads of the council's departments, such as the director of social services or the education director, tend to ensure councillors do not go beyond their powers, *ultra vires*, and will often stop councillors from making decisions which break the law.

There are four main types of committees:

*   *Standing committees*: an authority must have these if they run particular services. Hence a county must have an education and social services committee and a district must have a housing committee.
*   *Ad hoc committees*: these are set up at the discretion of the council and cover areas which are seen as important but not statutorily required. For example, these may include a women's committee, an employment committee or a race relations committee.
*   *Subcommittees*: these are smaller groupings of a committee handling specific issues or covering specific areas. The housing committee of Haringey Borough Council, for instance, has a subcommittee covering the Broadwater Farm housing estate.
*   *Policy and resources committee (P and R)*: the most important committee, it is the cabinet of the council. Composed of the leader, deputy leader and committee chairs, it co-ordinates policy and allocates finance to other committees.

Procedures in committee

Each committee will start by approving the minutes of the previous meeting and go on to consider reports prepared by the council's departments. In a social services committee, the director of social services may present a paper on the implementation of the Children Act 1989. This may be about the issue of taking children into care when parental abuse is suspected. A recommendation may be passed which will be sent to the full council. Journalists will be able to obtain such reports and may quote points made in the committee.

Officers

Officers are officially the servants of the council and try to resist attempts to politicise their role. However, as with civil servants in central government, politicians increasingly favour officers who are prepared to work with the policy of the ruling party group. The work of officers is circumscribed by legal constraints and they are greatly influenced by their professional training. Many still think of themselves foremost as engineers, architects, planners, social administrators or accountants.

A journalist usually has to go through the public relations or press department of the council. They have their own agenda, and the journalist must be careful to clarify the difference between publicity and news. Increasingly, press officers have found it difficult to be an intermediary between committed politicians and a more hostile national press and this has changed their role significantly. They are much more interested in negotiating a compromise between both sides.

The press office is likely to direct the reporter to the head of a department. The department will want to give a corporate view on an issue and will resent any attempt to contact and deal with a less senior officer who has only a partial view of the issue. Recent adverse reporting of issues related to social services and education have made officers much more sensitive as to what they say.

National politics

At the national level the main local contact is the constituency MP and there may be three or four in the area of a local newspaper. It is even better if a local MP is also a government minister or an outspoken critic on the backbenches. Speeches, general interviews, votes in the Commons, local party contacts and other public duties can provide material for stories. Background on an MP's personal and business life provides background for the local reporter.

A local paper will obtain a report of their local MP's speeches in the House from a stringer or news agency. Many regional and local papers have correspondents based at Westminster, some of whom are members of the lobby. The local newsroom will use Hansard Parliamentary Reports, and local MPs will be more than forthcoming in sending journalists copies of speeches This may also include speeches at party conferences in October, when a local paper may wish to send a reporter or will again use a stringer.

Local political parties

The local party holds regular meetings, selects the prospective MP or de-selects the sitting MP, chooses candidates for the local elections and, with other constituencies, for the European Parliament (Ball 1981). Again, the journalist should build up a relationship with local party activists because they can provide information about the content of local meetings.

Labour Party

The Labour Party has a federal structure controlled by a National Executive Committee (NEC), which is elected by the party conference. The NEC is made up of representatives from the trade unions, constituency parties, socialist groups, co-ops and a women's section. In recent years the NEC has strongly supported the process of reform in the party initiated by Neil Kinnock, and carried through by John Smith and Tony Blair. The leadership has moved power in the party away from the constituency parties and activists and has given ordinary members voting rights in the election of the party leader so replacing the old electoral college system which gave votes to the trade unions, MPs and constituency parties. The Blair leadership has also distanced the party from the trade unions, although most of its income still derives from the trade union political levy.

There are twelve regional councils with their own executive committees which co-ordinate activities in relation to local, national and European elections. At the local level the party is organised on a constituency basis, with an elected general management committee which has representatives from ward organisations. The ward may have twenty to thirty activists, whereas the constituency organisation may have a hundred representatives.

Blair has completed the process of policy reform, moving the party further to the right and away from policies which were associated with the left. This has involved, for example, a rewriting of the party's constitution, especially Clause 4, which advocated public ownership as an ultimate objective. After eighteen years in opposition New Labour won its largest majority in the 1997 general election, and carried this forward in their general election landslide in 2001.

Conservative Party

The Conservative Party has a more top-down structure with considerable power residing with the leadership. The party leader chooses the party chairman, who runs the party organisation. At the regional level there are the twice-a-year meetings of the Conservative Union, which has delegates from the constituency associations and which elects an executive committee. At the local level there are the associations made up of ward organisations and which appoint a committee.

The party conference is always a stage-managed affair. Speeches by the leadership tend to be orchestrated and representatives are mainly out to display their loyalty. It is not a policy-making body, although it is a good barometer of party feeling. In 1998 William Hague, the then Tory leader, changed the method for electing the party's leader. After his general election defeat in 2001, this new method was used, involving the party's rank and file for the first time. Nominated candidates are voted for by Conservative MPs in a secret ballot and the number is then whittled down to two candidates who are then voted for by party members. In 2001 around 240,000 ballot papers were returned and the candidate of the right, Iain Duncan Smith, was elected leader. In 2003 Tory MPs voted him out of office and to avoid using the same electoral procedures they put forward only one nomination, Michael Howard, who was then elected unopposed.

Liberal Democrats

The Liberal Democrats also have a federal structure, with different organisations in England, Scotland and Wales. There are twelve regional parties, which appoint representatives to the regional council. The conference is the most powerful body, electing a co-ordination committee to oversee the day-to-day running of the party. At the constituency level there is the local party. The party leader is elected by the party membership on the basis of one person one vote.

Scottish National Party (SNP)

The Scottish National Party was founded in the 1930s, although it began to make inroads into the British political system only with its victory at Hamilton in 1967. This gave the party a boost to membership and party organization across Scotland, although the party suffered a setback with the rejection of a Scottish Assembly in 1979. The SNP is the main rival of Labour in Scotland, especially with the general decline in Conservative support. The SNP campaign for Scottish independence has led them to take a more pro-European line, and Labour has had to toughen its arguments for a devolved Scottish Assembly to ward off further Nationalist inroads.

Welsh Nationalist Party (Plaid Cymru)

The Welsh Nationalist Party made a breakthrough at Carmarthen in 1966 and strongly contests seats against Labour in the valleys, West Rhondda and Caerphilly. Recently the party has moderated its illegal tactics, preferring constitutional means through self-government in the form of a Welsh senate. It has also dropped its linguistic nationalism, now accepting English as well as Welsh as national languages.

Ulster Unionist Party

The Ulster Unionist Party dominated Ulster politics from 1922 when Northern Ireland was established. However, Unionism was fractured in the 1970s when direct rule was imposed from Westminster in the wake of increasing violence. Unionism is now divided between the more traditional Official Unionist Party (OUP) and the more hardline Democratic Unionist Party (DUP).

Social Democratic and Labour Party (SDLP)

The Social Democratic and Labour Party replaced the old Nationalist Party in 1971 and has been prepared to negotiate within the existing political framework despite its ultimate goal of a united Ireland.

Sinn Fein

Sinn Fein is often referred to as the political wing of the illegal Provisional Irish Republican Army (IRA), which has been engaged in an armed struggle against the British presence in Ireland since the 1960s. Sinn Fein received semi-illegal status when Thatcher imposed a ban on Sinn Fein politicians talking directly to radio and television. This ban was lifted when the Major government sought to involve Sinn Fein in all-party talks on the future of Northern Ireland. In April 1998 the Belfast Agreement (Good Friday Agreement) was reached between the British and Irish governments and interested parties in Northern Ireland. A devolved Northern Ireland Assembly was established but then suspended in October 2002 when the Unionists withdrew over the issue of decommissioning of IRA weapons. In 2003 Assembly elections were held and created more polarised results. The DUP became the largest party with 30 seats (gain of 8 seats), with the UUP 27seats (+1), Sinn Fein 24 (+6), SDLP 18 (−6), others (−9).

Green Party

Founded in 1973, it was called the Ecology Party in 1975 and became the Green Party in 1985, emphasising its links with the more successful European green movement. The Greens had a partial breakthrough in 1989 when they took 15 per cent of the vote in European parliamentary elections, although their vote fell back to just 1 per cent in the following 1992 general election. Internally there has always been a basic division between those who want the Greens to be a conventional party and those who want to base the party's politics on alternative lifestyles. Recently Green representation has been improved by the use of the more proportional additional member system in elections. Greens now have three on the new Greater London Authority, one member of the Scottish Parliament, two members of the European Parliament (MEPs) and forty-three local councillors nationwide.

The United Kingdom Independence Party (UKIP)

UKIP made startling gains in the June 2004 European parliamentary elections. Calling for withdrawal from the EU, they polled 16 per cent of the vote, overtaking the Liberal Democrats, winning 12 seats and finishing just 7 per cent behind Labour. Established in 1993, with headquarters in Birmingham, the party has attracted a number of media celebrities, including the former TV chat show host Robert Kilroy-Silk, who is now an MEP.

Respect

Respect (Equality, Socialism, Peace, Environment, Community and Trade Unionism) is a broad leftist coalition building on the stop-the-war campaign which saw two million people taking to the streets of London on 15 February 2003 protesting against US–UK plans to invade Iraq. Headed by ex-Labour MP George Galloway, supporters include disaffected Labour members, film director Ken Loach, and trade union leader Mark Serwotka. The party has put up candidates in European, London Assembly and local elections.

Elections

People are most aware of politics and political parties at election times, and national elections especially provide journalists with a good source of stories. By-elections can be used as a barometer of government popularity and will always attract the leading MPs from all parties, including ministers and frontbench opposition speakers. The local agent for the candidates is the most important contact for the reporter, pointing them towards the appropriate meetings and photo opportunities. An agent may distribute a copy of a proposed speech in advance, highlighting the key passages which the party wants reported.

Otherwise most reports will be centred on candidates' comments on each other's parties' programmes and the personal stance taken by specific politicians. Journalists should be prepared to challenge candidates about issues and party commitments. Local issues are important and questions should be asked especially of candidates who have been brought in from outside the area by their respective parties.

Parliament

House of Commons

The House of Commons is the central focus for the reporting of national politics. Most political stories emanate from parliamentary reporting, and many local papers have their parliamentary specialists, often located at Westminster. Otherwise, local papers will employ London-based stringers and the task of the local reporter will be to follow such stories up with a local angle and local interview.

Constitutionally, Parliament is the sovereign body having power to choose, maintain and reject governments. For the media in general the system of adversarial party politics provides a dominant agenda. This view overemphasises the role and powers of ordinary MPs.

The power of government and especially that of the Prime Minister has increased in recent years. The government controls the business and procedures of the Commons, the Leader of the House outlining the timetable of business after Prime Minister's questions. The guillotine and closure motions are increasingly used to push legislation through, curtailing debate by putting a time limit on the discussion of amendments to bills. The Commons acts with the permission of government, most of its time devoted to the passage of public (government) bills through Commons procedures with the government's control of its majority ensuring legislation is passed.

The work of government has grown in complexity. The state intervenes through economic and welfare politics, and since 1945 this has led to a massive increase in public spending. Government requires more legislative time, and the length of bills and Parliamentary sittings have grown in recent years. In one annual session there are about 150 government bills to be considered, most receiving the Royal Assent, and about two thousand statutory orders and regulations. There were experiments with special standing committees to scrutinise policy during the passage of bills. Pressure groups were invited to play a part in the committee stage of the Education Act 1981 dealing with children with special educational needs. However, such experiments were quickly dropped (Norton 1991).

Backbenchers and the opposition parties can use the following limited devices for influencing government. Their interventions can provide copy for reporters:

- *Question time*: once a week for 30 minutes on Wednesday afternoons, Prime Minister's questions provide a set piece between government and opposition. There is little scrutiny here, with rhetoric crowding out information and the planted question from a government backbencher allowing the Prime Minister to attack the opposition.
- *Private Members' bills*: a good source of news. MPs ballot for the opportunity to introduce them and are then inundated with suggestions from pressure groups on suitable topics. There is very limited parliamentary time for such bills and few get through, the more controversial being usually talked out.
- *Ten-Minute Rule bill, Adjournment debate and Early Day Motions*: ways for backbenchers to draw public attention to specific issues.
- *Supply Days and Emergency debates*: used by the opposition parties to debate and vote on issues of importance. The government ensures it has a majority to ward off such attacks, the main intention of the opposition being to embarrass ministers and the government.

House of Lords

Since 1997 New Labour has been committed to the reform of the House of Lords, in 1999 doing away with all but 92 of the 650 hereditary peers and establishing a Royal Commission under the Conservative peer Lord Wakeham, who suggested that only 87 of 550 members should be directly elected. Labour committed itself to complete Lords reform in its 2001 election manifesto. However, the Blair government suggested only 20 per cent of peers should be elected by the public. Both the Tories and the Liberal Democrats argued there should be at least 80 per cent of members elected directly. In 2003, Blair backed a wholly appointed Lords, suggesting that elections would create a 'rival rather than a revising chamber'. The Commons rejected all options for reform, and since 2003 the issue has dropped off the political agenda.

Select committees

In recent years the most notable attempt to increase the Commons' influence over government has been the introduction of new select committees. With the televising of Parliament these now have a much higher profile. They are made up of about twelve MPs and can call ministers, civil servants, union leaders and business chiefs to give evidence on particular topics. Since 1980 select committees have overseen the work of the main government departments, including Agriculture, Defence, Education, Employment, Environment, Foreign Affairs, Home Affairs, Social Services, Trade and Industry, Transport, the Military and the Civil Service.

They produce reports, sometimes critical of government policy, but are weakened by the evasiveness of ministers and civil servants, hiding behind collective Cabinet responsibility. Select committees hold sessions which journalists can attend. Usually, officials and ministers are questioned by MPs about aspects of a contemporary issue. Sometimes discussions can be a little heated, and notes from the meeting can be used in conjunction with follow-up interviews with interested parties. Civil servants have a set of instructions, the Osmotherly Rules drawn up in 1977, which govern their evidence before select committees. They are instructed to be helpful but guarded to ensure good government and national security. As a result many important issues relating to government are kept from select committees, including advice to ministers, how decisions are made in departments, the level of consultation, the work of Cabinet committees and how policy is reviewed.

The relative impotence of select committees was dramatically shown in the case of Clive Ponting, who leaked information to the Foreign Affairs Select Committee on the way Parliament had been deceived by the Ministry of Defence about the sinking of *General Belgrano* during the 1982 Falklands War. The chairman of the committee, Sir Anthony Kershaw, instead of establishing an inquiry about government accountability, gave the documents to the Minister of Defence, who immediately set up a leak inquiry to punish the person who had provided the information. Other members of the select committee tamely acquiesced in their chairman's actions.

Standing committees

Standing committees of between twenty and fifty MPs are appointed to examine the details of bills as they progress through Parliament. The committee can be of the whole House, as with the Maastricht Bill or the Finance Bill, and amendments to a bill can be tabled.

A local MP may be on a standing committee or may have a particular interest in the legislation. There is a *First Reading*, when a bill is formally introduced without a vote; a *Second Reading*, when the general principles of the bill are discussed; a *Committee Stage*; a *Report Stage*, when committee amendments are considered by the House; and a *Third Reading*, when the bill is reviewed and further amendments added. The bill then goes to the *Lords*, the Committee Stage usually being of the whole House, and the bill returns to the Commons with *Lords' amendments* and these then need to be resolved before the bill receives the *Royal Assent* and becomes an *Act*.

Government and the civil service

The decline in the power of Parliament is matched by a growth in the power of the executive, and in particular the power of the Prime Minister's office. Much of this power emanates from party control and the growth of the Cabinet office since the First World War. The anonymity of civil service procedures reinforces this power at the centre (Ponting 1986). The Prime Minister appoints the government, dismisses ministers, chooses appropriate ministers for Cabinet committees, controls Cabinet agendas and chairs discussions with the Cabinet Secretary writing the minutes on behalf of the Prime Minister. The Prime Minister also controls the system of patronage, approving ministerial preferments to the chairmanship of quangos such as the Independent Television Commission.

Cabinet government remains secretive, and divisions between ministers are usually concealed by the notion of *collective Cabinet responsibility*. Under this convention decisions of the Cabinet are collective and ministers are not allowed to contest the view emanating from the Cabinet Office. This makes it difficult for journalists to record the true flavour of the political debates and discussions taking place at the heart of government. The work of the civil service is also kept secret by means of *ministerial responsibility*. This convention states that the buck stops with departmental ministers, ensuring that, when questioned in select committees, senior civil servants can dodge answering by referring to their minister.

Cabinet committees

The issues concerning the resignation of Nigel Lawson and Geoffrey Howe from Thatcher's government raised questions about the relevance of the notion of collective Cabinet government. In the 1980s the Cabinet met less often, some forty-five times a year compared with nearly a hundred times in every year since 1945, and the number of Cabinet committees and papers also fell (Hennessy 1986).

Under Thatcher a large proportion of Cabinet work was determined by Cabinet committees. Many major items of public policy were dealt with by committees including the abolition of the GLC and six metropolitan authorities, the introduction of the poll tax, the banning of trade unions at GCHQ (the government's signals intelligence headquarters based in Cheltenham), the privatisation of British Telecom and reforms of the NHS.

The three principal committees deal with economics, overseas and defence, and home affairs. With more decisions made in committee, the whole Cabinet system has become fragmented with policy being decided by relatively isolated groups of ministers and civil servants.

Prime Minister's Office

Another recent trend has involved the bypassing of the Cabinet system altogether. Increasingly, policy has been determined by informal groupings centred around the Prime Minister. Government information flows as much through the Prime Minister's Office as it does through the Cabinet secretariat. As a consequence, policy reaches the Cabinet and departments in a fairly developed form, providing ministers with a *fait accompli* and little time to organise opposition to it. The Broadcasting White Paper of 1989 was developed in a series of breakfast meetings between Thatcher and like-minded newspaper editors.

Under New Labour there has been a burgeoning of political advisers and spin doctors. There has been a threefold increase in advisers, over a hundred being taken on since 1997 with a spiralling salary bill. Lord Waldegrave, giving evidence to Lord Neill's public standards inquiry, pointed to a 'new political apparatchik system equivalent to an alternative civil service'. Tony Blair is becoming the most prolific creator of life peers ever, having appointed more than two hundred since 1997. Patronage still remains an insidious part of British government and culture, and, with the wider culture of secrecy, places a question mark over democratic practice and accountability.

The lobby

The lobby is made up of some 250 journalists with privileged access to the corridors of power. Tunstall (1983: ch. 2) has outlined four types of access: off-the-record talks with MPs in the Commons lobby; receiving embargoed copies of official documents; attending regular briefings by press staff; and having permanent offices at Westminster. The price that journalists pay is in their collusion with a system which reinforces the culture of confidentiality and deference.

Lobby journalists do not write reports about the proceedings in Parliament. Rather, they provide background on current political issues, culled from ministerial briefings and gossip from MPs and press officials. Journalists become insiders, keeping their sources anonymous. Public documents, such as committee reports, are embargoed, with lobby journalists being given personal copies long before they are presented to Parliament.

A meeting of government information officers takes place every Thursday afternoon at the Cabinet Office, with the lead taken by the Prime Minister's chief press officer. Techniques involve ensuring that unwelcome news is managed in a way to reduce its damaging effect. No two ministers are allowed to announce unpopular measures on the same day, whereas bad news may be released on a strong news day when there are other important stories. Failing this, news can be released late on a Friday afternoon.

Every civil servant and journalist who has close links with Whitehall is subject to negative vetting. This involves an investigation by MI5 and Special Branch using the Criminal Record Computer of individuals' private lives, addresses, financial standing, politics and social views.

In March 2000 the prime minister's press secretary, Alastair Campbell, announced he would drop his anonymity when quoted speaking on behalf of the Prime Minister. In future briefings would be on the record and journalists could quote the prime minister's official spokesman (PMOS). This followed criticisms from press, radio and TV reporters about Campbell's unilateral decision to give access to Michael Cockerell to film lobby briefings as part of a BBC documentary programme. In other EU countries government spokespersons are often seen on TV. Campbell also put summaries of his briefings on Number 10's new website, suggesting that the purity of the government's message will be less likely to be filtered into hostile coverage by what Blair has called a 'negative media culture'.

Secrecy: the 'cover-up culture' of Britain

Linked to this centralisation of power is the secrecy which pervades British politics and the patronising assumption that the government knows best. Britain's culture of secrecy is buttressed by harsh libel laws, weak rights of access to official information, the Official Secrets Act and the D-Notice system. For local government a new cabinet system has allowed councillors to take decisions about education, social services and planning in much greater secrecy. People have lost their right to know compared with the previous system which required councils to take decisions at open meetings of the full council or its committees. The Terrorism Act 2000 went one step further in putting journalists in danger of arrest, search and questioning if they cover the activities of campaigning groups such as road protesters or environmentalist groups taking action against genetically modified (GM) crops.

The Regulation of Investigatory Powers Act 2000 further threatens journalists' sources and confidential information. The state is able to intercept email and telephone calls across private networks 'in the interests of the economic well-being of the United Kingdom'. This will be a powerful enhancement of what the Campaign for Freedom of Information has called 'the cover-up culture' of Britain.

Freedom of Information Act: BUT FREEDOM FOR WHOM?

An important innovation was the Freedom of Information Act which came into operation in January 2005. The Act was delayed for five years and was much watered down from the White Paper in 1997. In the 1996 Scott inquiry into arms for Iraq and the 2000 Phillips inquiry into BSE, effective government was seen to have been damaged by excessive departmental secrecy. For example, public health was threatened by the Department of Agriculture's failure to inform the Department of Health about potential health issues.

The new Act gives people a legally enforceable right to access information from ten thousand public bodies, including Parliament, government departments, local authorities and health trusts. However, ministers can veto requests if they believe disclosure would not be in the public interest. 'In most cases where information is exempted from disclosure there is a duty on public authorities to disclose where, in the view of the public authority, the public interest in disclosure outweighs the public interest in maintaining the exemption in question' (www.dca.gov.uk/foi/foiact).

A new office of information commissioner and a new Information Tribunal have been established to enforce rights. Each public body must draw up a scheme of publication approved by the commissioner. It is feared that departments will refuse access on public interest grounds. Moreover freedom of information campaigners were concerned after it became known that government departments had been eagerly destroying documents in the run-up to the legislation becoming law. For example, the number of files shredded nearly doubled in the Ministry of Defence. Some believed these files would no longer have been classified as confidential under the new Act – and so were destroyed.

10 All human life

Covering the courts

Mark Hanna

Stories of crime and the subsequent drama of court cases are the lifeblood of British newspapers. The front-page 'splash' of any newspaper is frequently a report of a criminal case. There are usually several reports of other cases, some brief, some long, on inside pages.

All types of human rashness, stupidity, greed, viciousness and malignancy are dissected in the courtroom, in a legal process framed and underpinned by human virtues – the bravery of police officers making a difficult arrest; the courage of testifying victims; the forensic ability of detectives, lawyers and judges; the commitment (in theory at least) to justice for all, including fairness to the accused.

What makes the best of these court reports so gripping, and therefore guarantees continuing media focus on crime and criminals, is that – perhaps more than in most other news stories – readers will imagine themselves standing in the shoes of those involved. How, in any serious case, would we have fared as victims in the same circumstances? Could we hope to avoid or defend ourselves from violence? Would we fall prey to fraud? Many of us fall prey to thieves.

We are all potential victims and witnesses, and potential offenders too. Most people's criminal potential is realised only in minor traffic offences. Yet a mundane car trip can flip into tragedy, making a thunderous story for journalists, yielding a morality tale for everyone. For example, in 2001 Gary Hart, aged 37, after staying up all night talking by telephone to a woman he had just 'met' on the internet, fell asleep next morning at the wheel of his Land Rover. It veered off the M62 motorway, down a bank and on to a railway track, where – shortly after he abandoned it to seek help – it was struck by a passenger express which, derailed, crashed into an oncoming coal train. Ten people died and there was a £30 million claim on his motor insurance. Hart, a construction company boss from Strubby, Lincolnshire, was sentenced to five years' jail for causing death by dangerous driving (Hall 2001; Wainright 2002; Clark 2004).

For media audiences, the court process is a layer of fascination in itself. In trials, quick-witted, adversarial lawyers unravel evidence in gentle questioning or fierce cross-examination of witnesses. This is real and, therefore, more powerful than any theatre. Anyone who has sat through a lengthy Crown Court trial knows the emotional charge generated as pain and suffering are recounted or lies are devastatingly nailed. That charge reaches new levels when, at last, the jury troops back from its private room to its courtroom seats to deliver a verdict. Court lore is that, if jurors have voted to convict, they do not meet the defendant's eyes while waiting for their foreman or forewoman to be asked to stand to announce their decision.

When the innocent (and, sometimes, not so innocent) are acquitted, reporters see their joy, their collapse in relief in the dock. When sexual predators are declared guilty, reporters may hear shouting from the offenders' victims, exultant in the public gallery as deep, corrosive anger is finally released. Reporters often seek, immediately after a murder trial ends, comment from relatives of the murdered, who – in their enduring grief – have some satisfaction to see the killer led, convicted, to the cells. It is in these raw, adrenalised moments that good journalists know they must coolly observe and listen, to gather compelling detail. A good journalist knows, too, that miscarriages of justice sometimes occur. The media should play a key role in exposing these.

Eyes and ears of the public

The idea that the media should be, in court, the wider public's eyes and ears, and therefore act as a watchdog scrutinising the police and the judicial system, is central to the concept of open justice. Courts must, in law, permit the public and press to be present during proceedings, unless there is an overriding reason to operate behind closed doors. Open justice is a main bulwark to protect the civil liberties enjoyed in democracies (Jaconelli 2002).

In a Court of Appeal case in 1998, the Lord Chief Justice, Lord Woolf, drawing on case law dating from 1913, listed reasons why legal proceedings should continue to take place in 'the full glare' of open court:

> It is necessary because the public nature of proceedings deters inappropriate behaviour on the part of the court. It also maintains the public's confidence in the administration of justice. It enables the public to know that justice is being administered impartially. It can result in evidence becoming available which would not become available if the proceedings were conducted behind closed doors or with one or more of the parties' or witnesses' identity concealed. It makes uninformed and inaccurate comment about the proceedings less likely. (Regina v Legal Aid Board, ex parte Kaim Todner, Court of Appeal (1999) QB 966)

Another benefit of open justice is that media reports from the courts provide fodder for public debate about the effectiveness of the police and the judiciary, and about social trends reflected in crime patterns and civil disputes. This triggers discussion about government policy on a wide range of issues. For various reasons, in Britain, where recorded rates of crime rose in the latter half of the twentieth century, the 'law and order' issue is, in particular, a key battleground in political controversy. A major study of British news stories in *The Times* and the *Mirror* from 1945 to 1991 showed that, until the mid-1960s, the overall percentage of stories primarily about crime averaged about 10 per cent in both papers, but that from the late 1960s the percentage doubled to around 21 per cent (Reiner, Livingstone and Allen 2000: 112; 2001: 183 and 2003: 13–32).

Of course, when making day-to-day decisions on what court cases to cover, news editors rarely consider their ethical duty to uphold the open justice principle. Their decisions are usually pragmatic, based on limited resources to deploy staff reporters or pay freelances, and commercial, based on which cases will most interest their audiences, and so maintain or increase their newspaper's sales. The seductive thrill of reading about some criminals' lifestyles, the frisson of fear engendered by crime reports, and the comfort provided by reports of justice done created much of the market demand in which our popular press evolved.

A multitude of crime 'pamphlets' flourished in the seventeenth and eighteenth centuries, describing – with great artistic licence – the lives of notorious thieves or murderers, to be sold at their execution or shortly afterwards (Chandler 1958: 139). By the early nineteenth century, murder and execution 'broadsides' were so popular that one – the 'last Dying Speech and Confession of William Corder, murderer of Maria Marten', published in 1828 – sold 1,166,000 copies (Anderson 1991: 25). In 1843, the first issue of the *News of the World*, a Sunday newspaper later to be dubbed a 'squalid recorder of squalid crime', included a front-page story headed 'Extraordinary charge of drugging and violation'. The motto of Lord Northcliffe – who in 1896 launched what is regarded as the first 'popular' daily newspaper, the *Daily Mail* – was 'Get me a murder a day!' (Bainbridge and Stockdill 1993: 13; Berrey 1933: 35; Williams 1998: 56).

The court system

All criminal prosecutions in England, Wales and Northern Ireland begin in the magistrates' courts and more than 95 per cent of cases are completed there, the majority being comparatively minor. The role of magistrates, also known as 'justices of the peace', to reach verdicts and impose punishment, is centuries old. Most are volunteers – ordinary citizens, selected as suitable, who for a few hours each week, without pay, help dispense justice in their communities. But some magistrates – those now called 'district judges' – are paid a salary. These are solicitors or barristers (in other words, trained lawyers), and deal with particularly complex cases. Magistrates also preside over Youth Courts, which deal with juveniles accused of crime. (See http://www.hmcourts-service.gov.uk/infoabout/magistrates/index.htm, accessed on 21 July 2005.)

The most serious cases – such as murder, rape, robbery – can be dealt with only at Crown Courts, and are sent there by the magistrates, either for trial or merely for sentence. Crown Court verdicts are decided by juries – citizens selected randomly from the electoral roll for that district. In English and Welsh trials there are 12 jurors.

Decisions on punishment and points of law are made by the Crown Court judges, who are trained lawyers.

The Scottish legal system has evolved independently, with different types of court. It, too, has juries (Bonnington, McInnes and McKain 2000).

The professional challenge of reporting the courts

When someone is charged with a newsworthy crime, news organisations will keep track of the case's progress by sending reporters to preliminary hearings at court, or by ringing the police or the Crown Prosecution Service. Most cases, of course, go unreported in the media. It is often pot luck what is covered.

In magistrates' courts, reporters can turn up early to scan the daily, computerised lists of cases. These give the defendants' names, addresses, the charges they face and other details. In Crown Courts written information about the day's cases is often confined to notices, pinned up on a general board or outside each courtroom, listing the defendants' names, case numbers, the presiding judge's name and the stage reached by each case.

A good reporter will sniff out interesting cases by being sufficiently personable, cheery and cheeky enough to gain help from the court community. Each courthouse has a network of officials and regular users such as the ushers (the personnel who fetch waiting defendants and witnesses into court), court clerks, lawyers, security guards, administrators and receptionists. Word of a pending case with an unusual twist may spread quickly among them. Occasionally, a reporter may find, in the public galleries of courthouses, ordinary citizens who regularly enjoy attending as visitors. These may have a good knowledge of cases awaiting trial, having sampled them in preliminary hearings. Harold Pearson, a retired coach-driver who, after he was widowed, visited Sheffield Crown Court regularly for 20 years, kept his own notes of pending trials which he often shared with curious journalists. He was so popular that on both his eightieth and ninetieth birthdays the courthouse threw a party for him, attended by judges, barristers, police, probation officers and court staff (Dawes 1999).

Media law: the ban on photographs

Court reporting is not a job for an amateur. Reporters need intensive training to avoid ending up in the dock themselves, with their editors, for breach of laws covering the media. Journalists face fines, and, in some circumstances, jail sentences if they break such law. For example, since an Act of Parliament in 1925 it has been illegal in England and Wales to take photographs (or to film) inside a courthouse or in its precincts. This ban was a response to the increasing use by journalists of discreet cameras, including a notorious incident in 1912 when the *Mirror* published a photograph, apparently taken covertly, of an Old Bailey judge passing a death sentence on a murderer. It was felt such photography distastefully pilloried defendants and witnesses (Stepniak 2003: 255–6; Jaconelli 2002: 315–40).

There has been *some* televising of British courts. Footage from trials in Scotland – where the ban on cameras is maintained by the judiciary, not by any statute – was broadcast with judges' consent as an experiment in 1994. Britain's highest appeal court, the House of Lords, has permitted TV to broadcast its proceedings. This poses few inherent problems because it has no juries and because witnesses rarely give evidence there in person. The Law Lords technically sit as a House of Lords committee, not covered by the 1925 Act. In 2004 the Government launched a pilot scheme to film in the Court of Appeal, and began consultations about what other types of courts might be televised (Department for Constitutional Affairs 2004; Stepniak 2003: 263–8) .

But it seems likely that, to avoid the problem of nervous witnesses (including crime victims) refusing to testify if they are to be televised, cameras will remain firmly banned from our lower courts, or else may be permitted there only during non-sensitive stages of cases, with strict conditions on what is broadcast. So the British public will continue to be denied, or spared, the 'court television' culture of America, where major trials (such as O. J. Simpson's acquittal in 1995 of murdering his wife) figure in the ratings war.

The British media, thus deprived of photographs or film from inside the courts, employ artists to produce sketches of the courtroom scene during newsworthy cases. But the same 1925 statute which prohibits cameras also bans sketching in the court itself, if the intent is publication. So these artists first make written notes to help them memorise, from the public gallery, the faces of defendants, witnesses, lawyers, the magistrates or judge, and then leave the courtroom to draw their sketches of the drama within.

Covering juveniles and sexual offences

Since 1933 it has been illegal, in most cases, for media reports to reveal the identities of juveniles (children aged under 18) concerned in Youth Court proceedings, as witnesses or defendants. In other types of court, magistrates or judges can use discretionary powers to grant a juvenile similar anonymity. It is also illegal for the media, in most cases, to identify victims and alleged victims of sexual or sex-related offences.

Contempt of Court

In addition to specific reporting restrictions, only some of which are referred to above, there is a raft of other law designed to ensure trials are fair, with verdicts determined only by the evidence presented in court. This law aims to prevent magistrates and potential or selected jurors being prejudiced by media reports. The 1981 Contempt of Court Act prohibits the publication of anything creating 'a substantial risk of serious prejudice or impediment' to 'active' proceedings. It severely limits, as soon as a person is arrested or sought by warrant or charged or summonsed, what background information can be published about them and the case, until the proceedings are complete. Therefore, if someone is potentially facing trial, it becomes dangerous, under contempt law, to publish references to any previous criminal convictions they have, because this could jeopardise their chance of a fair trial. Other statutes restrict, until the eventual trial is over, what can be reported contemporaneously from preliminary hearings.

Although trials can usually be reported freely as they take place, a court can, under the 1981 Act, order the media to postpone the reporting of all or part of a trial, to avoid prejudice to any linked trial yet to begin. Under the Courts Act 2003, a media breach of contempt law could, if it causes a trial to be abandoned, leave the publisher liable for the whole cost of the aborted trial, which – in a major case – could run into several million pounds. Contempt law also prohibits journalists from asking jurors how they voted in any trial. Reporters need to take legal advice before they consider revealing any juror's identity.

Libel

And then there is libel law. The basic rule – to promote the concept of open justice – is that the media are safe, under libel law, to report anything said as part of proceedings in open court, no matter how damaging any such allegation may be to anyone's reputation, provided that the report is a fair and accurate reflection of what was said (and obeys any reporting restriction in force).

Fair and accurate reports of such court cases, published contemporaneously (in the next edition of a daily or weekly newspaper, for instance), are covered in law by 'absolute privilege'. This defence against a libel action remains valid whatever motive the journalist and publisher have in airing the case. Such privilege means that the media can safely report, from the courts, that someone is accused of a crime, whether a parking offence or a murder, and the unfolding of evidence in court. So it is also safe, as regards libel, to report that a witness is alleged in open court to be lying, or that a policeman is accused in open court of faking evidence, provided the report is fair and accurate.

If such a report is not contemporaneous, but is published weeks, months or years after the court case ends, then it is still protected from libel actions. But the protection is then under another defence – 'qualified privilege'. This means it must not be published maliciously.

Fairness

It is, obviously, impossible to include, in a media report, everything said in a court hearing. But a fair report is sufficiently balanced – so readers are not misled. As regards a criminal case, this will involve presenting elements of both prosecution and defence evidence and arguments. In a lengthy trial, some days are dominated by the prosecution case, then later days dominated by defence evidence. Media reports should, while inevitably reflecting the stage of the case, continue to indicate that nothing is proven until the verdict. A report which accurately quotes the prosecution's opening speech but omits the fact that the defendant denies the charge would not be fair. For the same reason, a reporter, when covering an ongoing trial, must make clear, in each report until the verdict, that the case is still running, to indicate that evidence is still open to challenge. This can be done simply by stating, at the end of each report: 'The trial continues.'

What is fair and balanced depends on the circumstances of each case, and what is said in each session in court. For example:

> Farmer Joe Bloggs turned his shotgun on his sheepdog, blasting it in his kitchen, leaving the collie to bleed to death in agony. Bloggs, aged 45, of Bloggs Farm, Heavytown, admitted causing cruelty to an animal. Magistrates fined him £500.

If a morning newspaper reported this, but failed to report what was also said in court the previous day – that Bloggs shot the persistently barking dog when grieving, drunk and depressed after his only child died of leukaemia – then Bloggs could probably successfully sue for libel, despite his conviction for cruelty, because the mitigating circumstances of this family tragedy had not been aired, making the report unfair. (The character Farmer Bloggs, and all details in this hypothetical case, and all names and details in examples of reports used hereafter in this chapter, are fictitious, and are not intended to allude in any way to real cases or real people.)

But the law on fairness in court reporting is not totally clear. The authors of the famous textbook *McNae's Essential Law for Journalists* advise: 'The safest journalistic practice is that if the newspaper has reported allegations made by the prosecutor that are later rebutted those rebuttals should also be carried' (Welsh and Greenwood 2003: 260–1). A particular libel danger is to suggest in a media report, by unfairness or inaccuracy, that an *acquitted* defendant is really guilty.

Accuracy

A mistake, exaggeration, distortion or avoidable ambiguity in a court report could leave the publisher exposed to libel action by someone whose reputation was thereby affected, including the defendant. As each court case involves damaging allegations, reporters cannot be slipshod. They will find it hard to operate fairly, accurately and effectively – certainly in proceedings of any length – without shorthand of at least 100 words per minute. Tape recorders, or any types of recording equipment, are (almost always) not permitted in court, under contempt law. Notebooks should be stored safely for at least a year after a case ends. If the reporter thinks that further reference to the court case could be made later – for instance, as background in future stories – the notebook should be kept until and well beyond that time. Each time material from a court case is published, anyone claiming they have been libelled has a further 12 months in which to begin a libel action, whatever the date of the actual case.

To safeguard against the risk of a libel action, a report of an ongoing court case should not present the allegations made in it as being straight facts. These are matters in dispute. The report should make this clear by attributing each allegation to whoever made it, though – in a newspaper story's intro – it is safe to use the tagged-on phrase 'a court heard' or 'a jury was told' if the next paragraphs quickly reveal who made the allegation. For example:

> A farmer cruelly shot his sheepdog when he lost his temper over its barking, Heavytown magistrates heard.
> Joe Bloggs watched his collie Rover die in agony from the shotgun blast, said prosecution barrister Dick Emery.

In a lengthy court report, to attribute each statement directly (with phrases such as 'Mr Emery said . . .', 'he added') can leave the copy clogged up stylistically. Attribution can be achieved indirectly. If one sentence is not attributed but is sandwiched between other allegations made by the same person which *are* clearly attributed, then this may be safe. It depends on the context of each case, and the report's total effect. Alternatively, the reporter can attribute indirectly by using the grammatical convention of 'reported speech'. This involves shifting the tense of the verbs back in time; for example, shifting a verb in the present tense into the past tense.

Thus, a witness called Evans says, in the present tense: 'John Smith is always messing about when drunk. But he never carries a knife and is always very polite to strangers'. This can be rendered as a mixture of directly and indirectly attributed reported speech:

> Smith was always messing about when drunk, Mr Evans said.
> But Smith never carried a knife and was always polite to strangers.

Indirect attribution should not run over several sentences. Direct attribution must be inserted frequently to remind readers that trial evidence is not proven. If the speaker is using the past tense, that tense should be shifted back, in reported speech indirectly attributed, to the pluperfect tense. For example:

> A farmer cruelly shot his sheepdog when he lost his temper over its barking, Heavytown magistrates heard.
>
> Joe Bloggs watched his collie Rover die in agony from the shotgun blast, said prosecution barrister Dick Emery.
>
> Bloggs had then kicked the dog's corpse, and had buried it in the flower-bed.
>
> A neighbour had witnessed the burial, and Bloggs had confessed to the police that he shot the dog.
>
> 'But Bloggs lied, saying the dog was attacking him,' Mr Emery added.

Grammatical convention for indirect attribution is not always correctly followed in newspapers. Perhaps this problem is perennial. In his autobiography, the veteran investigative reporter Phillip Knightley (1997: 20) describes how, in the 1950s, a subeditor colleague was so maddened by a 30-minute lecture on the pluperfect that he grabbed a painting from the wall and smashed it over the pedantic editor's head. The subeditor was fired.

When a defendant admits the crime, or is convicted in a trial, there is no longer any need to attribute the crime allegation to anyone. It is now proven. But care must still be taken to attribute any evidence or argument which goes beyond what is proved by an admission or verdict, especially any allegation which affects the reputation of people other than the defendant – for instance, witnesses.

Journalists must remain accurate when trying to summarise charges. It would be libellous to report that someone is accused of *reckless driving* when the charge is, in fact, the lesser offence of *careless driving.*

A great danger of libel arises if a media report fails to include sufficient, available information to identify accurately the defendant and anyone else subject to defamatory allegations in the case. If you publish that 'Arthur Brown of Rotherham' is accused of indecent assault, every other Arthur Brown in Rotherham may be able to sue you for the libellous suggestion that they may be a molester, if they can prove that acquaintances could have reasonably thought the report referred to the Arthur Brown they know.

So media reports should include, as well as the defendant's name, their age, street address and occupation, as stated on the court list or in the proceedings or are officially made available by the court clerk. If you have gleaned such details merely from the court list, check, when listening in court, that these details are accepted there as correct. Similarly, you should always fully identify, in your report, any other person or organisation mentioned by name in the court proceedings, by including sufficient details officially given out by, or stated publicly in, the court. This reduces the risk of a libel claim from anyone or any organisation with a similar name.

If a document is referred to in court evidence, it is safe to quote from it as regards the material read out in open court. But a report of any other part of the same document which is *not* read out in open court (perhaps because a judge has ruled that part is inadmissible as evidence) is *not* privileged, even if a witness or lawyer helpfully shows it to you. Publishing such material could, if it defames someone, lead to a successful libel action. Similarly, quoting anyone about a case, even a lawyer involved, will *not* be protected by privilege if the comment was made outside of the court proceedings, e.g. in an interview in a corridor outside the courtroom.

The ethical journalist

Irrespective of legal restraints, journalists have ethical responsibilities in court reporting. The Code of Practice of the Press Complaints Commission states that journalists should not identify any victim of a sex attack, even in rare cases when the law permits it, unless there is adequate ethical justification. There is an ethical, as well as a legal, obligation to be fair and accurate.

Ethical duties go beyond codes. Journalists should not suggest crime in any community is worse than it actually is. Factors which create some people's overanxious 'fear of crime' are complex (Reiner, Livingstone and Allen 2000). But the media should ensure that exceptionally unpleasant crimes are not presented as any kind of norm.

Making detail work for you

In reports of preliminary hearings in criminal cases, legal restrictions usually prevent the airing of evidence, so information which can be conveyed from them is fairly basic. But in reports of sentencings or ongoing trials the intro should be a snapshot of the most newsworthy points of the case, and contain gripping detail to project a vivid verbal picture.

Which of these intros interests you most?

> The Crown Court trial has begun of an 18-year-old Heavytown man who allegedly murdered his mother.

Or this one?

> A teenager cut off his mother's head with an axe after she complained his room was untidy, a jury has heard.

The latter version has stark detail and contains a chilling contrast – the immensity of the alleged violence compared with the mundane nature of the alleged cause. Ideally, you use an active construction in an intro – someone doing something to someone else. Don't weaken your intro by overloading it with minor facts or subordinate clauses.

Imagine that the following, invented story – about an alleged swindler Jeremiah Tankard – is a court report in the mythical Heavytown's evening paper.

> A pub landlord swindled £250,000 from his customers and squandered all the money on prostitutes and gambling, a jury heard.
>
> Jeremiah Tankard, posing as a gemstone expert, persuaded 18 of his pub's regulars to speculate in diamonds, Heavytown Crown Court was told.
>
> Tankard, having got cheques from them, claimed he was off to Amsterdam to buy them diamonds, but instead visited London brothels and casinos, indulging in a 'massive spending spree', said prosecuting barrister Alfie Heren.
>
> Tankard, aged 45, of the Sparkly Arms pub, Facet Road, Heavyville, denies 18 charges of obtaining money by deception.

Notice how its intro hopes to seize the readers' gaze. The attention-grabbing allegations are succinctly elaborated and sufficiently attributed, in the second and third paragraphs. Without slowing narrative pace, other details are filtered into the copy, to state which court this is, and who is being quoted.

The story's fourth paragraph makes absolutely clear that Tankard denies the allegations. It accurately summarises them. The full wording of each charge, specifying the money allegedly obtained from each alleged victim, should be in the reporter's notebook, so they can justify this summary.

Once you, as a reporter, have drafted an intro and the early paragraphs, it is usually a good idea, to give readers context, to begin to set the alleged events in a clearer chronological order. The story could continue:

> In 2002 Tankard had arrived in Heavyville after buying the pub. He quickly grew friendly with local people, impressing them by running fund-raising events for the village school, Mr Heren said.
>
> Tankard's respectable image had led to him being voted on to the parish council.
>
> 'But Mr Tankard is really a charlatan without much conscience. Having won the trust of his village neighbours, he set out to exploit them with bogus talk of diamonds.
>
> 'He dishonestly lavished £250,000 of other people's money on his own selfish pleasures in vice-girls and roulette,' Mr Heren added.

Use of such direct (i.e. verbatim) quotations makes court copy lively, if the quotes have sharp focus or otherwise add a flourish. But verbose, rambling statements should be succinctly and fairly paraphrased, to keep the narrative brisk.

This court story is based mainly on the prosecuting opening of the case, in which the prosecution barrister – to help the jury gain quick understanding – outlines the main evidence against the defendant. But the need for journalistic fairness means that the newspaper's report should include indication of Tankard's apparent defence, if this is possible so early in coverage of this trial. For example, the story could conclude:

> One of the pub's customers, builder Ivor Packet, of Stash Street, Heavyville, told the court he handed £10,000 to Tankard in August 2003. 'Jeremiah told me his dad used to run a jewellery business, and that all his own family were busy putting all their money into diamonds, because diamond prices were soon to boom.'
>
> Cross-examined by Tankard's barrister Sheila Wigg, Mr Packet agreed he had not declared all his savings to the Inland Revenue, and that he had no receipt to prove he gave any money to Tankard. 'He was a mate. I trusted him. It was cash I had put away for a rainy day.'
>
> The trial continues.

For many newspapers, the convention is to deny a defendant any courtesy title – for instance, Mr, Mrs, or Ms – unless and until they are acquitted. Each media organisation has its own style conventions.

When major trials end, newspapers run background articles to accompany reports of the verdicts. Such 'backgrounders' remind readers of evidence given earlier in the case, discuss wider issues thrown up by the trial, and air material which contempt law prevented being published earlier, such as information about any previous crimes of the defendant. Usually, two versions of the backgrounder will have been prepared – one for use if the defendant is convicted, the other in the event of acquittal.

Other types of court

The legal and ethical principles of reporting from the criminal courts apply, in the main, to coverage of other types of court – for example, coroners' courts, the civil courts and family courts. Coroners hold inquests into certain types of death, and hold hearings to decide if ancient objects found by the public should be classed as 'treasure', and so be offered to museums.

In civil cases, heard in the county courts or High Courts, one party is suing another; for example, a former patient is suing a hospital or doctor after alleged medical negligence, claiming damages for suffering or injury allegedly caused. Again, allegations and evidence must be fairly and accurately reported, sufficiently attributed. If the parties agree an out-of-court settlement (i.e. to avoid more legal costs, they reach a financial deal in the case, so making the court's judgement unnecessary) this should not be reported as if the party being sued accepts liability, unless liability is definitely admitted. Otherwise, there could be libel problems.

In family proceedings, such as those concerning the upbringing of children, and possibly the intervention of social workers, there are – almost always – reporting restrictions preventing the media identifying any child (aged under 18) who is involved. The public are, by law, excluded from such hearings. Reporters may be allowed to attend, depending on the type of case.

The future of court reporting

In recent years, cost-cutting reductions in the number of reporters in newsrooms have undoubtedly led to fewer journalists attending court cases. As yet, there is little data available to quantify the decline in the number, and diversity, of court cases featured in the media, or how changes in news values may have contributed to this. But freelances complain that national news editors are interested only in the most sensational cases, or those involving a celebrity (Davies 1999, Skentelbery 2000).

Often journalists, juggling their work commitments, can merely dip in and out of a lengthy criminal trial, attending only at key stages, such as the prosecution opening. Media law experts Geoffrey Robertson and Andrew Nicol have condemned this trend, in which reporters only return 'vulture-like' for the verdict. 'If there is an acquittal, a newspaper will sometimes not even bother to report it, or will mention the matter without giving it anything like the prominence accorded to the discredited opening statement. This is *not* fair reporting' (2002: 487).

Increasing court usage of reporting restrictions is cited as another factor in the decline in court reporting (Battle 2003, Byrne 2003). Few journalists object to children, sex crime victims or blackmail victims being granted anonymity. But some recent laws seem to have been created primarily for politicians to be seen as supporting the rights of crime victims. Law which came into effect in 2004 gives each court discretion to rule that an adult witness must not be identified by the media, if the court feels that the quality of that witness's evidence, or his/her level of co-operation with the court, would be diminished by 'fear or distress'. But does great good result from such witnesses enjoying anonymity in the media, when the defendant (in all but the most exceptional cases) has a legal right to know who they are – if he or she does not know already – and is therefore able, anyway, to tell intimidating cronies who the witness is?

Each new reporting restriction undermines the open justice principle, making it harder for the media to produce interesting court stories. Ensuring anonymity for protected witnesses or victims means the reporter must exclude any evidential detail which could identify them, not just their name and address. Faced with such enforced self-censorship – with the risk of a court fine and professional embarrassment for the newspaper if a young reporter mistakenly includes too much – a news editor's instinct may well be to ignore 'difficult' cases altogether. (Against the general trend of and increase in reporting restrictions, since 1997 successive governments have passed laws to give the media greater opportunities to identify, 'in the public interest', persistent juvenile offenders, juveniles who commit serious crime and juveniles who have anti-social behaviour orders imposed on them.)

This reduction in court coverage diminishes journalists' ability to inform our society of the consequences of social division and of policy failures. The investigative reporter Nick Davies (1999) has warned:

The cases that flow through the courts reflect the tensions of the society around them, its poverty or racism or inequality; they present pictures of everyday anger and despair; they may reveal corruption and injustice in their preparation. Without publicity, these issues can be lost.

11 Investigative reporting

The times they are a-changin'?

Nick Nuttall

Investigative journalism enjoys a high reputation with the public. Its practitioners, along with the war correspondent, have become mythologised as titans of their trade – fearless, glamorous, noble, often reckless, always on the side of the 'people'. Strange, then, that at the beginning of the twenty-first century this reputation is contested territory – no one is really sure whether investigative reporting is in a healthy state or verging on extinction.

The clamour for a return to 'traditional' journalistic standards in the aftermath of the Gilligan 'affair' which exploded after the BBC *Today* reporter quoted an anonymous source on 29 May 2003 that a 'senior British official' had told him the British government's dossier on Iraq had been 'transformed in the week before it was published to make it sexier' and build a stronger case for war. The anonymous source turned out to be Dr David Kelly who, having been 'outed' by the government, went on to commit suicide. And Lord Hutton's subsequent report is considered by many journalists to be a thinly disguised attempt to muzzle the investigative impulse and return news agendas once more to the safe and non-confrontational. To such journalists these recent upheavals are just another example of a pernicious trend. Phillip Knightley, one of the world's most distinguished investigative journalists, noted one aspect of this trend in his February 2003 address on 'The Death of Investigative Journalism and Who Killed It' (2003: 7):

> All over the Western world, journalists, who should have been up in arms about the downgrading of foreign news, were bought off. Many became highly-paid columnists, celebrities in their own right, pushing their opinions rather than gathering facts. Or writers about lifestyle, relationships, gossip, travel, beauty, fashion, gardening and do-it-yourself which, although sometimes interesting in themselves, can hardly compare in importance with examining the human condition at the beginning of the 21st century, which is what serious journalists try to do.

And he concluded with some consternation: 'Investigative journalism is not dead yet, just moribund.'

The 'healthy state' exponents on the other hand offer a more sanguine critique of its status, although even here a note of ambivalence often creeps in. Deborah Chambers declares: 'Investigative journalism has been flourishing in the last three decades of the twentieth century' (De Burgh 2000: 89) whilst acknowledging also that 'there is evidence to suggest that the conditions that led to this boom are now changing' (2000: 104). The great investigative coups of the postwar years and particularly those carried out by the *Sunday Times*'s Insight team under the editorships of Denis Hamilton and Harold Evans, are usually cited in evidence:

- the Profumo affair (1963) which destroyed the career of a Cabinet minister and arguably helped bring down the Conservative government the following year (Knightley and Kennedy 1987)
- the Poulson scandal (1970) where politicians were bribed by architect John Poulson to award him lucrative building contracts. Paul Foot used *Private Eye* to highlight the work of local journalist Ray Fitzwalter in uncovering the scandal. It resulted in Poulson's bankruptcy and imprisonment and the resignation of the then Home Secretary Reginald Maudling (Tomkinson 1973; Fitzwalter and Taylor 1981)
- the Insight campaign begun in 1972 on behalf of the Thalidomide children. Distillers, the giant drinks conglomerate, made the drug Thalidomide under licence and marketed it as a safe anti-morning-sickness pill for pregnant women. Yet the drug wasn't safe as Phillip Knightley, one of the team assigned to the story, recalled in his autobiography, *A Hack's Progress*: 'Thalidomide crossed the placental barrier and with devilish precision sabotaged the developing limb buds of the foetus, so that children were born with hands emerging direct from their shoulders, and feet emerging direct from their hips and, in a few horrific cases, with both abnormalities' (1997: 156). Ultimately, Distillers compensated affected children to the tune of £28.4 million
- the DC-10 Paris air crash (1974) which killed 346 passengers and crew. As Harold Evans noted in *Good Times, Bad Times*: 'They died violently because the DC-10 had a lie in it' (1983: 27). The 'lie' was that a faulty door mechanism had not been modified adequately and the door blew off at altitude. Planemaker McDonnell Douglas eventually paid $62 million in compensation
- the *Guardian*'s reporting of the 'Cash for Questions' scandal (1994), in which MPs were paid £2,000 a time to ask questions in Parliament, effectively finishing the careers of two MPs and arguably tolling the death-knell of the Major government (De Burgh 2000: 56)
- and the long investigation by the *Guardian* into the expenses claims of government minister Jonathan Aitken (1994–9) which resulted in his eventual disgrace and imprisonment on perjury charges (Leigh and Vulliamy 1997; Spark 1999: 107–13)

There is much to be proud of in this long tradition, but the changing nature of modern journalism, its fragmentation, its cost-consciousness, its relentless pursuit of 'entertainment', is probably to blame for the more intimate ambitions of the modern investigative reporter. As Tessa Mayes, an award-winning journalist with extensive experience in both print and broadcast media, noted in a talk to Lincoln University students in November 2003:

Investigative journalism today is more concerned with a human interest approach to stories. When I worked as an undercover reporter in brothels on a story about eastern European girls who were illegal immigrants and were forced to work as prostitutes, the programme-makers wanted to concentrate on my emotions as a reporter and the women's feelings at the expense of analysing the subject more broadly.

What's it all about, Alfie?

Alfred Harmsworth, inventor of the modern press when he published the *Daily Mail* in 1896 and then the *Daily Mirror* in 1903, was quite clear about investigative journalism. He defined it as his 'talking points', stories designed to reflect readers' concerns on a day-to-day basis and thus not driven by or dependent on routine news agendas. Rather than just responding to events, the investigative journalist hijacks the news agenda on behalf of his or her readers. 'Cash for Questions' had nothing to do with the news agenda of the day until the *Guardian* broke the story, but it's generally accepted that this story, along with the 'Arms to Iraq' affair (De Burgh 2000: 292–8) and the Jonathan Aitken scandal were all significant in the defeat of John Major's government in 1997.

Naturally enough the power wielded by such journalism regularly causes alarm among the wider political and judicial classes. Lord Hutton, for example, is just the latest in a long line of judges who have excoriated the news media for failing to live up to some standard of probity probably more mythical than real. And the journalists' defence against all such charges has traditionally been the one-word battering ram – objectivity. Yet here again there are dissenting voices – from Martin Bell (1998) with his 'journalism of attachment', the idea that a journalist cannot remain neutral or objective when confronted by unspeakable evil, to the concerns of such eminent journalists as Paul Foot who was more interested in facts – unvarnished, unassailable, unalterable – rather than arcane discussion on the objectivity/subjectivity conundrum (De Burgh 2000: 77). Yet even facts, in the hands of a skilled practitioner, can tell a story in different ways merely by their selection or omission or by the context in which they are presented.

Despite these issues there is still a need to define the genre, at least from a vocational perspective, and to offer a more robust and forensic definition than Alfred Harmsworth's a century ago. David Spark (1996: 6) suggests the following:

> Investigative reporting seeks to gather facts which someone wants suppressed. It seeks not just the obvious informants who will be uncontroversial, or economical with the truth, but the less obvious who know about disturbing secrets and are angry or disturbed enough to divulge them.

Spark here touches on an important principle of investigative reporting: 'obvious informants' are not always the best or most reliable sources of information. John Pilger, too, alludes to this in his 2004 anthology of investigative journalism *Tell Me No Lies*. He recalls how Martha Gellhorn, doyenne of female war reporters, explained her technique to him: 'All I did was report from the ground up, not the other way round' (2004a: 1). In other words voices not normally heard are unearthed by intrepid journalists such as Gellhorn partly because such journalists understand that in any great organisation, whether public or private, you can probably learn more about what is really going on from the doorman than from the CEO.

What's the story?

It's important, then, to distinguish between true investigative journalism and the bogus stuff that often masquerades as the real thing. There's a lot of it about. But what is the difference? Usefully, the Press Complaints Commission (PCC) fleshes out a concept of 'The public interest' in its Code of Practice. This provides a series of ethical standards journalists are expected to follow, especially in stories concerning privacy, harassment, children, children in sex cases, hospitals, reporting of crime, and payment to criminals. However, there can be exceptions to these standards when the public interest is involved. Accordingly, the public interest includes, but is not confined to:

- detecting or exposing crime or serious impropriety
- protecting public health and safety
- preventing the public from being misled by an action or statement of an individual or organisation.

Furthermore the Code of Conduct of the National Union of Journalists (NUJ) states in Clause 5: 'A journalist shall obtain information, photographs and illustrations only by straightforward means. The use of other means can be justified only by over-riding consideration of the public interest.'

Editors and journalists alike have defended most of the following as legitimate examples of investigative journalism in 'the public interest'. Though typical of current offerings in the national press, few of them would pass the PCC and NUJ codes.

Sleazy does it

The story with no discernible public interest In 1994 the *News of the World* ran a story about the new Bishop of Durham being conditionally discharged by Hull magistrates for a gay sex act 26 years previously. The information was obtained from court records but it is questionable whether the public interest was served by running the story so long after the event.

Chequebook journalism

Kiss-and-tell Footballer Gary Flitcroft met 'C' in a public bar and had an affair with her in November 2001. 'C' sold her story to the *Sunday People*. Flitcroft (identified only as 'A' at this stage) obtained an injunction preventing Mirror Group Newspapers from publishing details of the affair. The Court of Appeal overturned this decision, ruling that a public figure had no right to block a newspaper's publication of 'kiss-and-tell' stories about his infidelities. The judge commented that Flitcroft was inevitably a figure in whom a section of the public and the media would be interested. Similarly, in April 2004, David Beckham was the target of a 'kiss-and-tell' exposé by Rebecca Loos, his former PA, who reputedly received £350,000 from the *News of the World* for her disclosure of their affair (Kelso 2004).

The sting

An individual is set up for a fall Sophie, Countess of Wessex, was invited to a meeting in February 2001 with an Arab she hoped to do business with. Unknown to her, the 'Arab' was *News of the World* reporter Mazher Mahmood, carrying a secret tape recorder and video camera. He recorded indiscreet comments about the royal family by the Countess, and 'Sophiegate' was born. Suggestions of her using her royal connections to further her PR business interests ultimately led to a change in royal protocol and the withdrawal of both the Earl and Countess from their private business interests. Once again there seems to be no public interest defence in this 'manufactured' story, just one example of many Mahmood stings. Others include his entrapment of various celebrities for 'supplying' drugs – *London's Burning* actor John Alford (1997), *Blue Peter* presenter Richard Bacon (1998) and Radio 2 DJ Johnnie Walker (1999).

Undercover agent

The journalist assumes a different identity to get the story In November 2003, *Mirror* reporter Ryan Parry used bogus references to get a job at Buckingham Palace as a footman. He was there during President Bush's visit and this exposed serious flaws in the royals' security arrangements. A few months previously Parry had infiltrated Wimbledon as a Securicor security guard, again using false references. Within two hours of starting work he was 'protecting' championship favourite Serena Williams. In both these cases there was a clear public interest in the information seeing the light of day.

Facts, facts, facts

The classic investigative story based on facts established by the journalist In October 2004, John Pilger exposed the fate of the islanders of Diego Garcia, a British colony in the Indian Ocean, midway between Africa and Asia, in a report for the *Express* (which accompanied an ITV investigative broadcast on the same theme) (2004c). In 1966, the islanders were forcibly shipped off to Mauritius to make way for an American military base. They have never been allowed to return. In 2000, the High Court ruled their expulsion illegal but the British government invoked a 'royal prerogative' decree banning the islanders from ever returning. Pilger, describing the British government's actions as a 'crime against humanity', used information from files found in the National Archives in Washington and the Public Record Office in London as well as interviews with the islanders. Investigative journalism as a genre requires no further justification.

Analysis of social surrogacy: THE ULTIMATE ASSIGNMENT?

Sunday Times, 8 July 2001
Career women 'rent' wombs to beat hassle of pregnancy
Tessa Mayes

A fertile 35-year-old business executive with three children hired another woman to carry her fourth child because she did not want to jeopardise her career.

The £43,000 procedure was organised by Conceptual Options, a private clinic in California. It not only enabled the woman to have her own fertilised egg implanted in a surrogate mother, but also allowed her to prearrange the sex of the baby.

'I want a daughter, but I don't want it to affect my career,' said the woman, who already has three sons aged five, six and nine.

An increasing number of women are 'renting' wombs for reasons of time pressure and vanity, with clinics in Britain as well as in the United States being asked to provide the service.

Successful businesswomen, actresses, athletes and models are among those opting for 'social surrogacy'. They cite career pressure, the pain of childbirth and the prospect of stretchmarks as the main reasons for avoiding pregnancy.

Theresa Erickson, a lawyer for Conceptual Options, said: 'It's not for us to judge why people do not want to carry a baby, although I have turned people away. Women can just say, "I need a surrogate", and doctors won't force her to allow them to check her fertility.'

Paul Serhal, medical director at the Assisted Conception Unit affiliated to University College Hospital London (UCL), said he was recently approached by an actress in her thirties.

'She was concerned about stretchmarks and wanted a surrogate to carry a baby produced from her egg and her partner's sperm,' Serhal said last week. 'If she came back, I would ask for the issues to be considered by the hospital ethics committee.'

The Los Angeles-based Egg Donation and Surrogacy Programme said that 5%–10% of surrogacy requests are for social rather than medical reasons. It added that nearly half of those are from men who do not want their wives to go through the physical endurance of pregnancy. Recent cases include:

- A Hollywood actress who hired a surrogate mother to carry a baby created from her egg and her lover's sperm. The surrogate had to sign a confidentiality agreement and, according to the clinic, 'probably did it for the money'.
- A model who approached a clinic in the American state of Georgia for a surrogate because she feared that a normal pregnancy would lower her income while she carried the baby.
- An American university professor who approached lawyers in Chicago to find out if she could have a social surrogacy. According to one lawyer close to the case she was worried about losing her tenure at the university if she became pregnant herself.

Cases of healthy women using surrogate mothers for social reasons are likely to anger campaigners for traditional families who believe that advances in fertility treatment have already gone too far.

These opening pars of a feature illustrate many facets of what might be termed 'issue-driven' investigative reporting, a genre that's become increasingly important in recent years. Not so much concerned with the exposure of wrongdoing, its main characteristics are a clear public interest element, an important moral or ethical question, and an angle that aims to illuminate and hopefully add to the public debate on the issue.

This investigation started as a general enquiry into new types of help available for infertile women who wished to have children and in particular what fees couples were paying clinics to help them achieve their 'dream' families through sex selection. In the UK, rules about sex selection are strict – IVF doctors are not allowed to select and implant embryos on the basis of gender. However, as reported in the *Sunday Times* on 7 October, 2001, under the headline 'Couples fly out for designer babies', British couples were jetting to America to have the procedure done anyway (Harlow 2001). Mayes decided to cold-call fertility clinics to find out what these couples were asking for.

It was while she was talking to these clinics that a new angle emerged. Mayes recalls: 'As I was chatting to a clinic director in California I was told that some women were too busy to have their own children and paid for surrogates . . . These women had social reasons for surrogacy, a new departure for the fertility industry which is used to having people approach them because they are infertile.' Calling other clinics confirmed this was no wild rumour. Several clinics put the phone down on Mayes while some confirmed they had, indeed, received such requests while others confirmed they provided such a service. So what began as an investigation into one fertility trend ended up as an investigation of another – women seeking 'social surrogacy'. It was also the first time this issue had been written about in Britain.

Issue-driven journalism in less subtle hands can easily become campaigning journalism, which, although it has an honourable heritage of its own, should not be confused with traditional investigative reporting. Whether journalists see themselves riding a white charger to the rescue of the public interest or lying in the gutter and looking at the stars is a matter of personal preference or inclination. Ultimately, however, moral indignation is a poor substitute for perseverance, analysis and a bit of luck.

WWW trouble: THE WORLD WIDE WEB AND THE INTERNET

Key the words 'investigative journalism' into a search engine such as Google and you'll get around 150,000 hits. Add the words '+UK' and the number falls to about 20,000. If each of these 'UK' sites was investigated for five minutes during a typical working day it would take one year to look at them all. This startling 'fact' perhaps best illustrates both the strength and the weakness of the internet. On the one hand it is potentially a huge resource only a click away. On the other hand there is often too much information and much of it is incorrect, useless or both.

Despite this the internet has become indispensable to journalists and newsrooms alike. Used intelligently it saves time and can occasionally produce spectacular results. For the investigative journalist there are a number of sites that can speed up research and can offer a simple and inexpensive way of getting information that would otherwise require visits to libraries, government offices such as HMSO, Companies House or other specialist organizations dotted around the country. But this requires an understanding not only of how it works but also of the limitations of the web itself.

A word of warning: The internet is constantly changing and mutating. No textbook or guide can hope to keep pace with its electronic momentum. What is correct today may well be out of date tomorrow. Sites are discontinued and new sites appear with frightening speed. Information, however beguiling, on any site last updated more than three months previously should be treated with extreme caution. For the investigative journalist, therefore, corroboration of all but the most basic or trivial information is essential.

Before looking at the way it works, however, a couple of words on terminology. The internet and the World Wide Web are not the same thing. The internet is a network of computers linked to each other for the purpose of exchanging information. The name is simply a contraction of '*inter*national *net*work'. There are three main elements: email, Usenet newsgroups and the World Wide Web. For journalists, the World Wide Web is the most useful research tool and it relies on the simple concept of hypertext links, those clickable words or phrases that interconnect pages on the web. And there are essentially three methods of searching on the web – keying in the web address or URL (uniform resource locator) if this is known, such as www.lincoln.ac.uk, using a search engine (such as Google) or navigating by clicking on the hypertext links embedded within websites. In practice most journalists use all three.

Keeping your secrets

As soon as you log on to the internet you leave an electronic trace of your activities so it's sensible to get some protection. Minimise the chances of being discovered by taking some basic precautions – especially important if you don't want to alert someone to your activities or the investigation is of a particularly sensitive nature.

• Install a firewall. Microsoft Windows has one built into its system but it is worthwhile downloading free firewall software from a site such as zonelabs.com. Firewalls protect your system from potential hackers by filtering information coming through your internet connection. Thus snoopers will find it more difficult to read or modify your files.

• Surf the net by proxy. Products like Anonymizer (www.anonymizer.com) enable you to shield your IP address and protect you from on-line tracking, SPAM harvesting, hackers and snoops. Your surfing is encrypted, your IP address hidden, thus allowing you to hide your tracks effectively.

• Set up a new email address for each search and ensure it cannot be traced back to you by the account name (the bit before the @) or the domain name (the bit after the @). Domain names can be customised, e.g. teacher.com, and could thus offer a clue to the owner. For free email providers look at sites such as www.emailaddresses.com or www.internetemaillist.com.

If you have serious reason to believe you are being or may be stalked on the net, or if you're just paranoid, consider also the following:

• Ensure only the intended recipient can read your message or file. For a small charge download encryption software from sites such as www.pgp.com. This is the PrettyGoodPrivacy programme which comes in a variety of packages from email protection alone to full system protection.

• Access your email account from a computer not traceable directly to you, for example, from a cybercafé. Snoopers could trace the location of the computer you are sending messages from, but if you're away from your home or work address and have not been caught on camera, they cannot tell who you are.

- Pay-as-you-talk mobiles make it harder for snoopers to tell who is using the handset, especially if you do not register your SIM card.
- To be absolutely certain of your privacy you should avoid all forms of electronic communication. Not feasible as a standard modus operandi but at sensitive moments in an investigation it might be better to pass on information directly or to handwrite messages.

Searching the web

Going straight to a website if you have the address is simple enough. But if you aren't sure what you're looking for, then the place to start is usually a search engine such as Google or Yahoo!. Here guesswork is often as effective as any other method. For example, suppose you want to find information about casualties among non-embedded journalists in Iraq.

Let's go to Google – www.google.com, the most popular search engine currently operating – and type the words 'non-embedded journalists in Iraq' in the search box. This results in about 1,900 hits. Too many for comfort. If we then enclose the words within double quote marks "non-embedded journalists in Iraq" the number of hits falls to only 55. The reason for this is that any words within double quote marks will appear together in all results exactly as you have entered them. Ideally, however, we want to reduce the number of hits still further and this can be done by using the '+' search feature. After the last double quote mark key a space then '+' followed immediately by 'friendly fire deaths' thus: "non-embedded journalists in Iraq" +"friendly fire deaths". This reduces the number of hits to five. The last of these links has details of journalists who were killed during the war and its aftermath and also suggests there may be something sinister in their deaths. This extra piece of information could even set you off on a new investigation.

A couple of other Google search aids are the '–' and 'OR' features. Sometimes your search word can have two meanings: 'cookies' can refer to a small computer file or a biscuit. If you are researching biscuits you can put a minus sign immediately in front of the term(s) you wish to exclude: cookies – "website OR internet OR computer". Remember, however, to put a space between the search word and the minus sign. The 'OR' operator allows you to search for pages that contain word A or word B. If you are looking for a holiday in Morocco or France, for example, you can key in holiday morocco OR france (the 'OR' must be upper case).

Search engines are only databases of web page extracts. No single search engine can store all the billions of pages on the web so it is worth checking others if Google, for example, doesn't cut the mustard on a particular search. Try Yahoo! (www.yahoo.com), AltaVista (www.altavista.com), or HotBot (www.hotbot.com).

Looking for Mr Right: PEOPLE SEARCHES ON THE WEB

Whatever information you have on an individual, it is still worth starting your search with the basics. You may discover some of the data already taken for granted is incorrect or out of date and this could hamper later trawls. Start with www.bt.com, www.royalmail.co.uk or www.b4usearch.co.uk. This should give you the full postal address and phone number so long as your quarry is in the phone book or on the electoral register.

If you have no luck with this and 192.com (see below) similarly comes up blank, then you are in trouble. However, before you give up on the web try inputting the name of your quarry into a search engine such as Google. Suppose you want information on the writer Graham Greene. Entering "graham greene" will give you a number of results but as it's a name you should also check for Greene, Graham as well. To find sites with either of these name phrases insert an 'OR' between them thus: "graham greene" OR "greene graham". It will soon become clear that there is an actor with the same name and, therefore, you need to eliminate him from your search. Do this by adding a '– actor' to the search terms: "graham greene" OR "greene graham" – actor. If your particular search still draws a blank and the search is crucial, then you will have to try other methods or ultimately use a private detective agency. To put it simply, such agencies have sources that will get specific information for a fee while your hands remain 'clean'.

No name no pack drill?

Sometimes you may be confronted with an email address alone and, moreover, one that gives no clue to its owner. How do you go about discovering whom it belongs to? There are a number of email directory sites (try http://mesa.rrzn.uni-hannover.de) but these are often either inadequate or inaccurate. However, if you take a punt that your target uses a newsgroup (Usenet news) either professionally or socially, or belongs to a chat room, chat forum or chat channel, then you may be able to discover who he or she is. Concentrate on those newsgroups that reflect your target's interests. If you know they like vintage cars, for example, then look at such newsgroups first.

Even if you know who your target is, there may be valuable information lurking in a chat room that could help your investigation. Check this by going to Google Groups (click 'groups' on the Google homepage) and entering the email address. If your target is a newsgroup or chat room user it should be revealed.

People sites

Most websites for tracing people have limitations, but the investigative journalist can sometimes find that elusive person, or a specific piece of information about him or her, by using one of the following:

- www.192.com   Accessing basic information – names, addresses, phone numbers, etc. requires the purchase of 'credits'. Entry level buys you 100 credits for £24.99. The 2004 electoral roll requires subscription to the premium service. If you register use an email address created specifically for the purpose. Don't use your normal email address.
- http://www.b4usearch.com   For people and business searches. Basic information is free.
- www.friendsreunited.co.uk   A dedicated reunion directory to find old school friends.
- www.lostschoolfriends.com   Useful but limited in scope.
- www.mesa.rrzn.uni-hannover.de   A search engine of large email directories.
- www.missing-you.net   Free online message-posting service for people seeking lost friends.

- http://order.internic.co.uk   (Click on the Whois tab) Should reveal your target if they have registered an internet domain name.

- www.servicepals.com   For finding people who were in the services.

- www.tracesmart.co.uk   People finder, address finder, database of all births, deaths and marriages in England and Wales between 1984 and 2002.

- www.gro.gov.uk and www.familyrecords.gov.uk   Government web sites for the tracking down of birth, death and marriage certificates. Records go back to 1837.

Looking for company? ORGANISATION SEARCHES ON THE WEB

Organisations, like people, leave traces of their activities. Commercial organisations produce a variety of information from annual reports to new product blurbs. Public sector and voluntary organisations tend to be less 'in your face', aware that their activities often involve the expenditure of public money. However, voluntary organisations, public authorities, trades unions, etc. also set up companies whenever they wish to take advantage of the limited liability offered by incorporation.

For company searches the best place to start is Companies House. All companies with limited liability are required by law to deposit at Companies House a range of documents including articles of association, shareholder, director and member details, subsidiary and parent company information, and yearly balance sheets, profit and loss accounts and annual reports. The free search will provide basic company details, register of disqualified directors, insolvency details and history of company transactions. Fees on a sliding scale from £4 per search are payable for the full 'monty', anything from mortgage charge details to the latest accounts, annual return, and company record.

Charities are similarly governed by statute. The Charity Commission website is the place to start looking. All registered charities are listed as well as Inquiry Reports that give details of formal inquiries of charities carried out in accordance with Section 8 of the Charities Act 1993.

Local councils all have websites and the *Municipal Yearbook* site is the best place to start looking for information. Online searches are by job function or council name. Your right of access to local government information is enshrined in the Local Government (Access to Information) Act 1985 (Northmore 1996: 116–32), the Local Government Act 2000 and the Freedom of Information Act 2000. Central government information is available from a myriad sources but a good starting point is the *Civil Service Yearbook*.

- www.charity-commission.gov.uk   The website of the Charity Commission, established to regulate charities in England and Wales.

- www.civil-service.co.uk   Extensive information on central government departments, the Royal Households, research councils. Search by department name, job title or name. Subscription required for full service but the book itself is usually available in reference libraries.

- www.companieshouse.gov.uk   Companies House is a government agency which contains records of all companies incorporated with limited liability. Its London address is 21 Bloomsbury Street, London, WC1B 3XD.

- www.municipalyearbook.co.uk Online searching for information on councils and local authorities. Search by keyword, job function, council name or interactive map. Subscription needed for full information but the book itself can be consulted in reference libraries.

- www.polis.parliament.uk POLIS is the Parliamentary OnLine Indexing Service, a database providing an index to the proceedings and publications of both Houses of Parliament including the full text of Early Day Motions since May 1997.

- www.statistics.gov.uk UK national statistics from government departments.

Looking for Mr Goodbar

Investigative journalism is often expensive and time-consuming and seldom carries any guarantee of success. So what can you do to minimise failure? The superstitious may consult a fortune-teller, find a four-leaf clover or buy a rabbit's foot, but we need a surer talisman, one that, without actually guaranteeing it, at least maximises our chances of success. Organisation and thoroughness are the key:

- *Go backwards* – Every effect has a cause. Find the cause by building a narrative of events, a time-line or something similar. Complex investigations may need multiple time-lines – for example, one for each of the protagonists in the story. Watch how they intersect and diverge. At some point you should discover the pivotal moment of your investigation – the 'big bang', if you like, of the universe you are briefly inhabiting.

- *Go public* – In any investigation there will be a wealth of information in the public domain. Search in libraries, the National Archive, Companies House, the Land Registry and so on. Perhaps advertise in local newspapers, shop windows or internet newsgroups for people with inside information to come forward.

- *Go looking* – Talk to everybody you turn up in your researches, regardless of how important they might seem to be. Anyone who is central should be face-to-faced. Others can be contacted by phone or email.

Apart from these working strategies there are a number of basic ground rules that apply to investigative reporting, from those you need to consider during the research phase to those that are paramount during the writing phase. No set of guidelines can be exhaustive but the following seem by common consent to be the most important:

- Ensure all significant facts are corroborated.
- Ensure all documents germane to the inquiry are checked for authenticity.
- Tape all conversations wherever possible and date all entries in your notebook. Sometimes these are your only defence against a potential action for defamation. In an ideal world you want a witness to everything.
- Visit the scene of the 'crime'. Neighbours talk, shopkeepers remember, employees divulge – but only if you talk to them face to face.
- Try to find sources prepared to be quoted and don't quote people if you don't know who they are or if their allegations seem too fanciful or outlandish.

- Protect your sources at all times, even if a refusal to divulge who they are constitutes a contempt of court. Prison might await, but if you can't be trusted to keep your word, you've no right to be an investigative journalist in the first place.
- Do not misrepresent who you are or what you are doing. This can often play badly if the lawyers are brought in. There are occasions when subterfuge is necessary e.g. exposing criminal activity, but it should be just that, necessary, and not just a wheeze or a sop to a reporter's vanity.
- Recent changes in the law, specifically the 'qualified privilege defence' (see Chapter 10), mean your allegations should be put to the person against whom you are making them, before publication.
- If you are researching in a strange town it's often a good idea to base yourself in the main library reference section. Virtually all the documents and books mentioned in this chapter are available there; you can usually access the internet and the staff are highly skilled and always helpful.
- Develop your interviewing skills. Remember you should attempt 'amiable conversations' rather than interrogations. Use open-ended questions and let your interviewee talk. In other words, don't interrupt all the time as if you're a tyro on the *Today* programme.
- Be aware that a minor error can undermine a whole investigation because it casts doubt on the credibility of your sources, your methods or your argument.
- Never prejudge the quality or value of potential information sources. You can reliably determine usefulness only after you have looked up that written source, tracked down and spoken to that individual. Even if you have doubts, do it anyway.
- Finally, consider the ethical dimension of your story – how will it impinge on the privacy or other human rights of your quarry? Do you have a convincing public interest defence?

There is one further test, however, that should be applied to the results of any investigation – have you presented the facts in such a way that readers can make up their own minds? As David Spark notes (1999: 94): 'The facts should be allowed to speak for themselves without loose and exaggerated expressions of opinion which could be hard to defend in court.'

And don't forget those non-electronic sources

What follows is an assortment of non-electronic sources that have proved valuable to researchers and investigative reporters alike – useful as a starting point, as a source of background detail or as a way of adding authority to your interviewing technique. It's a common yet nevertheless true dictum that you can never have too much information. All the volumes listed here should be available in good reference libraries.

People searches

- *Who's Who*   Biographies of some 30,000 individuals (the British 'Establishment')
- *The International Who's Who*   Ditto but world-wide
- *Debrett's Peerage and Baronetage*   A who's who of all titled citizens of the UK and Ireland and the British royal family

- *The Catholic Directory*   Lists Roman Catholic clergy in England and Wales plus details of schools, colleges, religious societies, etc.

- *Crockford's Clerical Directory*   Who's who in the Church of England. Lists all clergy and their livings throughout the UK

- Family Record Centre at the General Register Office, 1 Myddleton Street, London, EC1R 1UW   This office contains all birth, death and marriage certificates from 1837 onwards and wills before 1859. Copies of certificates are available for a fee of £11.50 or £7.00 if you visit one of their offices in person.

- Principal Registry of the Family Division of the High Court, 1st Avenue House, 42–49 High Holborn, London, WC1V 6NP   This office contains copies of all wills lodged for probate in the UK, from January 1859 onwards. A printed index is, however, available locally at County Records Offices. Check the website at www.courtservice.gov.uk

Organisation searches: COMMERCIAL, PUBLIC, VOLUNTARY

- *Annual Reports*   These are produced by public companies. The information is often very detailed and helpful to potential management, professional and technical employees. This information can be obtained from the company's public relations department.

- *The Municipal Yearbook* (Hemming Information Services)   An annual two-volume publication which gives comprehensive details of all local authorities in the UK plus health authorities, emergency services, etc.

- *Who Owns Whom* (Dun & Bradstreet)   Two-volume directory which shows the relationship between parent companies and their subsidiaries in the UK. Volume one lists over seven thousand parent companies and volume two lists all the subsidiary companies (over a hundred thousand) and matches them with their parent.

- *Key British Enterprises* (Dun & Bradstreeet)   Four-volume work giving financial data on turnover and capital, details of trade, trade names, trading styles and a full list of directors by name and function, of top fifty thousand businesses in the UK.

- *The Waterlow Stock Exchange Yearbook* (Caritas Data Ltd)   Provides a brief financial description of all quoted public companies on the London and Dublin Stock Exchanges.

- *Kompass* (Reed Business Information)   Published annually in three volumes. Volume one lists companies and gives basic facts on location, activities, staffing, directors etc.; volume two lists products and services; and volume three lists industrial trade names.

- *Britain's Top Privately Owned Companies* (Jordan Information Services)   A five-volume directory of major British companies providing trading and financial information. Alphabetically lists details of company address, nature of business, name and telephone numbers of chief executive.

- *International Directory of Company Histories* (Thomson Gale)   Detailed histories of more than 6,700 companies worldwide in 63 volumes. Full contact information, company history, key dates, etc.

- *Civil Service Yearbook* (The Stationery Office)   Gives details of all central and devolved government departments and key staff profiles.
- *Charity Choice UK: The Encyclopaedia of Charities* (Waterlow Professional Publishing)   Lists more than eight thousand charities with full contact details and areas of activity.
- *The Green Index* J. Edgar Milner (Cassell)   A directory of environmental orga- nizations in Great Britain and Ireland – name, contact details, interest area.
- *The Diplomatic Service List* (The Stationery Office)   A yearbook that lists all diplomatic staff at overseas embassies, high commissions and consular posts. Biographical notes on staff and ambassadors for previous twenty years.
- *Aslib Directory of Information Sources in the United Kingdom* by Keith Reynard   Contains listings of more than eleven thousand associations, clubs, societies, companies, educational establishments, institutes, commissions, government bodies and other organisations which provide information freely or on a fee-paying basis.

And finally . . . Where are the new Pilgers?

'Where are the new Pilgers?' is the title of an article by Cleland Thom (2004) in a *Press Gazette* supplement on journalism training. He suggested with some persua- sive evidence that more and more journalism students were likely to shun inves- tigative reporting in favour of the fun and glamour of showbiz journalism. Thom quoted a course leader in journalism at a new university:

> I'm immensely depressed by the poor standard of what passes for investigative journalism in British newspapers. You've got the occasional exception, such as Nick Davies in the *Guardian*, but generally it's sting-type stuff like Mazher Mahmood in the *News of the World*. When I trained, we all wanted to be John Pilger. Now all trainees see is the 3am girls.

Whether this course leader's depression will lift, whether there is a new generation of John Pilgers waiting in the wings, whether there are media organisations prepared to fund real investigative journalism again, all ultimately will depend on the desire, commitment and inspiration of a new generation of journalism students, whether on university courses, training schemes or through pure serendipity, deciding to take up the challenge and once again 'tell it like it is'.

12 Feature writing

Thinking visually, painting pictures with words

News features tend to contain more comment, analysis, colour, background, and a greater diversity of sources, than news stories and explore a larger number of issues in greater depth. It is the extra length that accounts for many of the distinguishing elements of features. In particular, their intro sections, where the overall tone of the piece is set, tend to be more colourful and varied in style than those of hard news. A news feature may argue a case; the personal views of the writer may be prominent. But the emphasis is still on the news.

The layout of a feature is often more colourful and imaginative than that of a news report. The headline, the standfirst (those few words that accompany most features summarising or teasingly hinting at its main point(s) and carrying the byline), the intro, the picture captions, and sometimes the graphic's contents are worked on together with the subeditor to convey the overall message of the piece. It helps then if the reporter is able to think visually while composing the feature. Adding extra, linked features to the package (such as a profile, a vox pop, a background chronology) will also help improve the overall display.

The intro

The news peg

Most news features do not start with the five Ws and the H of the traditional news opening section. The writing is more flexible – but the intro section still carries an urgency typical of straight news reporting. Occasionally a feature will begin in a news style but then break away to cover the issues in a distinctly 'un-newsy' way. For instance, the London *Evening Standard* (23 February 2000) began a feature on acquaintance rape with a straight news angle but moved on to carry the verbatim accounts of two women at length.

> Acquaintance rape is Britain's fastest growing crime, according to recent Home Office research. But the rising figures could well be the tip of an iceberg, women's groups believe, because many such attacks – where the woman knows, no matter how briefly, her attacker – go unreported.

The human interest focus

One of the most popular devices for helping the reader understand a complex event is to begin by focusing on the experiences or views of an individual. Thus, on the eve of the Knesset decision on the evacuation of Jewish settlers from Gaza, Donald MacIntyre in the *Independent* (25 October 2004), under the headline 'Gaza Jews say money cannot compensate for being thrown out of the place they call home', zooms in on a father and son:

> Avi Farham and his son, Ofer, have been here before. Twenty two years ago when Ofer was just two years old and had to ride on his father's shoulders, Avi was on the march to Jerusalem as he is this morning, in protest at the only other time Israel has ever evacuated a Jewish settlement beyond its 1967 borders. That evacuation was supervised by the then defence minister, Ariel Sharon, the man who as Prime Minister will be asking the Knesset tomorrow to approve the evacuation of Avi and 8,000 other settlers from Gaza.

Similarly, as part of Mansfield *Chad*'s 'Say no to doorstep callers' campaign, Paul Conboy focused (27 October 2004) on the plight of an anonymous pensioner:

> Again, the 94-year-old pensioner refused – no she was not going to sell her home, she was not going to succumb to pressure from the man repaving her drive.
>
> The Mansfield pensioner lives alone and is in the middle of a nightmare . . . just another victim of rogue doorstep sellers.
>
> Her story is just another shocking example of how these doorstep conmen will stoop to cheat their victims – and it is why *Chad* is demanding a ban on doorstep cold calling.

Quote intro

Most news intros (as we have seen) do not start with a direct quote. In contrast, features can often begin with striking quotes: they set the scene and tone effectively and concisely as well as convey the human dimension.

As here in *Socialist Worker* (23 October 2004) at the start of a feature on the campaign against council housing privatisations, Anindya Bhattacharyya reported:

> 'We're at a crossroads,' says Alan Walter, chair of Defend Council Housing (DCH). 'The government is on the back foot and isolated, with a broad alliance supporting the "fourth option" – direct public investment in council housing.'
>
> Alan Walter spoke as council tenants, housing activists, trade unionists and local councillors from across Britain were heading to London for the national conference of DCH. The conference will be held on Friday 29 October.
>
> The conference comes at a crucial moment for the movement against housing privatisation.

Or here in an *Observer* report (26 October 2004) on police racism:

> 'There's no Pakis round here,' spat the teenager. 'This is a white town.'
>
> The youngster was right: Llandudno's Asian community was nowhere to be seen. Inside the pubs of Mostyn Street, the patrons are exclusively white. So, too,

are those flitting among its string of shops. Maybe this is what drew PC Rob Pulling to the popular Edwardian seaside resort, a place he felt his hateful intolerance could be shared without reproach.

Eye-witness intro

Justin Huggler (in the *Independent*, 29 October 2004) visits Udaipur, one of India's leading tourist destinations, and describes what he sees to show, graphically, how drought is damaging the resort:

Where the waters used to lap at the entrance to the Lake Palace Hotel, today camels lazily graze on the green scrub that covers the empty lake bed. Water buffalow wallow in the last few puddles. A car from the city taking a short cut across the dry lake bed sends up a cloud of dust. Wild horses have come down from the hills to graze, and nose up curiously as you pass.

Historical background

A focus on the past can often throw a particular light on the news of today. Thus a few opening pars focusing on historical background can be an effective way of leading into the main angle, as here in the *Sunday Mirror* (13 February 2000):

For decades the world's tobacco industry has kept a tight lid on the list of deadly chemicals it uses to make cigarettes.

And governments, whose coffers bulge with tobacco taxes, have conspired to keep secret the full horror contained in a single lungful of cigarette smoke.

Today, for the first time, the *Sunday Mirror* can reveal the deadly cocktail contained in cigarettes.

(The *Sunday Mirror*, incidentally, exaggerated when it claimed an exclusive for the story. Other newspapers carried details from the same health department report, due to be released later in the week.)

Striking contrasts

Highlighting striking contrasts in descriptive language can be an effective way to inject urgency and special interest in the intro section. Here, in the *Guardian* (31 March 2003), Alfred Hickling, through vivid colour writing, contrasts a deprived Leeds suburb with the area around West Yorkshire Playhouse to highlight Mark Catley's background:

The south-Leeds suburb of Beeston is barely a mile from West Yorkshire Playhouse but it may as well be in another country. Situated on a windy hill over-looking Leeds United football ground, Beeston is one of the city's most deprived urban areas. Its most famous landmark is the desecrated graveyard featured in Tony Harrison's poem V. Many of the red-brick terraces are boarded up and abandoned; the only business that seems to be thriving is the bookies.

Nobody from Beeston ever goes to the Playhouse, including, until recently, the 32-year-old writer Mark Catley

The personalised intro

The 'I' of the reporter is only rarely prominent in news intros. But the tone of features can be far more personal, idiosyncratic, witty even. As David Newnham of the *Guardian* (21 November 1998) shows in his sparky, original, chatty style – combining slang, eye-witness colour and constant questioning.

> He's a dapper chappie my conductor – and a bit of a ladies' man, too. That pretty lady with the tenner, for example. She holds it up like a love letter and smiles a big red smile that matches the coachwork. Does he chuck her off into the rain? Does he lecture her on the need to proffer the exact fare? No chance. He sits down next to her – sits down, mark you, and counts out her change, nice as pie.
>
> Would I get the same care and consideration? I weigh the matter up and decide it's not impossible. For one thing, he's that type of conductor – a showman, a born party host. And for another thing, it's that type of bus.

In a fascinating *Independent* feature (10 November 2004) examining the decline of centuries-old Celtic languages, Marcus Tanner began:

> At the village of St Anne la Palud in western Brittany, I followed the Celtic saints as they went down to the sea at the annual religious fete they call the 'grand pardon'. A mission to find out what remained of Europe's Celtic cultures brought me to this most traditional of Breton folk festivals, and I noted down the names of the local saints embroidered on to the brilliant, red and green banners, hoisted by sturdy Bretons in traditional dress.

Questions

Questions rarely begin news reports. But in features they are OK. As, for instance, in this quirky report by Berlin correspondent Ruth Elkins in the *Independent on Sunday* (7 November 2004):

> Not long to live and don't want to give your relatives unnecessary stress? No problem: thanks to German innovation, you can now assemble your own gravestone in under an hour.

The sex angle

Sex is the favourite focus of the red-top tabloids. But often a puritanical agenda underpins the coverage with the stress on sex outside marriage being dangerous and sinful or on 'kinky' sex being a threat to the stability of marriage. As here in the *News of the World* (9 January 2000):

> Clare Holtby slipped into sexy red knickers and stilettos and writhed seductively on the bed as her husband took photo after photo.
>
> The next night, she steamed up the camera lens again – only this time she was completely naked.
>
> It was all a bit of fun to spice up their sex life. But the sizzling snaps ended up plastered all over top-shelf mags – and the couple's 'bit of fun' ended up leaving her feeling cheap and worthless and destroying their happy marriage.

Similarly, the *Sunday Mirror* (27 June 2004) introed:

> These shocking pictures capture drunken British youngsters engaged in a sordid mass orgy on the infamous 'love boat' Napa Queen.

In this way it manages to link sexuality with the 'shocking', 'sordid' and 'infamous'.

The narrative opening

Sometimes, features can begin in story mode: a familiar territory for most readers. Here, Helen Weathers in the *Daily Mail* (20 November 2004) began her 'shock' feature about a girl who had an abortion at 14:

> Two weeks ago, 15-year-old schoolgirl Melissa Smith walked nervously into her local chemist for an on-the-spot pregnancy test. Ten minutes later, she walked out shocked, clutching the positive result and wondering how she was going to break the devastating news to her mother.

The body of the text: THEMATIC STRUCTURE

While colour, description, opinion, analysis, narrative, quotes, dialogue and historical contextualising may be important in a news feature, they are all still built on the cement of factual detail and a sharp news sense. Just as in news stories the most important information comes first with the details declining in importance thereafter, so the same is true of news features.

At the same time, the writing style of features can be far more colourful and varied than that found in news stories. Emotional tones (angry, witty, ironic, condemnatory, adulatory) can vary along with the textual rhythms. Indeed, before launching into your writing, along with establishing the structure, it is crucial to identify the emotional core of your piece. Take these opening pars from a feature in the *Voice* (20 and 27 December 1999):

Youngsters flock to praise Christ

A Birmingham church is attracting large numbers from the city's youth.

Kenneth Taylor finds out how

In his expensive Timberland sports jacket, designer jeans and trainers, Mark Tennant looks as though he is heading for the nearest street corner to hang out with his friends.

The only indication that this trendy 22-year-old is actually making his way to Birmingham's Aston Christian Centre are a Bible in his left hand and the fact that it is 9.15am on Sunday.

But Mark, who gave up hard drugs when he became addicted to the Lord, is not alone. He is part of a procession of streetwise youths, in cars and on foot, heading for the Thomas Street church to worship.

The Pentecostal church, part of the Assemblies of God Churches of Great Britain and Ireland, is proving such a powerful magnet for young people that Pastor Calvin Young has to hold three services a day.

Souls

Recently an appeal was launched to raise £30,000 to buy a new building to house up to 1,000 people and leave enough space for various meeting rooms.

The church, on the embankment of the Aston Expressway and not far from the infamous Spaghetti Junction, is not much to look at from the outside, but inside is full of happy souls.

Pastor Calvin, in a maroon blazer, matching tie and slacks, looks more like a salesman than a minister.

Within minutes of the service getting under way, the congregation is whipped up into a spiritual frenzy.

Blessed

There is singing and clapping by the congregation while musicians are jamming away on keyboards, drums and guitars, accompanied by a trio of backing vocalists.

The Sunday I attended two people fainted when the 'Hallelujahs', 'Praise the Lords' and worshippers speaking in tongues reached fever pitch.

Pastor Calvin reckons about 80 per cent of the 250 people who regularly attend Sunday services are in their teens or early twenties.

He can't quite explain why his church – motto: 'A city church of many congregations, proclaiming God is love in the heart of the city' – is so blessed with youths at a time when others find it hard to attract them. But he feels the new millennium may play some role.

'If you look at human history, every 2,000 years something significant has taken place,' he says. 'I would not put a bet on it, but I believe this generation could be the one to witness the return of Christ.'

The thematic structure is clear:

- *Section 1: pars 1–4*: focus on Mark Tennant
- *Section 2: pars 5–7*: focus on Pentecostal church
- *Section 3: pars 8–11*: inside the church
- *Section 4: pars 12–14*: Pastor Calvin.

This piece is particularly interesting for the way in which the flow between these thematic blocks is helped through the use of subtly deployed transitional phrases. The intro spotlights Mark and then the phrase 'But Mark ... is not alone' leads effortlessly into the focus on the church and its popularity. The report first concentrates on the general facts about the church and then shifts its focus: 'but inside is full of happy souls'. That movement in the eye of the reporter (from outside to inside) helps provide an extra dynamic interest to the copy. It also provides the prompt for the new section of eye-witness description of people and events inside. Finally the focus falls on the Pastor. Factual details are combined with colourful description and

6 VOICE DECEMBER 20 & 27 1999

Youngsters flock

A Birmingham church is attracting large numbers from the city's youth. Kenneth Taylor finds out how

WE ARE FAMILY: The Aston Christian Centre is pulling in ever greater numbers of young people.   Pic: Jason Tilley

IN HIS expensive Timberland sports jacket, designer jeans and trainers, Mark Tennant looks as though he is heading for the nearest street corner to hang out with his friends.

The only indications that this trendy 22-year-old is actually making his way to Birmingham's Aston Christian Centre are a Bible in his left hand and the fact that it is 9.15am on Sunday.

But Mark, who gave up hard drugs when he became addicted to the Lord, is not alone.

He is part of a procession of streetwise youths, in cars and on foot, heading for the Thomas Street church to worship.

The Pentecostal church, part of the Assemblies of God Churches of Great Britain and Ireland, is proving such a powerful magnet for young people that Pastor Calvin Young has to hold three services a day.

Souls

Recently an appeal was launched to raise £300,000 to buy a new building to house up to 1,000 people and leave enough space for various meeting rooms.

The church, on the embankment of the Aston Expressway and not far from the infamous Spaghetti Junction, is not much to look at from the outside, but inside is full of happy souls.

Pastor Calvin, in a maroon blazer, matching tie and slacks, looks more like a salesman than a minister.

Within minutes of the service getting under way, the congregation is whipped up into a spiritual frenzy.

Blessed

There is singing and clapping by the congregation while musicians are jamming away on keyboards, drums and guitars, accompanied by a trio of backing vocalists.

The Sunday I attended two people fainted when the 'Hallelujahs', 'Praise the Lords'

and worshippers speaking in tongues reached fever pitch.

Pastor Calvin reckons about 80 per cent of the 250 people who regularly attend Sunday services are in their teens or early twenties.

He can't quite explain why his church – motto: 'A city church of many congregations, proclaiming God is love in the heart of the city' is so blessed with youths at a time when others find it hard to attract them. But he feels the new millennium may play some role.

"If you look at human history, every 2,000 years something significant has taken place," he says. "I would not put a bet on it,

but I believe this generation could be the one to witness the return of Christ."

He also points to a range of activities from lone parents' groups and a Saturday school to a diabetic support group, pastoral clinics and drama classes.

He is also not afraid to use technology to spread the word.

"We try to communicate in a manner relevant to this present generation," he says.

Sexuality

"We try to address real issues. We address single people and their sexuality.

"A lot of young people have got problems from some churches don't address them ".

Mark, who said he got his calling while watching the Vision Channel with a spliff in his hand, would certainly agree.

He readily admits to a past life of addiction to crack, marijuana, cocaine and lighter fluids, but within a few weeks of his calling he substituted them for the word of God.

"My mind was in a pretty bad way," he says. "My parents are Church of England but only in name.

"I had never been to church before I came here. It's like being in a family.

"This is the only church I've been to and it is the only one where I feel at home. It is God's will that no one should perish, but all

> **"Churches are changing and the face of Christianity is changing. It's not just about the way people dress and the fact that you don't have to wear a well-cut suit and matching handbag"**

to praise Christ

should come to repentance."

Mark, who now works as a croupier on a ship – a colleague at a casino introduced him to the church – got baptised at the Aston Christian Centre just before last Christmas.

A'-level student Le Ancia Donaldson got baptised two years ago at 15.

Dancing

She started going to the Aston Christian Centre with her mum, Colleen, but insists she has not been influenced in any way to give her life to the Lord.

Le Ancia, 17, says: "I grew up in the church. I used to go to a Methodist church with my grandmother but there weren't so many young people there and it was very formal.

"Here it is lively, friendly and welcoming. We have lots of different ministries like dancing, drama, youth clubs and sports and the church supports them all.

"The atmosphere here is really good and I come here to get spiritually uplifted."

Estate surveyor Steve McDonald, 27, quit the New Testament Church of God three months ago to start worshipping at the Aston Christian Centre.

He said: "I needed something more from a church than just worshipping on Sundays. Here they have activities all week long.

"The New Testament Church had nothing to offer young people. There was not much encouragement. Rather than catering for young people, they catered for people who enjoyed the traditional type of service."

Alternative

Barrister Patricia Hawthorne said there were other innercity churches in Birmingham, like Aston's King of Kings and the Ruach Inspirational Church of God in nearby Lozells, that also catered for young people.

Ms Hawthorne, 35, started worshipping at the Aston Christian Centre after becoming frustrated with the Baptist church where she was Christened.

"Churches are changing and the face of Christianity is changing," she said. "It is not just about the way people

dress and the fact you don't have to wear a well-cut suit and matching handbag.

"It is the fact that people can go to church and be themselves and that the church also acknowledges that, as an individual, you have weaknesses.

"Here everyone seems to be genuinely worshipping the Lord and are not watching what each other are wearing. Also, young people can see the problems in the world for themselves and are searching for an alternative way ahead.

"At my old church, when I tackled [them] about changing direction, [I was told that] a lot of the congregation were middle class and had no great needs. Only when they were in a crisis did they turn to the church to seek God."

If the Aston Christian Centre is considered middle-of-the-

road, then the Ruach is much more radical.

Its praise and worship leader, Nikki Munroe, said the church often held services in places such as Balsall Heath, a known vice girls' haunt, and Constitution Hill in the city centre, a gay haunt.

She said only about five of its 195-strong congregation were older than 45.

"Ruach, which means breath of God in Greek, is very radical," said Nikki. "We go that extra mile. We like to meet people who don't always go to church. Those who want to hear the gospel, we go to them.

"We are very loud, very outrageous and music-oriented. We're following in the footsteps of Jesus, who often associated with the less desirables in society."

> *"We are very loud, very outrageous and into music. We have this motto: 'Everybody is somebody' "*

PASTOR CALVIN YOUNG: 'This could be the generation to witness Christ's return.'   Pic: Jason Tilley

striking quotes backing up the main theme of the piece. This is excellent writing. Moreover, the variety of genres displayed in these few pars (human interest intro, factual detail, eye-witness descriptions, shifting focus) adds to its overall vitality and interest.

Use of parentheses

Parentheses are rarely seen in news stories: they break the urgent flow of the copy. But given the more flexible rhythms of features they can work. For instance, Jonathan Glancey, in his *Guardian* report (10 January 2000) on the newly restored Pompidou Centre in Paris, wrote:

> Below shop and cafe are a children's rumpus room (the sort of mimsy you expect to find at Ikea) and a bookshop twice as big as before.
>
> At the centre of this space is a stunted tree growing from a huge cube of earth rising from the basement (where four new performance and lecture spaces, including a second cinema, have been shaped) and a shoulder-shrugging information desk. (Don't try to speak a foreign language and, whatever you do, don't attempt your school French: this will only make matters all the more degrading for you.)

The final flourish

A hard news story carries information in order of news value. The last par is the least important and is cuttable without destroying the overall impact. A news feature can be different (Hennessy 1993; Adams 1999: 82–85). News values still apply but the final section can often carry its own importance. A feature may explore a range of views on a subject and conclude by passing a comment on them; another may argue a case and come to a conclusion in the final section. A final par may raise a pointed question; it may contain a striking direct quote or summarise an argument. Feature subs have to be particularly sensitive to this. Writers often include the words 'Must par' in brackets before a final sentence to stress its importance to the sub (who will not feel obliged to follow the advice).

Negotiating the subjective: THE EYE-WITNESS SPORTING EVENT

Journalists often attend sporting events, not to record the happenings and results from a specialist perspective but to describe simply the experience of being there. As Lynne Truss (1999: 127) commented: 'Uniquely in journalism, its appeal to the reader is entirely in the presentation of the simple fact: "I was there; I saw it with my own eyes; it happened once and it will never happen again."' The journalist becomes the outsider looking in. Such an assignment presents a varied challenge. You will need to extract a range of factual details relating to the event and highlight any news elements. It will provide you with opportunities for descriptive colour, eye-witness reporting, the development of sources and the use of quotes, and for the exploration of your subjective response.

The experience of attending an event as 'an ordinary member of the public' is very different from being a reporter there. As a journalist you are likely to have a notebook and tape recorder to record any interesting sights, interview and facts. You are on the look-out for the unusual, perhaps even the slightly bizarre, the newsworthy. You need to keep all your senses alive to collect a mass of details, quotes and impressions that will go towards the creation of your article. You are unlikely to provide a simple chronology of your experience: arrival, watching spectators, the highlights of the event, the results and departure. Instead, special journalistic values should come into play. You may want to intro on a lively quote or a striking incident which happens towards the end. It may be good to start with a colourful description of a participant and then pan out to take in the overall event.

Eye-witness writing is always overtly subjective. It should never be self-indulgent. If you are describing an underwater hockey match, the reader does not need to know at length your fears of underwater swimming originating in some early childhood trauma in Lake Ontario. This constraint does not apply to celebrity writers. Their own subjectivity is often, in journalistic terms, as interesting as the event they are describing and so their own self-indulgence is legitimate. But, in general, subjectivity works best when handled delicately. It is not easy striking the right balance between egotism and sensitive, effective 'subjectivity'.

Eye-witness features within this genre are usually aimed at non-specialist readers. Thus, you may need to explain the rules of the game if it is an unusual one and the level of support in the UK. Evidence of class, race and gender bias runs through whole segments of British life and is prominent in sporting activities. Certain sports are more distinctly working-class (football, ten-pin bowling, rugby league, darts) than others (polo, hunting, grouse shooting). There may be opportunities in your feature to explore these aspects.

Unusual sports are played all over the UK: it is a challenge to search them out in your own area. Do not worry if you have never seen them played before. The newness of the experience will make it all the more intense for you. All the same it is advisable to prepare as far as possible before covering the event. Consult local libraries for contacts and information; ring Sport England or the relevant national Sports Council or consult its website. Type your chosen sport into a web search engine and see what comes up. Ask friends and relations if they have any background information.

You may find the event boring and unintelligible. That merely presents you with the challenge of conveying that dullness in an interesting way. Always try to stay true to your feelings. Given the many pressures and constraints on journalists, that is not easily achieved. Try never to transform what you experience into a cliché you hope to be accepted by your news desk; try never to transform the 'dull' into something lively simply to 'beef up' your copy. It will, inevitably, appear inauthentic. The tone will be an important ingredient of your piece. Humour, irony, wry self-criticism, mock chauvinism: any of these may be appropriate. But the tone has to emerge from your own experience. The eye-witness piece will work only if that tone is genuine. To explore the subjective element in eye-witness reporting, I shall examine critically a piece I wrote in 1977 while on the staff of the *Cambridge Evening News*.

Analysis of 'Bingo: Eyes down for that elusive jackpot': *CAMBRIDGE EVENING NEWS* (15 JANUARY 1977)

I am with more than 450 people packed in a hall in the centre of Cambridge. And I'm staring – in the silent thrall of my bingo fling – at a small piece of paper full of figures.

A man stands on a balcony and reads out nothing but numbers. He commands total attention as we sit poised with pens and pencils praying for the elusive jackpot.

'All the eights, 88,' says the man on the balcony.

A cry of 'Yes' is heard. A whistle is blown. Great chattering breaks out. A young man dashes (so quick it is as if his life depended on it) towards the crier, takes a card from him and reads out again nothing but numbers. The crier is £80 richer: another game is over, another drama has been enacted.

Indeed, it is the theatrical, almost surreal, aspects of the surroundings that I find so fascinating in the Central EMI Bingo and Social Club in Hobson Street.

This converted cinema could quite comfortably have found a place in the zaniest of science fiction movies – with its brash, psychedelic, mish-mash of colours (silver, yellow, red, green, rust, cream to name a few) and its huge, electrically operated board that rises high behind the caller, a confusing conglomeration of figures blazing out like the strange invention of a mad mathematician.

And then there's the peculiar bingo lingo – housey housey, full house, last'un, flyer, ling double, quickie – that flows so naturally off the lips of the cognoscenti.

Since the game first burst upon the British public 15 years ago the number of participants has been growing dramatically. It's an even bet that at some time or other you've had a bingo fling.

The four-year-old Cambridge Central club has 10,000 members. And Britain's big four bingo businesses – Mecca, Rank, EMI and Ladbrokes – have between them 422 clubs dotted about the country.

Britain is, in fact, going through a bingo boom. But bingo players remain the great unnameables. It's an almost dead cert that if you play bingo you don't want your neighbour to know it.

Last Saturday I could find no-one prepared to give me his or her name, so strong is the social stigma attached to the game.

EMI's Press officer, Mr Eric Sullings, blamed this on the 'class consciousness of the town.'

'If you go to Lancashire and Yorkshire, the real bingo playing country,' he said, 'people are happy to talk freely about playing bingo but the further south you go the more careful people become.'

This wall of silence was not my only problem. Bingo, be warned, is almost submerged beneath rules and regulations.

Before you can play you have to be a member of the club. On my first approach to the Central I was membershipless and told I just could not play.

I had to sign like everyone else a free application card and wait a week for my membership. My second visit revealed still more hazards. I arrived at 8.15 p.m. expecting to launch into a game but was told it was impossible – no cards are sold after 7.45 and members are not allowed guests.

- *Par 9*: more background about bingo in Cambridge and in Britain generally.
- *Par 10*: more general background with 'an almost dead cert' continuing the gambling theme. Social stigma theme emerges.
- *Par 11*: social stigma theme developed and related to my own experience.
- *Pars 12–13*: strong quote to back up social stigma theme from good source.
- *Pars 14–16*: details, rules and regulations of game drawn from my own experience.
- *Par 17*: 'third time lucky' continues gambling theme as I continue narrative of my visits. Return to social stigma theme with indirect quote from manager.
- *Par 18*: new 'bashing bingo/addiction' theme.
- *Pars 19–20*: extra detail about Cambridge club continuing addiction theme.
- *Par 21*: short quote to support continuing addiction theme.
- *Par 22*: eye-witness reporting supporting the addiction theme.
- *Par 23*: quote to present positive view of the game in the interests of 'balance'.
- *Par 24*: balancing comment from myself plus extra details about costs and prize money.
- *Par 25*: short snappy concluding remark which is somewhat surprising: a 'sting in the tail' ending. In retrospect, I regret using this quote. Mr Jones did say it (a photographer was there to confirm after he protested) and it did provide me with a quirky finishing flourish. But it reflected badly on Mr Jones and caused him unnecessary problems. I should have exerted some self-censorship in that instance. Looking back at the feature, written after I had been a journalist for around seven years, the detached, ironic tone is most striking. I think it probably emerged from my class orientation. Here I was, a middle-class man intruding into the world of the working class who felt themselves ostracised in academically dominated Cambridge. From this tension emerges the self-conscious, over-literary style of my writing. The tone of dry irony (common in the media), in fact, was my attempt to negotiate this feeling of being 'an outsider'.

Journalists' dilemmas

To what extent can and should journalists remain outsiders? How much do journalistic notions of neutrality, objectivity and balance conflict with inevitable feelings of sympathy, compassion, alienation, confusion and solidarity? George Orwell grappled with such dilemmas by going to live the experience he wanted to write about (see Inglis 2002). He became a plongeur (a dish-washer in a hotel kitchen) and tramp before writing *Down and Out in Paris and London* (1933); he fought alongside the Republicans in the Spanish civil war and wrote of his experiences in *Homage to Catalonia* (1938). Later Orwell (often considered one of the twentieth century's greatest journalists) largely ignored the prestigious Fleet Street outlets for his journalism and concentrated his attentions on small-circulation, left-wing and literary publications. But even the 'Orwell solution' is not without its problems and paradoxes. The best the journalist can do is seek to understand their own histories; their own subjectivities as well as the broader political dynamics of their society. It is perhaps a tall order – but worth striving for.

Painting a picture in words: PROFILE WRITING

Open a newspaper and you are likely to find a profile somewhere. People, according to Harold Evans, former editor of *The Times* and the *Sunday Times*, are news. The profile (in French, *portrait*), the drawing of a portrait with words, is the archetypal manifestation of this 'people/human interest bias' in the media. It need not be only of a person: organisations, buildings, cemeteries, roads, parks, schools, Father Christmas, even weapons (rather obscenely) can be profiled. But people profiles are the most common. Profiles succeed in satisfying a wide range of interests:

- *Readers*: profiles are immensely popular. They feed people's curiosity about other people. What makes them tick, what hurdles have they overcome, what is the person really like behind the public face, what accounted for their downfall? This kind of questioning has great appeal. The 'tot' (triumph over tragedy) story, in which people talk about their success against tremendous odds, is a particularly popular genre. We become voyeurs into private or professional lives.
- *Reporters*: writing profiles is fun and challenging, and can often help a journalist to build up contact with a useful source. Reputations can be made on the strength of profile writing.
- *Editors*: profiles often appear in series which guarantee a certain space being filled each week. Readers like the series format also, perhaps because they provide a feeling of continuity, stability and order. They occupy the same spot at regular intervals and so simplify the reading process.
- *Proprietors*: there is an important commercial aspect to profiles. In terms of cost-effectiveness they are particularly attractive to newspaper proprietors. An interview with accompanying picture can easily provide half a page (broadsheet) or a page or more (tabloid or magazine). Compare this with the cost-effectiveness of investigative reporting. A journalist may spend hours, months even, investigating a story and get nowhere.
- *People*: being profiled can pander to their vanity. Profiles can help promote business. A writer, for instance, hopes the publicity will help sell more of their books. The PR industry is forever pressurising the press to profile its clients.

Types of people profiles

There are many kinds of profiles and no standard format. There are no profile rules. To highlight a few styles within the genre:

- A short profile may highlight some newsworthy feature of the subject. A variation on this theme is the tiny portraits of people drawn in diary or gossip columns.
- There is a profile focusing on the person's views about a contemporary issue or experience or highlighting a recent achievement or failure.
- A longer profile will aim to provide an overview of a life. The person will be chosen probably because of a newsworthy element (a new job, a new book, film, television series, political campaign, or they are visiting the local region) which will be highlighted.

- A person may be profiled because of some unusual feature of their lives. They may have the largest collection of football or theatre programmes in the country or an unusual job such as travelling around advising gypsies on educational matters. The news element here is not significant.

- There is the 'authoritative' profile (such as in the *Sunday Times* and the *Sunday Telegraph*) in which the newspaper tries to present its definitive view on the subject. These will tend to carry other people's views of the subject but will not carry any byline since it is the publication speaking.

- There is a whole range of 'special focus' profiles which build a picture of a person around a specific angle. The *Sunday Times* has its 'Life in the Day' series and 'Relative Values' in which two members of the same family give their impressions of growing up with the other person. (A similar feature in the *Independent* is called 'A Family Affair'.) The *Guardian* has a 'My Media' and a 'My Big Break' column. *The Times* has a 'Love etc' column in which folk talk (often with amazing frankness) about their love and sex lives.

- Becoming increasingly popular are question-and-answer profiles around various themes. The *Guardian Weekend* supplement has its 'Questionnaire' in which celebrities answer a standard series of questions while the freebie *Metro* series has 'The 60 second interview'. The *Independent* runs a regular Q & A profile based on readers' submissions while its Monday-edition *Media Weekly* has a regular 'My mentor' column. The *Observer Magazine*'s 'This Much I Know' weekly column carries a list of usually fascinating direct quotes from the subject with no intervention by the journalist. Often these special-theme profiles are commentaries rather than interview-based features. *The Times* has 'The Test' in which personalities are assessed in various categories. The *Guardian* has 'Pass Notes' in which the subjects are dissected through a jokey, conversational style of questioning.

- Occasionally a couple are profiled in the same article; they may be married, close friends, living together or in a business partnership. Some newspapers profile families. The Doncaster *Free Press* has a regular 'School Report'. Football teams, golf clubs can be profiled: on 24 November 2004, *Horncastle News* profiled a local choral group, the Banovallum Singers, on their twenty-fifth anniversary (so providing lots of opportunities for people-packed pics).

Preparing the profile paint

Focus

The journalist has to be aware of the particular kind of profile sought by their publication. Is it to be an overview of the life or a focus on the latest achievements or affairs, or a 'life in the day' (very different from a 'day in the life')? In every case, the focus will influence the questioning. The journalist tends to identify to the subject during the initial contact the kind (and possible length) of profile envisaged.

Background research

Absolutely crucial. Quite simply the more knowledge of the subject and their special area you bring to the interview the more respect they will have for you and the more likely they are to 'open up'. Thus, if you are interviewing a writer, film director, television producer or sports personality, local council leader or political campaigner you should be aware of their previous achievements. People featured in *Who's Who* will not expect questions about fundamental details of their life. The challenge is very different when the subject is unknown. In that case, the journalist needs to convey an interest in their subject and their specialist area.

Before (and if possible after) the interview, ask other people about your subject. You may want to include some of these views in your profile. Consult the cuttings; check out Google, other search engines and their website (official and unofficial); consult the celebrity site http://www.celebritiesworldwide.com – but don't presume details are accurate without checking. Immerse yourself in your subject.

Place of interview(s)

Most profiles are built on the basis of one-off interviews. Describing the time and place of the interview might provide colour to the piece. Good journalists use all their senses. Sometimes, the profile is the result of a series of interviews. On one occasion the subject may be relaxed, at another completely different. They may be extremely busy; describing snatches of conversation in various places can convey a sense of their hectic lifestyle. The journalist may meet the interviewee before the formal meeting by accident – and describe the experience in their copy. Occasionally a person is so famous they are extremely difficult to get hold of. Describing the hunt can provide colour to the profile. If the hunt ends in failure, the non-story can become the story. Again some people are very shy of interviews. When they finally agree, the 'rareness' is worth highlighting.

Sometimes personalities are unwilling to be interviewed. Profiles of them are still written, often containing comments about the person from other people. The person may have revealed something about themselves in a rare television interview and quotes and details from that may be used. Occasionally a profile might be built around a press conference but then the copy loses the feeling of intimacy that a face-to-face interview provides. Increasingly profiles are amounting to nothing more than rewrites of cuttings with some newsy element in the intro, and concern is growing over the power of PR departments to shape celebrity profiles. According to Tad Friend (1998): 'Most profiles are almost scripted by the PR agency.'

Those important brush strokes: CONSTRUCTING THE PROFILE

The influence of the news

Profiles need not begin with the newsworthy aspect. They might seek to highlight a particularly significant or unusual event in the past. They might open with a partic-ularly revealing quote. They might be descriptive, focusing on the appearance of the person or the environment in which the interview takes place. But many profiles are influenced by the news agenda and in these cases their news aspect will never be buried in copy. It will be near the start. Take, for instance, this profile of Nia Long by Elsa O'Toole in the *Voice* (1 November 2004), which focuses, in chatty style, on her role in the recently released film remake of *Alfie*:

> Let's face it, most women would not require the Dutch courage of a stiff drink before bedding Jude Law. Even if it was on a pool table, with 30 hairy-arsed film crew members standing around ogling.
>
> For Nia Long, however, it's all part of the day job, so when it came to shooting love scenes with Britain's hottest hunk, alcohol was foremost in her mind.
>
> The film in question is the *Alfie* remake which stars Jude in the title role made famous by Michael Caine in 1966.

Other profiles, in contrast, are 'timeless' without a specific news angle. The person themselves may simply be newsworthy or there may be something particularly interesting about them.

The importance of quotations

Most profiles will carry the views of the person through the use of direct quotes. The importance of these to the profile cannot be overstated. Given that the profile is attempting to paint the most vivid portrait possible, the language of the interviewee is a vital ingredient of their personality. A profile in which all the views are in reported speech will be deadly dull.

Some profiles will carry snatches of conversation (sometimes remembered rather than noted) verbatim. It helps provide special insights into the subject as well as varying the rhythmic pulse and tone of the writing. As here from Joanna Coles's profile of the American novelist Joyce Carol Oates in *The Times* (7 April 2000): the novelist Edmund White, who has an office opposite at Princeton University, 'bursts in'.

> 'We're talking about the role of illusion,' says Joyce by way of introduction.
>
> 'She's being very modest,' I complain.
>
> 'Well she's great,' says White.
>
> 'Oh isn't that sweet,' Joyce giggles.
>
> 'Ever since I've been here, she's taken me under her wing and introduced me to everybody. She's incredibly sweet and has more energy than anyone I know,' says White 'And she's also incredibly smart.'
>
> 'Oh my, *blush!*' cries Joyce.
>
> 'Very good, very good,' beams White sweeping up his raincoat and bustling out. 'See you later.'

Notice how Coles uses a range of attributive verbs ('says', 'complain', 'giggles', 'cries', 'beams'). Similarly, in her profile of Hollywood star Jamie Lee Curtis, Tiffany Rose (the *Independent*, 3 December 2004) used 'practically hollers', 'chatters away', 'rattles on', 'says wryly', 'shrugs', 'almost snorts', 'says, sighing'. That variety is typical of many features and profiles but be warned: poorly handled it can appear contrived.

Hard news hardly ever begins with direct quotes but profiles quite often do. A striking phrase can encapsulate so much of the person's personality. Other profiles will merge quotes from a conversation into one long, direct quote such as the 'Life in the Day' feature in the *Sunday Times* colour supplement. The interviewee will often be consulted to see if they approve of the editing. Some profiles carry quotes from people about the interviewee, their personality and/or their work. This is particularly the case in 'authoritative' profiles which attempt to provide an overview of the person and their achievements.

Descriptive colour

Many profiles carry descriptions of the person, their appearance, their mannerisms perhaps, their asides, the environment where they live, work or are interviewed. All this adds colour and variety to the copy. Thus, to capture the personality of Italy's famed foreign correspondent Tiziano Terzani, Peter Popham (the *Independent*, 21 April 2004) described his home in detail:

> Tiziano Terzani at home in Florence is reminiscent of one of those 18th century English nabobs, returned after a lucrative spell with the East India Company laden with treasures of the East. The home is fabulous, a house high up on the hills above Florence, in a district justly named *Bel Sguardo* (beautiful view). A cherry tree is in bloom outside the front door. The home he shares with his wife and frequent travelling companion, Angela, is full of the spoils of their journeys: an antique Chinese four-poster bed, chests and carpets, gleaming bronze buddhas, thousands of books.

Or take a look at the collection of marvellous profiles by drama producer and critic Kenneth Tynan (1990). This is how he describes Noël Coward's home, with such clarity, colour, metaphorical inventiveness and meticulous attention to detail (1990: 34):

> His house in Kensington is like a smart tavern in a market-town: hidden in a mews, with doors of glass and wrought-iron, and new-smelling panelling on the walls. A chic but quiet rendezvous, with a good cellar, you might judge, until you enter the studio – a high, airy room which might belong to a landscape painter with a rich Italian mistress. There are paintings everywhere except on the floor, which is board as often as it is carpet; over the door, an excellent oil of the owner by Clemence Dane; deep, snug and unshowy armchairs; and two grand pianos on rostrums in opposite corners.

(As an exercise, why not attempt to describe the room you are sitting in now? It's not easy!)

But do not be tempted to invent descriptive colour to brighten up a phone-based profile. In its 1992 report, the Press Complaints Commission criticised a reporter who said of the interviewee 'Watching her, sitting up in bed', though they had never seen her face to face.

Chronology

Only rarely do profiles begin at the beginning of a life and end with a focus on the present. That chronology will appear extremely dull since it reflects no concept of journalistic values. Instead, profiles can highlight a newsworthy or specially interesting aspect of the person and then, in the body of the article, take up the chronological theme, finally returning to the main theme. But be careful not to make confusing chronological jumps (first talking about 1975, then 1965, then 1999, then 1962). In his *Independent on Sunday* profile of Brian Keenan, held captive by Islamic militants in Lebanon during the 1980s, Cole Moreton begins by exploring his search for self-understanding (7 November 2004). Then, mid-way through the profile, Moreton offers a concise narrative of Keenan's life up until that fateful day in 1986:

> He was restless, in the first three decades of his life. After school in east Belfast he worked as a plumber's apprentice but then went on to university to read English literature. He kept returning to Belfast after working in Spain, Brussels and Scotland but at the age of 34 he decided to cut free of a city that was 'falling apart'. He took up a year's contract to teach English and Russian literature at the American University in the Lebanon, intending to travel on to Australia when it expired. One early morning in April 1986, after four months in Beirut, he was surrounded at the gates of his villa and bundled into a car.

Newspapers often carry the biographical details briefly in a box accompanying the article leaving in the profile the space to concentrate on more up-to-date matters. Such 'fact boxes' are useful also for giving textual and visual variety to the page.

The presence of the reporter

In any representation of an individual there is bound to be a subjective element. Many profiles rely on an entertaining mix of quotes and background detail, the journalist subjectively selecting the material and remaining invisible in the copy. But some profiles exploit the journalist–interviewee relationship and make the journalist intentionally intrusive. Reporters may present their own views on the subject or on some of the issues raised in the interview. They may describe the dynamic in the relationship and how the interviewer responded to some of the questions (abruptly, hesitantly). This is how Miranda Sawyer, in the *Observer Magazine* (31 October 2004), describes actor Bill Nighy:

> When I say to him, I'd like to talk to you about your clothes, he almost whoops with joy, and we spend a good 20 minutes on suits, including which buttons to do up your jacket: 'Middle: always. Top: sometimes. Bottom: never. Younger men do this unbearable thing where they do all these buttons up, and you just want to kill them.'

Top interviewer Lynn Barber, in the *Independent on Sunday* (30 January 2000), was not afraid to admit her insecurities to her readers when profiling Jimmy Savile. Notice how she makes no attempt to soften the impact of the question ('I hope you don't mind me asking, but'); she goes straight to the point:

> Still, I was nervous when I told him: 'What people say is that you like little girls.' He reacted with a flurry of funny-voice Jimmy Savile patter which he does when he's getting his bearings.

And in her *Independent* profile of Hollywood star Jennifer Tilley (19 November 2004), Tiffany Rose uses both her eyes and her ears, observing her subject's droll reactions to passers-by:

> At our early-morning rendezvous in the lobby of the Sutton Place Hotel, Toronto, Tilly is glowing. She is oblivious to the admiring glances from onlookers who clearly recognise 'that face' but are having trouble placing it. 'They're probably thinking, "Did we go to college together? Were you a bridesmaid at my first husband's wedding? Or something,"' she muses.

The bias of the newspaper

When newspapers of the left carry profiles, they often promote strong political points, rather than the subjective bias of the individual reporter. As here, *Socialist Worker* (3 June 2000):

> Brian Souter, head of Stagecoach, has tried to pose as the voice of the people with his funding of the referendum over the anti-gay law, Section 28, in Scotland.
>
> Really, he is a shark who has spent the last 20 years building a multi-billion transport company by ruthlessly forcing other companies off the road.

The finishing touches

Profiles usually end on a significant note. Copy doesn't just die away meaninglessly. A common device is to end on a positive note, particularly if the subject has been open in the interview about their difficult times. Thus a profile of singer Russell Watson by Rebecca Hardy, in the *Daily Mail*'s Weekend section (20 November 2004), which has focused on his childhood difficulties and 'the hell' of his early career struggles, ends with this telling quote:

> 'I appreciate what I have because I did go through the mill,' he says. 'I'll never forget what it was like to have nothing.'

The tone

This is the most vital ingredient of the piece. Is it to be an affectionate piece? Is it to be respectful, gently mocking, a damning exposé, intellectually discursive, witty, 'neutral' (hope you will never write a sycophantic one!)? In each of these the language used will be different. You may spend a couple of hours, even days, with your subject. They may offer you a meal. Some form of human contact is established. It is then very tricky to write a damning (though obviously non-libellous) profile of that person. Equally there is a danger of solving this dilemma by lavishing praise on your subject. There can be no standard response. At all times, passing judgement should always be handled delicately. A crook, a racist or a sexist needs to be exposed. But the interview is an extremely artificial environment and the impression that the subject provides should always be viewed as partial and superficial.

13 Some specialist areas

Personal columns, reviewing, freelancing

The 'I' witness: PERSONAL COLUMNS

All news emerges from a dialectical process in which the subjective confronts the objective. Its subjective element is particularly evident in the complex process of selection. Personal columns make this subjectivity overt. The 'I' speaks loud and clear. Personal columns 'work' when the voice speaks in particularly original tones. They may be witty, controversial, no-nonsense, hard-hitting, culturally eclectic, conversational, quirky, bitchy, whimsical, confessional, authoritative, subversive, irritating. At their worst they combine crude ranting with personal abuse. But the writer's personality should always shine through the copy.

The reader enters into a kind of relationship with the writer. Often accompanying the column is a head-and-shoulders picture or drawing of the writer to help 'personalise' this relationship further. Readers can come to love them – or hate them. The worst fate for a columnist is to be ignored. Yet, at the same time, as Christopher Silvester (1997: xi) argues:

> a column appears in the same publication on a regular basis usually in the same position and with the same heading and by-line. The presence of the column is reassuring, therefore, not primarily because of what it has to say but because of its appearance in a particular spot, on a particular day or days and at an approximately predictable length.

Personal column styles, language and tones are also appropriate to their newspaper. They make up and are influenced by the overall 'personality' of the newspaper. Quotations from novels by contemporary East European novelists might appear in a column in the *Observer* but not in the *Star*. A slow-moving narrative about a strange appointment at the hairdresser's may be appropriate for a local weekly but not for the *Guardian*.

The value of good columnists is acknowledged by all newspapers. As Andrew Marr records (2004: 43): 'Star columnists, such as Simon Jenkins and Matthew Parris of *The Times* and Richard Littlejohn at the *Sun*, are paid more than some national newspaper editors . . . One tabloid columnist is said by colleagues to be on £500,000. There is a broadsheet writer on £300,000.' And he muses: 'The best columnists are hugely prized by their editors, though there is no evidence I have ever seen that the loss of a writer visibly moves circulation at all.'

Similarly local papers will use personal columns strategically. Rather than attempt to be journals of record like their daily rivals, a weekly may carry an opinionated column from either a staff journalist or a reader. In this way, the paper is striving to make its mark on the local community, intervening with a column aimed at getting people talking and possibly provoking letters (either for or against).

There are many forms of personal columns. They might be straight opinion or involve a small amount of journalistic research. John Pilger's prominently displayed columns in the *Daily Mirror* in the lead-up to the 2003 invasion of Iraq carried powerful arguments against the US–UK aggression but were always based on extensive research of the historical record. Or a column may comprise a selection of short features or news stories reflecting the interests of the writer. Sketch writers, such as Simon Hoggart (the *Guardian*), Quentin Letts (the *Daily Mail*), Simon Carr (the *Independent*) and Matthew Parris (*The Times*), are associated particularly with lighthearted, eye-witness (and over-affectionate) pieces on Parliament.

Most personal columns respond a little too slavishly to the dominant news agenda; too many journalists end up talking about other journalists, other media. Female confessional columnists, such as India Knight, Anna Blundy and Zoë Heller, became all the rage in the 1990s. Helen Fielding became the most famous exponent of the genre, and her *Bridget Jones's Diary* went on to become a global best-seller. Kathryn Flett's outpourings in the *Observer* on her marriage breakdown drew an enormous response from readers. 'I wasn't resorting to journalistic tricks to fill the inches. There was no longer a place for endless puns, alliteration and smarty-pants irony; instead I was stuck with the truth,' she wrote (Flett 1997).

Also during the 1990s concern grew over the explosion of columns throughout the press. As Suzanne Moore (1996: x) commented:

> As more and more people get their news from other forms of media, the role of newspaper journalism has become more interpretative and subjective. In these times of media saturation and its subsequent neurosis – information anxiety – columnists in their idiosyncratic ways wade through the mire of information about the world we live in.

But, critics argued, instead of hard news and hard-hitting investigative pieces, frothy features full of the mindless musings of over-important, over-paid celebrity journalists were filling up the columns. According to Brian McNair (2000: 64): 'The rise of the political commentator is a direct consequence of the commodification of the public sphere which makes it necessary for news organisations to brand their output (give it exchange value in a market place containing many other superficially similar brands).'

Tips for budding columnists

Maintaining a constant stream of (ideally original) opinion is not easy. Indeed, according to Stephen Glover (1999: 290–1), the columnist's skill is 'in writing about matters of which one is ignorant'. Certainly, the columnist must be interested in, and reasonably informed about, a wide range of issues. Many journalists pick the brains of experts on their current subject – and then pass them on as if they were their own.

The American columnist Max Lerner had this advice: 'I keep a notebook and a file into which I jot down ideas for columns as they occur to me. Before I write I look through the papers and often some headline event will converge with one of these ideas' (Silvester 1997: xxiii).

Keith Waterhouse (1995), the eminent Fleet Street columnist, has provided his own 25-step plan to writing the perfect column. It included:

- Every columnist needs a good half-dozen hobby horses. But do not ride them to death.
- On cuttings: 'The more cuttings you accumulate, the more you will be tempted to offload them on to your readers ... Packing the column with other people's quotes is the columnar equivalent of watering the milk. Assimilate material and then discard it.'
- Never try to fake it. 'Nothing is so transparent as insincerity – pile on the adjectives though you may, false indignation has the ring of a counterfeit coin.'
- A column should not be used to pursue a personal grudge unless it is going to ring bells with most of your readers.
- Allow your readers only a few restricted glimpses into your private life.
- Columnar feuds are amusing to other columnists and may even yield them copy providing they don't mind living vicariously. The reader, or what Craig Brown describes as 'that diminishing minority of people who do not write newspaper columns', find them bemusing.

Analysis of Anne Robinson's column:
The Times (15 April 2000)

> ● I can't quite work out why Kathleen Turner getting her kit off every night in *The Graduate* in the West End is causing such a stir. The first time around, when Dustin Hoffman starred in the film with Anne Bancroft, it was wonderfully radical for Mrs Robinson to shamelessly seduce her daughter's boyfriend. But now I am Mrs Robinson's age-plus, I think it would take no time at all to get Benjamin into the sack.
>
> If only because these days Elaine, her daughter, would be a terrifyingly ambitious young woman with her sights set on merchant banking and million-dollar bonuses, doubtless scaring Benjamin witless with her power and desire for success. In contrast one can see the middle-aged Mrs Robinson as a very comforting alternative and needing to do little more than whistle to persuade an insecure lad to jump into bed alongside her.
>
> ● Madam Speaker has made it clear where she will and will not tolerate breast feeding in the House of Commons. Which surprised me because I thought we had sorted all that years ago when a young Labour MP called Helene Hayman fought to be allowed to bring her baby to Westminster.
>
> By co-incidence the now Baroness Hayman, and an Agriculture Minister, was on *Watchdog* last week talking about Pet Passports.

After we came off air I raised the breast-feeding episode and she told me firmly that she held no particular brief for women wanting to feed in public. Her problem was a tiny ten-day-old baby, an even tinier Labour majority and an insistence by the whips that she be around to vote.

As she explained, her only hope of keeping baby and party happy was to fight to be allowed to nurse in between debates. Baby Ben, incidentally, is now 23.

● Back to Covent Garden last week to see Sylvie Guillem in *Manon*.

It was sensational and, quite rightly, the audience howled its approval at the end.

My friend Sally, who was kind enough to get the tickets, was dreadfully disappointed with our view from Row D because the incline of the seats, intended to improve your view, is negligible so near the front and it was tricky seeing the footwork.

Then, at the interval, two women who turned out to be devoted fans of the Russian dancer Irek Mukhamedov, and had already seen him dance the role of Lescaut four times within a fortnight, came up to say hello. They looked pityingly at us when we told them where we were sitting.

'You have to go for Row A, or after Row H,' said one of them shaking her head in disbelief that none of us possessed such obvious House intelligence.

Why should we? When you book no one offers you that sort of advice and it prompted me to step back into the auditorium early to ask one of the opera house staff where he would sit if he was paying.

'A22 upstairs,' he said without hesitating, adding that when the Queen really wants to see the action she doesn't bother with the Royal Box. She and her party are there with the people in the front row of the circle.

● It's usually only Vivienne Westwood's most outrageous designs that are chosen by picture editors to feature in newspapers. A shame because it causes the public to view her, unfairly, as way out and silly.

A much better range of her work from the collection of Romilly McAlpine has gone on show at the Museum of London and is well worth a visit. Penrose absolutely fell in love with several of the numbers.

But then he loves women in men's clothes and would prefer me to dress the same as Katharine Hepburn in *On Golden Pond*. Even though I keep telling him that without the cheek bones, the hair and the slim hips, Katharine Hepburn would look like a bag lady.

● The party to launch the exhibition was swarming with glittery people. Nicky Haslam, the designer who looks about thirty instead of sixty and unlike Ms Westwood is still in his punk rock phase, introduced me to Hilary Alexander, from *The Daily Telegraph*.

Ms Alexander does one of those daytime shows where housewives are taken out of their own clothes and put into daring new outfits. I often think half of them look better before the hordes of makeover artists get to work. But the television team clearly believes it is taking part in important life-saving or at least face-saving surgery.

Dangerously so. Ten seconds after we were introduced, Ms Alexander started fiddling with my fringe and moving it around and telling me it was better "spread out". I was very tempted to give her a slap.

Anne Robinson

> 'Now I am Mrs Robinson's age-plus, I think it would take no time to get Benjamin into the sack'

● I CAN'T quite work out why Kathleen Turner getting her kit off every night in *The Graduate* in the West End is causing such a stir. The first time around, when Dustin Hoffman starred in the film with Anne Bancroft, it was wonderfully radical for Mrs Robinson to shamelessly seduce her daughter's boyfriend. But now I am Mrs Robinson's age-plus, I think it would take no time at all to get Benjamin into the sack.

If only because these days Elaine, her daughter, would be a terrifyingly ambitious young woman with her sights set on merchant banking and million-dollar bonuses, doubtless scaring Benjamin witless with her power and desire for success. In contrast one can see the middle-aged Mrs Robinson as a very comforting alternative and needing to do little more than whistle to persuade an insecure lad to jump into bed alongside her.

● MADAM Speaker has made it clear where she will and

will not tolerate breast feeding in the House of Commons. Which surprised me because I thought we had sorted all that years ago when a young Labour MP called Helene Hayman fought to be allowed to bring her baby to Westminster.

By coincidence the now Baroness Hayman, and an Agriculture Minister, was on *Watchdog* last week talking about Pet Passports.

After we came off air I raised the breast-feeding episode and she told me firmly that she held no particular brief for women wanting to feed in public. Her problem was a tiny ten-day-old baby, an even tinier Labour majority and an insistence by the whips that she be around to vote.

As she explained, her only hope of keeping baby and party happy was to fight to be allowed to nurse in between debates. Baby Ben, incidentally, is now 23.

● BACK to Covent Garden last week to see Sylvie Guillem in *Manon*.

It was sensational and, quite

rightly, the audience howled its approval at the end.

My friend Sally, who was kind enough to get the tickets, was dreadfully disappointed with our view from Row D because the incline of the seats, intended to improve your view, is negligible so near the front and it was tricky seeing the footwork.

Then, at the interval, two women who turned out to be devoted fans of the Russian dancer Irek

Mukhamedov, and had already seen him dance the role of Lescaut four times within a fortnight, came up to say hello. They looked pityingly at us when we told them where we were sitting.

"You have to go for Row A, or after Row H," said one of them shaking her head in disbelief that neither of us possessed such obvious House intelligence.

Why should we? When you book

no one offers you that sort of advice and it prompted me to step back into the auditorium early to ask one of the opera house staff where he would sit if he was paying.

"A22 upstairs," he said without hesitating, adding that when the Queen really wants to see the action she doesn't bother with the Royal Box. She and her party are there with the people in the front row of the circle.

● IT'S usually only Vivienne Westwood's most outrageous designs that are chosen by picture editors to feature in newspapers. A shame because it causes the public to view her, unfairly, as way out and silly.

A much better range of her work from the collection of Romilly McAlpine has gone on show at the Museum of London and is well worth a visit. Penrose absolutely fell in love with several of the numbers.

But then he loves women in men's clothes and would prefer me to dress the same as Katharine Hepburn in *On Golden Pond*. Even though I keep telling him that without the cheek bones, the hair and the slim hips, Katharine Hepburn would look like a bag lady.

● THE PARTY to launch the exhibition was swarming with glittery people. Nicky Haslam, the designer who looks about thirty instead of sixty and unlike Ms Westwood is still in his punk rock phase,

introduced me to Hilary Alexander, from *The Daily Telegraph*.

Ms Alexander does one of those daytime shows where housewives are taken out of their own clothes and put into glamourous new outfits. I often think half of them look better before the hordes of makeover artists get to work. But the television team clearly believes it is taking part in important life-saving or at least face-saving surgery.

Dangerously so. Ten seconds after we were introduced, Ms Alexander started fiddling with my fringe and moving it around and telling me it was better "spread out". I was very tempted to give her a slap.

● THE DAUGHTER is due home from New York for Easter. I am taking time off to bake and to cosset. Kirsty Young, who knows a thing or two about television presenting but has yet to experience the joys of being a guilty working mother, will be delighting you for the next three weeks.

anne.robinson@the-times.co.uk

Overview: critics might suggest this is a typical example of the 'dumbing down' of the broadsheet press: a TV celebrity penning a few gossipy thoughts based on her somewhat privileged lifestyle flitting from TV studio to Covent Garden and on to a glittery party. Until a decade ago this kind of column was reserved for the tabloid press (where Ms Robinson, in fact, developed her journalistic reputation). Others may argue it is all a necessary part of *The Times*'s moves to shake off its dull and sombre, pre-Murdoch past. Intriguingly Ms Robinson depicts a very feminine world: all her subjects are women, bar one.

Byline: The byline (in a large font) is accompanied by an unusual mug shot. Her expression is pleasantly cheeky-cum-whimsical. But most intriguing is the position of that right hand. It is held tightly around her front – as if protecting her from attack and that fist seems ready to punch anyone who dares intrude on her private territory. The few words drawn from the text (a 'pull quote' in a 'panel' in the jargon) accompanying the mug shot highlight significantly a passing remark that dwells on sex.

Gossip point one: 'I' is the first word, setting the tone for the highly individualised copy. Significantly, to draw in her readers, she begins by focusing on a sexual theme. The largely male journalists of Fleet Street were, indeed, getting into something of a sweat over middle-aged Kathleen Turner, star of Hollywood (that ultimate dream machine), stripping on the West End stage. Acres of news, columnar and review copy (in both tabloids and broadsheets) were devoted to the event, even though it lasted for no more than a split second. (Similar hysteria later followed news that the former Mrs Mick Jagger, Jerry Hall, was to succeed Turner in the role.) Turner herself (and her publicists) fed the frenzy by turning up to a press conference draped in a towel. There are many possible ways of explaining all this: a Freudian might focus on the failure of male journalists to outgrow their Oedipal adolescent fantasies about naked women – and particularly their mothers; a Marxist, for instance, might stress the commodification of women's bodies. Robinson avoids all these issues and moves on to a separate point: the supposed shock of seeing a middle-aged Mrs Robinson seduce the much younger Benjamin. It is intriguing to see how columnist Robinson sympathises and even identifies with Benjamin. Thus a determined careerist woman becomes, in her view, 'terrifying' – perhaps because she threatens men's traditional seats of power. Is there not a subtle anti-feminist agenda at work here?

Gossip point two: from sex we shift to the glittery world of TV celebrities and MPs. Betty Boothroyd, former Speaker of the House, had recently ruled against allowing MPs to breastfeed in the Commons chamber or committee rooms, though they were still permitted in their private rooms and in lavatories. Ms Robinson wants to convey this but her 'will and will not tolerate breast feeding' would be merely confusing to most of her readers. But she cleverly uses the column to give her readers a little insight into the goings on behind the camera, since what is unseen is far more interesting than the visible. It appears that her television guest Helene Hayman 'years ago' (a rather vague term) came to prominence over the Commons breastfeeding issue. But not through any sense of solidarity with her feminist sisters: she did it simply because of her concern to preserve the wafer-thin Labour majority. Robinson's failure to express any regret here is as significant as anything said.

Gossip point three: notice it's 'Back to Covent Garden' not 'To Covent Garden'. Robinson is clearly part of that exclusive set who can afford regular visits. By reading her column we vicariously mingle. 'Dreadfully disappointed' uses alliteration to stress the point but it is not a phrase that would trip off the lips of the average man or woman on the Clapham Omnibus. An interesting narrative develops with a whiff of the investigative about it. She chats with two other Garden-goers about the best seats available. Dialogue helps vary the rhythm of the text. And it transpires that 'A22 upstairs' is the best. So you have been advised. But the most important fact is missing. Precisely how much is that seat? That kind of basic financial question is not raised in this dreamy, wealthy world by Robinson (who, a profile in the *Guardian* of 6 October 2000 revealed, had earned £2 million in 1999). Also, intriguingly, it appears that when the Queen mixes with 'the people' it is not out of any democratic instinct: she is simply aiming to get the best seat. Ms Robinson fails to draw out the irony here.

Gossip point four: and so to the launch of an exhibition of clothes by Vivienne Westwood. Tabloid values dominate this column – and yet here she takes a swipe at them for distorting the achievements of Vivienne Westwood. Then suddenly a 'Penrose' arrives on the scene with definite views about women's dress. Who is this person? Is it her lover, her husband, her butler? I think we should have been told. And why this reference to *On Golden Pond*? Katharine Hepburn was well known for wearing trousers but this preference has never been particularly associated in the public consciousness with this specific film.

Gossip point five: and so to her meeting another journalist at the exhibition launch party. Ms Robinson is critical of the kind of television programme her new acquaintance hosts, at the same time attempting to 'balance' her view. But in saying 'the television team clearly believes it is taking part in important life-saving or at least face-saving surgery' she exaggerates their case and thus subtly reinforces her own. Ms Alexander then attempts to invade Ms Robinson's personal space, fiddling with her fringe. From her mug shot we know how important that space is to Ms Robinson. It is no surprise, then, when she writes: 'I was very tempted to give her a slap.' Perhaps Ms Alexander should feel herself lucky not to have been punched in the face.

The art of reviewing

Reviews serve many functions. They provide basic information: for example, that a film has just been released and can be seen at the cinemas indicated. For people who intend to see, read or hear a work (or, in the case of broadcasting, have already seen or heard it) the review gives an opinion carrying some authority to compare with their own. Yet often the vast majority of readers will never experience directly the work under review. A concert may have been attended by no more than a few hundred people. The review must then exist as a piece of writing in its own right. It must entice in the reader through the quality and colour of its prose. It must entertain, though different newspapers have different conceptions of what entertainment means.

For the producers of the work the review (good, bad or indifferent) offers some vital publicity. Many journalists like reviewing. They often come from a humanities academic background where arts reviewing is common. Science is still on the margins of the journalists' culture. And, for the newspaper, reviews can attract advertisers. A newspaper carrying substantial book reviews, for instance, is more likely to attract advertising from book publishers than one which largely ignores books.

On many local weeklies, the review might serve a different purpose. The newspaper is acting as a journal of record for the local community, carrying all the names of the performers, say, in a school play. Accompanied by a photograph of a scene, the report will serve as a souvenir for many. Just as in news, an overall consensus operates in the selection of works to review. For instance, in the area of films, the global economic power of Hollywood means that, every week, its latest products receive automatic priority. In the area of books reviewing, a consensus means that out of the hundreds published every week just a few receive prominent attention throughout Fleet Street. At the heart of reviewing lie some basic journalistic challenges. A great writer does not necessarily make a great reviewer.

- Names of performers, producers, writers and of any fictional characters and places must be carried correctly. Where relevant their titles must be given. In other words, the reviewer must be able to take an accurate note (see Gilbert 1999: 107).
- Direct quotes from the works, similarly, must be given correctly.
- Plots (or, say, the contents of an exhibition) should be summed up clearly and in accessible language.
- Any esoteric elements should be conveyed in a language likely to be understood by the majority of readers.
- In some cases, special sensitivity is required. A reporter, for instance, approaches a work by a group of committed amateurs or by children with different aesthetic standards from when reviewing a work by professionals. The reviewer may do the reader a service by not spoiling the suspense of a thriller; they may choose not to reveal a sudden twist in the plot at the end.
- In criticising the work, the journalist must not stray into libel by saying something that can damage a person's reputation.
- The journalist has to be true to their own experience and find the words to convey that accurately and concisely without falling into cliché.
- The reviewer must be able to write, handling variations of tone and sentence structure confidently in accordance with the overall style of the newspaper. The thematic structure (as in all features) must be clear and not contain any contradictions or repetitions.
- As in all journalistic writing, the intro section must carry sufficient weight to attract the reader. It might encapsulate the main theme of the piece, it may contain a striking quote or description, a joke or a narrative. If it is dull, pretentious, long-winded or off-target it has failed.
- Reviewers usually write to a specific length. As Irving Wardle, veteran theatre critic, commented: 'Reviewers soon learn to write to length knowing that if they overwrite it is their opinion that will be cut while all the plottery will be kept intact' (*Independent on Sunday*, 12 July 1992).
- The reviewer must be able to convey their enthusiasm for their specialist area. As critic Nigel Andrew comments: 'There is no such thing as an uninteresting film, wherever it came from, however much or little it cost and whatever it is trying to say' (*Press Gazette*, 15 January 1999).
- The style, length, content and tone of an arts review are influenced by many factors. Reviews in the popular press, often by celebrities, tend to be short, focusing on the entertainment level of the work. The language, as in the rest of the paper, is usually brisk and straight-to-the point. Any sexual, sensational, human interest elements are highlighted. The tone can be varied: mocking, ironic, damning,

praising. But it is rarely analytical. In films and theatre/showbiz reviews, the focus is often on the performance of the leading 'star', particularly if they are British.

* And the reviewer needs to be aware of the style of their newspaper, the expectations and cultural biases of its readers (Gilbert 1999: 103–5)

Many local papers tend to mix elements of the popular with those of the middle brow. The language and sentence length follow the style in the rest of the paper. But an extra overall length gives the chance for a more idiosyncratic approach. Plots can be explored in greater depth; themes can be explored further. Often in local and middle-brow papers, the emphasis tends to be more on the personalities involved. Heavies tend to put greater emphasis on reviewing, though there is a distinct London bias in their coverage. They draw important advertising from the arts and many of their readers, educated past the age of 18, have either an active or passive interest in 'culture'. Reviewers in the heavies aim to impress with the depth of their knowledge and appreciation. But as Edward Greenfield, for forty years *Guardian* music critic, commented (30 July 1993): 'My own belief is that the music critic must aim at appreciation above all, trying never to let the obvious need to analyse in nit-picking detail to get in the way of enjoyment.'

Analysis of 'Back row with Alan Frank:

YET MOORE FIBS FROM SPIN KING'. REVIEW OF MICHAEL MOORE'S *FAHRENHEIT 9/11*: THE *DAILY STAR* (9 JULY 2004) BY ALAN FRANK

Tony Blair may be wiping egg off his face after admitting that Iraq may not have had any weapons of mass destruction after all.

But he can thank his lucky stars that American film-maker Michael Moore was after his buddy George W. Bush and not him.

WMDs appear to have been a lie – and that's fine with Moore, who seems to believe that one good lie deserves another.

He fiddles with facts, manipulates movie clips and screws around with statistics as he bludgeons Bush with his side of events.

His examination of 'the Bush administration's action in the wake of the tragic events 9/11' is brilliant documentary film-making and won the coveted Palme D'Or at the Cannes. But its content needs to be taken with a huge pinch of salt.

It could well win an Academy Award, too, especially if there's a new Oscar category for Best Propaganda.

Moore is a brilliant spin-doctor, but in the end Moore is less.

VERDICT: 2/10

This is in many ways a typical *Star* review. It's short and snappy (just 161 words) (compared with, say, Mark Kermode's 1,294-word review of the same film in the *Observer* of 11 July 2004). All the sentences are short: 24 words, 22, 23, 21, 28, 13, 18, 12. The review is clearly intended to be read at speed. Three 'but's and four 'and's help provide that pace. The structure is clear: the opening par highlights Prime Minister Blair's embarrassment over WMD claims before the Iraq invasion of 2003;

the second par moves on to Moore's film; the next three pars make some very gener-alised criticisms (none of them supported by any evidence); the penultimate par suggests, ironically, the film could win an Academy Award. The final par ends with a concise, pun-laden flourish.

The reviewer is strangely ambivalent throughout, mixing praise and condemna-tion in equal measures. On the one hand Blair is lucky not to have been the subject of Moore's film because he is ruthless in exposing the lies surrounding WMD. On the other hand, Moore, he says, embellishes his argument with a stream of lies and spin. It is a 'brilliant documentary' but the content 'needs to be taken with a huge pinch of salt'. It could win a major award – but, Frank adds ironically, for Best Propaganda. And so on. Perhaps this ambivalence arises from the author's attempt to reconcile his newspaper's stance of fervid support for the 2003 invasion of Iraq with his admiration for the documentary qualities of the film.

It's a highly contrived, literary piece with puns and alliterations featuring throughout. This linguistic play begins in the headline ('Moore fibs') and comes to a head in par four: notice here the alliterations in 'fiddles with facts', 'manipulates movie clips', 'screws around with statistics' and 'bludgeons Bush'. And he finishes deliberately with the phrase 'in the end' and the conclusive, concise and witty pun 'Moore is less'. In other words, in place of a serious grappling with the political issues in the film, the reviewer has indulged in a sort of hedonistic, linguistic game.

And, in keeping with the conventional tabloid style, Frank uses a range of colourful, vernacular, slangy words and phrases: such as 'wiping egg off his face', 'thank his lucky stars', 'buddy', 'taken with a huge pinch of salt'. In this way, he is reaching out to his imaginary audience, addressing them directly in a language he thinks they will relate to. But is he right in thinking that?

Moreover, reviews, like all newspaper copy, are interesting as much for what they omit as for what they include. There is no time here to refer to Moore's other films, to explore the journalistic issues surrounding blockbuster documentaries, to compare it to other films about the invasion (such as Errol Morris's *The Fog of War*) or to examine Moore's sourcing techniques. A reviewer sounds off – and for the *Star* that's fine. That mark of 2/10 offers the final damning verdict.

Analysis of 'A Few Wisps of Smoke', review of *Burning Issues*: MORNING STAR (4 MAY 2000)

Compared to the Vaughan review, the sentence lengths here are much longer (25, 2, 44, 64, 44, 11, 38, 36, 61, 43, 35, 17, 16, 21, 22). In places they are too long. The piece is analytical and eclectic in its literary references. Larkin, Kafka, Proust, Powell, Rushdie, Orwell are all mentioned en passant without any explanations – the writer presuming a certain level of literary knowledge among his readers. There is a certain flattery involved which endears him to his readers. The text effectively mixes abstract musings (on say 'the nature of creativity', the 'credibility of biography', 'the source of great art') with slang and cliché ('the shit has really hit the fans', 'stabbing him in the back', 'whacky'). Though it appears in the newspaper which describes itself as 'the daily paper of the left', there is nothing particularly socialist or Marxist about the review. The London bias of the mainstream press is reflected here also in the *Morning Star*'s choice of plays to review.

A few wisps of smoke

BURNING ISSUES
Hampstead Theatre,
London NW3

WHEN poet Philip Larkin was revealed — after his death as racist, misogynist, porn-loving and small-minded, there was much debate about whether his reputation would survive. It did.

In Ron Hutchinson's new play, when a small publishing company newly acquired by a US conglomerate discovers that the diaries of its star author, Mallowan (Kenneth Colley) — a potential Nobel winner — contain little more than racist abuse, the shit has really hit the fans.

The publishers need the author's final instalment of his 12-volume novel; the contract to publish the journals is watertight; Mallowan's biographer, second-rate academic Watkins (William Chubb), failed to discover their existence; the US company's placeman, Richter (Rob Spendlove), sees a threat to profits; the editor who signed the contract fears for his Tuscan villa and his colleague is not-so-subtly stabbing him in the back.

When, in the space of a couple of hours, Mallowan is flattened by a gas boiler explosion and Watkins walks in front of a bus, the question becomes - by way of simplistic reference to Mein Kampf — whether the journals should go under the match.

There are some incidental pleasures, some funny lines and good performances. But for all Hutchinson's attempts to pose serious questions — about the nature of creativity, the credibility of biography, the morality of suppressing an author's beliefs to protect his literary reputation — his characters and situations are consistently unbelievable.

Mallowan, is constructed from bits of other writers — being a former insurance clerk (sort of Kafka), living "up north" in isolation except for his charlady (sort of Larkin), writing a novel sequence (sort of Proust/Powell).

But when we meet him, it is impossible to believe that this man, who keeps his custard creams in a lockable tin, could have written anything more profound than a complaint to the Gas Board, let alone a 12-novel humanistic piece about art and morality and the basic plot for The Satanic Verses, for which Rushdie has written to thank him.

Hutchinson is certainly arguing that the most banal life and personality can harbour the profound, a la Larkin, and - as one of the characters quotes from Orwell — that almost any world view, however whacky or extreme, can be a source of great art.

But with only hearsay to go on in respect of his literary talents, belief in Mallowan simply can't survive, particularly as his explanation for the disparity between his fiction and his journals is so unconvincing.

As the publishers, John Gordon-Sinclair and Andrew Woodall are entertainingly implausible but Miranda Pleasance's part is underwritten. As their accountant boss, Spendlove does well to make a last act double-U-turn only mildly preposterous. Chubb has the best turn as he discovers to his horror the extent to which his contemptuous subject has misled him.

But overall, Burning Issues is like the bonfire at its end, giving off little more than a few wisps of smoke.

Plays until June 3. Box office: 020 7722 9301.

MIKE PARKER

The review begins dramatically with a focus on Larkin. The piling on of the striking adjectives ('racist, misogynist, porn-loving and small-minded') effectively attracts attention. It is like the opening movement of a symphony which concludes with the staccato sentence 'It did'. But then the next pars ignore the Larkin theme and so the intro is left high and dry, bearing no apparent relation to the rest of the text. The intro implies that the play is primarily about Larkin. But it turns out it isn't; in par 6 we learn it is only loosely based on Larkin as well as a number of other writers. Confusing. The reviewer also in many places appears to be attempting to cram in too many details. Sentences become overloaded with subordinate clauses and text in parentheses. Pars 2–4, in which Parker tells the story of the play, are particularly convoluted.

The structure is entirely clear. Par 1: the Larkin allusion; pars 2–4: the plot; pars 5–9: analysis of main themes; par 10: assessment of actors' performances; par 11: conclusive remarks; final par: booking details. Most of the analysis is constructed around contrasts (on the one hand this, on the other hand that) which becomes repetitive and clichéd. Thus, in par 5, he writes: 'There are some incidental pleasures . . . But . . .' In the next par we hear about Mallowan. Par 7 begins: 'But when we meet him'. Again the focus is on Hutchinson's argument. And the next par begins: 'But with only hearsay to go on'. And so on. There is some imaginative writing based on acute observations, such as 'it is impossible to believe that this man, who keeps his custard creams in a lockable tin, could have written anything more profound than a complaint to the Gas Board [strikingly down-to-earth], let alone a 12-novel humanistic piece about art and morality'. And the short conclusive par in which he playfully and almost poetically puns around the 'Burning Issues' theme works well (and provides the sub with a useful headline phrase).

Freelancing: A SURVIVAL GUIDE

Just as there are many kinds of staff reporters so there are many kinds of freelances. Some are the best-paid and busiest writers. Many are finding life extremely difficult with widespread cuts in newspaper journalists' jobs intensifying competition among freelances. Such trends are not limited to the UK: an International Labour Organisation world survey in 1999 on the economic and social status of freelances revealed a 'scandalous exploitation expanding rapidly over the globe'. All the same, if you are determined, organised, imaginative, talented and can cope with stress, opportunities are still available to break into the freelance world.

A survey by the NUJ in 2004 found the average age of a freelance was 46, and 68 per cent had worked previously as staffers, typically for 11 years before going it alone. The overwhelming majority enjoyed being freelance with only 30 per cent wanting to return to a staff job. Some 87 per cent rated producing high-quality work as their most important motivation – even higher than getting paid (Leston 2004).

There are clearly good and bad sides to the freelance life. To a certain extent freelances enjoy some 'freedoms' not permitted to staff writers. They can work from home, they are not forced to abide by a strict daily routine, they can avoid all the hassles of office politics. They may even be given the opportunity to pursue a specialism which no other journalistic route has allowed. They may be fascinated by food and wine. A full-time food specialist is a rare commodity on daily and weekly newspapers. Freelancing for a number of publications in this area is more of a possibility.

But freelances can rarely free themselves from the constraints of the market. You may be contemptuous of the capitalist rat-race of the newspaper world but freelancing hardly provides a refuge from this. Freelances have to go where the money is. George Orwell, for instance, committed himself to small-scale, left-wing, literary journals and largely ignored the seductive appeal of Fleet Street. But until his last two novels, *Animal Farm* and *Nineteen Eighty-Four*, achieved global success he lived in relative poverty. It was his ethical and political choice (Keeble 2000). If you are interested in progressive journalism then secure a steady job (with a charity, progressive think-tank or pressure group) and build up your freelance experience on that foundation.

A freelance's working day is in many respects more demanding and stressful than that of a staffer. Not only do they have the problems of finding work, promoting new ideas and meeting deadlines, but also they have a range of other issues to worry about. They have to sort out taxation problems. They may have to chase finance departments to pay up. They have to negotiate rates and make sure all their equipment is maintained properly. Without the regular inflow of money enjoyed by staff journalists, freelances have, in short, to be far more financially organised. In the 2004 NUJ survey of freelances, 58 per cent reported having some or lots of money worries.

On top of all this, the freelance has no job security. When jobs are on the line, they are invariably the first to suffer. Without the companionship that goes with a full-time job, the freelance's life can be lonely. Significantly, the NUJ survey found 64 per cent reporting depression and 47 per cent having serious drinking or smoking habits (Leston 2004). And Michael Durham warns that working from home is a 'la-la land for the unwary' (2004): 'Even with an au pair, an after school helper, school hours, multitudes of labour-saving devices and people in to cook and clean, you will always end up at the mercy of the school run, the washing up, the taxi service to the judo club, the window cleaners, the radiator repair man, the doctor ... However disciplined you try to be, you will never, ever get any proper work done.'

Starting up

Launching into a freelance career is not easy. Many freelances are former full-time staffers who have developed a specialism, sent out linage (freelance copy paid by the line) to nationals and then, through either choice or redundancy, taken the plunge and gone solo or started a small agency. Sometimes a non-journalist professional may build up contacts and a specialist knowledge. They may have enjoyed close links with the media and even contributed occasional articles to the press. On this basis they may decide to switch to journalism as a career. The feature linking all these examples is a specialism which can be exploited journalistically. Very few freelances are generalists. As Stephen Wade (1997: 45) comments:

> The besetting sins of writing freelance are over-confidence and naivety. Never assume that editors are clamouring for your work. The competition is massive and there is a lot of talent around. Do not be naive enough to think that you can compete immediately with the full-time professionals. You have to put everything into your first article and submit to a realistic market, with a good covering letter. If you are sure of why you are writing, then these will all be more attainable.

Basic requirements

- A personal computer and printer: freelances have to have internet access and provide copy through email.
- Telephone and answering machine; many freelances have mobile phones and pagers so they are contactable at any time. Some have a built-in facility for taping telephone conversations. For tax purposes it is necessary to keep separate records of business and personal calls.
- A fax machine: given the speed of newspaper operations, the normal mail is often too slow and many publications still like to see the original hard copy.
- A small tape recorder or Dictaphone for interviews.
- A television: many freelances follow Ceefax and Oracle services to keep up with breaking news. And a radio.
- An accountant: to advise on tax and a pension plan. If you become particularly successful you will have to pay VAT. Most freelances keep in regular touch with their local tax inspector. Remember to log for tax purposes all relevant expenses such as stationery, office equipment, books and travel expenses.
- A solicitor: to help on copyright (see Howard 1994) and libel issues and looking into the small print of contracts.
- An office with a working desk: there are problems relating to capital gains tax if you sell your home and have used a room exclusively as an office. Consult your accountant on this. Your office will normally contain a library of reference books, dictionaries, collections of quotations, newspapers and magazines (often small circulation and specialist). In addition, the *Writer's Handbook* (Macmillan, annually) and *Writers' and Artists' Yearbook* (A. & C. Black, annually) are essential tools, providing tips, freelance rates and valuable lists of newspaper contacts. You may want on hand a collection of titles on freelancing such as Dobson (1992), Davis (1988), Dick (1998), Read (1992), Clayton (1994), Randall (2000) and McKay (2000: 31–43). Access to public and specialist libraries is essential. Established freelances will also take the opportunity to use the library facilities at newspapers to which they file copy. A filing cabinet: this should be used to store cuttings, photocopies of crucial articles and chapters, notes from interviews and written sources, copies of correspondence and invoices. Organising a tidy filing system is a special art providing enormous rewards. So much time can be lost looking for information when the filing system is chaotic.
- Headed writing paper and business cards.
- Transport: most reporters drive (and set some of the costs against taxable income) but it is not essential. Some freelances rely on bikes, others on public transport.
- Membership of the freelance branch of the NUJ: the union, along with local education centres, runs courses for starting-up freelances which can help develop skills and confidence.
- Capital: Christopher Browne (1999: 17) suggests that beginning freelances should negotiate an overdraft facility of at least £3,000 to £4,000 with their bank manager after presenting them with a business plan drawn up by an accountant.
- Stamina: Many freelances have to work evenings and weekends. As Dan Roberts comments (2004): 'Writer's block, insecurity, crises of confidence and rejected ideas are daily realities.' So it's important to develop strategies for dealing with stress.

Finding an outlet

Get to know the market for your specialist area of interest. Study the different writing styles, the lengths of sentences and articles in the different publications. Try to establish by examining byline patterns the amount of freelance work accepted and in which specific areas: it may be in celebrity profiles, in authoritative, fact-based comment or in timeless features. Read carefully recent issues to make sure that you do not duplicate anything already done. It is not a good idea to ring a publication to gather this kind of information or even their general views about freelancing. You are expected to do all the basic groundwork and then approach the publication with a potential article.

With a hot news story you will obviously contact the paper by phone. But with other kinds of stories there are no rules. Some prefer contact by phone, others by letter or fax or email. Always direct your approach to the most appropriate person on the editorial staff. If you have a feature, ring the features editor (asking the switchboard operator their name before speaking). Expect to have to travel through a range of protective secretaries before speaking to them in person.

Explain the main point of your story and the likely length you envisage. In covering news, there is always a danger the paper will take down the details and then send out their staffer to handle it. Try to convey the story's importance and the fact that you have it ready to send over by phone, fax or email. Do not give too much away on the phone. Even if they use your call as a simple 'tip off' for a story they cover themselves, you are still owed a payment for that. If you are not known to the paper, they are unlikely to commit themselves to carrying a story on the basis of a rushed phone call. They are likely to say: 'That sounds interesting. Send in the copy, but I can't promise anything.'

The perils of pitching

If you are pitching an idea for a timeless feature, explain your original angles, your main sources, the basic structure of the piece and wordage, why you are particularly suited to covering it and why you have chosen their particular publication. There are dangers here. The publication may steal your ideas and give them to someone else to follow up. And the freelance has absolutely no protection in law against this kind of theft. While written work can be copyrighted, ideas can occur to two people at the same time and can also be stolen. There is no easy solution to this problem. One approach is to provide only a bare minimum of background information before the idea is accepted. Personal contact with the commissioning editor also helps in creating mutual trust and confidence. The best solution is to prove your abilities to the newspaper in a series of stories sent on spec or to commission so they will be concerned not to lose your work to other competitors. It is also worth emphasising that you are the only person with the unique knowledge, contacts, idiosyncratic viewpoint or desire to complete the article. Clearly, freelances have to develop special negotiation skills.

Do not expect to have your hard copy returned. Even a stamped addressed envelope offers no guarantee. But always make sure you have a copy of all your submitted work. If it is rejected you may want to direct it to another newspaper or rearrange it with some new angles for a different outlet. Be persistent: remember *Gone with the Wind* was rejected 25 times before it was published and *Zen and the Art of Motorcycle Maintenance* 121 times. There may be queries over the story which can be cleared up only with reference to your original copy; you may need to protect yourself against libel where the paper has subbed in a comment or error.

Once the idea is accepted

If the commissioning editor has said, 'OK, I'll be pleased to look at your story but I can't promise we'll use it', they are free to reject your story without incurring any financial liability. But if they have commissioned your piece and then do not publish it they should pay you a 'kill fee' comprising part or all of the original amount agreed. But not all newspapers do. Many of the freelances in the NUJ survey complained of having their ideas stolen or of not receiving responses from editors after spending hours preparing and submitting ideas.

How much should you expect to be paid for your hard work? Well, the NUJ draws up a list of minimum freelance rates which are regularly updated and which will give you some idea of what to expect. The union also at its 1986 annual conference agreed a ten-point code on the use of freelance work. For example, Clause 1 stated 'Staff journalists hiring freelances have a duty to see that their freelances are treated reasonably'; Clause 2 ran: 'Conditions and rates of pay should be established clearly when the work is accepted or commissioned, preferably in writing'. According to Clause 3: 'Freelances should be paid in all cases for providing background information, tips, research materials, expertise etc.'. Certainly make sure you also negotiate expenses when your piece is commissioned since without that agreement you may end up using the payment simply to fund your research. And send in an invoice soon after the appearance of your copy.

Remember that if you are a self-employed freelance you own the copyright in your work: it is your 'intellectual property' whether submitted on spec or commissioned. Thus you are strongly advised to hold on to your copyright. This does not mean refusing further use of the material; you can license it, giving permission for a specific use for an agreed fee. Freelances, however, have become increasingly concerned over newspapers' use of journalists' copy in a range of electronic outlets. In September 1999, a three-judge panel decided that the *New York Times*, LexisNexis and other publishers could not resell freelance newspaper and magazine articles by means of electronic databases unless they had the author's express permission. And judges in Britain and Ireland were expected to follow the US lead. By 2004, many newspaper publishers had amended their commissioning terms to include the right to store and display material on electronic databases and to authorise others to do the same.

14 New technology

....

How journalism can damage your health

ournalism can damage your health. Many in the industry find it extremely stressful. A survey of media workers by Anthony Delano and John Henningham (1995) found that 51 per cent considered that they experienced high levels of stress while 24 per cent felt that the levels were very high. Another survey, commissioned by Guardian Financial Services and published in July 1996, found that more than 75 per cent of media employees had seen stress play a significant part in causing physical ill-health. Migraines, headaches, ulcers, irritable bowel syndrome, digestive problems and heart disease were among the stress-related conditions suffered. Almost half of those surveyed felt their bosses were doing nothing to reduce stress levels. By 2004, the NUJ was claiming that stress amongst journalists had reached 'epidemic levels' (Hardy 2004).

Occupational psychologist Dr Stephen Williams (1996) has studied hundreds of workplaces but says journalism beats all for stress. According to government figures (published in 1996) journalists are out-performing other professions at booze and tobacco consumption, and dying young as a result. Deadlines can be short, competition can be fierce, criticisms from colleagues can be sharp. Get some information wrong and not only is your mistake very public but also a costly libel action may result. Pressures from all sides (news desk, editors, sources, advertisers, politicians, proprietors) are faced every day. As cutbacks in the industry deepen, job security dwindles and the pressures to conform and work harder to justify the job grow.

The introduction of new technology has, for many, brought new stresses. Over recent years the newspaper industry has gone through a revolution. In the late 1960s, photocomposition (by which page images were composed photographically) began to replace hot-metal setting in the provincial press. The compositor would retype journalists' copy on a keyboard attached to a visual display unit (VDU). Text would be automatically hyphenated and justified, and strips of bromide from the photosetter would be pasted down to form the page. But in Fleet Street the introduction of photocomposition was delayed until the mid-1970s, the result of management incompetence and trade union conservatism. Even as late as 1985, three Fleet Street newspapers were hot-metal-set while five others used a mix of hot and cold systems. Then came Eddie Shah's launch of the new-tech, all-colour *Today* on 4 March 1986 and the sudden shift of Rupert Murdoch's News International titles from Gray's Inn Road to Wapping. *Today* was launched with an editorial staff of just 130, less than a quarter of the staff levels then at the *Express* or the *Mail*. So began a wave of editorial staff cuts throughout Fleet Street which are still continuing. One of the consequences of these jobs cuts is inevitably extra stresses for those remaining.

The silent sufferers

Journalists have always suffered from writer's cramp (though this is little covered in the media). New technology has brought many new hazards. Indeed, research suggests that up to 25 per cent of the population as a whole suffers from techno-anxiety (Macleod 1999). Particularly notorious among journalists is repetitive strain injury. This swept the industry from the mid-1980s so that a decade later the NUJ was claiming that it knew of more than a thousand sufferers. Nationally, with 7 million keyboard users, RSI became the biggest cause of time lost through illness in office work, and in 1994 the TUC was claiming an 'epidemic' of RSI injuries, causing two hundred thousand people a year to take time off work. A 1997 survey at the giant IPC Magazines group in London found that one-third of journalists had some symptoms of RSI. Research by the GMB union in 2000 suggested that left-handers were particularly prone.

By the late 1990s most of the larger newspaper companies had come to terms with RSI and were dealing with affected journalists compassionately. At the *Guardian*, for instance, a technology committee was set up, combining management and the NUJ. The emphasis was on supporting people in continuing to work, not on getting rid of them. As Tim Gopsill, NUJ health and safety officer, commented: 'The bigger the company the better. After all, they've got the money to spend. The *Financial Times*, for instance, has spent a fortune getting their newsroom up to acceptable ergonomic standards.' He said that, apart from 'some judges and bent doctors', most people now acknowledge RSI as a serious injury. But in smaller newsrooms journalists could still be 'badly treated', and throughout the industry there remained many silent sufferers afraid that if they revealed their symptoms they could be unemployable or sacked.

What is RSI?

Research into RSI is already considerable, but explaining its causes (why it strikes one person and not another) remains difficult. RSI and its associated symptoms have been around for more than 150 years. Piano players, factory workers, tennis players, farmers, anyone involved in repetitive activities with their limbs, are prone to suffer. But it is only recently, since journalists have been seriously affected, that concerns about it have been widely expressed in the media.

Symptoms can develop slowly over a period of time or appear suddenly as a devastating shock. One journalist recorded: 'I simply woke up one morning unable to move my neck or use my hands properly. I dropped newspapers, couldn't grasp a cup and, panic-stricken, didn't know what could be wrong.' While using a computer is often the main problem, first symptoms might appear while turning a screwdriver, mowing the lawn, writing, washing your hair, carrying shopping, turning taps, knitting, or playing the piano.

How to avoid RSI

If you are a staffer, try to insist through your union that your employer follows the European Union regulations which came into force on 1 January 1993. These insist that chairs must have height-adjustable seats and backs that are height and tilt-adjustable. Employers are obliged to provide stands to raise screens and footrests when these are required.

Concentrate on getting your posture right at the keyboard. Your forearms should be parallel to the floor when you type and both feet should be firmly on the floor. If you have short legs, you may need a footstool, a specially adjustable chair or both. In front of the keyboard there should be sufficient space to place wrists during rest periods or while reading the screen. You should be able to sit straight, using the back-rest of the chair, with relaxed shoulders and chin up, looking down at the screen at an angle of 15 degrees. There should be no pressure on the thighs from the chair since this can limit circulation and put pressure on the sciatic nerve.

You need to take regular breaks from the screen. The NUJ recommends breaks of 15 minutes in every 75 minutes of continuous VDU work or formal breaks of 15 minutes after each hour. Lunches should be taken away from the desk. All the same, lunch-at-the-desk is an increasing trend among hard-pressed, under-staffed newsrooms across the UK, and even in-built RSI warning sounds on computers are routinely ignored.

If symptoms emerge

If you suffer pain during or after working at the keyboard but not at other times when using your hands, take regular breaks, reduce your typing speed and adjust the height of your chair so that you can type more efficiently. And talk to your NUJ representative if there is one where you work. They should be able to advise on what to do.

If the pains persist during other uses of the hands, seek medical advice immediately: fear, anxiety and guilt do not help. Robert Jones, Emeritus Fellow at City University's journalism department, stresses the importance of being treated by an experienced doctor. He said: 'Physiotherapy can help but it can also make the condition worse unless there has been a diagnosis first and unless the physio is really experienced in dealing with RSI.' For some people RSI can have a devastating effect on their careers. The inflammation and pains remain, and they have to quit regular employment. Subs are generally worse-affected than reporters and, where employers are sensitive, sufferers are moved to work in a reporter's post requiring much less screen work.

But not all RSI sufferers remain permanent sufferers. Some respond to treatment, others find a period of rest from the screen and careful attention to all possible precautions thereafter clears the pains. Often a change of job and a shift away from a stressful situation can remove the symptoms. The RSI Association, set up to support sufferers, has a website at http://www.rsi-uk.org.uk.

Other ailments

In addition to RSI, people have suffered eye complaints from sitting at VDU screens. Headaches, blurred vision, fuzzy images, stress and irritability can result. The NUJ recommends that keyboard, desk, walls and other major surrounding areas should be non-reflective and avoid excessively bright or dark colour schemes. No VDU or operator should face a window.

Dust is attracted to a switched-on screen and this, together with positive ions and static, can lead to blocked pores, dry eyes and irritated skin. Author Peggy Bentham (1991) suggests that every operator should have a dust cover to put over the screen when not in use, an antistatic floor mat and an antistatic desk mat. In addition, she advises people to wear natural fibres at the VDU to reduce static. Because of the radiation risks in sitting in front of VDUs, the NUJ recommends that pregnant women should have the right to switch to non-VDU work without loss of pay, status and career prospects.

Photocopiers and laser printers which produce ozone can pose health risks if they are poorly positioned or maintained or used for long runs. Areas in which they are sited should be well ventilated, and no one should have to work within 3 metres of the machine. Health concerns have also been raised over the use of mobile phones. Research by US experts Dr Henry Lai and Dr Narenda Singh warns that exposure can damage the body's genetic building-block DNA, leading to Alzheimer's and cancer. A study by Polish scientists of soldiers (published in March 2000), found a direct link between mobile phone use and cancer. A major report by twelve independent experts in Britain, in May 2000, concluded that mobile phones were not a proven health risk to users. All the same, if you have to use a mobile phone, keep calls short; if you have to make a lengthy call, then switch the phone from ear to ear. In 2004, adding more fuel to the mobile phone scare, a group of Hungarian researchers published findings which suggested that men who carry mobile phones in their trouser pockets could be damaging their sperm count (Boseley 2004b). Another 2004 study by the Karolinska Institute in Stockholm suggested that using a mobile phone for 10 years or more might increase the risk of a non-cancerous tumour which could damage hearing (Meikle 2004). You have been warned!

15 On or off the job – or both?

Training and careers

The best way to learn about journalism is 'on the job'. You may have great ideas about the nature of reporting, you may know all about ideology and the history of the press in eighteenth-century England. But if you cannot bash out a quick story on a local murder you are useless. That was the dominant view in the industry at the beginning of the twentieth century. It remains largely the same at the start of the twenty-first. There have been slight changes. Training courses have developed with the support of newspaper managements and trade unions. They have even spread into the learned corridors of universities. But mutual suspicion persists between the press and academia.

On the one hand there is a prevalent belief that journalists are born, not made. You've either got the nose for news or, sadly, you haven't. As Sir David English, former editor of the *Daily Mail*, said: 'Journalism is a skill that can only be acquired on the job and at the end of the day it depends on whether someone has a burning individual talent.' On the other hand there is the belief that journalism is a profession with its own ethical and work-related standards which can be both taught and assessed. Thus, certain educational qualifications are laid down for entrants while the development of training courses becomes an essential part of the formation of the journalist's professional identity. Caught between these two views are students and trainers. A further twist emerges when attempts are made by educators to promote reflective, critical approaches to dominant professional attitudes (as, for instance, reflected in this text). Scepticism about the value of theoretical studies for aspiring reporters remains widespread.

The contrasting US/UK traditions of training

The training of journalists in Britain is a relatively new phenomenon. In the United States, university training started in the late nineteenth century with the first journalism school founded in 1908 at the University of Missouri. Ten years later there were 86 schools offering at least some journalism coursework while by 1940 this figure had jumped to 542.

In Britain, in contrast, it was not until the mid-1960s that any major programme of journalism training was launched. A diploma course had run at King's College

London between 1922 and 1939 but this was not restarted after the war. After the 1949 Royal Commission on the Press drew attention to the need for better training, the National Advisory Council for the Training and Education of Junior Journalists was set up in 1952 (Stephenson and Mory 1990). Three years later this body changed its title to the National Council for the Training of Journalists (NCTJ) and brought together representatives from the NUJ and the Institute of Journalists (the two trade unions), the Newspaper Society (owners of provincial newspapers in England and Wales and suburban London weeklies) and the Guild of British Newspaper Editors. Later they were joined by the Newspaper Publishers' Association (linking owners of national newspapers) and by the two bodies formed by the owners and managers of newspapers in Scotland.

Since the 1960s many colleges and universities have developed courses in journalism. Initially, the media were considered largely within their sociological or broader theoretical contexts in courses usually titled Mass Communications. But over recent decades the focus has shifted, largely in response to student demands, to the development of practical skills. Many mass-communication courses have integrated a practical element while both postgraduate and (since the early 1990s) undergraduate journalism degrees have emerged. By 2004, the Universities and Colleges Admissions Service (UCAS) handbook listed more than 600 undergraduate courses with 'journalism' in their titles. In addition, 28 higher-education institutions were listed as offering postgraduate courses in journalism and related subjects. Yet, despite all this, many newspaper journalists still learn the ropes on local papers.

Educational qualifications

In 1965 the trade unions and the Newspaper Society agreed that the minimum qualification for entry to the profession was three GCEs, one being in English. Since 1970 the required minimum has been five passes at O level or GCSE at grades A, B or C with English language still being among them. Some other examinations have been approved by the NCTJ as being educationally equivalent, and in exceptional cases (when the editor has their eye on an individual) the qualifications are waived. For those who seek to enter via a college course, the requirements are two A levels and two GSCEs including English at either level.

The trend over recent decades has been towards the formation of an increasingly graduate profession. In 1965 only 6 per cent entering local newspapers had a university degree while a further 33 per cent had one or more A levels. In 1990 53 per cent of entrants to provincial papers boasted degrees while most of the others had two or more A levels. By 2002, a survey by the Journalism Training Forum found that, of the sixty thousand print journalists in the UK, 98 per cent had degrees while 43 per cent had a postgraduate qualification too (Hargreaves 2002). As many as 68 per cent had some sort of journalistic qualification.

Even so, academic qualifications in themselves have never been sufficient to guarantee a chance to become a trainee journalist. As Sarah Niblock (1996) comments: 'Some editors may feel journalists who are well read in media criticism may lead them to question editorial policy, so do not think having such a qualification will automatically give you a head start.' In addition to showing academic abilities, the successful applicant must be able to demonstrate a special commitment to working in the field. Many school pupils go to newspapers on work attachments, others manage to persuade editors to let them observe the newspaper operations during their holidays.

Some students help with hospital radios; others send in letters and articles to their local newspapers. All this counts well for any applicant whether to a newspaper or to a college.

Pre-entry training: post A level

One-year pre-entry courses are provided at centres dotted about the UK, such as at City College Brighton and Hove; Crawley College; Darlington College; East Surrey College, Redhill; Harlow College; Sutton Coldfield College; Warwickshire College; West Kent College and Wolverhampton College. If you are lucky, you may win sponsorship from a local paper.

Pre-entry training: the postgraduate diploma route

In 1970, the first university journalism course was launched at University College, Cardiff. Largely the inspiration of Tom Hopkinson, former editor of *Picture Post*, and modelled on a programme at Columbia University, New York, it initially attracted between fifteen and twenty postgraduate students. A similar one-year postgraduate diploma course was begun at City University, London, in 1976, initially with thirteen students. By the late 1980s postgraduate courses had grown in numbers enormously, spanning a wide range of diplomas and MAs: newspaper, periodical, broadcast, European (linking Cardiff and City with colleges in Utrecht, the Netherlands, and Aarhus, Denmark) and international. In the late 1990s, City University launched an electronic publishing MA.

Also during the 1990s, one-year postgraduate diplomas were started at centres such as City of Liverpool Community College; De Montfort University, Leicester; Strathclyde University; Trinity and All Saints College, Leeds, and the University of Central Lancashire, Preston. Trent University, Nottingham, launched a diploma in investigative journalism. Napier University, Edinburgh, launched an international journalism MA. By 2004, there were 20 providers of journalism MAs. But suspicions of universities by the press persisted. As Professor Hugh Stephenson, of City University, commented: 'The academic community in this country has always been distrustful of courses in journalism and media employers have been distrustful of people with education.'

The degree route

In the early 1990s, for the first time the US-style undergraduate route to journalism emerged with the launch of degrees at five centres: Bournemouth University; University College, Cardiff; the University of Central Lancashire, Centre for Journalism; the London College of Printing; and City University, which offered a Journalism with a Social Science course (with an optional third year 'out' studying abroad or on work attachments). They were to be later joined by a host of others, including Teesside University, Wolverhampton University, Liverpool John Moores University, Surrey Institute of Art and Design University College and Harlow College/Middlesex University.

Journalism can now be studied alongside an extraordinary range of subjects: Staffordshire University offers Journalism and Citizenship; Sheffield University offers Journalism and Russian; Sunderland University offers Journalism with Comparative

Literature. By 2004, UCAS was listing 638 degrees (attracting 4,870 students) with journalism in their titles. Some national and local newspapers offer awards (watch the publications themselves for details). For instance, the *Hull Daily Mail*, the *Grimsby Telegraph*, the *Scunthorpe Telegraph* and the *Lincolnshire Echo* have linked up with the University of Lincoln. There are also special awards for applicants from ethnic minorities.

On-the-job training

Roughly 40 per cent of entrants to newspaper journalism start by training on a local. Take a look at media directories (such as *Benn's* and *Willing's Press Guide*), which your local library should hold: these list all newspapers and periodicals in the UK. It is advisable before writing to ring any chosen newspaper just to make sure it is worth your while and to get the editor's name correct on the letter. Editors tend to come and go. Remember that trainees are appallingly paid. An NUJ survey in 2004 found that rates were at least £7,000 less than the median starting salary for graduates. Once accepted, a direct entrant for their first six months tends to take a course of home study in addition to receiving on-the-job training and experience. Most will then attend a twelve-week block release course (such as at Darlington College, Highbury College or Norton College, Sheffield).

Each trainee will have to pass seven qualifying examinations of the National Council for the Training of Journalists (www.nctj.com): newspaper journalism, handling handouts, law (two parts), local and central government (two parts), and shorthand to 100 words per minute. For direct entrants the qualifying period is two years, for pre-entry and postgraduate diploma students it is eighteen months. Once through all these hoops, the journalist can then take the NCTJ National Certificate Examination (NCE) to be fully qualified. In 2004, under the dynamic leadership of new chief executive Joanne Butcher, the NCTJ aimed to boost its profile in the industry with the appointment of high-profile journalists such as Alan Rusbridger, editor of the *Guardian*, and Kim Fletcher, editorial director of the Telegraph Group, to its board.

A number of regional and national newspapers have set up their own training schemes. Even the *Sun* joined forces with City University, London, to launch a graduate training scheme.

National Vocational Qualifications

In the early 1990s, the National Vocational Qualifications (and Scottish Vocational Qualifications) in newspapers emerged. Organised by the Newspaper Society, the NVQs were almost entirely focused on work-based assessments. Following the setting up of the National Council for Vocational Qualifications in 1996, the Newspaper Society's steering group drew up a set of standards at Level 4 under three headings – writing, production journalism and press photography (a graphics journalism option at Level 3 followed). A reporter covering a diary event, for instance, is required to display accurate fact-gathering skills, an appreciation of any legal and ethical issues arising and the ability to file copy to a deadline. Students take from one to three years, so candidates working part-time can complete the course.

In recent years, the NVQs (awarded by the RSA Examinations Board together with the Newspapers Qualifications Council) have come under severe criticism from the NCTJ, Society of Editors and the Periodicals Training Council. But some groups, such as Eastern Counties Newspapers, remained committed to them, and by mid-2000 the number studying for NVQs was roughly equivalent to those studying for an NCE.

And in April 2004 the Level Four NVQ in Journalism was relaunched as the Diploma in Newspaper Journalism.

Other routes

In addition to these entry routes there are many others. For instance, there are two-year HNDs, BTECs, and many evening-class centres now run courses in freelancing, feature writing and press photography. There are privately run journalism train-ing centres (most of them claiming extraordinary success for their graduates in gaining jobs in the industry), and you can even learn journalism via a correspondence course on the internet. The range of courses is, in fact, bewildering.

Many universities provide media studies courses. During the 1990s media-related courses became the most fashionable to study and inevitably attracted the suspicions of Fleet Street once reserved for sociology and peace studies. Many editors argue that they require applicants with broad interests and knowledge rather than bookish experts in the narrow academic discipline of communications. Yet, increasingly, theo-retical media courses are incorporating practical vocational elements. It is to be hoped that journalists' traditional reluctance to encourage the reflective, critical approach will dwindle as more media graduates enter the industry. There are conflicting research findings over the job success rate of media graduates. But Angela Phillips and Ivor Gaber of Goldsmiths' College, London, conclude (1996: 63–4):

> Despite myths to the contrary, employment prospects for graduates of communi-cations and media degrees are good. The Standing Conference on Cultural, Communication and Media Studies, which brings together all relevant university departments, studied the destination of their graduates and found, gratifyingly, that the percentage of those in employment, six months after graduation, was slightly higher than the average for all graduates.

Further reading and contact addresses

Careers in Journalism: National Union of Journalists, Acorn House, 308 Gray's Inn Road, London WC1X 8DP. Tel: 020–7278 7916; fax: 020–7837 8143. (The NUJ also provides a list of useful books on journalism, drawn up by Humphrey Evans.)

How to be a Journalist, Newspaper Society, 74–7 Great Russell Street, London WC1B 3DA. Tel: 020–7636 7014; fax: 020–7631 5119; email: ns@newspapersoc.org.uk; website: http://www.newspapersoc.org.uk.

National Council for the Training of Journalists, Latton Bush Centre, Southern Way, Harlow, Essex CM18 7BL. Tel: 01279–430009; fax: 01279–438008; email: Info@NCTJ.com; website: http://www.nctj.com.

University and Colleges Admissions Service (UCAS) PO Box 28, Cheltenham GL52 3LZ. Tel: 01242–222444; website: http://www.ucas.ac.uk.

The foot in the door: GETTING THE FIRST JOB

Journalism has always been a notoriously difficult world to enter. With staff cuts in virtually all newspapers since the late 1980s, the job hunt has become still more difficult. Admittedly, the internet is beginning to provide large numbers of new jobs for journalists, but not only are colleges producing more trained young aspirants but also the newspaper jobs market is becoming jammed full with experienced journalists made redundant and on the hunt for employment.

Contacts are crucial. Spend time while training concentrating on building up sources and links in the industry. Also try to get freelance work published. After completing work attachments on newspapers, get your supervisor to write you a reference. Compile an attractive portfolio of your cuttings and references and attach an up-to-date CV: that will provide an invaluable aid to you during job interviews. You may even want to post your CV on the internet, including links to other works you have completed. As Damian Barr (1999) advises: 'Provide the URL (the name of your website) in your prospective letter or email so that an employer can click to it easily without having to bother with attachments.'

The application

Because newspapers are inundated with job applications there is little need to advertise many of the jobs that fall vacant. But a number are still advertised in *Press Gazette* (published every Friday) and the *Guardian* Media section every Monday. See also www.holdthefrontpage.co.uk (excellent for the locals), www.mediauk.com and www.journalismuk.co.uk while internet jobs are advertised at Recruitmedia (http://www.recruitmedia.co.uk).

The letter of application should be brief and to the point. The accompanying CV should summarise your achievement to date. It should list your name, address, date of birth, education (school, college, university, evening classes etc.) with dates and qualifications (briefly), professional qualifications, work on student or university publications; any job(s) you have held (perhaps on a local hospital radio), desktop publishing skills, publications, special interests, languages, references (with addresses and contact details) (see Corfield 1992). It is also advisable to have your CV printed out in an attractive font: it is an important document, and you are more likely to impress if it looks good. (Websites advising on CVs include http://www.free-resume-tips.com; http://www.provenresumes.com; http://www.cvspecial.co.uk.)

The interview

It is vital to prepare for any job or college interview. Find out about the paper, get some copies and look at them critically. The interviewer will also expect you to be able to speak confidently about the national media – both print and broadcast, and the internet. It also impresses if you can use some journalistic jargon. If words like 'follow-up', 'page lead', 'splash' and 'stringer' flow off your lips (at the appropriate moments, of course), this shows that your newspaper ambition is more than a Hollywood-induced fantasy. Dress tidily and be prepared to show off your portfolio. And always go prepared to ask questions. Good luck.

Glossary

....

ABC – Audit Bureau of Circulation: organisation providing official figures for newspaper *circulation*

access provider – a company that sells *internet* connections (also known as an internet access provider or *internet service provider*)

ad – abbreviation for advertisement

add – additional copy, as when the Press Association (*PA*) follows lead of major story with new paragraphs

advance – statement/speech issued in advance to the media

advertorial – where distinction between editorial and advertising becomes blurred

agency – main news agencies are *PA*, Reuters, Agence France Presse, Itar-Tass, Associated Press. Also a large number of smaller agencies serving specialist and general fields. Copy known as wire copy. See also *snap*

agony aunt – woman offering advice to people who write to newspapers with personal or emotional problems. Agony uncle is the male equivalent, but there are not many of these around

alignment – ranging of copy text (and headlines) over columns. Copy ranged or aligned or set left begins on extreme left of column; all lines of copy ranged right are flush to the extreme right of the column and ragged on the left

alternative press – loose term incorporating wide variety of non-mainstream newspapers. Can include leftist, religious, municipal, trade union publications

ambush interview – when an interviewee is surprised by a suddenly different line of questioning or by a sudden appearance of a journalist (or group of journalists). Has dramatic flavour when done on television

angle – main point stressed in story usually in *intro*. Also known as hook. US: peg

AP – Associated Press news agency

apology – a newspaper may admit error and publish correction in apology. Complainant can still claim libel in court, and publication of apology provides no defence for newspaper. But, if newspaper loses case, the fact that it took prompt and adequate steps to correct error and to express regret provides plea in mitigation of damages, tending to reduce size of damages awarded

artwork – all illustrations, maps, charts or cartoons that accompany copy

asterisk – * occasionally used in text to link footnote or to indicate letters of words considered obscene

attachment or work experience – time spent by student journalists training (or occasionally just observing) at media organisation. US: internship

attribution – linking information or *quote* to original source

author's marks – changes made by author on *proof* of copy

backbench – group of top-level journalists who meet to decide the overall shape and emphases in newspaper

background – section of news or *feature* story carrying information which serves to contextualise main elements. Also, in computer jargon, indicates hyphenation and justification system is operating while copy is being input

backgrounder – *feature* exploring the background to main story in the news

back issue – previous issue of paper

back-up – fallback supply of equipment, data or copy

banner – front-page headline extending across full page

baron – newspaper proprietor. Other words: mogul, magnate, boss

beat – when a story is gained before rival. US: refers to specialist area covered by reporter e.g. education, defence, health

bill or **billboard** – poster giving headline of main story of the day

black – in days of typewriters this was carbon back-up copy of top hard copy typed by reporter. Many contemporary computer systems still call copies of top story blax

blackout – organisation or government imposes ban on all news releases for specific period

blob par(s) – follows small black marking (usually a square, outline of square, a circle or sometimes in tabloid a star) at start of paragraph. *Bullet* in computer jargon

body – copy following *intro*

boil down – shorten copy

bold face – heavy-face type (in contrast to lighter *roman* type of most stories' body text) used for emphasising in copy, headlines, subheadings; see also *italic*

Boolean search – internet search allowing the inclusion or exclusion of documents containing certain words through the use of AND, NOT and OR

box – copy with rules around all four sides; see also *fact file*

break – moment when news story emerges. But bad break refers to ugly-looking hyphenation at end of line of text

breaker – any device (such as *crosshead* or *panel*) which breaks up text on page

brief – short item of news often of just one *par* but occasionally with up to four or five pars. Other names: snip/nib/bright/filler; also short advice given to journalists before they cover a story

broadsheet – large-size newspaper such as *Daily Telegraph*, *Financial Times*. A number of national newspapers previously broadsheet, such as the *Independent* and *The Times*, have recently turned *tabloid*, though calling themselves the more respectable *compacts*

browser – software program for navigating the internet, in particular the World Wide Web

bureau – newspaper office in foreign country

bury – when important information or *quote* is carried within the body of text so its impact is lost

bust – when copy text or headlines run over allotted space

buy-up – see *chequebook journalism*

byline – gives name of journalist(s) who have written article. Otherwise known as credit line. Subs sometimes call it blame line. When appears at end of story known as *sign-off*

calls (or **check calls**) – routine telephone calls (or sometimes face-to-face visits) by reporters to bodies such as police, ambulance, hospitals, fire brigade (usually supplying information on tapes) to check if any news is breaking

campaigning journalism – overtly partisan journalism promoting particular cause. US: advocacy journalism

caps – see *upper case*

caption – words accompanying any picture or *artwork*. A caption amounting to a small story is a caption story

casting off – estimating length of story

casual – journalist employed by newspaper on a temporary basis. Since it is cheaper for employers, numbers are growing

catchline – usually single word identifying story which is typed in right-hand corner of every page. Subeditor will tend to use this word to identify story on layout. US: slug

CD-ROM – abbreviation of compact-disc-read-only-memory. CD holding computer-accessible data. For instance, dictionaries and back issues of newspapers are available in this form

centre spread – copy and pictures running over two pages in centre of newspaper

chapel – newspaper branch of National Union of Journalists. Chair, if male, is father of the chapel; if female, mother of the chapel

chequebook journalism – activity in which newspapers compete to purchase rights to buy up someone's story

circulation – total number of copies of each issue sold; see also *readership*

city desk – section of newspaper running financial pages

classified ads – small ads classified according to subject area and carrying no illustrations (cf. *display ads*)

clips or **clippings** – stories cut from newspapers and usually filed. Most newspapers have *cuttings* libraries to assist journalists' research. Individual journalists will have their own cuttings files. Increasingly computerised

colour – section of newspaper copy focusing on descriptions or impressions. Thus a colour *feature* is one which puts emphasis on description and the subjective response of the journalist, though the news element may still be strong

column – vertical section of article appearing on page. Also known as leg

columnist – journalist who provides comment in regular series of articles

column rule – usually light line between columns of type

compact – tabloid version of former broadsheet newspaper e.g. the *Independent*, *The Times*

conference – meeting of editorial staff to discuss previous issue/s and plan future ones

contact – journalist's source

contacts book – pocket-sized booklet carried by reporter listing contact details of sources

copy – editorial material. Hard copy refers to editorial material typed on paper

copy approval – allowing a person to see and approve copy before publication

copy tasting – see *taster*

correspondent – usually refers to journalist working in specialist area: defence, transport; or abroad e.g. Cairo correspondent

credit – byline of photographer or illustrator

crop – to cut a picture

crosshead – small heading usually of one or two words within body of text of larger type size than body text sometimes with *underline*. Used for design purposes to break up grey area of text. Word is usually drawn from text following but carries no great news value. Written by subeditor and not reporter

cross-ref – abbreviation of cross-reference: indicates story continues or begins on another page

cub reporter – trainee

cursor – usually dash or arrow on the computer screen indicating position of the next input

curtain raiser – story which provides background to forthcoming event. Otherwise known as scene setter

cut – remove copy from script, screen or page proof

cut-out – illustration with background cut, masked or painted out so that the image appears on the white of the page background

cuttings – stories cut from newspapers or magazines; a cuttings job is an article based on cuttings; also known as *clips* or *clippings*

database – storage of electronically accessible data

dateline – place from which story was *filed*, usually applied to stories from abroad

'day in the life of' profile – *feature* focusing on particular day of subject. Not to be confused with 'life in the day of' profile, which covers subject's life but in context of talking about currently typical day

deadline – time by which copy is expected to be submitted

death knock – when a journalist breaks news of a death to a member of the public

deck – unit of a headline

Deep Throat – secret *whistleblower* on major scandal. First given to secret source/s for Woodward and Bernstein in Watergate scandal. Derived from title of (in)famous pornographic film starring Linda Lovelace. In May 2005, Mark Felt, the FBI's No. 2 at the time, admitted being Deep Throat

delete – to cut or remove

desks – departments of newspapers: thus news desk, features desk

diary column – gossip column; also a day-to-day personal account

diary piece – article derived from routine sources (press conferences, press releases, council meetings, Parliament) listed in diary (originally in written form but increasingly on screens) which helps news desk organise news-gathering activities. Off-diary stories come from reporter's initiative and from non-routine sources

dig – to do deep research

direct entry – entry to journalism through publication which runs its own training programme

direct input – process by which text goes straight from editorial screen into computer for typesetting thus cutting out process in which printers typed out copy

discussion list – individuals communicating via email subscribe to the list and then receive all messages other subscribers send

disk – hard or floppy disk containing computer information (but note: compact disc)

display ads – large advertisements usually containing illustrations (cf. *classified ads*) and appearing on editorial pages. Advertising department will organise distribution of ads throughout the newspaper which is usually indicated on a *dummy* handed to subs before layout begins

district office – any office away from newspaper's main one

domain name – system of names to describe precise position of computer on the internet (e.g. city.ac.uk is the domain for City University, London)

doorstepping – journalists pursuing sources by standing outside their front doors. Now journalists often wait in cars

double column – text or headline or graphics over two columns. Double-page spread is a feature occupying two facing pages

download – to transfer data from one computer to another

downpage – story appearing in bottom half of newspaper page

downtable – subs other than the chief and deputy chief subs (who often used to sit at the top table of the subs room)

drop cap – capital letter at start of *par* occupying more than one line of text

dumbing down – claim that media standards, in general, are falling with increasing emphasis on sensationalism, celebrities, 'human interest' stories, sexual titillation, scandal and sleaze; see also *tabloidisation*

dummy – small version of editorial pages used for planning overall contents and usually containing details of *display ads*

editor – person in overall charge of the editorial content of the newspaper

editorial – all non-advertising copy; also a column in which newspaper expresses its views on issues (sometimes known as leader)

email – electronic mail carried on the internet

embargo – time (often found on press release) before which information should not be published

exclusive – story supposedly unique carried by newspaper. System becomes devalued when attached to stories too frequently or when the same story is carried in other newspapers (as often happens)

eye-witness reporting – presence of reporter at news event can provide unique opportunities for descriptive writing

e-zine – electronic magazine

fact file – listing of facts (often *boxed*) relating to story. Useful way of creating visual and copy variety on page

feature – as distinct from news story, tends to be longer, carry more background information, *colour*, wider range of sources, and journalist's opinion can be prominent

feedback – response from colleagues or public to journalist's copy

file – (verb) to send story from foreign country; (noun) anything stored on a computer such as a document, program or image

filler – short story, usually of one or two pars, filling in space when a longer story runs short (also known as brief)

fireman – person sent from newspaper's headquarters to cover major story (either at home or abroad). Notice gender bias in word

fit – when text, picture or headline does not overrun (bust) its allotted space

Fleet Street – though newspapers have dispersed from this street in East London (between the Strand and St Paul's Cathedral), national newspapers as a collective group are still known by this name. Often known as Street of Shame

floppy disk – flexible disk used for storage of information on computers

font – typeface of one particular size (incorrectly spelled as fount)

Fourth Estate – press supposedly occupying the position of fourth most powerful institution after Lords Spiritual, Lords Temporal and Commons (Lord Macaulay: 'The gallery in which reporters sit has become a fourth estate of the realm.')

free – free newspaper

freebie – range of services and entertainments (e.g. drinks, meals, trips abroad funded by organisations, concert tickets etc.) provided free to journalists. Some journalists believe acceptance of freebies compromises 'objectivity' and refuse them

freelance – journalist contributing to several media outlets and not on permanent staff of any one organisation; see also *stringer*. US: freelancer

FTP – File Transfer Protocol, used to transfer files across the internet

galley proof – see *proof*

gopher – a menu system allowing you to navigate the internet, largely displaced by the World Wide Web

graphics – illustrations and drawings used in designing pages

gutter – space between pages in centre spread; also space between any two columns on computer screens

gutter press – sometimes applied to *tabloid* press

hack – insult word for journalists which journalists are happy to use to describe themselves

hamper – story displayed horizontally, usually at the top of page

handout – story sent to media outlets by press relations office of organisation or PR company

hard copy – copy typed on sheets of paper (usually A4 size). Each page is known as a folio

hard news – news focusing on who, what, where, when, why based on factual detail and quotes and containing little description, journalist comment or analysis; cf. *soft news*

heavies – 'serious' papers such as *Guardian*, *The Times*, *Financial Times*

hold – instruction (usually known as set and hold) ensuring copy is prepared for publication but not printed, as for instance an *obituary* of some eminent person written in advance

home page – either the front page that is loaded at start-up by *web browser* or the main web document for a group, person or organisation

house – media organisation. Thus in-house (meaning within particular media organisation). House organ is company's own newspaper or magazine; see also *style*

HTML – hypertext mark-up language, comprising the codes for writing web pages

human interest story – story focusing on success, failures, tragedies, emotional/sexual histories of people, eliminating or marginalising more abstract and deeper cultural, economic, political, class-based factors

hypertext – divides a document into clickable links that connect web pages to each other

imprint – name and address of printer and publisher required by law on newspaper

indent – abbreviation for indentation providing white space at start or end of line

in-depth reporting – detailed coverage

index – front page (or sometimes elsewhere) listing of stories in rest of paper, to ease reading and 'sell' or 'flag' the contents in prominent place

in-house – see *house*

input – to type copy into computer

insert – copy injected into story which is already written or set

inside story – reporter bases investigation on their experience and research within organisation(s) at centre of controversy and/or quotes from insiders within organisation

internet – network of interconnecting computers communicating through the TCP/IP (Transmission Control Protocol/Internet Protocol)

internet service provider (ISP) – organisation providing access to the internet

intro – opening of news or feature story usually containing main *angle*. Not necessarily just single *par*. Also known as lead. US: nose

inverted pyramid – traditional representation of news stories (with main point at start and information declining in news value thereafter and ending with short background). Tends to oversimplify structure of news story. Better to imagine series of inverted pyramids within an overall large pyramid

investigative reporting – in one respect all journalism involves investigation. But investigative journalism tends to reveal something of social or political significance which someone powerful or famous wants hidden. US: muckraking

issue – all copies of the day's paper and its editions

italic – typeface sloping to the right *like this*; see also *bold* and *roman*

journalese – journalists' jargon

journo – jocular term for journalist

justify – line of text set to fit given measure

kill – to decide not to use (or drop) story or feature. Newspapers are supposed to pay 'kill fee' when they break an agreement to use freelance copy

knock down – to disprove story, usually in rival newspaper

label – headline merely categorising the news e.g. 'Interview with PM'

layout – design of the page, originally by *subeditor* using pencil and sent to compositor for guidance but normally now done totally on screen

lead (pronounced led) – space between lines of type (derived from former 'hot metal' printing system when strips of metal, or leads, were used for this purpose). Leaded-out copy has its lines spaced out to fit allotted space

lead (pronounced leed) – main story on page. On front page otherwise known as *splash*

leader – see *editorial*

legal (verb) – to send copy to lawyer to be checked for libel, contempt etc.

life in the day of – see *day in the life of*

lift – to use whole or section of story from one edition to the next; also to pinch story from other media outlet changing and adding only a little. When barest minimum is changed known as 'straight lift'

linage – payment to freelances based on number of lines of copy used

line drawing – drawing made up of black lines as in cartoon

listings – lists usually of entertainment events giving basic information: times, venue, phone numbers and so on

Listserv – software for organising an email discussion list

literal – typing error, either misspelling or mistranscription

lobby – specialist group of correspondents reporting House of Commons

lower case – small letters in *font* of type (as opposed to *upper case* or *capitals*)

masthead – newspaper's title on front page

middle-market – newspapers such as *Mail* and *Express* which lie (in overall style and appearance) between *heavies* and the *red-tops*

modem – telephone link-up for computers, most commonly used for sending email and accessing the internet

mole – a secret source for investigative journalist buried deep in the heart of organisation whose activities they are prepared to reveal

moonlighter – journalist who works during the evening for media organisation while holding another full-time job during day. Nice to be but it means moonlighter is depriving colleague of job

mug shot – photo showing just face (and sometimes shoulders), otherwise known as head and shoulders

must – editorial copy which must appear e.g. apology, correction

New Journalism – literary form of reportage pioneered in US in 1960s and 1970s by Norman Mailer, Tom Wolfe, Joan Didion and Truman Capote

newsgroups – discussion groups on the internet

New World and Communication Order – a concept promoted by UNESCO in 1970s and 1980s to counter dominance of international news flows by five major news agencies. Western countries, particularly US and UK, saw it as 'threatening the flow of information'

nibs – short news stories

obit – abbreviation of obituary, an account and appreciation of someone's life

off-beat – unusual story often with a humorous twist

offline – not connected to the internet

off the record – when statements are made not for publication but for background only. Information derived from comments should in no way be traceable back to source

online – connected to the internet

on spec – uncommissioned article submitted voluntarily to media

on the record – when there are no restrictions on reporting what is said

op ed – abbreviation of opposite editorial, being the page opposite one on which editorial or leader comment falls. Usually contains important features and commentary by prestigious columnists

opinion piece – article in which journalist expresses overt opinion

overline – see *strap or strapline*

PA – abbreviation for Press Association, an *agency* which supplies national news and features (as well as an international service from its link up with Reuters) to national and local papers. 'Page-ready' copy from PA is designed and can be slotted straight into newspaper

pack – collection of journalists (sometimes known as 'rat-pack') as in 'following the pack'

panel – text larger than body text with lines top and bottom. Serves to break up grey block of copy. Written by *subeditors*

paparazzi – horde of photographers

par – abbreviation for paragraph. Also para

pay-off – last par with twist or flourish

pic – abbreviation for picture meaning photograph; plural pix

pick-up – journalist attending function might pick up or take away a photograph supplied by the organisers, known as a pick-up job; also journalists following up an event after it has happened are 'picking up' news

picture-grabber – facility for taking pictures off television

podding – scheme originally promoted by Westminster Press in which multi-skilled subs, reporters and photographers worked in small teams

pool – privileged small group of journalists with special access to event or source. Their reports and findings are distributed to those news organisations outside the pool

pops/populars – mass-selling national *tabloids*; now known as *red-tops* because their *mastheads* are in red

PR – abbreviation for public relations

press release – announcement made by organisation specially for use by media (not necessarily just press)

probe – investigation

profile – picture in words which usually focuses on an individual, but an organisation, a car, a horse, a building, and so on can be profiled

proof – printout of part or whole page. This proof is read, corrected where necessary and the amended page (the revise) is then ready for final printing. Galley proof contains just columns of type

puff – story giving publicity

punchline – main point of story. Thus 'punchy' means story has a strong news *angle*

qualities – see *broadsheets*

quote – abbreviation for quotation; also, when a reporter files copy over phone, 'quote' then means first inverted commas. End quote marks are often known as 'unquote'

readership – number of people who read paper as opposed to the number of copies sold

red-tops – tabloid newspapers such as the *Mirror*, the *Sun* and the *People*, so-called because their *mastheads* are red

re-jig/re-hash – rearrangement of copy provided by reporter usually by *subeditor* to produce a better-structured piece

retrospective – *feature* looking back on event

re-vamp – change story or page in light of new material

revise – see *proof*

rewrite – to use information provided in story but compose it in completely new language. Known as rewrite job

ring-around – story based on series of telephone calls

roman – standard typeface (not *bold* or *italic*)

round-up – gathering together of various strands of story either under the same heading (otherwise known as umbrella story) or under variety of headings

roving reporter – reporter who travels around a lot

RSI – abbreviation for repetitive strain injury, which journalists can suffer through their use of a keyboard and a mouse

run – period of printing edition

running story – story which runs or develops over number of editions or days

run on – continue from one line, column or page to the next

scoop – exclusive

screamer – exclamation mark (usually in headline)

search engine – provides for subject searching on the internet through feeding terms on to a *database* and returning a list of 'hits' or correspondences

section – separately folded part of the paper

server – computer that makes services and data available on a network

set and hold – see *hold*

sexy story – story with popular appeal. But many 'sexy stories' give sex a bad name

sign-off – byline at foot of story

silly season – supposedly a time (usually in the summer holiday period) when little *hard* news is around and the press is reduced to covering trivia. For some newspapers the silly season can last a long time. Wars and invasions often happen in silly seasons, too

sister paper – when company owns more than one paper each is described as sister. Thus *The Times* is the *Sun*'s sister since both are owned by Rupert Murdoch

sketch – light, often witty article describing event. Most commonly used with reference to reporting House of Commons

slip – special edition for particular area or event

snap – brief information given by news *agency* before main story is sent

snapper – photographer

soft news – light news story that can be more colourful, witty and commenty than *hard news*

soundbite – short, pithy quote used by journalists. First coined by US radio and television journalists in the late 1960s

spoiler – story or picture run deliberately early to 'spoil' a rival's 'exclusive'

spike – to reject copy or other information (e.g. *press release*). Derived from old metal spike which stood on wooden base on which subs would stick unwanted material. Had advantage over 'binning' since material was accessible so long as it remained on spike

spin doctors – people who attempt to influence news or political agenda (the 'spin' in the jargon) such as press officers, communications specialists and other propagandists

splash – lead news story on front page

standfirst – text intended to be read between headline and story which can elaborate on point made in headline, add new one or raise questions which will be answered in story (a teaser). Sometimes contains *byline*. Helps provide reader with a 'guiding hand' into reading large slice of copy – thus mainly used for features and occasionally long news stories. Also known as the 'sell'

stet – ignore deletion (Latin for 'let it stand')

stop press – column on back page of newspaper left blank and allowing for slotting in of breaking news just before publication

strap or **strapline** – headline in smaller type appearing over main deck. Otherwise known as overline

stringer – *freelance*, in provinces, in London or overseas, who has come to arrangement with news organisation to supply copy on agreed basis. Super-stringer will contract to devote most of working for one organisation but still be free to freelance for other media outlets for rest of time

style – special rules adopted by newspaper relating to spellings, punctuation and abbreviation. Often contained within style book though increasingly carried on screen. Many newspapers somehow survive without them

subeditor/sub – responsible for editing reporters' copy, writing headlines, captions, laying out pages etc. Stone sub makes final corrections and cuts on page proofs. US: copy editor

tabloid – newspaper whose pages are roughly half the size of *broadsheet*. All *pops* or popular papers are tabloids as are *sections* of some of the *heavies*. Serious tabloids exist on the Continent (*Le Monde* in France, for instance) and in US (*Los Angeles Times*). Here in the UK *The Times* and *Independent* have turned tabloid (though they call themselves *compacts*)

tabloidese – shoddy, over-sensational, cliché-ridden copy most commonly associated with the *tabloids*

tabloidisation – claim that media in general are following tabloid values prioritising entertainment, sensationalism and scandal above 'hard facts'

take – page or number of pages comprising a section of longer piece

taster – journalist who checks copy, selecting good and removing unwanted. Process known as copy tasting

think piece – analytical article

tip-off – information supplied to newspaper by member of the public

top – story at the top of a page

tots – abbreviation for 'triumph over tragedy story', particularly popular human interest genre

trim – cut a report

umbrella story – see *round-up*

underline – to carry a line or rule under headline or *crosshead*

upper case – capital letters when used alongside small (*lower case*) letters. When just capital letters are used (as in headlines) they are known as *caps*

URL – uniform resource location: a string of characters identifying internet resource and its location; the most common ones begin http://

web browser – software for viewing websites, such as Internet Explorer and Netscape Navigator

whistleblower – person revealing newsworthy and previously secret information to media

widow – short line left at top of column

Bibliography

Adams, Sally (1999) 'Writing features', in Wynford Hicks with Sally Adams and Harriett Gilbert, *Writing for Journalists*, London: Routledge: 47–98.

Adams, Sally with Hicks, Wynford (2001) *Interviewing for Journalists*, London: Routledge.

Aitchison, Jean (1988) *Writing for the Press*, London: Hutchinson.

Alia, Valerie (2004) *Media Ethics and Social Change*, Edinburgh: Edinburgh University Press.

Allan, Stuart (2004) *News Culture*, 2nd edition, Maidenhead, Berkshire: Open University Press. First published 1999.

Almond, Gabriel and Verba, Stanley (1963) *The Civic Culture*, Princeton, NJ: Princeton University Press.

Always, Nicholas (2004) 'Advertisement black spot', *Press Gazette*, 26 November.

Anderson, Patricia (1991) *The Printed Image and the Transformation of Popular Culture, 1790–1860,* Oxford: Clarendon Press.

Arnot, Chris (2004) 'Muslim columnist trades Yorkshire Pudding for Currant Bun shocker!' *Independent*, 22 November.

Article 19 (2003) *What's the Story? Results from Research into Media Coverage of Refugees and Asylum Seekers in the UK*, London: Article 19 (www.article19.org.uk).

Atton, Chris (2002) *Alternative Media*, London: Sage.

—— (2003) 'Ethical issues in alternative journalism', *Ethical Space: The International Journal of Communication Ethics*, vol. 1, no. 1: 26–31.

Aubrey, Crispin (ed.) (1982) *Nukespeak: the Media and the Bomb*, London: Comedia.

Bagnall, Nicholas (1993) *Newspaper Language*, Oxford: Focal Press.

Bainbridge, Cyril and Stockdill, Roy (1993) *The News of the World Story,* London: HarperCollins.

Ball, Alan R. (1981) *British Political Parties*, London: Macmillan.

Barber, Lynn (1991) *Mostly Men*, London: Viking.

—— (1999) 'The art of the interview', in Stephen Glover (ed.) *Secrets of the Press: Journalists on Journalism*, London: Allen Lane/Penguin Press: 196–205.

Barker, Dennis (1998) 'The question posers', *Press Gazette*, 11 September.

Barr, Damian (1999) 'Let them read all about you', *The Times*, 8 November.

Barsamian, David (2002) 'John Pilger', *The Progressive*, November. Available online at http://www.progressive.org/nov02/intv1102.html, accessed 8 October 2004.

Baston, Lewis (2000) *Sleaze: the State of Britain*, London: Channel 4 Books.

Battle, John (2003) 'Silenced in court', *Guardian* Media section, 24 February. Available online at http://media.guardian.co.uk/mediaguardian/story/0,,901391,00.html, accessed 2 December 2004.

Beal, Joan C. (2004) *English in Modern Times*, London: Arnold.

Bell, Martin (1998) 'The journalism of attachment', in Matthew Kieran (ed.) *Media Ethics*, London: Routledge: 15–22.

Bentham, Peggy (1991) *VDU Terminal Sickness*: *Computer Health Risks and How to Protect Yourself*, London: Green Print.

Berrey, R. Power (1933) *The Romance of a Great Newspaper*, London: *News of the World*.

Bird, S. Elizabeth and Dardenne, Robert W. (1988) 'Myth, chronicle and story', in James W. Carey (ed.) *Media, Myths and Narrative*: *Television and the Press*, London: Sage.

Bloch, Alan (1992) 'Town hall turnover', *Municipal Review and AMA News*, 63(727): 40.

Bloch, Jonathan and Fitzgerald, Patrick (1983) *British Intelligence and Covert Action*, London: Junction.

Bonnington, Alistair, McInnes, Rosalind, and McKain, Bruce (2000) *Scots Law for Journalists*, Edinburgh: W.Green/Sweet & Maxwell.

Boorstin, Daniel (1962) *The Image*: *or What Happened to the American Dream?*, New York: Harper & Row.

Boseley, Sarah (2004a) 'Britons' "shocking" ignorance on Aids', *Guardian*, 1 December.

—— (2004b) 'Mobiles cut sperm count, says report', *Guardian*, 28 June.

Bower, Tom (1988) *Maxwell: the Outsider*, London: Mandarin.

—— (1992) 'Maxwell: a very British experience', Sixth James Cameron Memorial Lecture, City University, London.

Boyne, Gerry A. (1999) 'Managing local services: from CCT to best value', *Local Government Studies*, special edition, summer.

Brockway, Fenner (1986) *98 Not Out*, London: Quartet Books.

Brown, Gerry (1995a) 'Fines are just fine by me', *Guardian*, 24 July.

—— (1995b) *Exposed! Sensational True Story of Fleet Street Reporter*, London: Viking.

Browne, Christopher (1996) *The Prying Game: The Sex, Sleaze and Scandals of Fleet Street and the Media Mafia*, London: Robson.

—— (1999) *The Journalist's Handbook*, London: A. & C. Black.

Burchett, Wilfred (1981) *At the Barricades: Forty Years on the Cutting Edge of History*, New York: New York Times Books.

—— (1983) *Shadows of Hiroshima*, London: Verso.

Burkeman, Oliver (2002) 'Voice of America', *Guardian*, 1 March.

Burrell, Ian (2004a) 'We ARE the world', *Independent*, 29 November.

—— (2004b) 'MPs back moves for new law', *Independent*, 11 October.

—— (2004c) 'The wit and wisdom of Dan Rather', *Independent*, 29 November.

Byrne, Ciar (2003) 'Local hero', *Guardian* Media section, 17 March. Available online at http://media.guardian.co.uk/mediaguardian/story/0,7558,915404,00.html, accessed 2 December 2004.

Campbell, Duncan and Connor, Steve (1986) *On the Record: Surveillance, Computers and Privacy*, London: Michael Joseph.

Cassy, John (2003) 'DirecTV seals world domination', *Guardian*, 11 April.

Castells, Manuel (1997) *The Power of Identity*: Vol. 2 of *The Information Age: Economy, Society and Culture*, Oxford: Blackwell.

Chalaby, Jean (1998) *The Invention of Journalism*, London: Macmillan.

Chandler, Frank Wadleigh (1958) *The Literature of Roguery*, New York: Burt Franklin.

Chilton, Paul (ed.) (1985) *Language and the Nuclear Arms Debate: Nukespeak Today*, London: Frances Pinter.

Chomsky, Noam (1999) *The New Military Humanism: Lessons from Kosovo*, London: Pluto.

Chossudovsky, Michel (1998) *The Globalisation of Poverty: Impacts of IMF and World Bank Reforms*, London: Zed.

Christmas, Linda (2000) 'Road to enlightenment', *Press Gazette*, 10 March.

Clark, Andrew (2004) 'All policyholders may foot bill for expected record insurance payout', *Guardian*, 10 November. Available online at http://www.guardian.co.uk/uk_news/story/0,,1347331,00.html, accessed 2 December 2004.

Clarkson, Wendsley (1990) *Confessions of a Tabloid Journalist*, London: Fourth Estate.

Clayton, Joan (1994) *Interviewing for Journalists: How to Research and Conduct Interviews You Can Sell*, London: Piatkus.

Cockerell, Michael, Hennessy, Peter and Walker, David (1984) *Sources Close to the Prime Minister: Inside the Hidden World of the News Manipulators*, London: Macmillan.

Cohen, Stanley (1980) *Folk Devils and Moral Panics*, London: Robertson.

Coleman, Terry (1993) 'Best chat lines of our time', *Guardian*, 6 November.

Conboy, Martin (2002) *The Press and Popular Culture*, London: Sage.

—— (2003) 'Parochializing the global: language and the British tabloid press' in Jean Aitchison and Diana M. Lewis (eds) *New Media Language*, London: Routledge: 45–54.

—— (2004) *Journalism: a Critical History*, London: Sage.

Conley, David (2002) *The Daily Miracle: an Introduction to Journalism*, 2nd edition, Melbourne, Australia: Oxford University Press.

Corfield, Rebecca (1992) *Preparing Your Own CV*, London: Kogan Page.

Cottle, Simon (1999) 'Ethnic minorities and the British news media', in Jane Stokes and Anna Reading (eds) *The Media in Britain*, London and New York: Macmillan Press/St Martin's Press: 191–200.

Cramer, Chris (2000) 'I can still taste the cordite, 20 years later', *Independent*, 2 May.

Curran, James and Seaton, Jean (2003) *Power Without Responsibility: the Press, Broadcasting and New Media in Britain*, 6th edition, London: Routledge.

Curran, James, Douglas, Angus and Whannel, Gary (1980) 'The political economy of the human interest story', in Anthony Smith (ed.) *Newspapers and Democracy: International Essays on a Changing Medium*, Cambridge, Mass.: MIT Press: 288–316.

Curtis, Liz (1984) *Ireland and the Propaganda War*, London: Pluto.

Dalby, Andrew (2002) *Language in Danger: How Language Loss Threatens our Future*, London: Penguin Press.

Davies, Nick (1999) 'Getting away with murder', *Guardian* Media section, 11 January.

—— (2000) 'Keeping a foot in the door', *Guardian*, 10 January.

Davies, Russell (1995) *Foreign Body: the Secret Life of Robert Maxwell*, London: Bloomsbury.

Davis, Anthony (1988) *Magazine Journalism Today*, Oxford: Heinemann.

Dawes, Martin (1999) 'Brief encounter . . . but for crown court regular Harold the love affair has lasted for over 20 YEARS!' *Sheffield Star*, 17 February.

De Burgh, Hugo (2000) *Investigative Journalism: Context and Practice*, London: Routledge.

Delano, Anthony (2003) 'Women journalists: what's the difference?', *Journalism Studies* vol. 1, no. 2: 273–86.

Delano, Anthony and Henningham, John (1995) *The News Breed: British Journalism in the 1990s*, London: London College of Printing.

Dent, Susie (2004) *Larpers and Shroomers: the Language Report*, Oxford: Oxford University Press.

Department for Constitutional Affairs (2004) *Broadcasting Courts*, consultation paper CP 28/04, published 15 November. Available online at http://www.dca.gov.uk/consult/courts/broad-casting-cp28-04.htm, accessed 2 December 2004.

Department of National Heritage (1995) *Privacy and Media Intrusion*, London: HMSO.

Department of the Environment, Transport and the Regions (DETR) (1998) *A Mayor and Assembly for London?* London: DETR.

Department of the Environment, Transport and the Regions (1999) *Modern Local Government. In Touch with the People*, White Paper Cm 4014, London: Stationery Office.

Dick, Jill (1998) *Freelance Writing for Newspapers*, 2nd edition, London: A. & C. Black.

Dobson, Christopher (1992) *The Freelance Journalist: How to Survive and Succeed*, Oxford: Butterworth-Heinemann.

Dorner, Jane (2000) *The Internet: a Writer's Guide*, London: A. & C. Black.

Dorril, Stephen and Ramsay, Robin (1991) *Smear*, London: Fourth Estate.

Dougary, Ginny (1994) *Executive Tarts and Other Myths*, London: Virago.

Doyle, Margaret (1995) *The A–Z of Non-Sexist Language*, London: the Women's Press.

Durham, Michael (2004) 'Some of us are trying to work in here', *Guardian*, 29 September.

Ellwood, Wayne (1996) 'Seduced by technology', *New Internationalist*, December.

Empson, Martin (2004) 'You don't say', *Socialist Review*, November.

Evans, Harold (1983) *Good Times, Bad Times*, London: Weidenfeld & Nicolson.

Ezard, John (2004) 'Where to stick grocer's apostrophe', *Guardian*, 8 July.

Fedler, Fred (1989) *Reporting for the Print Media*, 4th edition, San Diego, Calif.: Harcourt, Brace, Jovanovich.

Fiske, John (1989) *Understanding Popular Culture*, London: Unwin Hyman.

—— (1992) 'Popularity and the politics of information', in Peter Dahlgren and Colin Sparks (eds) *Journalism and Popular Culture*, London: Sage: 45–63.

Fitzwalter, Raymond and Taylor, David (1981) *Web of Corruption: Full Story of John Poulson and T. Dan Smith*, London: Granada.

Flett, Kathryn (1997) 'When I bared all . . .', *Guardian*, 16 June.

Fowler, Roger (1991) *Language in the News: Discourse and Ideology in the Press*, London: Routledge.

Franklin, Bob (1994) *Packaging Politics: Political Communication in Britain's Media Democracy*, London: Edward Arnold.

—— (1997) *Newszack and News Media*, London: Edward Arnold.

—— (1998) 'No news isn't good news: the development of local free newspapers', in Bob Franklin and David Murphy (eds) *Making the Local News*, London: Routledge: 125–39.

—— (2005) 'McJournalism: the local press and the McDonaldization thesis', in Stuart Allan (ed.) *Journalism: Critical Issues*, Maidenhead: Open University Press: 137–50.

Franklin, Bob and Murphy, David (1991) *What News?*, London: Routledge.

Friedlander, Edward Jay and Lee, John (2004) *Feature Writing for Newspapers and Magazines*, Boston, Mass./New York/San Francisco, Calif.: Pearson Education Inc.

Friend, Tad (1998) 'Stars in their eyes', *Guardian*, 20 April.

Frost, Chris (2000) *Media Ethics and Self-Regulation*, London: Longman.

—— (2002) *Reporting for Journalists*, London: Routledge.

Gilbert, Harriett (1999) 'Writing reviews', in Wynford Hicks with Sally Adams and Harriett Gilbert, *Writing for Journalists*, London: Routledge: 99–123.

Gilster, Paul (1996) *Finding it on the Internet: The Internet Navigator's Guide to Search Tools and Techniques*, London: Wiley.

Glover, Stephen (1999) 'What columnists are good for', in Stephen Glover (ed.) *Secrets of the Press: Journalists on Journalism*, London: Allen Lane/Penguin Press: 289–98.

Golding, Peter and Murdock, Graham (2000) 'Culture, communications and political economy', in James Curran and Michael Gurevitch (eds) *Mass Media and Society*, 3rd edition, London: Arnold: 70–92.

Goodwin, Eugene (1994) *Groping for Ethics*, Ames, Iowa: Iowa State University Press.

Gordon, Paul and Rosenberg, David (1989) *Daily Racism: the Press and Black People in Britain*, London: Runnymede Trust.

Greenslade, Roy (1992) *Maxwell's Fall*, London: Simon & Schuster.

—— (1995) 'Breaking the silence', *Guardian*, 6 February.

—— (2000) 'No more news of the screws', *Guardian*, 24 April.

—— (2003) *Press Gang: How Newspapers Make Profits from Propaganda*, London: Macmillan.

—— (2004a) 'Have the regional takeovers run out of steam?', *Guardian*, 29 November.

—— (2004b) 'The great pay divide', *Guardian*, 6 December.

Gripsrud, Jostein (1992) 'The aesthetics and politics of melodrama', in Peter Dahlgren and Colin Sparks (eds) *Journalism and Popular Culture*, London: Sage: 84–95.

Gun, Katharine (2004) 'The truth must out', *Observer*, 19 September.

Hall, Jim (2001) *Online Journalism: a Critical Primer*, London: Pluto Press.

Hall, Sarah (2001) 'Tiredness and cruel luck led to tragedy', *Guardian*, 14 December. Available online at http://www.guardian.co.uk/selby/story/0,7369,618352,00.html, accessed 2 December 2004.

Halloran, James, Elliott, Phillip and Murdock, Graham (1970) *Demonstrations and Communications*, Harmondsworth: Penguin.

Hanlin, Bruce (1992) 'Owners, editors and journalists', in Andrew Belsey and Ruth Chadwick (eds) *Ethical Issues in Journalism and the Media*, London: Routledge: 33–48.

Hanstock, Terry (1999) 'The thirteenth pillar: the death of Di reconsidered', *Lobster*, no. 38.

Harcup, Tony (2004) *Journalism: Principles and Practice*, London/Thousand Oaks, New Delhi: Sage.

Hardy, Rebecca (2004) 'Stress busters', *Press Gazette*, 6 June.

Hargrave, Sean (2004) 'The blog busters', *Guardian*, 9 August.

Hargreaves, Ian (2000) 'In search of the elusive first rung', *Press Gazette* (journalism training special edition), 4 April.

—— (2002) 'Young, graduated and white', *Press Gazette*, 12 July.

—— (2003) *Journalism: Truth or Dare?* Oxford: Oxford University Press.

Harlow, John (2001) 'Couples fly out for designer babies', *Sunday Times*, 7 October.

Harman, Harriet (2000) 'A house of men', *Guardian*, 27 March.

Harris, Nigel (1992) 'Codes of conduct for journalists', in Andrew Belsey and Ruth Chadwick (eds) *Ethical Issues in Journalism and the Media*, London: Routledge: 62–76.

Harris, Robert (1990) *Good and Faithful Servant*, London: Faber & Faber.

Hay, Colin (1999) *The Political Economy of New Labour: Labouring under False Pretences?*, Manchester: Manchester University Press.

Hellinger, Daniel and Judd, Dennis R. (1991) *The Democratic Façade*, Belmont, Calif.: Wadsworth.

Hennessy, Brendan (1993) *Writing Feature Articles*, Oxford: Focal Press.

Hennessy, Peter (1986) *Cabinet*, Oxford: Blackwell.

Herman, Ed and Chomsky, Noam (1994) *Manufacturing Consent: the Political Economy of the Mass Media*, 4th edition, London: Vintage.

Hicks, Wynford (1998) *English for Journalists*, 2nd edition, London: Routledge.

Hicks, Wynford and Holmes, Tim (2002) *Subediting for Journalists*, London: Routledge.

Hillyard, Paddy and Percy-Smith, Janie (1988) *The Coercive State: the Decline of Democracy in Britain*, London: Fontana.

Hogan, Daniel (1998) 'Sobriety in the last chance saloon', in *Self Regulation in the Media*, papers from the annual conference of the Association for Journalism Education, London.

Hollingsworth, Mark (1990) *The Press and Political Dissent*, London: Pluto.

—— (2000) 'Secrets, lies and David Shayler', *Guardian*, 17 March.

Hollingsworth, Mark and Fielding, Nick (1999) *Defending the Realm: M15 and the Shayler Affair*, London: André Deutsch.

Howard, Clive (1994) *Journalists and Copyright*, London: National Union of Journalists.

Howard, Philip (1984) *State of the Language*, London: Hamish Hamilton.

Hughes, Lotte and McCrum, Sarah (1998) *Interviewing Children*, London: Save the Children.

Humphrys, John (2004a) *Lost for Words: the Mangling and Manipulating of the English Language*, London: Hodder & Stoughton.

—— (2004b) 'Lost for words', *Independent*, 8 November.

Inglis, Fred (2002) *People's Witness: the Journalist in Modern Politics*, New Haven, Conn./London: Yale University Press.

Jaconelli, Joseph (2002) *Open Justice: a Critique of the Public Trial,* Oxford: Oxford University Press.

Johnson, Andrew (1996) 'The rising tide of shutdown culture', *Press Gazette*, 15 November.

Jones, George and Stewart, John (1998) 'Committees not all over yet', *Local Government Chronicle*, 6 November: 8.

Keeble, Richard (1997) *Secret State, Silent Press: New Militarism the Gulf and the Modern Image of Warfare*, Luton: John Libbey.

—— (1998a) 'The politics of sleaze reporting: a critical overview of the ethical debate in the British press of the 1990s', *Recherches en Communication*, Catholic University of Louvain, Belgium, 9: 71–81.

—— (1998b) 'The myth of Saddam Hussein: new militarism and the propaganda function of the human interest story', in Matthew Kieran (ed.) *Media Ethics*, London: Routledge: 66–81.

—— (1999) 'The three secret wars in the Balkans 1999', in Peter Goff (ed.) *The Kosovo News and Propaganda War*, Vienna: International Press Institute.

—— (2000) 'George Orwell – the journalist', *Press Gazette*, 21 January.

—— (2001) *Ethics for Journalists*, London: Routledge.

—— (2004a) 'Agents of the press', London: *Press Gazette*, 27 July.

—— (2004b) 'The unknown quantity', London: *Press Gazette*, 6 August.

Kelso, Paul (2004) 'Beckham assistant ready to take affair claim to court', *Guardian*, 15 April. Available online at www.guardian.co.uk/print/0,3858,4901831-103690,00.html, accessed 25 November 2004.

Kennedy, Paul (1986) 'A. J. P. Taylor and profound causes in history', in Chris Wrigley (ed.) *Warfare, Diplomacy and Politics*: *Essays in Honour of A. J. P. Taylor*, London: Hamish Hamilton.

Kiernan, Ben (ed.) (1986) *Burchett: Reporting on the Other Side of the World*, London: Quartet.

Kiley, Robert (1999) 'Easy as falling off a log', *Guardian*, 12 January.

King, Graham (2000) *Punctuation*, Glasgow: HarperCollins.

Knightley, Phillip (1997) *A Hack's Progress*, London: Jonathan Cape.

—— (2003). 'A permanent casualty: the death of investigative journalism and who killed it?', Sydney: Evatt Foundation. Available online at http://evatt.labor.net.au/publications/papers/79. html, accessed 25 November 2004.

Knightley, Phillip and Kennedy, Caroline (1987) *An Affair of State: the Profumo Case and the Framing of Stephen Ward*, London: Atheneum.

Kovach, Bill and Rosenstiel, Tom (2003) *The Elements of Journalism*, London: Guardian Books.

Lamont, Duncan (2004) 'Is libel back in fashion?' *Guardian*, 12 January.

Lashmar, Paul (2000) 'Is a good story worth a prison sentence?', *Independent*, 28 March.

Leach, Steve (1999) 'Introducing cabinets into British local government', *Parliamentary Affairs*, January: 77–93.

Leapman, Michael (1983) *Barefaced Cheek*, London: Hodder & Stoughton.

Leigh, David (1980) *The Frontiers of Secrecy: Closed Government in Britain*, London: Junction.

—— (1989) *The Wilson Plot*, 2nd edition, London: Heinemann.

Leigh, David and Vulliamy, Ed (1997) *Sleaze: the Corruption of Parliament*, London: Fourth Estate.

Leslie, Ann (1999) 'Female firemen', in Stephen Glover (ed.) *Secrets of the Press: Journalists on Journalism*, London: Allen Lane/Penguin Press: 221–36.

Leston, Jean (2004) 'Debunking those myths of the freelance working life', *Press Gazette*, 26 November.

Leyland, Adam (1998) 'The pen mightier than the sword but not the tape', *Press Gazette*, 17 July.

Lloyd, John (2004) *What the Media Are Doing to Our Politics*, London: Constable & Robinson.

Lowndes, Vivien (1999) 'Rebuilding trust in central–local relations: policy or passion?', *Local Government Studies*, Winter: 116–36.

MacArthur, Brian (2004) 'Editors get hooked on the web as they seek global audience', *The Times*, 23 July. Available online at http://business.timesonline.co.uk/article/0,,9071-1188596,00.html, accessed 12 October 2004.

McCann, Paul (2000) 'Make way for TV briefings', *The Times*, 17 March.

McKane, Anna (2004) *Journalism*: *a Career Handbook*, London: A. & C. Black Publishers.

McKay, Jenny (2000) *The Magazines Handbook*, London: Routledge.

MacKinnon, Kenneth (2003) *Representing Men: Maleness and Masculinity in the Media*, London: Arnold.

Macleod, Louise (1999) 'Eek! It's a mouse', *Guardian*, 12 January.

McNair B. (2003) *News and Journalism in the UK*, 4th edition, London: Routledge.

—— (2000) *Journalism and Democracy: an Evaluation of the Political Public Sphere*, London: Routledge.

McQuail, Denis (1992) *Media Performance: Mass Communication and the Public Interest*, London: Sage.

Mair, Peter (2000) 'Partyless democracy: solving the paradox of New Labour?', *New Left Review*, vol. 2. no. 2 (March/April): 28–35.

Manning, Paul (2001) *News and News Sources: a Critical Introduction*, London: Sage.

Marr, Andrew (2004) *My Trade: a Short History of British Journalism*, Basingstoke/Oxford: Macmillan.

Mayes, Ian (1999) 'Disaster watch', *Guardian*, 16 October.

—— (2000) 'My word', *Guardian*, 1 July.

Mayes, Tessa (2000) 'Submerging in "therapy news"', *British Journalism Review*, vol. 11, no. 4: 30–6.

—— (2002) *Restraint or Revelation? Free speech and Privacy in a Confessional Age*, London: spiked-online. Available online at http://www.spiked-online.com/articles/00000006DAC6.htm, accessed 27 March 2004.

Meikle, James (2004) 'Study points to tumour risk from older mobiles', *Guardian*, 16 October.

Melin-Higgins, Margareta (1997) 'The social construction of journalist ideals: gender in journalism education', paper presented at conference 'Journalists for a New Century', London College of Printing, 24 April.

Merritt, Stephanie (2003) 'Speaking for myself, I'm as guilty of using tired old cliché as the next man', *Observer*, 13 April.

Metzler, Ken (1997) *Creative Interviewing*, Boston, Mass.: Allyn & Bacon.

Meyer, Christopher (2004) 'Court isn't the place to argue over privacy', *Independent*, 11 October.

Miller, David (2004) *Tell Me Lies: Propaganda and media distortion in the attack on Iraq*, London: Pluto Press.

Mills, Jane (1991) *Womanwords*, London: Virago.

Milne, Seamus (1995) *The Enemy Within: the Secret War against the Miners*, London: Pan.

Milner, Annalisa (2000) *Browsing the Web*, London: Dorling Kindersley.

Milstein, Sarah and Dornfest, Rael (2004) 'Discover the web's hidden treasures', *Sunday Times*, 30 May.

Moore, Alison (1999) 'Articles of faith', *Press Gazette*, 2 February.

Moore, Suzanne (1996) *Head over Heels*, London: Viking.

Moore, Wendy (1999) 'Poverty still a killer', *Guardian*, 22 December.

Morgan, Jean (1998) 'Judge backs right of reporter and paper to protect source', *Press Gazette*, 3 April.

Morris, Steven (2004) 'Fleet Street editors and media law experts give their verdict', *Guardian*, 7 May.

Morton, Andrew (1992) *Diana: Her True Story*, London: Michael O'Mara.

Naughton, John (2000) *A Brief History of the Future: The Origins of the Internet*, 2nd edition, London: Orion.

Newton, Kenneth (1986) 'Mass media', in Henry Drucker (gen. ed,) et al., *Developments in British Politics*, London: Macmillan.

Niblock, Sarah (1996) *Inside Journalism*, London: Blueprint.

Nolan, Lord (1996) *Aspects of Conduct in Local Government in England, Scotland and Wales*, London: Committee on Standards in Public Life.

Norris, Bill (2000) 'Media ethics at the sharp end', in David Berry (ed.) *Ethics and Media Culture: Practices and Representations*, Oxford: Focal Press: 325–38.

Northmore, David (1990) *Freedom of Information Handbook*, London: Bloomsbury.

—— (1996) *Lifting the Lid: a Guide to Investigative Research*, London: Cassell.

Norton, Phillip (1991) 'Committees in the House of Commons', *Politics Review*, vol. 1, no. 1.

Office of the Deputy Prime Minister (2001) *Strong Leadership – Quality Public Services*, London: ODPM.

Office of the Deputy Prime Minister (2002) *Your Region, Your Choice: Revitalising the English Regions*, London: ODPM.

Orwell, George (1984 [1957]) 'Politics and the English language', in *Inside the Whale and Other Essays*, Harmondsworth: Penguin: 143–57.

Oxford, Esther (1992) 'Pay your money and pick your man', *Independent*, 18 November.

Page, Ben (1998) 'Making voting attractive again', *Local Government Chronicle*, 16 October: 16–17.

Page, Bruce (2003) *The Murdoch Archipelago*, London: Simon & Schuster.

Paglia, Camille (1995) *Vamps and Tramps*, Harmondsworth: Penguin.

Peak, Steve and Fisher, Paul (1999) *The Media Guide 2000*, London: Fourth Estate.

Phillips, Angela and Gaber, Ivor (1996) 'The case for media degrees', *British Journalism Review*, vol. 7, no. 3: 62–5.

Pierce, Andrew (2000) 'Whispers in the corridors of power', *The Times*, 7 July.

Pilger, John (1996) 'The hidden power of the media', *Socialist Review*, September.

—— (1998) *Hidden Agendas*, London: Vintage.

—— (2004a) *Tell Me No Lies: Investigative Journalism and Its Triumphs*, London: Jonathan Cape.

—— (2004b) 'Iraq: the unthinkable becomes normal', *New Statesman*, 15 November.

—— (2004c) 'Paradise lost: how Britain betrayed innocent islanders', *Express*, 13 October.

Platell, Amanda (1999) 'Institutionalised sexism', in Stephen Glover (ed.) *Secrets of the Press: Journalists on Journalism*, London: Allen Lane/Penguin Press: 140–7.

Ponsford, Dominic (2004a) 'Reduction of bulks drives decline in regional dailies', *Press Gazette*, 3 September.

—— (2004b) 'Press freedom threatened by "no win, no fee", MPs told', *Press Gazette*, 1 October.

—— (2004c) 'Editors toughen up code to outlaw phone text grabs', *Press Gazette*, 14 May.

Ponsford, Dominic and Slattery, Jon (2004a) 'European privacy protection grows', *Press Gazette*, 3 December.

—— (2004b) 'Legal pitfalls of online archives', *Press Gazette*, 3 December.

Ponting, Clive (1986) *Whitehall: Tragedy and Farce*, London: Sphere.

—— (1990) *Secrecy in Britain*, Oxford: Basil Blackwell.

Porter, Bernard (1992) *Plots and Paranoia: a History of Political Espionage in Britain 1790–1988*, London: Routledge.

Pöttker, Horst (2003) 'News and its communicative quality: the inverted pyramid – when and why did it appear?' *Journalism Studies*, vol. 4, no. 4: 501–11.

Preston, Peter (2004a) 'Are newspapers burnt out?', *Observer*, 21 November.

—— (2004b) 'When race is a numbers game', *Observer*, 24 October.

Privacy International and the GreenNet Educational Trust (2003) *Silenced: an International Report on Censorship and Control of the Internet*. Available online at www.privacyinternational.org/survey/censorship, accessed 1 December 2004.

Project Censored (1998) *Censored: the News that Didn't Make the News*, New York: Seven Stories Press.

Randall, David (2000) *The Universal Journalist*, 2nd edition, London: Pluto.

Read, Sue (1992) *The Complete Guide to Working from Home*, London: Headline.

Reddick, Randy and King, Elliot (1997) *The Online Journalist: Using the Internet and Other Electronic Resources*, 2nd edition, Fort Worth, Tex.: Harcourt Brace.

Reece, Damian (2004) 'Net search engines rev up for battle', *Independent*, 30 January.

Reeves, Ian (1999) 'Reaping the whirlwind', *Press Gazette*, 18 May.

—— (2002) 'Is the demon just a pussycat?' *Press Gazette*, 10 May.

Reiner, Robert, Livingstone, Sonia and Allen, Jessica (2000) 'No more happy endings? The media and popular concern about crime since the Second World War', in Tim Hope and Richard Sparks (eds) *Crime, Risk and Insecurity*, London: Routledge: 107–25.

—— (2001) 'Casino culture: media and crime in a winner–loser society', in Kevin Stenson and Robert R. Sullivan (eds) *Crime, Risk and Justice*, Cullompton: Willan Publishing: 175–93.

—— (2003) 'From law and order to lynch mobs: crime news since the Second World War', in Paul Mason (ed.) *Criminal Visions: Media Representations of Crime and Justice*, Cullompton: Willan Publishing: 13–32.

Richards, Ian (2005) *Quagmires and Quandaries: Exploring Journalism Ethics*, Sydney: University of New South Wales Press.

Roberts, Dan (2004) 'Stumbling block', *Press Gazette*, 23 July.

Robertson, Geoffrey (1983) *People Against the Press: an Enquiry into the Press Council*, London: Quartet.

Robertson, Geoffrey, and Nicol, Andrew (2002) *Media Law,* 4th edition, London: Penguin Books.

Robinson, James (2004) 'Malone gears up for kill at News Corp', *Observer*, 5 December 2004.

Rock, P. (1988) 'News as eternal recurrence', in Stanley Cohen and Jock Young (eds) *The Manufacture of News: Social Problems, Deviance and the Mass Media*, London: Constable: 64–70.

Rooney, Ben (2004) 'How to navigate cyberspace', *Press Gazette*, 12 November.

Rose, Richard (1965) *Politics in England*, London: Faber & Faber.

Roszak, Theodore (1996) 'Dumbing us down', *New Internationalist*, December.

Rowlands, Barbara (1993) 'Don't call me, please, and I won't call you', *Independent*, 24 August.

Rozenberg, Joshua (2004) *Privacy and the Press*, Oxford: Oxford University Press.

Rudin, Richard and Ibbotson, Trevor (2002) *Introduction to Journalism: Essential Techniques and Background Knowledge*, Oxford: Focal Press.

Sanders, Karen (2003) *Ethics and Journalism*, London: Sage

Sarikakis, Katherine (2004) *British Media in a Global Era*, London: Arnold.

Schudson, Michael (1978) *Discovering the News*, New York: Basic Books.

Searle, Chris (1989) *Your Daily Dose of Racism*, London: Campaign for Press and Broadcasting Freedom.

Sebba, Anne (1994) *Battling for News: the Rise of the Woman Reporter*, London: Hodder & Stoughton.

Sereny, Gitta (1998) *Cries Unheard*, London: Macmillan.

Seymour-Ure, Colin (1974) *The Political Impact of the Mass Media*, London: Constable.

Shawcross, William (1992) *Murdoch*, London: Pan Books.

Silvester, Christopher (ed.) (1994) *Interviews: an Anthology from 1859 to the Present Day*, Harmondsworth: Penguin.

—— (1997) (ed.) *The Penguin Book of Columnists*, London: Viking.

Skentelbery, David (2000) 'Journalism now comes second to costs', *Press Gazette*, 7 January.

Smith, Anthony (1978) *The Politics of Information*, London: Macmillan.

Smith, Geoffrey, Hemder, Derrick and Kett, David (1992) *Local Government for Journalists*, London: LGC Communications Information and Research.

Snoddy, Raymond (1993) *The Good, the Bad and the Unacceptable*, 2nd edition, London: Faber & Faber.

Spark, David (1999) *Investigative Reporting: a Study in Technique*, Oxford: Focal Press.

Sparks, Colin (1992) 'Popular journalism: theories and practice', in Peter Dahlgren and Colin Sparks (eds) *Journalism and Popular Culture*, London: Sage: 24–44.

—— (1999) 'The press', in Jane Stokes and Anna Reading (eds) *The Media in Britain: Current Debates and Developments*, London: Macmillan: 41–60.

—— (2003) 'Inside the media', *International Socialism*, no. 98: 31–55.

Spender, Dale (1980) *Man Made Language*; London: Routledge & Kegan Paul.

—— (ed.) (1983) *Feminist Theories: Three Centuries of Women's Intellectual Traditions*, London: Women's Press.

Stafford, David (1988) *The Silent Game: the Real World of Imaginary Spies*, London: Viking.

Stephenson, Hugh and Mory, Pierre (1990) *Journalism Training in Europe*, Brussels: European Community.

Stepniak, Daniel (2003) 'British justice: not suitable for public viewing?', in Paul Mason (ed.) *Criminal Visions: Media Representations of Crime and Justice*, Cullompton: Willan Publishing: 254–75.

Stevenson, Nick (1995) *Understanding Media Cultures: Social Theory and Mass Communication*, London: Sage.

Stoker, Gerry (1999) 'Slow road to regionalism', *Local Government Chronicle*, 22 January: 8.

Stone, Richard (2002) *Textbook on Civil Liberties and Human Rights*, Oxford: Oxford University Press.

Taylor, Noreen (2000) 'The national ladies in waiting', *Press Gazette*, 7 July.

Teather, David (2004) 'Microsoft takes on Google with new search engine', *Guardian,* 12 November.

Tench, Dan (2004) 'The law of secrets', *Guardian*, 8 March.

Thom, Cleland (2004). 'Where are the new Pilgers?', *Journalism Training: A Press Gazette Supplement*, March.

Tiffen, Rodney (1989) *News and Power*, London: Unwin Hyman.

Todd, L. (2001) *Cassell's Guide to Punctuation*, London: Cassell.

Todd, Paul and Bloch, Jonathan (2003) *Global Intelligence: the World's Secret Services Today*, London: Zed Books.

Tomkinson, Martin (1973). *Private Eye Extra: Guide to the Poulson Case*, London: Pressdram.

Trelford, Donald (2000) 'The freedom to be irresponsible', *Press Gazette*, 24 March.

Trkulja. Maria (2003) 'Vows and rows', *Observer Magazine*, 21 December.

Truss, Lynne (1999) 'On the terraces', in Stephen Glover (ed.) *Secrets of the Press: Journalists on Journalism*, London: Allen Lane/Penguin Press: 125–32.

Tulloch, John (1998) 'Managing the press in a medium-sized European power', in Hugh Stephenson and Michael Bromley (eds) *Sex Lies and Democracy: the Press and the Public*, London: Longman: 63–83.

—— (2004) 'What universe are you from? Everyday tragedies and the ethics of press intrusion into grief', *Ethical Space: The International Journal of Communication Ethics*, vol. 1, no. 3: 25–30.

Tumber, Howard (ed.) (1999) *News: a Reader*, Oxford: Oxford University Press.

Tunstall, Jeremy (1983) *The Media in Britain*, London: Constable.

Turner, John (2000) *The Tories and Europe*, Manchester: Manchester University Press.

Tynan, Kenneth (1990) *Profiles: Selected and Edited by Kathleen Tynan and Ernie Eban*, London: Nick Hern Books.

Ullmann, John and Honeyman, Steve (1983) *The Reporter's Handbook: an Investigator's Guide to Documents and Techniques*, New York: St Martin's Press.

Van Dijk, Teu (1988) *News as Discourse*, Hillsdale, NJ: Lawrence Erlbaum.

—— (1991) *Racism and the Press*, London: Routledge.

Wade, Stephen (1997) *Freelance Writing*, London: Straightforward.

Wainwright, Martin (2002) 'Dozing driver who caused 10 deaths gets five years', *Guardian*, 12 January. Available online at http://www.guardian.co.uk/uk_news/story/0,,631657,00.html, accessed 2 December 2004.

Wallace, Milverton (1996) 'Death of the deadline', *Press Gazette*, 12 April.

—— (2004) 'The internet revolution: new challenges for journalists', talk at the University of Lincoln, 11 October.

Ward, Mike (2002) *Journalism Online*, Oxford: Focal Press.

Wasley, Andrew (2000) 'Grief encounter', *Guardian*, 6 March.

Waterhouse, Keith (1981) *The Mirror's Way with Words*, London: Mirror Books.

—— (1991) *English our English (and How to Sing It)*, London: Viking.

—— (1995) 'Talking of which . . .', *Guardian*, 25 September.

Welsh, Tom and Greenwood, Walter (eds) (2003) *McNae's Essential Law for Journalists*, 17th edition, Oxford: Oxford University Press.

Wheen, Francis (2000) 'The Sun's gypsy curse', *Guardian*, 22 March.

Widdicombe, D. (1986) *Report of the Committee of Inquiry into the Conduct of Local Authority Business*, London: HMSO.

Williams, Granville (1994) *Britain's Media: How They Are Related: Media Ownership and Democracy*, London: Campaign for Press and Broadcasting Freedom.

Williams, Kevin (1998) *Get Me a Murder a Day!*, London: Arnold.

Williams, Paul N. (1978) *Investigative Reporting and Editing*, Englewood Cliffs, NJ: Prentice Hall.

Williams, Stephen (1996) 'A job to die for?', *Journalist*, June–July.

Wilson, David and Game, Chris (1998) *Local Government in the United Kingdom*, London: Macmillan.

Wilson, John (1996) *Understanding Journalism: a Guide to the Issues*, London: Routledge.

Wingfield, John (1984) *Bugging: a Complete Survey of Electronic Surveillance Today*, London: Robert Hale.

Wintour, Charles (1990) *The Rise and Fall of Fleet Street*, London: Hutchinson.

Wright, Peter (with Greengrass, Paul) (1987) *Spycatcher*, Melbourne: Heinemann.

Wroe, Martin (2003) 'Stirring in the sticks', *Sunday Times*, 25 May.

Zobel, Gibby (2000) 'Rights mess', *Guardian*, 3 May.

Index

....

Related titles from Routledge

Print Journalism

Edited by Richard Keeble

Print Journalism: a critical introduction provides a unique and thorough insight into the skills required to work within the newspaper, magazine and online journalism industries. Among the many highlighted are:

- Sourcing the news
- Interviewing
- Sub-editing
- Feature writing and editing
- Reviewing
- Designing pages
- Pitching ideas

In addition separate chapters focus on ethics, reporting courts, covering politics and copyright whilst others looks at the history of newspapers and magazines, the structure of the UK print industry(including its financial organisation) and the development of journalism education in the UK, helping to place the coverage of skills within a broader, critical context.

All contributors are experienced practising journalists as well as journalism educators from a broad range of UK universities.

Hb: 0–415–35881–7
Pb: 0–415–35882–5

Available at all good bookshops
For ordering and further information please visit:
www.routledge.com